Developing Performance Support for Computer Systems

A Strategy for Maximizing Usability and Learnability

James R. Williams
Synergetic Applications
Bloomsbury, NJ

CRC Press
Taylor & Francis Group
Boca Raton London New York

CRC Press is an imprint of the
Taylor & Francis Group, an **informa** business

CRC Press
Taylor & Francis Group
6000 Broken Sound Parkway NW, Suite 300
Boca Raton, FL 33487-2742

© 2004 by Taylor & Francis Group, LLC
CRC Press is an imprint of Taylor & Francis Group, an Informa business

First issued in paperback 2019

No claim to original U.S. Government works

ISBN 13: 978-0-367-45436-4 (pbk)
ISBN 13: 978-0-415-32640-7 (hbk)

Visit the Taylor & Francis Web site at
http://www.taylorandfrancis.com

and the CRC Press Web site at
http://www.crcpress.com

Library of Congress Cataloging-in-Publication Data

Williams, James R. (James Richard), 1932-
  Developing performance support for computer systems : a strategy for maximizing usability and learnability / James R. Williams.
    p. cm.
  Includes bibliographical references and index.
  ISBN 0-415-32640-0 (alk. paper)
  1. Computer sytems. 2. Performance—Mangement. I. Title.

  QA76.W5185 2004
  004—dc22
                                                    2004042811

Library of Congress Card Number 2004042811

Contents

Preface ix
Acknowledgments xi

CHAPTER ONE
Introduction..1
  Why Performance Support?...1
    Usability...2
    Learnability..3
  What is Performance Support? 4
  Design approach 6
  Types of Performance Support 9
    Documentation..9
    Online Help..10
    Performance Aids 11
    Coaches, Advisors and Wizards 11
    Instruction 12
    Performance Support System (PSS) 13
  Performance Support System Model 15
  How to Use This Book..16
  References..18

CHAPTER TWO
Design Environments and Strategies 19
  Introduction..19
  Ideal Environment..19
    Impact 19
    Strategies...20
  Typical Environment 22
    Impact 22
    Strategies...22
  Late Involvement Environment 24
    Impact 24
    Strategies...25
  References..26

CHAPTER THREE
Project Planning...27

Introduction...27
Planning Environment 27
  Software Development Environment..27
  Centralized Performance Support Development Environment 28
  Separate Performance Support Development Organizations.........29
Estimation Factors and Impacts..29
  Steps in Cost Estimation 29
  Estimation Approaches..35
Planning Methodology and Tools..35
  Methodology...36
  Personnel Requirements – Design Team 37
  Personnel Requirements – Product Developers.........................38
  Tools 39
Sample Plan for Performance Support Projects...........................41
Planning for Electronic Performance Support Products................47
  Planning Phase..48
  Requirements Phase..48
  Design Phase...49
  Development Phase...49
  Developmental (Alpha) Test Phase 49
  Usability Test Phase...50
  Beta Test Phase...50
  Production Test Phase...50
References...51

CHAPTER FOUR
  Needs Assessment and Task Analysis......................................53
  Introduction..53
  Development Environment Constraints......................................54
    Limited to Existing Data...55
    Limited Access to Using Organizations 55
    Limited Access to Users 55
    Limited Impact on Data Collection Planning 55
  Needs Assessment Methods..55
    Identifying Target Population...56
    Determining Current Deficiencies...57
    Determining User and Management Needs..............................69
    Developing Usability Objectives...72
    Needs Assessment Reporting 75
  Task Analysis for Performance Support.....................................77
    Analyzing and Describing Current Performance..........................77

Designing New Performance 84
Task Characteristics 101
Potential Performance Support Solutions 101
Sample Task Analysis Report Template 101
Needs Assessment and Task Analysis Data Checklist 103
References 104

CHAPTER FIVE
Matching Performance Support Methods to Task Requirements 105
Introduction 105
Determining Skill and Knowledge Requirements 105
Defining Skill 106
Defining Knowledge 108
Process Related Knowledge 108
Environment Related Knowledge 111
What Must Be Done before Skill and Knowledge Derivation? ... 114
Assumptions 115
Skill and Knowledge Derivation Process 116
Performance Support Considerations and Alternatives 122
Techniques for Enabling Immediate Performance 122
Techniques for Enabling Learning 123
Performance Support Selection Aid 125
References 128

CHAPTER SIX
General Design Guidance 129
Introduction 129
User Considerations 129
Physical Aspects 129
Information Processing Capability 131
Perceptual Characteristics 132
Individual Differences 137
Information Presentation 140
Categories of Information Presentation 140
Task/Information Use Dependencies 141
Steps for Determining Information Requirements 141
Data Forms 142
Layout and Structuring Consideration 154
Display Density 154
Complexity 154
Grouping 154

Arranging Information...155
Windows 158
Labeling 158
Text Presentation 158
Aesthetic Factors...160
General Layout Guidelines 160
Media Selection 161
Use of Color..171
Color Definitions 171
Color and Information 172
Choosing Colors to Display...172
Icons...180
Icons for Informational Purposes..181
Icons for Navigation and Media Control 181
Accessibility..184
Input and Outputs..185
User Preferences 185
Object Descriptions..185
Presentation..186
Color 187
Accessibility Features 187
User Control..188
Online Documentation and Help 189
Internationalization 190
References...190

CHAPTER SEVEN
Developing Performance Support Products.......................................195
Introduction..195
Documentation...195
Development Approach 196
Developing Deliverable Documents.....................................200
Guidelines...203
Performance Aids 208
Development Approach 209
Guidelines...215
Online Help..217
Development Approach 218
Guidelines...232
Coaches, Advisors and Wizards 238
Coaches...238

Advisors 239
Wizards 239
Development Approach 240
Guidelines 246
Instruction 247
Development Approach 248
Guidelines 262
Electronic Performance Support...265
Development Approach 265
Guidelines 275
Iterative Approach to Electronic Performance Support.........277
Moving Performance Support Products Online..................278
Restructuring Existing Performance Support Products 278
Revamping the Online Help System into an Integrator.......278
Testing the Integrated System...279
Adding New Performance Support Components..................279
References..280

CHAPTER EIGHT
Testing Performance Support Products 283
Introduction..283
Evaluation Methods 283
When to Test...285
Test Planning 286
Test Cases (Alpha, Usability and Product Tests) 286
Traceability (Alpha, Usability and Product Tests) 286
Data to Be Collected 287
Test Procedures..287
Testing Resources 287
Developmental Testing – Heuristic Evaluation 288
Developmental Testing – Alpha Testing 291
Usability Testing..295
Usability Criteria..295
Participant Requirements...297
Task Scenarios 298
Test Sessions..299
Observed vs. Non-observed Tests 299
Test Data..301
Test Materials 301
Procedures..305
Recording Tools..306

Beta Testing 308
   Call for Participants 308
   Participant Agreement 309
   Data Collection Forms 309
Product Testing..310
Follow-up Evaluation 310
   Interviews..311
   Performance Observations 312
Test Reporting..312
References..315

Appendix A
Instructional Strategy Selection Aid...................................317

Appendix B
Documentation Evaluation Checklist 323

Appendix C
Performance Aid Evaluation Checklist..................................331

Appendix D
Online Help Evaluation Checklist 337

Appendix E
Coaches, Advisors, Wizards Evaluation Checklist................345

Appendix F
Instruction Evaluation Checklist...349

Appendix G
EPSS Evaluation Checklist..355

Index 361

Preface

This book is the result of my forty plus years of experience in developing and managing the development of various performance support products for both software and hardware systems. However, the majority of my experience has been in the development of large software systems used to support telecommunications personnel. I have learned a great deal during this time about what works and doesn't work and the purpose of this book is to share my knowledge with individuals who have the responsibility for producing various performance support products, such as online help, instruction, performance aids, documentation, coaches/advisors/wizards and electronic performance support systems. This book provides a practical approach to development, rather than theoretical, and presents many guidelines for designing and developing performance support products. All of the processes and guidelines have been applied in the development of real projects.

I have been involved with computer systems for my entire career and actually used a computer to analyze the data for my master's thesis back in 1959. My first job in industry was to develop a computer system to capture and analyze attendance data for the Chicago school system. I also had the good fortune of being a staff member at the System Development Corporation during the early 1960s when it pioneered the systems approach in the development of large computer-based information systems for the US Air Force. Having degrees in both industrial psychology (specializing in human factors) and education, I have been particularly interested in methods that can optimize both the usability and learnability of software systems. While a member of the AT&T Training Research Group during the late 1970s, my colleagues and I became convinced that research data could be successfully utilized to improve the quality of performance support products. Utilizing both research data and the practical experiences of training developers, the AT&T Training Research Group developed a set of training development standards that were successfully used to develop training throughout the Bell System.

Since I am a strong proponent of the use of standards and have been active in the development of software ergonomic standards for over fifteen years, this book frequently refers to and advocates the use of appropriate standards where ever possible. Having applied standards in the development of numerous projects, I have never found the use of formal standards to constrain creativity or make products less useful (contrary to some opinions).

To facilitate the use of the checklists provided in the Appendices of this book, readers can obtain an electronic copy of the Appendices by going to the following website:

http://www.crcpress.com/e_products/downloads/download.asp?cat_no=TF1741

Acknowledgments

I could not have written this book without the encouragement and support of my wife Jonetta. She has endured the many hours spent in my office working on the book. Our children, Janise Wolocen and Jason Williams, have provided moral support throughout the writing process. Also, Jason and his wife, Amber, provided editorial comments on a number of chapters.

This book owes a considerable amount to my interaction with my colleagues over the years in the Bell System and its successors (i.e., Bellcore and Telcordia Technologies). My colleagues in Telcordia's Learning Support Organization were particularly influential in the evolution of my views on the development of performance support. I would particularly like to thank Rick Mosley and Ed Russell at Telcordia Technologies for their encouragement and efforts in obtaining Telcordia's permission to use a number of screen shots from the Telcordia Performance Support Project Estimator in the book. The many students who took my courses at Bellcore also helped shape my thinking on many of the topics in this book.

I also owe a special thanks to Thomas Geis, Managing Direct ProContext, whose comments on the title and introduction to the book led to some major improvements. In addition, Jim Carter, University of Saskatchewan, provided very useful comments that led to a reorganization of Chapter 1.

CHAPTER ONE

Introduction

The purpose of this book is to provide a strategy for maximizing the usability and learnability of computer systems by the application of an integrated performance support systems approach. Detailed planning, design and development guidance is provided for designers, developers and managers responsible for developing performance support for users and supporting staff members of new and revised computer systems. This book covers the entire area of performance support, rather than just a few specific topic areas. In addition, performance support is presented as an integrated development process that optimizes the use of resources and "how to" guidance is provided so developers can apply the information directly to the design of their performance support products. Many books are available on some of the specific performance support products covered in this book (e.g., training, documentation, and online help) and electronic performance support systems, but these books do not cover the integration of different products into a performance support system. This book has the following major objectives:

- Present a pragmatic definition of performance support, and its importance, and describe the different types of performance support products
- Describe different types of design environments and strategies for working within them
- Provide guidance for planning performance support projects and estimating resource requirements
- Present a practical method for performing needs assessment and task analysis
- Provide guidance on matching performance support methods to task requirements
- Provide general design guidance on information presentation, layout and formatting, media selection, the use of color and icons, and accessibility
- Present procedures and specific guidance for developing the various types of performance support products
- Provide a method for testing performance support products

While the following chapters primarily address the development of performance support for large software systems (e.g., business information systems), the principles and approaches presented can be applied in any computer system development environment.

WHY PERFORMANCE SUPPORT?

Due to intense competition and the need to cut costs, organizations have been looking for methods that would improve the way their employees work. The goal is to improve the quality of the work and also get it done faster and at lower costs. Also, with downsizing, many senior experienced employees are leaving the organizations. As a result, much of the expert knowledge about how to accomplish many organizational activities is being lost. These problems are particularly pronounced in the use of computer systems to support organizational functions. Thomas Landauer, in his book *The Trouble with Computers, Usefulness, Usability, and Productivity* (Landauer, 1995), states that over the last twenty years computers have failed to provide the increases in productivity that they were intended to. While Landauer targets usefulness and usability as the main causes, the lack of good performance support also played a large part in the productivity story. Of course, one could argue that the usefulness of the performance support itself has a considerable effect on the usefulness of the system. Landauer conservatively estimates productivity could be increased 20 to 40 percent if User-Centered Design was utilized in the design of systems (Landauer, 1995, pg. 233). Performance support can help resolve some of the above problems by providing:

- Performance-oriented instruction to allow new employees to learn the job quickly and other employees to quickly learn/relearn a seldom performed task
- Quick access to step-by-step procedures for accomplishing the task at hand
- Context-sensitive information related to error resolution and problem solving
- Reference material where additional information is required
- Coaches and advisors for assisting in completing inputs and analyzing outputs
- Wizards for performing complex and tedious tasks

Early system developers typically did not include performance support with their products and left it up to the users themselves, or third parties, for information on how to learn and use the system. Training, performance aids and documentation were the only kinds of support provided with most systems until online help started appearing in consumer software products. Most of the early online help products, however, were just online versions of the user manuals. Since the user manuals were not specifically developed for use online, users had a great deal of difficulty finding the information that they needed. After a few attempts to find important information relevant to their current task, users quit using the help and relied on printed documentation instead. Therefore, the online help provided with many of these systems did not support performance. As a result, online help had a bad reputation with the user community. A key point to be made here is if a product does not support performance, it will not be used.

In many system development organizations, developers of training, performance aids, documentation and online help are in different organizations (e.g., training, technical communications) and do not interact with each other. Products developed to support users and support personnel in such environments are not integrated into a performance support framework. As a result, there is a great deal of duplication of information, inconsistent formats and terminology, and confused users. Integrating performance support product development allows the development of products that are consistent and complementary. Analysis and design activities are centralized so duplication of effort is minimized.

Usability

As noted in the beginning of this chapter, the intent of performance support is to maximize the usability and learnability of the product or system. Usability is defined in the ISO standard: Guidance on usability (ISO 9241-11: 1998) as "A concept comprising the effectiveness, efficiency and satisfaction with which specified users can achieve specified goals in a particular environment." If the product or system was completely intuitive and required no explanation or assistance to the user, performance support would not be necessary. However, the existence of such products is extremely rare, particularly since different users have different experiences and skills related to the use of a product. In addition, products are used in various environments and users tend to have different goals. Figure 1.1 depicts the performance support features (and associated products) that can enhance the usability of a computer-based system or application. A performance support feature's contribution to usability depends on the appropriateness of the support and its quick availability. Performance support can maximize usability by providing timely assistance to the user relevant to accomplishing their specific goals and solving problems which may occur along the way. As a result, effectiveness, efficiency and satisfaction are improved.

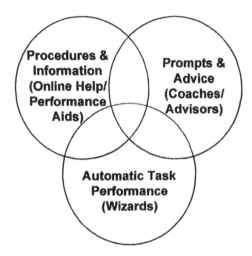

Figure 1.1 Performance Support Features Contributing to Product Usability

Learnability

Learnability relates to how well a product or system supports the user in learning to use it. The ISO ergonomic standard on dialogue principles (ISO 9241-10: 1995) includes learnability as one of the seven principles important for the design and evaluation of human-computer dialogues. These principles include:

- Suitability for the task
- Self-descriptiveness
- Controllability
- Conformity with user expectations
- Error tolerance
- Suitability for individualization
- Suitability for learning

According to ISO 9241-10, "a dialogue is suitable for learning when it supports and guides the user in learning to use the system." While all of these principles are important to both user interface design and performance support design, suitability for learning (or learnability) is the dialogue principle most supported by performance support. Good performance support is intended to maximize the ability of the user to learn to use the product as quickly and effectively as possible.

As can be seen in Figure 1.2, the slope of the learning curve determines how quickly a user can reach full productivity with a product. The availability of appropriate instruction, in addition to the optimization of the dialogue principles listed above affect learnability (and hence the slope of the learning curve). Usability and learnability are closely interrelated in that the more usable a product is the easier it will be to learn. Therefore, the performance support products that support usability also support learnability. For this reason, it is very important that the use of performance support be included in any training provided.

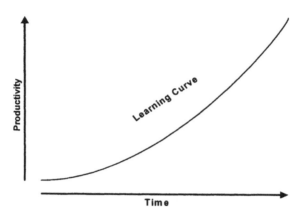

Figure 1.2 Effect of Learning Curve on Productivity

WHAT IS PERFORMANCE SUPPORT?

Performance support (sometimes called "user support") includes all of the user-oriented materials, in addition to the user interface, that will support the user in learning and using the system. Such materials include overviews, online help, performance aids, documentation, coaches, wizards, tutorials and training. Performance support materials may be online or in paper form, but the trend is to provide all performance support online as part of the system software. The term "performance support" is preferred over "user support" because the emphasis is on performance. The goal of performance support is to provide effective and efficient user performance. Optimum performance support (i.e., a well designed performance support system) provides users with all the information they need, when they need it, so they can perform their jobs successfully. Organization and system procedures are presented in the context of the users' job functions in formats most appropriate for completing specific tasks.

Performance support systems are often referred to as "electronic performance support systems" (EPSS), a term made popular by Gloria Gery (Gery, 1991). Gery defines electronic performance support as: "… an electronic system that provides integrated, on-demand access to information, advice, learning experiences, and tools to enable a high level of job performance with a minimum of support from other people." There also have been various other terms used for systems intended to deliver performance support by electronic means. Griffin and Beagles (2000) use the term Training and Performance Support Systems (TPSS) for a system that included computer-based training modules, electronic job aids, classroom training modules, case-based practices and performance tests, electronic performance support systems and other media. Callahan et al (2000) developed a framework for using personal computers to learn concepts, knowledge and information and get feedback and performance support to accomplish specific tasks. They called this approach "Learning, Information, and Performance Support (LIPS)."

Additional terms that have been used for the material provided to users with a system include: "learning support", "knowledge support" and "e-learning" (when provided in electronic form). While learning support mostly relates to training materials supplied with a system, some organizations have expanded the meaning of the term to include documentation and online help as well as training. Knowledge support (and the associated knowledge management system) is usually included as part of an EPSS (Raybould, 2000) and refers to the organization and presentation of domain knowledge related to the work to be accomplished. However, there are a number of systems called Knowledge Support Systems (KSS). Often online help, advisors and CBT are included as part of knowledge support systems. Due to the popularity of providing information by electronic means (i.e., by computer, or via the web), often anything remotely related to learning and knowledge is being called e-learning. As is the case for learning support, many developing organizations are including electronic documentation and online help as part of e-learning. Broderick (2001) points out that e-learning in often used for a combination of learning from instruction, knowledge management and performance support. He particularly takes issue with the inclusion of performance support as learning which he describes as intended to guide the user to perform something without the user needing to fully understand or know the topic.

Terms such as "User Assistance" (Microsoft, 2001) and "Interactive Assistance" (Marion, 2000) have been used to describe help systems that have evolved into including other performance support components. Within user assistance, Microsoft includes "What's This?" help, Help buttons, Status bar messages, ToolTips, Reference help, Procedural help, Conceptual help, Wizards, Tours, and Tutorials. Marion includes interactive books, online help systems, pop-ups, rollovers, moving and animated information, and audio, visual, and multimedia information as explanatory interactive assistance. As can be noted by the above discussion, the background of the developers of these various kinds of performance support systems has a large influence on what they are called. In addition, the great overlap between these different approaches and systems is readily apparent.

One of the major problems confronting developers and managers of performance support products is all of the different terminology used to represent similar design processes and outcomes. While coming up with unique names may help sell consulting services and books, it provides little to help developers and managers for sorting out best practices. Therefore, in this book, we will use the term "performance support system" (PSS) because this term is more general and does not assume all of the support elements are provided electronically. As noted above, a PSS may contain non-electronic elements for enhancing performance (e.g., paper performance aids). In addition, a PSS can contain any of the elements included in the various types of systems discussed in the previous paragraph. While an Electronic Performance Support System is a worthwhile goal, it is not attainable in many design environments. Electronic Performance Support Systems are typically developed to support a limited number of specific operations, whereas large software systems usually support a multitude of functions and organizations. An EPSS is so tightly integrated with the system that it is part of the interface and, therefore, requires a high level of cooperation between the developers of the EPSS and the developers of the application. It is rarely practical to develop an EPSS in a large system development environment due to the additional resource and time requirements. On the other hand, a PSS (as defined above) can be developed within any environment.

While software organizations often include "help desk" operations under user support, we will not cover help desks or other kinds of people support operations in this book. Help desks are essentially ongoing live human interactions with users to resolve problems, whereas performance support (as described in this book) consists of concrete materials or products. Performance support for a system, however, may include materials to aid help desk personnel.

DESIGN APPROACH

Since "performance" is the key word in developing performance support products, some practitioners refer to the design approach as "performance-centered design" rather than the more typically used "user-centered" or "human-centered" design. Human-centered design is defined in the ISO standard (ISO 13407: 1999, Human centred design processes for interactive systems, clause 5.1) as "An approach to design that is characterized by the active involvement of users, and a clear understanding of user and task requirements, an appropriate allocation of function between users and technology, iterations of design solutions and multi-disciplinary design." User-centered (or human-centered design) has become a very popular design approach (with many variations) for creating various kinds of products, interfaces, websites, media, etc., used by people. One of the major tenets of user-centered design (UCD) is the inclusion of a product's end-users throughout the design process. In some cases, the concentration on end-user needs in user-centered design leaves out important organizational and financial goals. As a result, the product may be popular with users but be a financial failure. One approach, where the focus is on users within user-centered design, is called "participatory design." In participatory design, actual representative users participate in the entire design process, including specifying requirements. One of the problems with relying solely on participatory design is design solutions are limited to the knowledge and innovativeness of the sample users. However, it can be a useful approach when used in addition to other user-centered design approaches. Another take-off on user-centered design is "learner-centered" design often used by developers of learning support and e-learning systems. The emphasis, however, is essentially the same (i.e., ensuring that the consumer of the product is well represented during design) whether you call the individual a learner or a user.

Gery (1995) states that "The goal of performance-centered software design is 1) to integrate the knowledge, data, and tools required to be successful in performing a task, and 2) to provide task structuring support to help performers create required deliverables." Massey, Montoya-Weiss and O'Driscol (2001) define Performance-Centered Design as: "PCD involves defining needs and performance goals, analyzing performance problems and identifying comprehensive interventions to improve performance and achieve goals." However, most of the definitions (probably derived from Gery) of performance-centered design, have an EPSS focus and state "Performance-Centered Design (PCD) infuses tools with knowledge, structures tasks, and enables performers to achieve the required level of performance as quickly as possible – at the very most, within a day -- with minimum support from other people."

Many performance-centered design practitioners include user-centered design within performance-centered design (e.g., Raybould, 2000), expand on UCD or consider UCD different (not as appropriate) as PCD (Winslow and Bramer, 1994). Raybould differentiates user-centered design from performance-centered design by using a narrow definition of user-centered design to only include the design of the computer-human interaction. On the other hand, he states that performance-centered design "applies to both the work and the computer-human interaction." Winslow and Bramer state that the concentrating on "system users" puts the focus on systems in that "system users are oriented, not toward the work they are performing, but rather toward the system on which they are working" (page 46). They stress that the focus should be performance-centered and not how to use a system. However, it is important to remember that a system is usually comprised of functions done by the computer as well as done by the human (or user). In those cases where system functions are accomplished by a combination of the computer and the human, it is important to put the focus on how to use the system. The inclusion of knowledge management and organizational learning/training as part of PCD is also often used as a differentiator between PCD and UCD. However, the definition of "human-centered design" in the ISO Standard, as quoted above, is compatible with Gery's "goal for performance-centered software design", and can easily accommodate the design activities defined by most performance-centered design practitioners.

It is worth noting that the focus on "performance" is not new and was considered quite important in Industrial Psychology and Human Engineering in the 1950s and 60s. For example, McCormick (1957) in his text on *Human Engineering* stated that the broad goals of human engineering are those of "human economy, or efficiency, in work activities – of so creating situations in which human activities are carried on that the objectives of the activities are accomplished adequately with reasonable human costs." Sounds like it could be a definition for "performance-centered design" doesn't it? The military had also begun to pay attention to the human performance aspect of military system during the 1960s and those efforts resulted in the identification of the "Personnel Subsystem" as an important part of the system design.

During the late 1960s and early 1970s, Bell Laboratories embarked on a huge project to develop business information systems for the Bell Operating Companies. In order to develop effective procedures for the development of the "human performance part" of these systems, Bell Laboratories contracted with Research Associates Incorporated (mostly comprised of ex-military officers) to investigate and propose a methodology for developing a personnel subsystem for an industrial information system environment. Their report (Gardner, 1970) recommended approximately 20 end products that would result from a comprehensive design of a personnel subsystem to support an information system. Frank Kirk describes this work in his book *Total System Development for Information Systems* (Kirk, 1973). In addition, Bell Laboratories hired a number of experienced human factors people, including the author, to help implement and support the development organizations in producing personnel subsystem products. This approach was called Personnel Subsystem Development (PSD) and was a part of the Total System Development (TSD) process described in Frank Kirk's book. The Bell Labs PSD process was comprised of nine functional areas:

1. Management and Planning
2. PSS Analysis
3. Position Design and Documentation
4. Manual Interface Design
5. Training Development
6. Development of Personnel Planning Information
7. PSS Test
8. Preparation of Deliverable Documentation
9. Installation, Conversion and Maintenance

This process evolved during 1970s and the term "Personnel Subsystem Development" was replaced, due to its military connotations, with the term "Human Performance Engineering." Bob Bailey describes the evolved process in his book *Human Performance Engineering* (Bailey, 1982). Unfortunately, part of the evolution resulted in the organizational separation of human performance engineers (human factors people) from the performance support people (documentation and training). Documentation and Training were also put into separate organizations (Technical Publications and Training).

After the break-up of the Bell System, Bellcore inherited the operations support system development responsibilities from Bell Laboratories. At that time and until the early 1990s, documentation and training were in different organizations within Bellcore. However, as a result of a re-engineering study, documentation and training were merged into a new "Learning Support" organization. In addition, online help, which had been the responsibility of the human performance engineers working in the software development organizations (later called usability engineers), was assigned to the new organization. Encouraged by the potential synergies offered by this new organization, the author and several colleagues proposed a performance support model and prototype (Williams. and Larson 1994) to spur future development of electronic performance support within the organization. The model's major components were: online help, online training and an information browser. Goals of each of the components were:

- Online Help: to provide small chunks of task-relevant information to facilitate the user's completion of immediate and related tasks.
- Online Training: to provide small chunks of training (capable of simulating system functions), spaced over time, using the same system interface that the user will use on the job.
- Information Browser: to provide quick access to any information that a user feels that they need to perform their job. The browser was intended to provide both user related documentation and associated reference materials.

The Information Browser was to use "SuperBook" as the document browsing system. SuperBook not only provided hyper-text features, but also provided "fish-eye view" indexes and sophisticated search tools. For a description of SuperBook and the research that went into it, see Landauer (1995). Unfortunately, Bellcore dropped support for SuperBook so we were never able to implement the model.

During the late 1990s, the Learning Support Organization at Telcordia Technologies (previously Bellcore) began to actively pursue online delivery of performance support materials for the software applications that they supported. To cultivate this endeavor, a number of developer special interest groups (SIGs) were formed to help developers apply new technology, including one for Performance Support Systems (which I chaired). The design approach promoted in the PSS SIG, and in this book, is essentially a blend of performance-centered design and user-centered design. This design approach has the following tenets:

- A team approach is used in the design process that includes representatives of all of the relevant disciplines (e.g., performance technology, training, usability, documentation, online help and software development).
- User requirements and objectives are based on both user and organizational needs.
- Performance support requirements are based on the analysis of performance deficiencies (if they exist), user requirements and task requirements.
- Users and managers are actively involved in the requirements and testing process (but not in the actual design of the system).
- The choice of performance support methods to enable performance is based on an analysis of the skill and knowledge requirements of the tasks.
- Performance support is designed to optimize performance and minimize time away from the task (i.e., support should be quickly available and supply appropriate guidance when it is needed).
- Prototypes are developed (whenever possible) to test proposed design features. Prototypes are particularly important for products for use online (e.g., online help, wizards).
- Heuristic evaluation is used to evaluate performance support products prior to delivery for testing.
- Usability testing is performed on each performance support product using representative users.

- Performance support products are iterated based on heuristic evaluation and usability testing.

TYPES OF PERFORMANCE SUPPORT

Performance support includes a large number of different types of products. Most performance support products can be classified as documentation, online help, performance aids, coaches and wizards, instruction and Performance Support Systems (PSS).

Documentation

Documentation is probably the most common form of support material provided with a system. While the trend is to move all of the system's documentation on line, it is important to note that many users still prefer documentation in paper form. Also, the design of a document to be viewed online is different from one which is to be read in printed form. For example, if a two-column paper document is put online in the same format, readers will have difficulty reading the document because the page size of the printed document rarely fits within the display window on the computer. Scrolling through the one column also moves the second column before it is read.

Three types of documentation are typically supplied with larger software systems, system overviews, user documentation, and administrative or support documentation.

System overviews

A system overview describes the system at a high level. They generally include what the system accomplishes for the customer, what other systems it interacts with, how typical users use it, and what kind of platform it runs on. While the document should focus on the benefits of the system, it should also tell the customer what the system doesn't do. System overviews may be written for several different populations, e.g., managers, users, support personnel.

User documentation

Examples of user documentation include:

Getting Started Guides – describe the basic concepts a user will need to know to use a product or system, and instructions on how to get to further, more detailed information, such as other paper documentation, online help, online tutorial. Getting Started Guides are used primarily to introduce new users to a product/system and guide them into the product/system and to other performance support.

User Manuals – are intended for end-users of a product or system. They should include all the information a user will need, whether the user is new or experienced.

Administrative/support documentation

Examples of administrative/support documentation include:

System Administrator's Guides – are intended for the people who install and turn up the system's features, and who support users of the system, particularly when they have problems.

Database Administrator's Guides – are intended for a subgroup of the administrators of a software system, that is, for the people responsible for entry and maintenance of the data that allows the system to do its job.

Online Help

Basic online help consists of online text and graphics that is contextually linked to the application at the screen or field level. Online help should contain information about the system; its screens, fields, and commands; and provide instructions on how to complete tasks using the system. If the user knows the topic, online help should provide a means to find the content (search). Help systems can include a number of different types of help, such as:

Context-sensitive object/field help – provides information about a particular object or field and its context. It specifies what the characteristics of the object or field are and how to use the object or enter appropriate data. Context-sensitive help is usually accessible directly by clicking on the item in a prescribed way or pressing a key (e.g., F1).

Window/dialog help – is similar to context-sensitive object/field help, but relates to the whole window or dialog box. Window help explains the purpose of the window and may describe all of the window's elements such as menu bars, functional groupings, fields, buttons, etc. In addition, it may provide information concerning alternative paths to get to the window. A dialog help topic would explain the purpose of the dialog and describe the dialog's elements and associated procedures.

Procedural help – provides the specific procedures for accomplishing a task in a step-by-step format. Procedural help typically presents the steps in a short, concise manner to minimize reading time.

"Show me" help – provides a static or graphic example of a procedure or steps being accomplished (e.g., a video depicting the sequence of mouse clicks to access a particular screen and enter the appropriate information).

Information (about) help – provides descriptive information about the system and components. Information-about help is particularly useful to new users in that it provides "what" and "why" information about various system features, functions and processes. Microsoft calls this type of help "conceptual help."

Much of the research about the use of online help indicates users want the help system to answer the following questions:

• What is it?
• How do I do it?

Performance Aids

Performance aids are documents or devices that contain information for on-the-job use to specifically support the performance of a specific task or tasks. They may be in paper (or plastic) or online. More specifically, its function is to extend human capability to store and process information. A performance aid may simplify a step or steps in a task or may even eliminate steps. Some common examples of performance aids are checklists, decision tables and codebooks. Performance aids can be differentiated from other elements that support human behavior, such as tools, training aids and specialized equipment features. Many software and hardware products include performance aids for quick setup, use and maintenance of the product (e.g., a reference card for changing the ink cartridge for a printer).

A performance aid differs from a training aid in that training aids are documents or devices designed to encourage learning of particular skills or knowledge, while performance aids are designed to support work activities on the job. Training aids often contain small segments of information presented in planned sequences making them easier to learn. Performance aids, on the other hand, contain information in the form most suitable for direct use on the job by a trained individual. Therefore, the information segments in a performance aid may be larger than those contained in the training aid and are organized to facilitate use on-the-job rather than for ease of learning.

Performance aids have a number of benefits, including:

- Reducing errors because the reliance on the user's memory for accurate task performance is eliminated.
- Improving task efficiency and increasing the speed of task performance.
- Reducing training requirements. Although usually the user must be trained to use the aid, it is not necessary to train the user to learn the information in the aid.
- Lowering minimum selection requirements. Well-designed performance aids may allow a person to perform the job at a lower skill and knowledge level.
- Increasing safety when a task is performed involving dangerous equipment.
- Improving performance during contingencies, such as strikes, when people without experience must step in.
- Increasing reliability of performance. Performance aids provide standardization when several people perform the same activity. The use of performance aids allows better prediction of how quickly and/ or accurately a task will be performed.
- Increasing job satisfaction because a more efficient system enables the user to complete the task easier.

Coaches, Advisors and Wizards

Coaches – provide specific 'how to' information to help a user over a minor hurdle. Coaching typically consists of basic information, context-sensitive hints or tips, or procedural steps required to complete a specific, complex task. One type of coach "cue cards," often used in conjunction with help systems, provides step-by-step instructions while a user is performing a task, without the rest of the help interface appearing.

Advisors – provide hints, explanations of complicated concepts, and decision aids when a complex tasks requiring expertise must be performed. Advisors can help novices perform tasks and make decisions close to experts and can contribute to continued performance improvement. They are particularly useful when users need to perform complex tasks and need information as to when and why a step needs to be done or what information is required to make a specific decision.

Wizards – help users complete tasks by providing brief, action-oriented assistance in response to the users need. Rather than simply telling the user how to perform an activity, wizards present choices, prompt for input, transform data, screens or states and automate tasks. Wizards help users accomplish tasks that may be very complex and/or require experience to perform. For example, a graph wizard will lead the user through the steps of producing various kinds of graphs to display their data. The Wizard then creates the graph based on the information the user provides. Afterward, the user can make changes to the graph as desired. Install programs associated with many software products are also good examples of wizards. Such programs ask the user a few questions about their configurations and where they want the program installed and the software does the rest. Another good example is a tax program (such as Intuit's TurboTax) where the user answers questions and the program completes all of the tax forms based on the user's responses.

Instruction

Instruction, training and education are often used synonymously. In this book, we will differentiate between instruction and education, but will include training as part of instruction. The goal of education is to provide knowledge that can be applied to various tasks in various environments (e.g., courses provided in college).   Instruction (or training), on the other hand, is intended to impart the skills and knowledge needed to perform specific work activities. The term "instruction" will be used instead of "training" because training infers a formal delivery environment. Instruction can be provided by an instructor, by a paper self-instructional text or by a computer. Media presented during instruction may vary from straight text to highly interactive graphics and video. The following kinds of instruction may be provided as part of performance support:

Instructor-led Training – is training delivered by an instructor. Instructor-led training is particularly useful when the material to be learned is quite complex and the instructor is an expert. Instructor-led training also is frequently used when the system delivery time is too short to develop online training. In the case of a new system, for example, instructors are often subject matter experts involved in the development of the system.   Expert instructors can more easily keep up with the typical frequent changes to a system as it nears completion than online instructional developers.

Self-instructional Text – is training provided in self-instructional paper format. One of the major advantages of self-instructional text is that students are able to take the training at their own pace. In some cases, instructors or monitors may be available to provide additional help to students.   The use of self-instructional texts has diminished considerably over the last ten years due to the growing popularity (and declining cost) of online delivery of training materials. Since the same self-paced material can be delivered online without the cost of printing, it is typically cheaper to deliver it online.

Online Tutorial – is an interactive tutorial provided online that does not contain testing of student performance. Online tutorials may be delivered by means of various media, e.g., CDs, downloaded from a server to the users desktop computer or via the web.

Computer Based Training (CBT) – is similar to an On-line Tutorial, but is typically more performance oriented and includes testing and tracking of student performance. CBT may be comprised of various smaller components that also can be used for training on a specific task or function.

Task Tutor – is an interactive dialog that simulates the task or function to be learned. The purpose for the task tutor is to facilitate learning of the task so even novices can quickly attain competent performance. Tutors are particularly useful for tasks that are extremely difficult to learn, complex, or critical.

Performance Support System (PSS)

A PSS would typically contain several, interrelated pieces of more traditional performance support such as online help, online tutorials, online reference material and computer-based training, as well as coaches and wizards supported by an integrated, sophisticated user interface.

In addition to the performance support elements listed above, a PSS may contain features that automate repetitive, simple tasks without user intervention (e.g., automatically fill in spreadsheets, auto-correct spelling). While the goal of a performance support system is to provide all support materials online so that they can be accessed as needed, it is often necessary to include non-online components to facilitate performance (e.g., instructor-led training, paper performance aids). The most important attribute of a PSS is all of the performance support components (both computer-based and non-computer-based) are designed and developed as an integrated whole.

It also is often possible to migrate the non-computer components to online as a system matures and the software becomes more stable. In such cases, however, the structure of the non-computer components is a consideration. The more modular the structure, the easier it will be to incorporate them into the online system. If possible, the design of the overall performance support system should take into consideration any plans to integrate non-computer components later. It also is important to note that a performance support system may contain one or more electronic performance support systems as components. If all of the components used are in electronic form, the system is often referred to as an electronic performance support system.

A performance support system includes five main components representing guidance, knowledge, instruction, automation and the user interface. However, as noted above, a given performance support system may not include all five components.

Guidance component

The guidance component provides immediate help on accomplishing tasks and making decisions. Guidance includes online help, cue cards, advisors, performance aids and decision aids. In some cases, guidance components may be in non-electronic form (e.g., paper job aid).

Knowledge component

Information relevant to performing the job is provided by the knowledge component. Such information includes description of system components and functions, best practices, supportive information and reference materials (e.g., documentation, reference tables).

Instructional component

The instructional component provides instruction on performing job and system functions. It may include overviews, tutorials, computer or web-based training, task specific instruction and simulations exercises. While it is preferable for all of the instruction to be computer-based, in some cases instructor-led training may be included because of the nature of the training (e.g., requires human interaction), volatility of the software (e.g., new system) or development time constraints.

Automation component

Automating tasks users, either do not like to perform (e.g., are tedious and repetitive), or perform poorly, is an important goal of performance support systems. The automation component automates such tasks when they can be successfully performed by the computer. Wizards, for example, can accomplish certain activities with minimal user inputs and as a result allow users time to perform job activities more suited to their skill and knowledge.

User interface component

The user interface component ties all of the performance support components together in a logical easy to understand and use fashion. It is particularly important that the various parts of the performance support system use the same terminology and function in the same manner. Style guides can help ensure all of the performance support components are consistent with each other.

Performance Support System Attributes

A number of authors have suggested attributes relevant for performance support systems. For example, Gery (1995) lists twenty-six attributes and behaviors for a performance-centered system. These attributes/behaviors include: creating a "big picture," establishing and maintaining a work context, aiding goal establishment, structuring work process and progression through tasks and logic, reinforcing and linking activity to business strategy, institutionalizing current best approach, reflecting natural work situations (language, metaphors, actions), providing alternative views of the interface and support resources and alternative search and navigation mechanisms, providing contextual feedback, showing evidence of work progression, providing advise, automating tasks (where possible), layering information, providing access to underlying logic, allowing customization (individual differences and needs), providing obvious options and next steps and using consistent interface conventions and system behavior.

Raybould (2000) lists 22 heuristics for performance-center design, including: advance warning, affordance, answers descriptive, functional and procedural questions, automates tasks, captures best practice, consistent, feedback, forgiving, goal establishment, interprets, layered, matches work flow, minimizes translation, proactive support, recognition, relevant, resources, search, stimulus response path and task or process focused.

In supporting designers at Telcordia Technologies, we stressed performance support should help performers:

* Grasp the big picture
* Set goals and understand consequences
* Get definitions

- Understand concepts
- Carry out job tasks
- Know where they are in the process
- Get feedback
- Interpret results
- Get coaching or guidance when needed
- Learn
- Get help geared to their actions and knowledge
- Get access to a knowledge base
- Make decisions and solve problems

While the above attributes/heuristics are all relevant to the design of a performance support system, it will be a rare case when all of the attributes are fully represented in any given performance support system, particularly those associated with a large software system. Nevertheless, it is a worthwhile task for managers and developers to determine at the very beginning of their project what heuristics they expect to apply to their performance support system.

PERFORMANCE SUPPORT SYSTEM MODEL

As noted in the beginning of this chapter, the purpose of performance support is to maximize the usability and learnability of a product or system. The conceptual model depicted in Figure 1.3 illustrates some of the key relationships and concepts in this book.

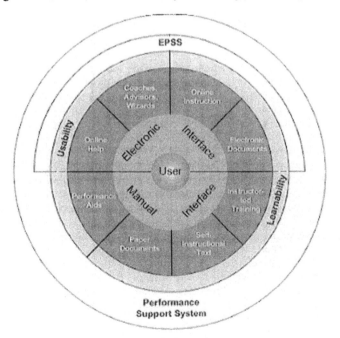

Figure 1.3 Conceptual Performance Support System Model

This conceptual model shows the relationships of performance support products, type of interface (manual or electronic), whether the product primarily supports usability or learnability and differentiates between Electronic Performance Support Systems (EPSS) and Performance Support Systems (PSS).

Note that Figure 1.3 depicts the user at the center of the model (reflecting the view of user centered design). Surrounding the user is the type of interface, either manual (i.e., typical paper or person interaction) or electronic, used to access the performance support product (the user interface component of the PSS). Segmented areas in the next ring list those products electronically delivered and those manually delivered, separated by the line in the middle of the model. The next ring separates the performance support products into two groups, those that typically support usability and those that typically support learnability. Those products that support usability are: performance aids, online help and coaches and wizards (i.e., the guidance and automation components of the PSS). Products that support learnability include online instruction, electronic documents, instructor-led training, self-instructional text and paper documents (i.e., the knowledge and instructional components of the PSS). The next semi-ring at the top of the model denotes those products that could be included within an Electronic Performance Support System (EPSS). Finally, the outer ring shows that all of the performance support products, including those in an EPSS, are part of the performance support system.

HOW TO USE THIS BOOK

As noted previously, this book is intended to be used by managers, designers and developers of performance support deliverables. Figure 1.4 shows the overall performance support development process. This figure depicts the sequence of the development activities and indicates the chapters in this book that provide relevant guidance.

Managers will be most interested in Chapter 2 (Design Environments and Strategies), Chapter 3 (Project Planning) and Chapter 9 (Testing Performance Support Products). However, managers also should be generally familiar with the material in the other chapters, particularly Chapter 7 (Developing Performance Support Products). Chapter 3 provides managers with useful information on both scoping and planning their projects. The samples included can be used directly in the planning process.

While performance support developers with design responsibility should read all of the chapters in the book, they should pay particular attention to Chapter 4 (Needs Assessment and Task Analysis), Chapter 5 (Matching Performance Support Methods to Task Requirements) and Chapter 6 (General Design Guidance). The principles and approaches presented in Chapters 4 and 5 can be directly applied to determining the requirements for performance support deliverables. Chapter 6 should be helpful in specifying the overall design characteristics of the various deliverables.

Performance support developers with specific product development responsibility also should read all of the chapters, but should concentrate on Chapter 6 (General Design Guidance), Chapter 7 (Developing Performance Support Products) and Chapter 8 (Testing Performance Support Products). Chapter 6 provides guidance that can be applied to the design of all of the various products, while Chapter 7 provides design and development information for each of the specific products. Chapter 8 presents important guidance for testing products both individually and as an integrated performance support system.

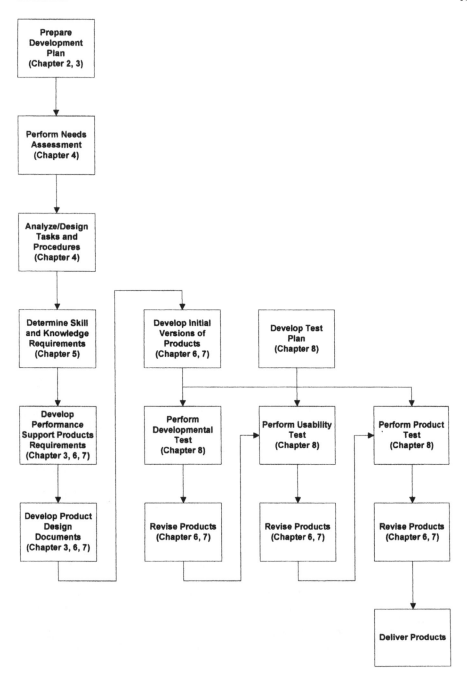

Figure 1.4 Performance Support Development Process

REFERENCES

Bailey, R. W. (1982) *Human Performance Engineering,* Englewood Cliffs, NJ: Prentice-Hall.

Broderick, C. (2001) Learning from Instruction, Knowledge Management and Performance Support, *eLearning Age Magazine,* Nov/Dec.

Callahan, E., Shim, J., Oakley, G. (2000) Learning, Information, and Performance Support (LIPS): A Multimedia-Aided Approach, *Interfaces,* 30, pp. 29-40.

Gardner, J., Kirk, F., and McClure, G. (1970) *Identification and Definition of Personnel Subsystem Analysis and Design Products and Services – Phase 1; A compilation of Developmental Information,* Research Association.

Gery, G. (1991) *Electronic Performance Support Systems,*Tolland, MA: Gery Associates

Gery, G. (1995) Attributes and Behaviors of Performance Centered Systems, *Performance Improvement Quarterly,* 8, No. 1, pp. 47-93.

Griffin, S. and Beagles, C. (2000) Training and Performance Support System (TPSS): A Case Study from Needs Assessment to Return on Investment, *Educational Technology,* September-October, pp. 34-42.

ISO 9241-10 (1996) *Ergonomic requirements for office work with visual display terminals (VDTs), Part 10: Dialogue principles,* Geneva, International Organization for Standardization.

ISO 9241-11 (1998) *Ergonomic requirements for office work with visual display terminals (VDTs), Part 11: Guidance on usability,* Geneva, International Organization for Standardization.

ISO 13407 (1999) *Human centred design processes for interactive systems,* International Organization for Standardization.

Kirk, F. G. (1973) *Total System Development for Information Systems,* New York: John Wiley & Sons.

Landauer, T. (1995) *The Trouble with Computers, Usefulness, Usability, and Productivity,* MIT Press, Massachusetts Institute of Technology, Cambridge, MA.

Massey, A., Montoya-Weiss, M. and O'Driscoll, T. (2001) A Methodology to Structure Ill-Structured Processes: Performance Centered Design, *Proceedings, 34th Hawaii International Conference on System Sciences, 2001* (HICSS-34) – Vol. 3, pg 3041, IEEE.

Marion, C. (2000) Make Way for Interactive Assistance. Online. Available HTTP: <http://www.chesco.com/~cmarion/PCD/MakeWayforInteractiveAsst.html> (accessed 6 February 2003).

McCormick, E. (1957) *Human Engineering,* New York: McGraw-Hill.

Microsoft (2001) Design Specifications and Guidelines – User Assistance. Online. Available HTTP: <http/www.microsoft.com/library/bookds/winguide/ch13b.htm> (accessed 12 February 2003).

Raybould, B. (2000) Building Performance-Centered Web-Based Systems, Information Systems, and Knowledge Management Systems in the 21st Century, *Performance Improvement,* July.

Williams, J. and Larson, G. (1994) Electronic Performance Support System Model, In *Proceedings of 1994 Human Factors and Ergonomics Society 38th Annual Meeting,* October 24-28.

Winslow, C. and Bramer, J. (1994) *Future Work,* New York: Free Press.

CHAPTER TWO

Design Environments and Strategies

INTRODUCTION

Computer system performance support products are developed in many different environments, but the most common environment is where the user interface has been developed and the software has progressed to the code stage before the writers, online help developers and trainers begin their development. In an ideal environment, the performance support personnel are involved upfront in the setting of requirements and the development of design documents that determine how the system looks, functions and interacts with users. Often, however, performance support is developed in a "worse case scenario" where performance support developers need to produce performance support just before the system is due to ship. In this chapter, we will discuss these three different environments, the impact they have on performance support development and strategies that can be used to overcome obstacles.

IDEAL ENVIRONMENT

The ideal environment is the environment usually assumed for the development of an EPSS. In this environment, performance support is considered an integral part of the system, and, if not the major focus, certainly a very important one. Design is done on a team basis with software designers, usability engineers and performance support developers all working together from requirements specification to the deployment of the system. In this ideal environment, the system requirements are developed on the basis of organization and user needs determined by system analysts and performance technologists analyzing business functions, work flows and processes, current performance and desired performance. Performance deficiencies are determined, intervention strategies are developed and user interfaces and support mechanisms are built to implement them. Prototypes are constructed for testing various user interface designs prior to implementation.

Impact

While the above environment is ideal for developing the best performance support for a system, it does present a number of challenges for managers and developers. The following factors will impact the development process:

- Organization. The organizational structure will affect how smoothly the development proceeds. For example, whether the organizational structure is hierarchical (with all of the members of the project reporting to a single organization), or a matrix structure (with some or all of the developers reporting to another organization but assigned to work on the project under a project manager). The organizational structure is likely to have a strong impact on how well members of the design and development teams work together.

- Coordination. The integrated development approach requires a considerable amount of coordination between the various specialists represented on the design and development teams. Often, performance support specialists assigned to design and development teams are not fully integrated into the teams. In addition, it may be difficult to develop appropriate coordination between specialties that have similar responsibilities, e.g., system analyst and performance technologists.
- Access to users. The degree to which users are involved in the design and development of the project will have a large impact on the usefulness of the resultant product.
- Developer Skills. In integrated development projects, higher levels of team work and "system" skills are required due to the interaction of team members with different specialties.
- Standardization. Lack of standardization of the development process and products will slow down development and make products less useful.

Strategies

Organization

Having worked on projects developed by means of a matrix organization as well as projects utilizing a straight hierarchical structure, I have found that the matrix approach leads to more problems and sometimes poor morale. Often, those project members reporting to organizations other than the developing organization are treated as second class citizens and do not receive as much credit for their project contribution as those reporting directly to the developing organization. Gery (1991) also points out that a hierarchical organizational structure is preferred for developing an EPSS because the organization can make all of the decisions required to fund the project and controls all of the resources to complete it.

If a matrix organizational approach is chosen for developing the performance support system, it is important to ensure that all project members (whether in the development organization or in a supporting organization) are treated equal in terms of both responsibility and rewards. If possible, the developing organization's project management should be directly involved with the performance reviews of team members reporting to other organizations. That way, the team member's efforts on the project will be visible to the matrix organization managers.

Coordination

Coordination between teams and team members is essential for an integrated development project to work properly. System Development Corporation back in the 1960s had an interesting and successful approach towards ensuring coordination between team members with different specialties on a project. Specialists (e.g., human factors, programmers, operations research, technical writers) were promoted to a higher-level job category (in the case of SDC, a Systems Consultant) only when they demonstrated that they could work together with other specialists on a team and had some understanding of the other specialties involved with the project. Extending from the SDC approach, I would highly recommend that members of inter-disciplinary teams (particularly performance support members) get involved in and contribute to as many design and development activities as possible to enhance their role as team members.

In the case of specialties with overlapping functions, e.g., system analyst and performance technologist, it is important for each of the specialties to understand and value each other's unique approach so as to optimize their combined contribution to the project. For example, system analysts have a great deal of experience analyzing business functions and existing work flows, while performance technologists have considerable experience in determining performance deficiencies and task performance. Coordination between the two specialties would be enhanced if each specialty performed those functions that they had the most experience in accomplishing and then produced a combined product, reviewed and approved by both.

Access to Users

Access to users is critical for the success of any performance support system. The ideal design environment assumes that users are involved throughout the process. However, it is often very difficult to obtain users frequently and in sufficient numbers to adequately assure meeting usability objectives. It is particularly difficult to obtain typical users to test prototype versions of the system during early design. One way around this is to use people within the organization (but not involved with the product) that have similar backgrounds and skills to the intended target population for initial prototype testing. Another suggestion is to convince a target customer organization to partner in the development and become the first organization to receive the performance support system. This approach works quite well if the product or system could significantly improve the customer's productivity. As part of the partnership, the customer would be asked to provide intended users as participants in the design and testing process. The customer benefits from the partnership by not only getting the product first, but also by influencing the design. In such a partnership situation, care must be taken to involve other potential users in later stages of testing, e.g., usability testing and beta testing.

Developer Skills

In addition to the need for a high level of skill in their own discipline, multi-discipline project team members must have teaming skills to be successful. One way to enhance teaming is for team members to learn all they can about the technologies used by other team members. This can be accomplished by taking courses related to other disciplines and/or reading books and journal articles on the subject area. However, a critical component of teaming skills is the ability to listen to people with different views and backgrounds and try to understand and incorporate their viewpoints whenever possible.

It also is important for performance support developers to be skilled in the use of the development tools (e.g., online help authoring tools, CBT authoring tools, word processing tools) selected for the production of the project deliverables. Skill in using development tools is particularly critical in projects where there are a limited number of developers for specific product types.

Standardization

To standardize the development process, I highly recommend the use of the ISO standard for the human centered design of interactive systems (ISO 13407, 1999). This standard specifies the various design and development activities necessary to ensure that users are adequately considered throughout the process. In addition, both developmental products (e.g., requirements, design documents) and deliverable products (e.g., software, performance support products) should follow standardized format and content requirements (e.g., style guides). The use of standardized formats and content also will contribute towards easier and faster development.

TYPICAL ENVIRONMENT

As noted above, the most typical performance support development environment is that in which performance support developers begin their development after most of the design decisions have already been made. User interfaces, dialog components and screen designs have been specified and may be in early implementation stages. Technical writers, trainers and help developers obtain their basic information from analyzing system documents (e.g., requirements and design documents) and talking to the various software developers and usability engineers (if involved).

Impact

The typical performance support development environment presents many challenges for managers and developers. For example:

- Funding. Since funding for performance support will generally come from the developing organization, it may be insufficient to create high quality performance support products.
- Information. The degree to which performance support developers can obtain access to design and development documents and subject matter experts will have a large impact on performance support product development. When essential information is not available, performance support developers typically assume details that may not be correct.
- Coordination. The coordination between system designers and developers, as well as various performance support developers, is critical to the success of the project.
- Access to Users. In the typical environment, it is rarely possible for performance support developers to obtain direct access to users. The lack of user access will impact on the usability of the performance support products.
- Developer Skills. Due to the lack of direct involvement in the project development, performance support personnel will need additional data collection and analytical skills.
- Standardization. Lack of standardization of the development process and products will slow down development and make products less useful.

Strategies

Funding

The lack of sufficient funding for performance support is often a problem in the development of computer systems within the typical design environment. Funding for performance support may be on a "head count" basis, or may be a specific budget amount allowed for the work. Funding requirements are often based on estimates made by managers that have not developed performance support products and relate the development to the production of system support documentation by technical writers. To get around this problem, performance support developers should prepare development time estimates for their products as soon as they have read the relevant system documentation. The resultant estimates can then be used to negotiate with the project management concerning any need for funding or schedule changes. While it may not be possible to obtain additional funding or schedule changes, such data will help explain problems meeting schedules.

Information

Access to system documentation and subject matter experts is critical to accurate and timely performance support product development. Performance support developers will need to obtain and become familiar with all of the requirements, design and development documents relevant to the development of their performance support products. Managers of performance support development will need to obtain and become familiar with the system development plans and schedules in order to develop realistic performance support development plans and schedules. In addition, developers will need to be able to interact with subject matter experts to obtain clarification and details about the design as well as feedback on material that they develop. In this environment it is crucial for all performance support material to be reviewed by appropriate subject matter experts to ensure accuracy.

Coordination

Coordination between performance support developers and other developers on the project is particularly important in the typical design environment. Since performance support developers have not been involved in most of the design decisions, they will need to ask many questions about the "why" and "how" of the system and its components. This interaction can best take place if the performance support developers are able to get themselves on the design or development team responsible for the development of the subsystem or component corresponding to the performance support product. It also is important for performance support developers to interact frequently to both share information and avoid duplication of effort.

Access to Users

As noted above, typically performance support developers do not have direct access to users and must rely on information supplied by others (e.g., user interface developers). If a front-end analysis or task analysis was done, it is essential for performance support developers to obtain and become familiar with them. In some cases, information about users will need to be extracted from other types of documents such as system descriptions, system requirements, etc. Performance support developers also should read any material available relevant to the intended users and their work.

One strategy for obtaining access to users for testing performance support products is to "piggy back" onto any other user testing activities scheduled. For example, if a usability test is to be done on the user interface, try to get the person conducting the test to include the use of online help and supporting documentation as part of the test of the interface. If possible, the online help developer should sit in on the test and observe firsthand any problems that the user may have with the help system. Another situation that can accommodate user testing of performance support products is "guest testing" where potential users test the computer system prior to its release. If the documentation is provided to the guest testers and online help and other online support products are included in the test environment, a great deal of information can be obtained on the usability of the products.

Developer Skills

In the typical design environment, interviewing skills, analytical skills, and skill with the development tools are all important. It is crucial for performance support developers to be able to obtain accurate and complete information from subject matter experts as quickly as possible. Performance support managers should select development personnel with the necessary skill sets to optimize the probability of delivering acceptable products.

Standardization

As was the case with the ideal environment, the use of standardized development processes and products will contribute to easier and faster development. The use of style guides for performance support products is highly recommended.

LATE INVOLVEMENT ENVIRONMENT

Unfortunately, performance support is often an afterthought in many software development projects. In such cases, performance support developers are brought in at the last minute to develop documentation and online help for the product. If training is provided, it is usually in the form of instructor-led courses with the instructors typically subject matter experts, rather than experienced training developers. Writers and help developers are provided system documentation developed by system designers and software developers from which they must extract important information and procedures that are relevant for users and support personnel. If they are lucky, a pre-delivery version of the system is running so that they can observe how the system really works. User-centered design or human factors efforts may or may not have been involved in the design or development.

Impact

In the late involvement environment, the following factors will impact the development process:

- Development Time. Since development time is very short, the completeness and usability of performance support products is likely to suffer.
- Information. The ability to obtain accurate and complete information about system components, functions, features and user interfaces is critical, but very difficult to obtain due to the lack of time.
- Coordination. Since system developers will be engaged in final development and testing activities (driven by meeting schedules), it will be very difficult to establish the necessary coordination with subject matter experts.
- Product Testing. Due to the lateness of the development of the performance support products, it is unlikely that the products can be thoroughly tested.
- Developer Skills. In this environment, performance support personnel will need higher levels of skill in data collection and analysis and product development.
- Standardization. Lack of standardization of the development process and products will slow down development and make products less useful.

Strategies

Development Time

Sufficient time to develop quality products is critical to the success of any performance support developer. Obviously, the first solution to the insufficient time problem is to negotiate for additional time. However, this is rarely possible due to delivery schedules already established for delivery of the system. Project managers never want to miss target dates, particularly where the delivery of support material is the holdup. It may be possible to obtain additional time for completion when the performance support product is delivered as part of the software (e.g., online help). But this only will be likely when project managers see the product as an important feature of the software.

If budget is not a problem and the system has many individual components or subsystems, it may be possible to break up the performance support product development into equivalent pieces and assign individual developers to each piece. However, a sufficient number of qualified performance support developers must be available to use this approach. In addition, projects with numerous developers require more coordination and management.

Information

As noted above, the availability of sufficient information about the system to develop performance support products is critical. Due to the shortness of time, initial data collection should be concentrated on those performance support aspects that are critical to using the system or application, e.g., procedures and steps for accomplishing user tasks. If time is available, additional information related to system features and other explanatory material can be added later.

Coordination

In the late environment, coordination is particularly important between the subject matter experts (typically the component or subsystem developers) and the performance support developers. It will be very important for the subject matter experts, and their management, to understand the contribution that the performance support product will have to the successful use of their components or subsystems. If possible, the subject matter expert should be paired with the performance support developer as the "team" responsible for the performance support product. This would assure the full commitment of the subject matter expert.

Product Testing

Since time will not be available to fully test performance support products, it is important to get them into the system test stages as quickly as possible. If the system or application will perform usability testing, developers should try to get their performance support products tested as part of that test. Due to the shortness of time, this may mean that the product is not fully completed when submitted for testing. But it is better to test an incomplete product than not test it at all. In any case, it is essential for all performance support products to be available and tested as part of the final system and product testing to ensure that they work properly and contain accurate information.

If sufficient testing cannot be done within the system test environment, follow-up evaluation on the performance support products should be done (see Chapter 8). Data from follow-up evaluation will be very useful in the development of the next version of the product.

Developer Skills

The late involvement environment will require the assignment of developers with the highest level of skills in developing their particular product type. It is essential that these developers are highly skilled on the development tools being used and have developed many products of the same type using these tools. If possible, performance support developers also should be chosen that have had previous experience in developing performance support for the type of system or application being developed. Such "double expertise" will optimize both the speed of development and the quality of the performance support product.

As was noted for the typical development environment, developers will also need to obtain accurate and complete information from subject matter experts as quickly as possible. Therefore, good data collection and analytical skills are a must.

If training needs to be provided in this environment, it can only be developed by subject matter experts that fully understand the application and its components and features. In such cases, it is important to utilize standardized formats for the development of training materials (e.g., PowerPoint presentations). It is highly recommended that such training include "hands on" use of the application. Also, a training technologist should supervise and coordinate the development effort to ensure that the instruction contains the appropriate content and utilizes appropriate instructional strategies.

Standardization

As was the case with the other design environments, the use of standardized development processes and products will contribute to easier and faster development. To focus the development effort on content rather than style, the use of style guides for performance support products is critical in the late involvement environment.

REFERENCES

Gery, G. (1991) *Electronic Performance Support Systems*, Tolland, MA: Gery Associates.

ISO 13407 (1999) *Human centred design processes for interactive systems*, International Organization for Standardization.

CHAPTER THREE

Project Planning

INTRODUCTION

A very important aspect of developing performance support for a system is determining the necessary resources and time required to do the job properly. The most accurate planning is obviously done on the basis of experience in developing the same sort of support for previous systems. Unfortunately, most managers responsible for developing performance support do not typically keep track of important details concerning the resources spent to produce the various types of deliverables. In addition, it is quite common for development personnel not to report additional time (overtime) required to meet tight schedules. While different planning environments will affect the project planning process and accuracy, the use of appropriate time and cost estimation factors and a comprehensive project plan will help improve the likelihood of producing performance support deliverables on time within available resources.

PLANNING ENVIRONMENT

The development of performance support for a system usually takes place in either an environment where performance support is in the same organization as the software development, an environment where performance support is developed in a central organization that is not part of software development or in an environment where performance support is developed by several different organizations.

Software Development Environment

When performance support is part of the software development organization, performance support project planning is closely tied to the software development plan. The delivery of performance support milestones and the receipt of materials from software development typically are dictated by the software development schedule. In such cases, performance support managers usually determine how much time they have to produce their deliverables (based on the software schedule) and assign sufficient resources to meet that schedule. When sufficient resources are not available, development personnel work overtime and/or the quality of the product suffers. This environment does have the advantage of having all of the development people in the same organization. Planning in the software development environment primarily involves a determination of what information is available about users and task requirements, when requirements and design documents can be obtained, when stable software can be expected, and making accurate estimates of the development time required to produce the various types of performance support. In the software development environment, it is important for performance support developers to establish formal working relationships with both the individuals responsible for developing the various system features and the user interface designers supporting those features. Planning should include the review and approval activities of the performance support developers of the software requirements and design documents, as well as the review and approval by software and user interface developers of performance support documents.

Centralized Performance Support Development Environment

In those cases that performance support is the responsibility of a centralized development organization, close coordination is required between the software development organization (or organizations) and the performance support development organization. This is the type of environment that was present at Telcordia Technologies until 2002 when downsizing resulted in the merging of performance support into software development. Prior to the merging, the Telcordia Learning Support Organization was responsible for developing performance support for many different operations support systems being developed by a number of software development organizations. As noted in the Introduction, Learning Support was comprised of performance technologists, online help developers, technical writers and training developers and instructors. In this type of environment, Learning Support was responsible for developing schedules for producing the various performance support products within the overall software development schedule. While the development schedules were primarily based on the requirements of the software development schedule, modifications could be made on the basis of Learning Support's analysis of the resources required to meet that schedule and still produce quality products.

The advantage of the centralized performance support development environment became evident when Telcordia contracted with SBC Communications to integrate seven operations support systems into one integrated system. Each of these systems had totally different types of user interfaces, online help, documentation and training. A software development organization was created to oversee the revisions of the existing software and develop new integrating software and common features. One of the important benefits of this project was that it forced standards to be developed to ensure compatibility of the various system components, including performance support. The software development organization was responsible for overall planning and development schedules for the integrated software. Learning Support was responsible for preparing a development plan and schedule that was then reviewed and approved by the various software development stakeholders (e.g., project management, usability, software design and programming). In addition, Learning Support was responsible for developing requirements and design documents for performance support products. These documents also were reviewed and approved by the software development stakeholders. It also is important to note that the responsible Learning Support developers were stakeholders for the various requirements and design documents prepared by software development. This approach allowed the performance support developers to have an impact on the design before it became finalized. Our experience indicated that this involvement of the performance support developers in the review and "sign-off" of software requirements and design documentation was an important contributor to developing accurate, complete and comprehensive performance support products.

One of the problems with the Telcordia centralized development environment was that the usability engineers were in the software development organization rather than in the organization responsible for performance support. Ideally, all of the human performance components should be developed by a team of performance technologists, interface designers, online help developers, documentation developers and trainers. That way, analytical activities (e.g., user needs and task analysis) and overall design activities can be done on a team basis. Fortunately, there was good cooperation between Learning

Support developers and the usability engineers responsible for the various user interface components.

In some cases, a centralized performance support development organization acts as a contractor to produce various performance support products for inside, and/or outside organizations. When functioning in this type of environment, the centralized organization typically submits a development plan and schedule to the client organization for approval.

Separate Performance Support Development Organizations

Where there are a number of different organizations (e.g., online help, training, technical publications) involved in developing performance support products for a system, coordination between the different organizations is critical to any successful development. A common overall plan should be developed as a cooperative effort of the involved organizations. If possible, the development activities across the different organizations should be standardized so that effort involved can be uniformly represented. It is important for the developing organizations to include in the plan the sharing of resources and information, particularly during the analytical stages of development. As noted above, it is very important to include review and approval activities of both the system developers of performance support products and performance support developers of system products.

ESTIMATION FACTORS AND IMPACTS

Inaccurate estimating of the time and cost of developing performance support products often has devastating results, such as: poor quality deliverables, demoralized and burnt-out staff, loss of credibility, lost market opportunities, budget overruns, etc. Most estimates are done by project managers, either on the basis of their own experience, or from best-guess estimates supplied by developers. While a number of authors have made recommendations on the development time and factors to consider in pricing the development of various performance support products, none of the recommendations provided a parametric method for ensuring consistent and reliable results. Since a considerable amount of work has been done in the development of parametric estimation tools for software projects, the methods and approaches used for software estimation are used as a general frame of reference in this book.

Steps in Cost Estimation

Cost estimation generally is comprised of three basic steps:

- Estimating the size of the development product.
- Estimating the effort in person-months or hours.
- Estimating the project cost in dollars.

Estimating Size

For software products, size is usually in terms of Lines of Code, Function Points, Feature Points or Objects. Similarly, for performance support deliverables it would be pages of a manual, number of online help topics, hours of instruction, etc. While a great deal of research has gone into estimating the size of software products, not much research has been done on estimating the size of performance support deliverables. One author assumed a particular size deliverable in developing estimates of development time by means of experts and later massaged the deliverable size assumption based on input from the raters (see Golas, 1994). Typically the size of a performance support deliverable is estimated on the basis of its likely similarity to existing deliverables.

Estimating Effort

Much more research and expert judgments have been offered in terms of the amount of effort required to develop various performance support deliverables. One set of ratios of development time to hours of instruction that has been around for at least twenty years (and quoted frequently) is:

- Instructor-led = 70/1 (hours of development/hours of instruction)
- Self Instruction = 120/1
- CBT (regular) = 200-300/1
- CBT (complex) = 300-500/1

Other general estimates have been given by several authors. For example, Kruse (2002) suggested development times of 300/1 for web/computer-based without audio or video and 600/1 for high quality multimedia. Parks (2002) suggests 100/1 for drill and practice, text based, page turner types of material; 300/1 for tutorial, graphics, limited animation, audio; 500/1 for simulation, graphics, animation, video, audio; and 600/1 for first effort, undocumented content, HTML programming.

However, the most extensive estimates that have been presented for the effort required to develop various types of performance support products are from Greer (1992), Golas (1994), the Dublin Group (1996), and the Telcordia Technologies Performance Support Project Estimator© (2000). Table 3.1 presents a comparison of the development time estimates provided by these four sources.

It should be noted that Greer's estimates were for various kinds of training materials and the estimates provided by Golas related only to the development of interactive courseware. Nevertheless, there is a fair amount of agreement between the various estimates. Based on the data listed above and my own experience in developing various kinds of deliverables, I propose the time estimates listed in Table 3.2 as a reasonable starting point in estimating development times.

Variables Impacting on Effort

A number of studies and recommendations have suggested variables that need to be taken into account when determining development time for various performance support products. Greer, in conjunction with the estimates of development time listed in Table 3.1, noted that development time should be increased by 50% for inexperienced developers.

Table 3.1 Summary of Time Estimates for Developing Various Performance Support Deliverables

Deliverable Type	Development Time Estimates*			
	Greer 1992	**Golas 1994**	**Dublin 1996**	**Telcordia 2000**
EPSS				6 hrs/screen
Expert Systems			.5-8 hrs/topic	
Online Help			.25-2 hrs/topic	2 hrs/topic
Wizards, Cue Cards			8-10 hrs/item	4 hrs/screen
Online User Guide/Reference		2-5 hrs/page		4 hrs/page
Online Tutorial				300 hrs
CBT (general)	150 hrs	50-200 hrs	150-400 hrs	300 hrs
CBT – Multimedia		200-600/hrs	400-1500 hrs	450 hrs
Self-instruction Guide			80-200 hrs/pub	
Instructor-led Training			40-200 hrs	50 hrs
Instructor Materials	1 hr/page			4 hrs/page
Exercises	5 hr/exercise			
Test Items	.5 hr/item			
Paper-based Training Materials				4 hrs/page
Job Aid			10-100 hrs/item	4 hrs/page
Paper Documentation			1-4 hrs/page	4 hrs/page
Reading Material	1 hr/page			
Video	3 hrs/min			3 hrs/min
Analytical Studies (FEA, TA, FUE)				50 hrs/page

*Instruction per hour of instruction, other deliverables in units

Golas (1994) collected data from 20 Interactive Courseware (ICW) experts, with an average of 18 years of experience in developing CBT, concerning both development time and variables that affected development time. She originally identified 10 factors that affected ICW time estimates, but later increased this to 13 factors after evaluating feedback from her experts. Broadbent (1998) identified 12 variables that should be considered in the development of an instructor-led program. The "Telcordia Performance Support Project Estimator" (Telcordia, 2000) includes 12 parameter values for estimating the cost of various kinds of performance support deliverables (see Figure 3.1). For the development of training on the internet, Parks (2002) lists such variables as: the use of templates, experience, authoring tools, stability of content, complexity of media, and the use of simulation. Kruse (2002) listed 8 factors affecting the cost of developing e-learning. Table 3.3 summarizes and compares the development time factors identified by Golas, Broadbent, Telcordia, Parks and Kruse. It should be noted that, except for Telcordia, the factors identified mostly concerned the development of training. However, most of the factors that impact training development time also will impact on the development of other performance support products.

Table 3.2 Time Estimates Proposed for Developing Various Performance Support Deliverables

Deliverable Type	Development Time Estimates*
EPSS	7 hrs/screen
Advisors	6 hrs/topic
Wizards	6 hrs/screen
Online Help	2 hrs/topic
Cue Cards	6 hrs/item
Online User Guide	5 hrs/page
Online Reference	3 hrs/page
Online Tutorial	300 hrs
CBT (general)	300 hrs
CBT – Multimedia	450 hrs
CBT – Multimedia, Highly Interactive	700 hrs
CBT - Simulation	1000-1500 hrs
Self-instruction Guide (paper)	150 hrs
Instructor-led Training	50 hrs
Instructor Guide (paper)	4 hrs/page
Paper-based Training Materials	4 hrs/page
Job Aid	50 hrs/item
Paper User Guides	4 hrs/page
Paper Administrator Guides	5 hrs/page
Video	3 hrs/min
Analytical Studies (FEA, TA, FUE)	50 hrs/page

*Instruction per hour of Instruction, other deliverables in units

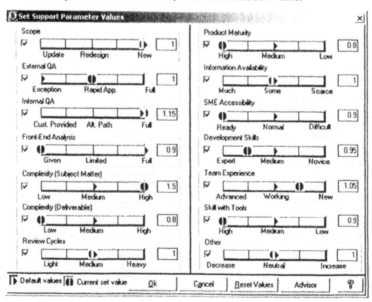

Figure 3.1 Parameter Values Screen (Source – Telcordia Performance Support Project Estimator, Copyright © 2000 Telcordia Technologies, Inc. Produced with Permission)

Table 3.3 Summary of Variables Impacting the Development of Performance Support Deliverables

Variable Identified	Golas 1994	Broadbent 1998	Telcordia 2000	Parks 2002	Kruse 2002
Analysis Information (e.g., performance req.) Availability	X	X	X		
Quality of Data Available		X			X
Subject Matter Knowledge	X	X	X		
Subject Matter Complexity	X		X		X
Content Stability	X		X	X	
Target Population Info		X			
Familiarity with Target Population	X				
Following Best Commercial Practice	X				
Following Standards	X		X	X	
Quality of Planning	X	X			
Course Length	X	X			X
Degree of Interactivity		X		X	
Complexity of deliverable (media)			X	X	X
Elements Included (e.g., participant, instructor)		X			
Packaging Requirements (delivery media)		X			X
Scope of development		X	X	X	
Level of Interaction with Client (review cycles)		X	X		
Client's Level and Quality of Involvement	X	X	X		
Maturity of Development Tools (skill with)	X		X	X	
Resource and Time Availability for Project	X				X
Experience of Project Team	X		X	X	
Development Skills			X		
Student Tracking					X

On the basis of the above data and my experience in developing and using the estimation variables in Estimator, I have concluded that there are four major variable types that impact upon the development time of performance support deliverables, i.e., information variables, content variables, development variables and developer variables. Table 3.4 lists the various variables associated with each of the variable types and their potential impact on performance support development time.

Table 3.4 Variables and Impacts on the Development of Performance Support Deliverables

Variable	Impact on Development Time
Information Variables	
User/Organizational Needs	None or minimal increases, complete decreases
Performance Requirements	None or minimal increases, complete decreases
Target Population Information	None or minimal increases, complete decreases
Quality of Data Available	Lower the quality the longer the time
Subject Matter Expert	Low availability increases, high decreases
Content Variables	
Subject Matter Complexity	High increases, low decreases
Content Stability	Low stability increases
Content Length	Long lengths increase, short decreases
Elements Included	Large number increases, small decreases
Degree of Interactivity	High interactivity increases, low decreases
Complexity of Deliverable (media)	High complexity increases, low decreases
Packaging Requirements	Complex increases, simple decreases
Tracking and Reporting Requirements	Requirement for increases
Development Variables	
Scope of Development	All new increases, simple revision decreases
Quality of Planning	Low planning increases, high quality decreases
Following Standards	Following standards increases initially, but decreases in the long run
Product Maturity	Low increases, high decreases
Development Tools Maturity	Low increases, mature tools decrease
Review Cycles	More cycles increase
Client Involvement	High client involvement increases, but may save maintenance time
Developer Variables	
Experience with Deliverable Type	Low experience increases, high decreases
Subject Matter Knowledge	Low knowledge increases, high decreases
Familiarity with Target Population	Low familiarity increases, high decreases
Development Skills	Low skills increase, high skills decrease
Team Skills	Low team experience increases, high decreases

Estimating Costs

Estimating costs is based on the estimates of size, development time, personnel costs and other costs to develop the deliverables (e.g., travel, equipment). Often mathematical expressions of various complexities are used to express cost as a function of one or more cost driving variables. For example, the complexity of the system, difficulty of obtaining information and experience of the developers would all affect development time and associated costs.

To estimate costs accurately, it is important to be able to determine the different salary levels, and percentages of each, that will be working on the project. Also, you will need to know what your organization's loading (or overhead) factor is in relation to your direct (salary) costs.

Estimation Approaches

Estimation approaches are based on the use of a particular model such as analogy, functionality, expert judgment, or parametric.

Analogy Models

Analogy models are used to estimate the deliverable's size, costs and/or development time, through comparison with one or more similar deliverables developed in a previous project (where costs and schedules are known). In software estimation, database analogy models are sometimes used to estimate size. Where analogy estimating techniques are used, it is important to make careful comparisons between previous and new deliverables in terms of similarities and differences.

Functionality Models

In functional models, the deliverable's size, and or development time, is computed from components of known size (and development time) from a database. For software estimation, size estimates for various software functions are contained in a database. Users can list the functions they expect their product to perform and obtain a size estimate for each. Then, all of the function estimates can be added together as an estimate of the total size for the software product.

Expert Judgment Models

Expert judgment models estimate size, and or development time, from the opinions of one or more subject matter experts. A number of software cost models use the expert judgment approach. PERT (Program Evaluation and Review Technique) is a method used to size a software (or hardware) product and calculate the standard deviation for risk assessment purposes.

Parametric Models

Parametric models use statistical relationships between historical data (such as size and development time) and other variables (technical, physical, environmental, personnel characteristics) to compute costs. Many software project estimation tools use parametric models to develop estimates through mathematical formulas (e.g., regression-based models) that use statistical relationships between the size and software characteristics that affect size. Parametric models are similar to database analogy models since historical data are used in their development. Instead of direct comparisons, regression models use equations that are developed based on analysis of the historical data.

PLANNING METHODOLOGY AND TOOLS

Successful planning for any project requires both a good planning process and appropriate tools. The process must include a methodology that will produce the information necessary to plan the project with an acceptable degree of confidence.

Methodology

When a performance support development project is comprised of many different deliverables, it is particularly important to use the same planning methodology across all of the deliverables. Otherwise, the data going into projections of development time and resources will be inconsistent and lead to inaccuracies that will cause management difficulties. A consistent methodology also is critical to the collection of historical data that can be used for planning future projects. The availability of a detailed process flow of all of the performance support development activities and relationships to other activities is essential for the development of a good plan. Such a process flow should include the analytical activities that are common to the design of the various products (e.g., user needs assessment, task analysis). In addition, it should include activities related to evaluating and responding to requirements and design documents prepared by software development. Reviewing activities often are not included in planning, but such activities take time and need to be accounted for in the overall plan. The list below depicts general tasks that are appropriate for planning an integrated development of performance support deliverables for a computer system.

1. Prepare Requirements and Design Documents

    *   Collect and Analyze User Needs and Task Requirements Data
    *   Review System Requirements and Design Documents
    *   Develop Performance Support Release Plan
    *   Prepare Online Help Requirements
    *   Prepare Documentation Requirements
    *   Prepare Training Requirements
    *   Develop Design Document
    *   Develop Online Help Prototype

2. Prepare Initial Drafts of Deliverables (e.g., online help, guides, performance aids, and reference materials)

    *   Develop structures according to requirements
    *   Review and analyze system detailed design documents
    *   Develop drafts of deliverable (test links for online materials)
    *   Perform heuristic evaluation on drafts and revise as required
    *   Distribute drafts for unit test
    *   Revise and update deliverables based on comments

3. Prepare Performance Support Deliverables for Product Test

    *   Update drafts of deliverables and prepare drafts of training materials
    *   Perform QA on drafts and revise as required
    *   Distribute drafts for Product Test
    *   Revise and update deliverables based on Product Test comments

4. Prepare Performance Support Deliverables for Pre-Delivery Test

    *   "Build" online help for Pre-Delivery Test
    *   Distribute deliverables for Pre-Delivery Test
    *   Revise and update deliverables based on Test results
    *   Build final versions of online materials for release
    *   Issue final versions of paper deliverables for release

It should be noted that for actual planning purposes the general tasks above would be broken down into more detail. In addition, each deliverable would have its associated development tasks listed separately so that appropriate start/complete dates and dependencies can be assigned.

Personnel Requirements – Design Team

To prepare a comprehensive performance support development plan, it also is important to identify the personnel requirements needed to design the performance support system and develop the various kinds of deliverables. As noted previously, a team approach is recommended for the integrated analysis and design activities. The team should be comprised of experienced developers of the various types of products (e.g., online help, training, documentation) as well as performance technologists and human factors personnel (if available). If Electronic Performance Support components are included in the system, one or more software developers also will be needed on the design team. In addition to having strong team skills, design team members should have the following qualifications:

Performance Technologists

Performance technologists on the design team should have at least five years of experience in analyzing and specifying user needs and task requirements as well as designing appropriate performance enabling mechanisms. If possible, performance technologists should have a graduate level degree in performance or educational technology from a recognized educational institution. It is recommended that a senior performance technologist function as the design team leader.

Human Factors/Usability Engineer

The human factors/usability engineers on the design team should have at least five years of experience in performing human factors analysis and design activities. If the performance support system will have any EPSS components, it is particularly important that they also have had experience in designing and developing user interfaces.

Online Help Designer

Online help designers should have at least five years of experience developing online help products. They also should have experience in designing the look and feel of online help. In addition, online help designers should have human factors training and experience, particularly in regard to user interface design. If possible, they should have a degree in human factors or performance technology, or a degree from a university that has a curriculum related to the design of online performance support materials. A background limited to technical writing skills and experience is not acceptable for this position.

Instructional Designer

The instructional designers on the design team should have at least five years of experience in both the analysis and specification of user needs and task requirements and the development of training intervention strategies. They should have experience in completing a number of instructional development projects from inception to conclusion. Instructional designers should have a graduate level degree in instructional technology or related subjects from a recognized educational institution.

Senior Technical Writer

Senior technical writers should have at least five years of experience in preparing performance support documentation. If possible, they also should have experience in the preparation of online documentation. Their responsibilities should have included the design of the document structure and formats as well as preparing the content. Senior technical writers should have a degree from an educational institution that has a curriculum related to developing system support materials.

Software Developer (EPSS components)

Software developers on the design team should have at least five years of experience in developing user-related software for computer systems. In addition, software developers should have three to five years of experience with the programming language used for the EPSS application. Knowledge of user interface design issues will be particularly helpful. If possible, software developers for an EPSS project should have developed the software for one or more previous electronic support components (e.g., wizard, decision support system) or systems.

Personnel Requirements – Product Developers

To maximize the likelihood that performance support products will be developed in a reasonable time frame and meet the needs of their users, product developers need to have product specific qualifications. Developers for the various deliverables should have the following qualifications:

Online Help Developer

Online help developers should have at least two years of experience developing online help products. If possible, they should have a degree in human factors or performance technology, or a degree from a university that has a curriculum related to the design of online performance support materials. Online help developers with a background limited to technical writing skills and experience should be encouraged to obtain additional training in human factors, particularly user interface design.

Instructional Developer

The instructional developers should have at least two years of experience in the development of instructional materials. They should have prepared several training courses and, preferably, developed the training intervention strategies for those courses. If possible, instructional developers should have a graduate level degree in instructional technology or related subjects from a recognized educational institution. Where subject matter experts serve as instructional developers, they should be encouraged to take courses in the development of training materials.

Technical Writer

Technical writers should have at least two years of experience in preparing performance support documentation. Experience in the preparation of online documentation is an additional plus. Technical writers should have a degree from an educational institution that has a curriculum related to developing technical documentation.

Performance Technologist or Human Factors Engineer (EPSS components)

Performance technologists or human factors engineers that have responsibility for developing EPSS components should have at least three years of experience in designing appropriate performance enabling mechanisms as well as experience in designing and developing user interfaces. Experience in the development of interactive media also would be helpful. If possible, performance technologists or human factors engineers assigned to develop EPSS components should have graduate level degrees in their particular disciplines from recognized educational institutions.

Software Developer (EPSS components)

Software developers should have at least three years of experience in developing user-related software for computer systems. In particular, software developers should have at least three years of experience with the programming language used for the EPSS application. If possible they should have some knowledge of user interface design issues. In addition, previous experience in the development of an electronic support component or system would be helpful.

Tools

The use of estimation tools during planning and early design forces project managers to consider more carefully both the characteristics of the products they expect to deliver to the customer and the development environment. Since much of the power of these tools is based on the quantification of previous experience in developing similar products, managers that use estimation tools are more likely to accurately scope out the design and development activities and effort required. Another benefit of estimation tools is that they can be applied both during the requirements and design phases of the project. As the design becomes more detailed, the estimation process becomes more accurate. Estimates are later compared with "actuals" and the tool is refined on the basis of accumulated experiences and becomes progressively more accurate. In addition to estimating tools, project scheduling tools (e.g., Microsoft Project) can be very useful in planning and managing a performance support project.

Telcordia Performance Support Project Estimator©

The Telcordia Performance Support Project Estimator© (or "Estimator") is an electronic performance support system (EPSS) that provides a consistent methodology to create estimations for analytical deliverables (front-end analysis, task analysis and follow-up evaluation reports) and specific performance support deliverables (paper documentation, paper-based training, computer-based training, computer-based support, video and web sites). Estimator is a knowledge-based tool that provides access to integrated information, advice and accumulated experiences for the estimating process. First time users are able to create accurate estimates on the basis of the guidance provided by the program.

Advice is provided for both estimating the size of the deliverables and setting the parameters throughout the process. Experienced users can directly prepare estimates without using the available guidance and can prepare "quick estimates" without providing project information.

Estimator, like similar software estimation tools, uses two major inputs types to produce development time and cost estimates. These are:

1. Probable size of the deliverable (number of screens, topics, web pages, etc.)
2. Parameter setting to reflect the development environment (e.g., extent of quality process, expertise of the developers, skill with tools, whether the system is new or a revision)

It is important to note that Estimator is very user configurable and new types of deliverables can be added (e.g., a "wizard") and parameter values can be easily modified to match local development environments.

Project Scheduling Tools

The use of a project scheduling tool (e.g., Project Scheduler, Microsoft Project) can help a performance support project manager specify the performance support activities and resources required to develop the various performance support deliverables. Scheduling tools also require the identification of interrelationships and dependencies with other activities that impact development. For example, the availability of software requirements and design documents will impact on the development of related performance support products.

Project scheduling tools provide sophisticated features that simplify the task of scheduling and tracking project phases, tasks, milestones and workloads. They also typically provide charts (e.g., gantt charts), calendars, task sheets, graphs and reports to indicate progress. On the basis of dependencies and critical path information, project scheduling tools can depict the effect of task levels and completions on the overall project schedule. However, a project scheduling tool's accuracy and usefulness is based on the quality of the data that is entered in to it about the project. To use a project scheduling tool, all of the important development tasks, their dependencies on other activities and resource requirements must be available. First time use obviously will be the most difficult since the required data need to be obtained from knowledgeable performance support developers and managers within the organization. For successive projects, the original data can be refined on the basis of experience with the previous project and the use of the tool will be much easier.

Development time estimates from a cost estimating tool (e.g., Estimator) can be useful input to a project scheduler. However, the development time estimates provided by Estimator are for an entire project or the individual deliverables for that project. Develop times for the phases and tasks within a project are not provided. Therefore, the project manager will need to estimate the amount of total time that will be allocated to each of the development tasks. Ideally, a performance support estimating tool should be able to allocate development time projections across the various development tasks and directly input this data into a project scheduler.

SAMPLE PLAN FOR PERFORMANCE SUPPORT PROJECTS

In order to develop a plan for the development of performance support deliverables, it is necessary to prepare a list of major tasks that need to be accomplished during the development. As noted in the section on Methodology, such major tasks would include:

1. Develop performance support requirements and design documents
   - Collect and analyze user needs and task requirements data
   - Prepare performance support release plan
   - Prepare online help requirements
   - Prepare documentation requirements
   - Prepare training requirements
   - Prepare design document
   - Develop online help prototype

2. Prepare initial drafts of deliverables for software unit test
   - Develop initial drafts of Online Help, Getting Started Guide, User Guide, Installation Guide, System Administration Guide and Database Guide
   - Perform heuristic evaluation on product and revise as required
   - Distribute draft product (or initial "build") for software unit test
   - Revise based on comments

3. Prepare deliverables for product test
   - Update drafts of Online Help, Getting Started Guide, User Guide, Installation Guide, System Administration Guide and Database Guide and prepare user training materials
   - Perform quality assurance assessments on products and revise as required
   - Distribute updated product (or new "build") and training for product test
   - Revise based on comments

4. Prepare deliverable for pre-delivery test
   - Distribute drafts (or builds) of Online Help, Getting Started Guide, User Guide, Installation Guide, System Administration Guide and Database Guide
   - Test help and training materials on target population samples
   - Revise products based on comments and test results
   - Issue final versions of performance support products

Table 3.5 provides a list of the above major tasks and the typical activities required to develop various performance support products for a software system. This table can be used as a performance aid to develop "start" and "finish" dates and assign personnel responsibilities for completing the various activities. If a project scheduling tool is used by project management, data from the Performance Support Development Tasks table can be provided as input for the overall project schedule.

Table 3.5 Performance Support Development Tasks

Activity	Start	Finish	Responsibility
Requirements and Design			
Collect and Analyze User Needs and Task Requirements Data			
Develop data collection plan			
Distribute plan for review			
Review comments and update plan			
Collect user needs and task requirements data according to plan			
Analyze data			
Prepare report			
Develop Performance Support Release Plan			
Prepare draft of Release Plan			
Distribute Release Plan for review			
Review comments and update Release Plan			
Baseline Release Plan			
Online Help Requirements			
Prepare Online Help Requirements			
Distribute Online Help Requirements for review			
Review comments and update Online Help Requirements			
Baseline Online Help Requirements			
Documentation Requirements			
Prepare Documentation Requirements			
Distribute Documentation Requirements for review			
Review comments and update Documentation Requirements			
Baseline Documentation Requirements			
Training Requirements			
Prepare Training Requirements			
Distribute Training Requirements for review			
Review comments and update Training Requirements			
Baseline Training Requirements			
Design Document			
Review available performance-related information			
Prepare Design Document			

Activity	Start	Finish	Responsibility
Distribute Design Document for review			
Review comments and update Design Document			
Baseline Design Document			
Online Help Prototype			
Develop Online Help prototype			
Test Prototype and revise Prototype			
Demonstrate Prototype			
Revise Prototype as required			
Software Unit Test			
Online Help			
Develop Online Help content and associated links			
Test content and links			
Develop TOCs, Index, Glossary			
Perform heuristic evaluation on help and revise as required			
"Build" Help for software unit test			
Comments on unit test Help version due to author			
Revise help based on Comments			
Getting Started Guide			
Develop document structure according to requirements			
Develop draft of Getting Started Document			
Perform heuristic evaluation on draft and revise as required			
Distribute draft for software unit test			
Comments on unit test draft due to author			
Revise and update document based on comments			
User Guide			
Develop document structure according to requirements			
Develop draft of User Guide			
Perform heuristic evaluation on draft and revise as required			
Distribute draft for software unit test			
Comments on unit test draft due to author			
Revise and update document based on comments			
Installation Guide			
Develop document structure according to requirements			

Activity	Start	Finish	Responsibility
Develop draft of Installation Guide Document			
Perform heuristic evaluation on draft and revise as required			
Distribute draft for software unit test			
Comments on unit test draft due to author			
Revise and update document based on comments			
System Administration Guide			
Develop document structure according to requirements			
Develop draft of System Administration Guide			
Perform heuristic evaluation on draft and revise as required			
Distribute draft for software unit test			
Comments on unit test draft due to author			
Revise and update document based on comments			
Database Guide			
Develop document structure according to requirements			
Develop draft of Database Guide			
Perform heuristic evaluation on draft and revise as required			
Distribute draft for software unit test			
Comments on unit test draft due to author			
Revise and update document based on comments			
Product Test			
Online Help			
Update Online Help content and associated links			
Test content and links			
Update TOCs, Index, Glossary			
Perform QA on help and revise as required			
"Build" Help for Product Test			
Comments on Product Test help version due to author			
Revise help based on Product Test Comments			
Getting Started Guide			
Update draft of Getting Started Document			
Perform QA on draft and revise as required			
Distribute draft for Product Test			

Activity	Start	Finish	Responsibility
Comments on Product Test draft due to author			
Revise and update document based on Product Test comments			
User Guide			
Update draft of User Guide			
Perform QA on draft and revise as required			
Distribute draft for Product Test			
Comments on Product Test draft due to author			
Revise and update document based on Product Test comments			
User Training			
Develop user training materials			
Perform QA on draft and revise as required			
Distribute draft for Product Test			
Comments on Product Test draft due to author			
Revise and update training material based on Product Test comments			
Installation Guide			
Update draft of Installation Guide Document			
Perform QA on draft and revise as required			
Distribute draft for Product Test			
Comments on Product Test draft due to author			
Revise and update document based on Product Test comments			
System Administration Guide			
Update draft of System Administration Guide			
Perform heuristic evaluation on draft and revise as required			
Distribute draft for Product Test			
Comments on Product Test draft due to author			
Revise and update document based on Product Test comments			
Database Guide			
Update draft of Database Guide			
Perform heuristic evaluation on draft and revise as required			
Distribute draft for Product Test			

Activity	Start	Finish	Responsibility
Comments on Product Test draft due to author			
Revise and update document based on Product Test comments			
System Administration Training			
Develop system administration training materials			
Perform QA on draft and revise as required			
Distribute draft for Product Test			
Comments on Product Test draft due to author			
Revise and update training material based on Product Test comments			
Pre-Delivery Test			
Online Help			
"Build" Help for Pre-Delivery Test			
Test help on sample of target population			
Comments on test version due to author			
Revise help based on Test Comments			
Build final version of Help for release			
Getting Started Guide			
Distribute document for Pre-Delivery Test			
Comments on test version due to author			
Revise and update document based on test comments			
Issue Final version of document			
User Guide			
Distribute document for Pre-Delivery Test			
Comments on test version due to author			
Revise and update document based on Test comments			
Issue Final version of document			
User Training			
Test user training materials on target population			
Revise as required			
Issue Final version of training			
Installation Guide			
Distribute document for Pre-Delivery Test			
Comments on test version due to author			
Revise and update document based on Test comments			
Issue Final version of document			

Activity	Start	Finish	Responsibility
System Administrator's Guide			
Distribute document for Pre-Delivery Test			
Comments on test version due to author			
Revise and update document based on Test comments			
Issue Final version of document			
Database Guide			
Distribute document for Pre-Delivery Test			
Comments on test version due to author			
Revise and update document based on Test comments			
Issue Final version of document			
System Administration Training			
Test system administration training materials on target population			
Revise as required			
Issue Final version of training			

PLANNING FOR ELECTRONIC PERFORMANCE SUPPORT PRODUCTS

The planning activities for electronic performance support products or systems are somewhat different than the activities described above due to the fact that such products are essentially software. If the organization has software development standards and policies, these standards and policies will need to be followed when developing electronic performance support software. The approach that will be described in this section is essentially compatible with most software development processes that meet the requirements of the quality assurance standards ISO 9000 and 9001.

Software development processes typically include the following development phases:

- Planning – In which the plan for the project is developed and baselined.
- Requirements – In which requirements for the software are defined and baselined.
- Design – Where the software design documents (specifying the database content, data processing, screen designs and user interfaces) are developed and baselined.
- Development – Where the databases, screens and interfaces are developed and the software is coded.
- Developmental Test (Alpha Test) – In which the initial version of the software and interface is tested to ensure that it works as specified.
- Usability Test – In which the software is tested on a sample of users in a controlled environment. It should be noted that software development process do not always require usability testing.
- User Test (Beta Test) – In which the software is tested by "guest" users in their own environments (essentially a "real life" test).
- Product Test (Pre-shipment Test) – Where the final version of the product is tested prior to shipping it to customers.

Planning Phase

In the planning phase, the initial plan for the electronic performance support product is developed and circulated for review and approval by the various stakeholders in the project. Stakeholders typically include management, members of the project team and users (or representatives of users) that are expected to use the product. The project plan includes sections such as:

- Project Definition – Describes the background for the project; scope of the project; assumptions, constraints, dependencies and risks; development phases; deliverables and milestones; and support requirements.
- Development Tasks – Describes development tasks to be accomplished including duration and dependencies; cost estimates; and project schedule (see example of a project schedule in Table 3.6).
- Resource Requirements – Identifies project team members; staffing plans; and organizational structure.
- Project Oversight – Provides information on quality management, change control, and other project oversight features.

The project plan is reviewed and commented on by stakeholders and then baselined. Any changes in the project plan would be subject to review and sign-off by these same stakeholders.

Requirements Phase

Requirements may be very detailed or they may be brief (sometimes referred to as "thin" requirements) depending on the nature of the project and the development process. A requirements document is essential for both design guidance and as a primary source on what the product is expected to produce and how the product is expected to perform (test criteria). The Requirements document includes such sections as:

- Introduction/General – Describes purpose and scope of the document, target audience, review and concurrence requirements, traceability requirements, and change control process.
- Rationale – Describes business opportunity, product description and features, benefits and value of product, and assumptions/dependencies/constraints.
- Processing Flows – Provides initial structure and functionality of data processes.
- System Architecture – Describes basis system components and interrelationships.
- Detailed Requirements – Lists the specific requirements for the system in sufficient detail that they can be tested against.
- Testing Considerations – Provides requirements for testing (e.g., requirement for a test plan).

The requirements document is reviewed and commented on by stakeholders and then baselined. Any changes in the requirements would be subject to review and sign-off. The test plan (see Chapter 8 for more information) should be developed either late in the requirements phase or earlier in the design phase and would include such sections as:

- Description of the product (system).
- General description of the test levels (e.g., developmental, beta and product).
- Overall testing requirements (e.g., traceability, reporting)
- Developmental (alpha) test

      o   Test cases (use scenario to test where product meets a specified requirement or functionality)
      o   Traceability (association of test case to specific requirement)
      o   Data to be collected (specifies the types of data to be collected, e.g., start/end time, number of errors, type of error)
      o   Test procedure (describes the step by step procedure to be followed)
      o   Testing resources (describes the people that will conduct the tests and the facilities required, e.g., hardware, environment)
      o   Test materials (e.g., test scenarios, checklists, test logs)

- Usability Test (contains the same elements as listed for the developmental test)
- Beta Test (lists instructions and materials to be provided beta testers and feedback mechanisms)
- Product Test (contains the same elements as listed for the developmental test)

Design Phase

In the design phase, the detailed specifications for the product are developed. Usually a design document (or a number of design documents depending on the complexity of the product) is developed, reviewed by stakeholders and baselined. The design documents should have sufficient detail on the design so that screens can be developed and the software coded. The design document typically would include the following sections:

- Introduction – Describes purpose of the document, target audience, special definitions, assumptions, dependencies and constraints.
- Product (System) Overview – Describes purpose of the product (or system), description of primary target population, product objectives and usability objectives.
- Product (System) Design – Describes general product (or system) structure, requirements to design traceability approach, functional descriptions, system architecture and impacts, data administration, format and style requirements, accessibility, module design, user interface and interface objects (e.g., screens and fields) and associated attributes, process, module relationships and troubleshooting.
- Open issues – Lists design issues that need further resolution.

    Design documents also are reviewed and commented on by stakeholders and then baselined. Any changes to the design would be subject to review and sign-off.

Development Phase

During the development phase, the databases, screens, screen objects, and interfaces are developed according to the design document(s) and the software is coded and initially tested. Embedded support components such as tutorials and online help also would be developed during this phase, but somewhat later due to their dependency on the development of the user interface objects.

Developmental (Alpha) Test Phase

In the alpha test phase, the initial version of the product is tested according to the test plan to ensure that it functions as expected. Test cases are developed against each of the products requirements and these test cases are run by project team members and others to determine that all processes and interface elements function according to the requirements. Most of the major software "bugs" are discovered during this phase. Problems and bugs are fixed, based on their severity, and a new "build" of the software is produced.

Usability Test Phase

While usability testing shares many of the objectives of the previous test phase, its main focus is on ensuring that the usability objectives stated for the product are met. Since usability testing requires testing the product with representative users, issues regarding difficulties in understanding and using the product and interface elements are more likely to surface during this phase.

Beta Test Phase

When all of the significant user problems and additional software bugs are corrected, the product is sent out to typical customers for beta testing. Beta testing may vary from simply making the product available and asking users to comment if they have a problem, to user instructions and feedback forms.

Production Test Phase

Based on the results of the beta test phase, identified problems and suggestions are evaluated for importance and cost-effectiveness and the product is modified accordingly. After the modifications are complete, the product is tested again prior to release. The purpose of this test is primarily to ensure that all of the changes work properly and that the product functions according to requirements and is reliable (has no known faults).

Table 3.6 Sample Electronic Performance Support Project Schedule

Activity	Start	Finish	Responsibility	Comments
Draft requirements				
Review & baseline requirements				
Draft Test Plan				
Review & baseline Test Plan				
Develop Design Document				
Review & baseline Design Document				
Develop content & screens				
Code content/screens (Alpha)				
Develop Alpha test cases				
Perform Alpha Test				
Revise as per test results				
Prepare additional support material				
Develop usability test materials				
Conduct usability test sessions				
Report test results				
Revise as per test results				
Code Beta				
Update additional support materials				
Perform Beta Test				
Report Beta Test results				
Revise as per test results				
Code Product Test				
Develop Product Tests cases				
Perform Product Test				
Revise as required				
Code release version				
Package product				
Release product				

REFERENCES

Broadbent, B. (1998) The Training Formula, *Training and Development,* October.
Golas, K. C. (1994) Estimating Time to Develop Interactive Courseware in the 1990s, *Journal of Interactive Instruction Development,* Winter.

Greer, M. (1992) *ID Project Management: Tools and techniques for instructional designers and developers*, Englewood Cliffs, NJ: Educational Technology

Kruse, K. (2002) How much will it cost? Estimating e-learning budgets, Web article, Available HTTP: <http://www.e-learningguru.com/articles/art6_1.htm> (accessed 10 February 2003).

Parks, E. (2002) How much will it cost to develop training on the intranet? Ask International, Online. Available HTTP: <http//askintl.com/index.cfm/1,0,852,4712,661,0.html> (accessed 10 February 2003).

Telcordia (2000), Telcordia Performance Support Project Estimator, Guided Tour Online. Available: HTTP: <http//www.800teachme.com/tools/estimator.html> (accessed 20 February 2003).

CHAPTER FOUR

Needs Assessment and Task Analysis

INTRODUCTION

This chapter provides a systematic approach to determining user needs, developing usability objectives, analyzing and modifying existing tasks, and designing new tasks. Appropriate data collection methods are covered, as well as analytical approaches such as input/output analysis, contingency analysis and decision analysis. Additionally, principles and guidelines associated with user needs and task analysis methodologies will be covered.

Needs assessment is essentially the collection of appropriate data from managers and potential (or current users) about how the system should function, what outputs it should produce and the requirements for accuracy, efficiency, etc. If the system is a revision of an existing system, needs assessment also may include the collection and analysis of data concerning performance deficiencies. Performance deficiency information also may be used in the design of an entirely new system if this system will be supporting organizational functions previously done differently. It should be noted that the term "needs assessment" has been used for many years by performance technologists and instructional designers for the "front-end analysis" activities preceding training development. Most of these needs assessment processes are concerned with determining and eliminating deficiencies by means of training or other performance interventions (e.g., job aids). While, as noted above, deficiency information may be important in the determination of user needs for a system, there are many other factors that must be considered. For example, user needs in relationship to performance support products also must be considered. In fact, user and management needs will be used to develop usability objectives for the performance support products.

Task analysis is the analysis of work activities and breaking them down to an appropriate level of detail to enable the determination of behaviors, skills and knowledge. In this book, task analysis will include both the analysis of existing tasks and the creation of new tasks.

Both the design environment and the development environment affect user needs assessment and task analysis activities. The design environment relates to whether the design is for a revision of an existing system, the development of a new system within a family of related systems or an entirely new system. On the other hand, the development environment relates to the organizational and personnel factors that will affect the data collection and analysis activities.

If the design is for a revised system, then a great deal of the analysis is on the existing system in terms of deficiencies, enhancements, etc. In the development of a new system within a family of existing systems, the analysis will be quite different since the new system does not yet exist. The analysis can look at related systems, however, and it will need to take into account how the new system will relate to the existing systems. If the design is for an entirely new system, it is possible to look at similar systems, but much of the analysis will involve the synthesis of new user needs and activities (see Figure 4.1).

Revision of an Existing System

New System within a Family of Related Systems

Entirely New System Design

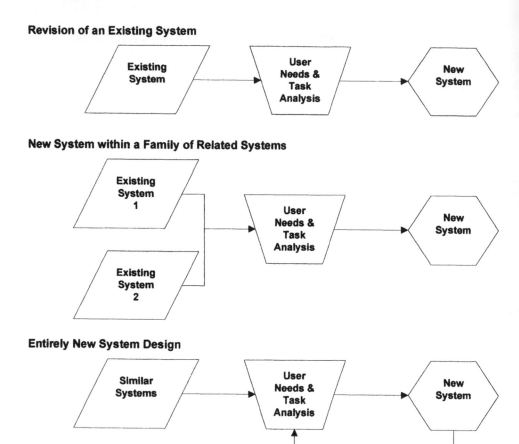

Figure 4.1 Design Environments (Modified from Stammers et al 1990)

DEVELOPMENT ENVIRONMENT CONSTRAINTS

Constraints brought about by the development environment have considerable impact on the quality and quantity of data collection. In most system development environments, information on potential users and system and user requirements is collected by business or systems analysts. Sometimes human factors or usability people are involved in the data collection and analysis. In rare cases, performance technologists conduct needs assessments within the organization(s) that will be using the system.

The following types of constraints are typical encountered when attempting to collect needs assessment and task analysis data:

Limited to Existing Data

In this situation, either the system development organization or the using organization will not allow the collection of data in the using organization. There may be many reasons for this, but in some cases it is essentially a lack of understanding of the importance of obtaining data from real users. If it is not possible to change the minds of management, relevant data on users and user needs must be culled from any existing documentation such as system planning information, requirements and system descriptions.

Limited Access to Using Organizations

Often some access to the using organizations will be permitted, but on a very limited basis. For example, if the using organization has five locations, they may permit access to only one of the five. This may be a problem unless all of the locations have identical operations and the same types of users and support personnel. Obviously, the best solution is to get management to change their minds so that appropriate sampling can take place across the various sites. If this is not possible, try to get the user organization management to allow data collected for the one location to be circulated to the other locations for verification.

Limited Access to Users

This situation is similar to the above situation, but may cause even more complications. It is common for organizations to have managers, supervisors or system support personnel speak for end users, particularly in terms of user's needs. Managers and supervisors often feel that they understand the needs of users, but this is rarely the case. Again, the best solution is to convince managers that it is important to get to real users in order to ensure that any performance support developed will have maximum effectiveness. If it is possible to obtain data from a few users, try to obtain users that are as representative as possible.

Limited Impact on Data Collection Planning

In this situation, data collection planning is under the control of another organization, e.g., system analysis. This organization may be the only organization authorized to make contact with the using organization and schedule data collection activities. If this is the case, it will be important to have a close relationship to controlling organization and convince their management of the importance of obtaining user data relevant to the development of performance support. Where ever possible, try to schedule joint data collection sessions with the controlling organization's analysts so as to optimize the use of the using organization resources.

NEEDS ASSESSMENT METHODS

Needs assessment methods include document analysis, interviews, surveys, critical incidents, questionnaires and rating scales. The selection of assessment methods and the amount of data collected depends on the scope of the project, the availability of information sources and the resources of the needs assessment team. Some of the key questions to be answered during needs assessment are:

- What information will be required from the system?
- Who needs that information?
- Why do they need the information?
- When and in what form will it be required?
- What degree of accuracy is necessary?
- What deficiencies exist in using the current system? (In the case of an existing system.)

For the purpose of developing performance support, needs assessment will usually require the following three or four steps:

1. Identify target population
2. Determine current deficiencies (for an existing system)
3. Determine user and management needs
4. Develop usability objectives

The first three steps usually can be accomplished by a visit or visits to the using organization as part of a specific needs assessment project. In such cases it will be important to obtain high-level management approval and buy-in for this activity to ensure the cooperation of all of the people to be interviewed. The first visit should be with high-level management to work out the scope of the project and schedules for subsequent interviews.

Identifying Target Population

One of the most important prerequisites of performance support development is the identification of the people that will be using and supporting the system. If the system is currently in operation, users and support individuals can be determined on the basis of actual involvement. However, for a new system or a significantly revised system, intended users and support personnel may need to be identified on the basis of system planning or requirements documentation. If user information is not available in current documentation, it may be necessary to interview managers responsible for implementing the system in their organization(s). In addition to identifying users and support personnel for the purpose of collecting job and task data, the following additional types of information are important for performance support development:

1. User Experience/Sophistication

    - With computers
    - With application subject area (including typical length of job experience)
    - From relevant training courses

2. User Skills – such as typing, problem solving, etc.
3. Frequency of Use – Examples of frequency of use are:

    - Dedicated users – are users that generally have been trained to use the system on the job and typically spend the entire day using the system.
    - Casual users – are users that make occasional use of the system, but spend most of the day doing something else. Examples would be a salesperson checking

the status of an order, or a manager varying some budget parameters to make a decision.

4. Job Pressures – include time pressures and high penalties for the occurrence of errors. Usually such job pressures are based on the importance of meeting job standards in obtaining successful ratings by supervisors.

In identifying the target population, it is important to obtain as much information as possible on the number of different organizations and locations that will be using, or are using, the system. Organizations tend to have unique environments that often changes the way people use a system. As noted above, users tend to vary in the amount that they will use a system. Also, the difference between experienced users and novice users must be considered. Some of the experienced users also may be "experts" on the system. Therefore, data should be collected across the using organizations and locations from the following types of users and support personnel:

- Expert system users
- Subject matter experts
- Typical dedicated users and support personnel (with average amount of experience)
- Typical casual users and support personnel (with average amount of experience)
- Novice users and support personnel (with limited experience)
- Supervisors of the above populations

Once the types of users and locations are identified, the number of people needed to obtain reasonably reliable data must be determined. Since needs assessment is intended to identify user's needs and to determine current performance deficiencies, far fewer people will need to be included in the analysis than would be the case for a task analysis. The amount of data collected also will depend on the time frame available and the importance placed on the needs assessment by the using organization and its willingness to provide personnel for participation in the study. As a general rule, only enough data needs to be collected to verify performance deficiencies and to define user needs. The availability of documented materials (supervisor reports, trouble reports, event logs, etc.) can lessen the need to collect data from members of the target population. However, representative members of the target population should be interviewed to verify any data available in documentation.

While some data may be collected by surveys during needs assessment, interviewing is the most powerful technique for obtaining reliable data. Interviewing yields the best results because the interviewer is able to change questions and probe for more information based on the responses of the interviewee. When looking for the cause of deficiencies and clarification of user needs, the flexibility of the interviewer is a very powerful tool.

Determining Current Deficiencies

Information about current performance deficiencies is an important factor to consider both in the improvement of performance in an organization and the development or modification of systems supporting that performance. The goals of deficiency analysis are to identify performance deficiencies, their probable causes, penalties, value of solving, and whether performance support mechanisms are potential solutions. There have been a number of different methods proposed to determine and analyze performance deficiencies in an organization, particularly in relationship to training development (e.g., Harless, 1970; Gilbert, 1978; Kaufman, 1986). The approach that will be used in this book is a variation of the process developed at AT&T by the Training Research Group. It consists of obtaining information about deficiencies in an organization at three levels:

- *1st Level* – Information from those individuals that requested the study (including customer surveys, etc.).
- *2nd Level* – Information currently available from subject matter experts, trouble reports, etc.
- *3rd Level* – Information collected directly from job incumbents.

Typically, data are collected one level at a time; however, in some cases data are collected at all three levels in an organization to maximize the efficient use of personnel. Deficiency analysis data can be captured for each of the three levels using a Deficiency Analysis Summary Form (see Table 4.1 for an example). This form would be used to capture data for each deficiency.

Table 4.1 Deficiency Analysis Summary (Example)

Condition (under which output produced)	Attempting to read quantity from a file created from a different module of the program directly from a sequence table.
Who (produced output)	Program user
Output (alleged deficient)	Program module (not accessed)
Standard (for output)	Correct module accessed
Deviation (from standard)	Error message received instead of accessing correct module
Source (of data)	Trouble Report
Method(s) of measurement	Error message
Cause(s) (of deficiency)	Used incorrect command (Declare) which does not work when module invoked directly from a sequence table. Should have created module stating a call without a "declare."
Penalties	User had to contact trouble desk to resolve.
Value of solving	Increased productivity, decrease in trouble reports.

Determining Standards of Performance

One of the most critical aspects of deficiency analysis is the determination of required (or expected) standard of performance for a given job and associated tasks. The standard may be a minimum level of performance or it may be a level of performance that the organization feels is required to be competitive (desired level). A deficiency is the difference between the required (or desired) level of performance and the actual performance. The criteria for performance may be in terms of time (how long it takes), accuracy (the correctness of the output) and/or completeness (when the performance ends). The establishment of standards consists of the following three steps:

1. Specify the job (or responsibility) outputs – These outputs specify the accomplishment or results wanted. The outputs of the job or responsibility must be obtained from the organization. In some cases, this information is available in

written documentation. However, it may be necessary to interview managers or supervisors to obtain it.

2. Determine criteria for each output – The criteria specify the dimensions that the results of the output will be measured in (e.g., quality, efficiency).

3. Establish the standard for each output – This step identifies the level of the dimension required for acceptable performance. As noted above, there may be a level appropriate for current performance and another level for desired performance.

An example of an output, associated criteria and standards is shown below:

Output	Criteria	Standards
Customer Trouble Report	a. Accuracy	a. 100% accuracy
	b. Timeliness	b. Within 10 minutes of receipt from customer

Another example of a standard from a telephone operator's "customer connect" output might be to connect the customer within 50 seconds with 100% accuracy.

Identifying 1st Level Deficiencies

As noted above, deficiencies should be identified at three successive levels. The first level is essentially the "symptoms" level because it is based on information that led the using organization's management to believe that performance deficiencies that need to be corrected exist in the organization. Such information may include failures to meet organizational targets, customer complaints, trouble reports, etc. 1st level performance deficiencies are analyzed first in order to ensure as much information as possible is collected concerning the suspected deficiencies. Individuals providing the information on the suspected initial deficiencies are interviewed and a Deficiency Analysis Summary (see Table 4.2) is completed for each reported deficiency. For those deficiencies indicated by other sources (e.g., reports, customer surveys, etc.), the analyst reviews the source information and completes a Deficiency Analysis Summary on each deficiency based on the data provided by the source document. The data are then summarized across deficiencies. At this stage of the analysis, it is important to identify and resolve disagreements in the data, i.e., differences between different individuals as to what the standards are and the current degree of deviations from those standards. This may require discussions with higher management to verify the standards. There also may be discrepancies in the data about the causes of deficiencies. However, such discrepancies are not too important at the first level because cause data will be reported more reliably when collected at the lower levels of the deficiency analysis.

Identifying 2nd Level Deficiencies

The 2nd level performance deficiency analysis is essentially a refinement of the data collected at the 1st level. At this level, the analyst looks for more specific information concerning suspected deficiencies both to verify their existence and to obtain more detail about their cause and effect. In addition, information about any other relevant deficiencies is collected at this stage. 2nd level deficiency information is typically collected from supervisors and subject matter experts (SMEs) in the using organization. The first step in a 2nd level deficiency analysis is to obtain a list of supervisors and SMEs relevant to the job incumbent population in which the performance deficiencies are suspected. Supervisors and SMEs are then interviewed, using the structure provided in the Deficiency Analysis Summary, about each output associated with the different system users, or support persons job. Additionally, trouble reports or other reports describing specific deviations from expected ranges may be analyzed to provide more data. Examples of questions to ask supervisors include:

- What are the desired or ideal accomplishments (outputs) required on this job?
- What are the actual outputs?
- Who produces these outputs?
- How do you evaluate these outputs? (Standard of performance, e.g., quality, time.)
- Are there deviations from the expected performance standards? If so, what is the actual range of performance?
- What sources do you use to obtain information about performance?
- How are the deviations measured (e.g., planned vs. actual time)?
- In your opinion, what is the cause(s) of the deficiency?
- What are the penalties for the occurrence of this deficiency (e.g., missed installation date)?
- In your opinion, what would be the value for eliminating this deficiency (e.g., increased productivity, lower customer complaints)?

Information collected during the 2nd level deficiency analysis should be summarized to determine the prevalence and seriousness of the deficiencies. As was the case at the 1st level, discrepancies between the data should be identified and resolved. This may involve discussions with higher-level management and/or group discussions with the interviewees to obtain a group consensus.

Identifying 3rd Level Deficiencies

On the basis of information collected at the 2nd level deficiency analysis, sample incumbents performing the activities alleged to be deficient should be observed and/or samples of incumbents should be interviewed to determine their views and experiences concerning the deficiencies reported at the two previous levels.

Observational data has the advantage of not relying on the subjective memory of the individual, but takes considerable time and requires a great deal of coordination with the using organization. In addition, observations of performance would need to be done at the work location which may impinge on the work environment, both in terms of the performance of the incumbent being observed and the performance of fellow workers. The major advantage of observation is that it provides the analyst with much greater insight into how the work is performed and any problems that might be encountered.

The use of interviews is less invasive than observation and can be done at a location outside of the workplace. However, there are advantages in interviewing people at their workplace. For example, if they refer to any performance aids, system documentation or actual system screens, the interviewer can ask to see them. Examples of questions that incumbents may be asked are:

- What are the accomplishments (outputs) that you are expected to produce?
- Are you producing these outputs?
- How are these outputs evaluated? (Quality, quantity, time)
- How are these requirements for the outputs conveyed to you?
- What is your level of performance in regard to those requirements?
- If you are not meeting the requirement(s), what is the problem, or cause?
- What is the penalty for missing the requirement(s)? (In terms of effect on the organization, the customer or yourself.)
- In your opinion what would be the value of eliminating this problem?

When collecting information from incumbents on the cause of deficiencies, it is important to obtain as much insight as possible as to whether the cause is due to a lack of skill or knowledge or due to some other cause. Causes of deficiencies can be classified as due to:

- Deficiencies of skill.
- Deficiencies of knowledge.
- Deficiencies of execution.

Identifying the type of cause can be very useful in initial determinations as to appropriate solutions using performance support. For example, deficiencies in skill would require performance support mechanisms that provide for practice. On the other hand, deficiencies of knowledge may be solved by training, performance aids or online help. Deficiencies of execution, however, are a function of task interference, lack of feedback, or insufficient consequences to the performer. Therefore, deficiencies of execution usually must be addressed by re-engineering the job or by organizational changes.

After completing all of the incumbent interviews the individual Deficiency Analysis Summary Forms are summarized. As with the previous levels, discrepancies in the data should be resolved by further interviews or discussions with management. During such interviews or discussions, it will be particularly important to obtain management consensus on the costs and value of solving the deficiencies reported to ensure that the validity of this information during the later step of determining cost/effectiveness of various potential solutions.

Determining Potential Efficiencies

In addition to determining deficiencies, it may be useful to obtain information from managers, SMEs and job incumbents on potential efficiencies. An efficiency differs from a deficiency in that a deficiency is defined as a lack of meeting the standard, while an efficiency improves upon the current acceptable level of performance. Often, an efficiency analysis can yield suggestions on improving procedures, support materials, etc. that may not come out of a deficiency analysis. This information can be very useful in situations where a system is being revised. Users can be asked about potential efficiencies for both system procedures and performance support products. An example of a potential efficiencies data collection form for performance support products is shown in Figure 4.2. Information on potential efficiencies can be collected at the same time deficiency data are being collected.

Performance Support Product Analysis Summary
Potential Efficiencies – Form 2

Equipment/System: _____

Performance Support Product: _____

User of Product: _____

Source of Information: _____ Date: _____

Potential efficiency: _____

_____

_____

_____

_____

How identified: _____

_____

_____

Probable effect of efficiency: _____

_____

_____

_____

_____

Improvements in performance anticipated: _____

_____

_____

_____

Value of providing: _____

_____

_____

_____

Other comments: _____

_____

_____

_____

Figure 4.2 Potential Efficiencies Data Collection Form - Sample

Using Critical Incidents as a Means to Identify Deficiencies

The critical incident technique is a procedure for obtaining firsthand reports of satisfactory or unsatisfactory performance. It differs from the deficiency analysis approach described above in that the focus is on critical behaviors rather than general behaviors. This method, originally developed by Flanagan (1954), can reveal useful data about abnormal or unusual situations, but typically does not provide much information about normal events. However, it may be useful as another means of obtaining information on deficiencies particularly those that have great impact on the performer or the organization. Also, the critical incident technique is inexpensive and can provide rich information relative to the features of a system that are particularly vulnerable or valuable. In addition, this technique allows system users to report on near-misses that may otherwise not be discovered. This technique is especially appropriate for the identification of unusual events that are not likely to be picked up with techniques that rely on users' reports of their normal performance. Another important feature of the critical incident technique is that it forces respondents to provide specific incidents of a problem, rather than simply generalize about the existence of a problem. Generalizations are typically much less reliable than reports of critical incidents. Specifically, the critical incident technique calls for responses to the following questions:

1. What were the circumstances leading up to the incident?
2. What did the performer do or say that was significant?
3. Why was the action especially effective or ineffective?
4. What would the normally effective performance have been under these circumstances?

Answers to these questions could be collected from the employee who performs the task, his subordinates (if any) and his supervisor. While the critical incident technique has been validated to be highly effective in identifying performance problems due to lack of knowledge, it is not without problems. When used in an interview environment, considerable skill is required by the interviewer to obtain information using this approach. The interviewer must take care not to prompt the performer. However, the interviewer needs to assure that sufficient detail about incidents is provided by the performer so that they can be understood during later analysis. Success of user reported critical incidents depends on the ability of typical users to recognize and report critical incidents effectively, but all users may not have this ability. It is important for the interviewer to provide examples of critical incidents so that respondents have a better understanding as to what they are. Also, the critical incident technique requires more effort to complete than does other data collection devices. It is important to remember that the study must be validated each time it is to be used because its thrust will change with each job studied. Validation on a small scale should be done prior to the study using individuals typical of the target population.

If the critical incident data collection device is administered as a questionnaire, the following should be considered:

- As with any questionnaire-like device, many more must be forwarded for completion than are needed in the sample to ensure that a adequate sample number are returned.
- Number of returns needed is predicated solely upon identified variation patterns and sample percentage needed to canvass those patterns.
- If completion time is charged to the job, little cooperation can be expected.
- Steps must be taken to guarantee anonymity. Information regarding individuals' deficiencies must be kept confidential.

- Since the responses will be in a paragraph format the data cannot be processed by machine readily. Therefore, collation and analysis will be time-consuming.
- Data often will be returned which is useless. This data will be overwhelmingly interpersonal relations oriented ("He's a good guy because ... He's a bad guy because ...") or "exotic" (e.g., examples of effective behavior extremely atypical of the job population; the respondent is far above average, or examples of ineffective behavior also atypical since it reflects a blatant lack of common sense or reasonable foresight). Interpersonal relations data may be useful for other purposes; "exotic" data is of no use. Also some of the data may be too generic or vague. This may be due to poor focus of the study, inaccurate perceptions or memory of the respondent, or response bias or responses due to cultural norm response.

While the questionnaire version of the critical incident technique is often recommended for use during a needs assessment, it is typically not recommended for use in task analysis. However, I personally prefer to use the interview version for both needs assessment and task analysis. The interview version can be used as an additional data collection method when interviewing incumbents about their current performance and only adds a little extra time to the interview. I also have found that it is easier to obtain critical incident data from interviewees if separate questionnaires are used for obtaining effective and ineffective incidents. Utilizing this approach, the analyst can provide some examples of effective incidents and then ask the interviewee to think about any such incidents that they may have encountered. After exhausting the interviewee's recollection of effective incidents, the analyst then repeats the process for ineffective incidents. Examples of interviewing forms for effective and ineffective incidents are shown in Figures 4.3 and 4.4.

The analysis of critical incidents is done by sorting the incidents into like groups which are then defined and named. This process essentially involves identifying the content (or themes) represented by clusters of incidents and conducting "retranslation" exercises during which the analyst or others sort the incidents into content dimensions or categories. This step helps identify incidents that are judged to represent dimensions of the performance being investigated. Sorting and naming of incidents is usually most effectively done by a group of SMEs under the guidance of the analyst. Effective and ineffective incidents are initially sorted separately, but may be combined if they represent mirror images of the same problem. The number of incidents is counted and the percent of the total incidents is computed for each category. Categories can also be ranked according to the number of incidents reported. As a result, a taxonomy of critical requirements for performance can be created.

Collecting critical incident data by means of index cards (with one incident to a card) simplifies the sorting and classification process. Paper forms also can be used, but are easier to sort if only one incident is recorded per form. A simple spreadsheet also could be used to group the critical incident data where each item is entered as a separate incident at the beginning and then incidents are compiled into categories. Incidents could be categorized as: identical, very similar, similar, could be similar.

Critical Incident Survey
Effective Incidents

Introduction
The collection of information about particularly effective behaviors related to your job functions will be very useful in improving the overall performance of your organization.
An example of an effective behavior is: _____
_____
_____

Effective Incident Description
Can you think of a situation where such an example of effective behavior occurred?
If yes, please describe this situation: _____
_____
_____

Describe what led up to this situation:
_____
_____
_____

What was done that was particularly effective?
_____
_____
_____
_____

What was the specific result of this action?
_____
_____
_____
_____

Why was this action particularly effective and what might have been even more effective?
_____
_____
_____
_____

Can you think of another example of effective behavior?
(If yes, continue with questions for describing incidents as above.)

Figure 4.3 Example of Interviewing Form for Collection of Effective Incidents

Critical Incident Survey
Ineffective Incidents

Introduction
The collection of information about particularly ineffective behaviors related to your job
functions will be very useful in improving the overall performance of your organization.
An example of an ineffective behavior is: _____

_____
_____
_____

Ineffective Incident Description
Can you think of a situation where such an example of ineffective behavior occurred?
If yes, please describe this situation: _____

_____
_____
_____

Describe what led up to this situation:

_____
_____
_____

What was done that was particularly ineffective?

_____
_____
_____
_____

What was the specific result of this action?

_____
_____
_____
_____

Why was this action particularly ineffective and what might have been done to prevent it?

_____
_____
_____
_____

Can you think of another example of ineffective behavior?
(If yes, continue with questions for describing incidents as above.)

Figure 4.4 Example of Interviewing Form for Collection of Ineffective Incidents

Potential for Improving Performance

Another approach to looking at deficiencies proposed by Thomas Gilbert (1978) is the "potential for improving performance" (PIP) which is the ratio of the exemplar's performance to typical performance. Gilbert defines exemplary performance as the historically best performance and essentially would be the performance of the best performer in a particular job responsibility for a given accomplishment. The conceptual approach proposed by Gilbert is that by comparing the performance of the best performer with typical performers, methods such as training, information and motivation can be used to bring typical performers up to the level of the best performers. The development of PIPs would require collecting performance data from the best performers in the organization as well as the representative samples of performers typically utilized in the data collection process.

Estimating Value of Solving

Estimating the value of solving deficiencies is important to determining the cost effectiveness of any proposed solutions. To estimate the value of solving a deficiency, it is first necessary to determine the cost of the deficiency in terms of its effect on quality, response time, cost, etc. Data from the various analyses done during the previous steps can be used to provide this information, for example:

- "Value of solving" data from the deficiency analysis summaries
- "Value of providing" data from the efficiency analysis summaries
- "Results" data from the critical incident

However, if the data is not quantified in the summaries, it may be necessary to obtain better estimates on the costs of the various deficiencies from management. Also, some values of solving (e.g., customer satisfaction) may not be able to stated directly in monetary terms. Analyst may need to consult with the higher-level management to determine what value needs to be assigned in such cases. Some of the generic performance measures used to account for the value and impact in computer systems are:

- Improvements in process/product/service
- Cycle time reduction
- Customer Satisfaction
- Cost-effectiveness

After determining the costs of the various deficiencies (which is actually the value of solving), it is necessary to determine the most appropriate methods for solving these deficiencies.

As noted earlier, information collected during deficiency analysis concerning the "causes of deficiencies" can be used as initial determinates of possible solutions for deficiencies. Skill deficiencies are mostly likely to be solved by the use of performance support methods that provide practice (e.g., training or simulation). Deficiencies of knowledge may be solved by such performance support as training, performance aids or online help. As noted previously, there are also deficiencies of execution that typically are not solvable by means of a performance support solution. For example, performers may not be motivated to perform at the level required due to the lack of proper motivation (e.g., no rewards or penalties, rewards for incorrect actions, penalties for correct action). They may also not receive proper feedback on their actions (e.g., feedback may be late, infrequent or only negative). Such deficiency causes typically would need to be solved by some kind of organizational action (e.g., job redesign, modification of performer objectives).

Since more than one solution may be appropriate to resolve a given deficiency, it is important to identify various potential solutions so that the costs of these different solutions can be compared. At this point the costs of the potential solutions will be based on very limited information and will only provide "ballpark" figures. The accuracy of the estimates will depend to a great deal on the knowledge and experience of the analyst in identifying and costing out potential solutions. Cost estimating tools, as discussed in the previous chapter, can be very useful in developing such estimates.

Once the costs for the various potential solutions are estimated, cost-benefit estimates can be made. As its name suggests, in its simplest form the value of the benefits of a solution are added up and then the costs associated with it are subtracted. More complex forms of cost-benefit analysis (CBA) use a ratio approach such as the Benefit-Cost Ratio (BCR). The formula for calculating BCR is:

BCR = Benefits / Costs (The total benefits of a solution divided by the total costs of the solution)

If the value of the BCR is less than one, the project should not be continued. On the other hand, if the BCR is greater than one, then the solution has benefits that exceed costs. Using this approach, one can compare benefit/cost ratios of competing solutions. This is sometimes referred to as a "worth analysis" (Praxis, 1972) where worth is determined on the basis that "value" divided by cost is greater than one.

While cost-benefits can be computed for just the development costs of a solution, it is more accurate if the CBA time period matches the system life cycle. In other words, includes the feasibility study, design, development, implementation, operation and maintenance stages of a project. This is particularly true for solutions, such as training, that have long term costs and benefits associated with them. The end of a system life cycle is when the system is phased out or replaced by another system that is significantly different in terms of resource requirements, processing, operational capabilities or system outputs. In computing benefits and cost, it is important to include the "total" benefits and cost. Total benefits would include money saved by the organization, money made, and anything that adds directly or indirectly to the bottom line as well as the improvements in productivity, customer satisfaction, etc. mentioned above. When determining total costs, the obvious and not as obvious costs such as learner's time, organizational overhead, materials, time away from the job, facility costs, web development, CD production cost, etc. should be included.

Another term used frequently in comparing solutions is Return on Investment (ROI). The total benefits minus the total costs is typically referred to as the return or profit from an investment. The formula for calculating ROI is:

ROI (in %) = (benefits / costs) x 100

The term ROI is usually used to refer to the rate of return on investment, so it is important to differentiate between the ROI and BCR so that users of the analysis understand what is meant. Actually, the ROI is just other way of expressing the Benefit-Cost Ratio (BCR). ROI can be computed from a BCR by simply multiplying the BCR by 100 which then converts the BCR to a percent or rate of return. Since Return on Investment is very popular with many managers, it may be useful to include both ratios in describing the results of a needs analysis.

Determining User and Management Needs

The primary objective of a needs analysis is to determine the gap between "what is" and "what should be." Obviously, the data collection activities described above provide a considerable amount of data concerning this gap. In fact, if a deficiency or an efficiency analysis is being done, it is cost effective to collect information on user and management needs at the same time. This approach will minimize the time and resources needed by both the user organization and the organization conducting the study. However, needs go beyond job performance requirements because they relate to what users and managers expect of a system in terms of performance, outputs, ease of use, etc. In addition, if a deficiency analysis is not done, it still is important to collect data concerning user and management needs so that the system and associated performance support can target those needs.

It is important to stress that user needs must be derived from users and not others that may speak for users (e.g., supervisors, SMEs). Often supervisors or SMEs believe that they are able to speak for users because they themselves were once users and believe they fully understand the user's job functions and needs. However, this is rarely the case. There are actually three versions of a job:

- The supervisor's version.
- The job incumbent's version.
- The actual version (based on observation of performance).

It also is important to differentiate between management's needs and user's needs. While the satisfaction of user needs is an important consideration in supporting the performance of the work tasks, the outcome of the performance must meet the needs of management. So, in a sense, both must be met to optimize performance. User and management needs also may be based on either current requirements or some future requirements. An important distinction must be made about the difference between needs and tasks. Needs are essentially high-level and relate to goals. Goals are what the user is attempting to achieve as an end result. For example, a goal for a word processing task might be the preparation of a letter to a customer. A goal for an automated directory system might be: Users can rapidly find the number of the desired person and call that person without dialing. Tasks, on the other hand, are the activities that support goals, but are totally dependent on the current environment and system.

The process for determining user and management needs includes the following steps:

1. Determine the sample of users required
2. Interview users to determine:

    a) Major job functions supported by the system/software
    b) User's goals related to (supporting) responsibilities (i.e., what they want to accomplish).
    c) Operations, tools, methods used to accomplish goals.
    d) Problems with above.
    e) Information needed to accomplish goals.
    f) Usability objectives.

3. Interview managers to determine:

    a) Management's goals related to functions supported by the system/software.
    b) Gap between current capabilities and goals.
    c) Criteria for meeting goals

User Sampling

Since users with different job responsibilities tend to use a system differently, it is important to obtain data from representative samples of such users to ensure that user needs represent all the intended users. Data should be collected across the using organizations and locations from the following types of users: expert system users, typical dedicated users (with average amount of experience), typical casual users (with average amount of experience) and novice users (with limited experience). At a minimum, data from at least three to five of each type of user should be obtained. If there are different locations, user needs information for each type of user at each location also should be collected. To minimize travel and the use of resources, a useful strategy is to extend the data collected at one location by creating a checklist of the needs listed by users at the first location and sending this checklist to users at other locations for verification.

Interviewing Users

As noted above, when ever possible, user needs interviews should be done in conjunction with other needs assessment data collection activities. The procedure for user interviews includes the following steps:

1. Users are asked to list their job functions related to the system.
2. For each of these functions, users are asked to specify what their goals are and what procedures, system operations and outputs currently are used to satisfy those goals.
3. Users should then be asked to describe any problems that they have satisfying their goals, particularly in regard to system operations and outputs.
4. Finally, users are asked to describe what changes could be made that would allow them to meet their goals.

In addition to the type of needs expressed above, collecting data relevant to the user's perceived need for various types of data can provide useful information. Such data includes:

*   Information items needed – Specific information items that are important to accomplishing a job function (either currently available or desired in the future).
*   Users – Indicates the primary and secondary users of the information.
*   Information item importance – Rating in terms of importance of the item to accomplishing the job function.
*   Frequency – How often the information item is typically used on the job.
*   Required response time – Specifies how quickly the information is required to meet job requirements.
*   Current response time – Specifies how quickly the information is currently provided.

A "Critical Information Survey" can be developed to collect information from various users concerning the information dimensions listed above (see Figure 4.5 for an example).

Critical Information Survey

Information	Importance					Needed for			Frequency			Needed in			Obtained in		
Item Name	Low ← → High 1 2 3 4 5					Self	Mgr.	Other	X/day	X/wk	X/mo	No. min.	No. hrs.	No. days	No. min.	No. hrs.	No. days

Figure 4.5 Sample Critical Information Survey Data Collection Form

Interviewing Managers

Ideally, managers should be interviewed after data are collected from typical users. In this way, managers can obtain both an understanding of users' reports of needs and provide their own views on such needs. Managers also have their own needs for system data and performance. Collecting needs data from managers involves having managers list the organization's goals for the system and then quantifying those goals in terms of what the system needs to produce to meet these goals (i.e., criteria for success). If the system or manual version of the system is currently in operation, management's views concerning the current performance and the "gap" between current performance and management's goals also should be collected at this time.

If the system is an information system, it may be useful to collect data from managers as to their information needs. The Critical Information Survey described above also can be used in collecting data from managers.

Developing Usability Objectives

Usability objectives are important to both the development and testing of systems, software, user interfaces and performance support products used by people. They essentially state how the product is expected to perform in order to meet the expectations of users. Information concerning usability objectives should be collected in conjunction with interviews done during needs assessment to collect other data (e.g., deficiencies, needs) to optimize the data collection process. In fact, having users and managers specify usability objectives is a logical follow-up to their description and quantification of their needs.

Usability is defined in the ISO standard: Guidance on usability (ISO 9241-11: 1998) as "A concept comprising the effectiveness, efficiency and satisfaction with which specified users can achieve specified goals in a particular environment." Other characteristics of usability defined in ISO 9241-11 include:

- Effectiveness: "Measures of the accuracy and completeness of the goals achieved."
- Efficiency: "Measures of the accuracy and completeness of goals achieved relative to the resources (e.g., time, human effort) used to achieve the specified goals."
- Satisfaction: "Measures of the comfort and acceptability of the work system to its users and other people affected by its use."
- Usability Criteria: "Required levels of measures of usability, the achievement of which can be verified."
- Usability Attributes: "The features and characteristics of a product which influence the effectiveness, efficiency, and satisfaction with which specified users can achieve specified goals in a particular environment."

It is important to define usability objectives in measurable terms for effectiveness, efficiency and satisfaction so that usability testing performed later in design can verify that those objectives have been met. There are a number of criteria that can be used to measure effectiveness, efficiency and satisfaction (see Table 4.2 for relevant examples of measurement criteria). In setting usability objective, the criteria established must be meaningful to both users and their organization. Following are examples of some usability objectives for a telephone company service that is intended to allow customers to adjust their lights and temperature remotely:

- Customers will be able to successfully (with no more than 2 attempts) set their lights and temperature for each room in their house by using their telephone, for periods up to one week.
- 99% of customers age 16 and up will be able to use the service to set their lights and temperature.
- Customers will rate this service as easy to use on a rating scale (average score of 5 on a 7 point scale).
- Unauthorized persons will not be able to access the customer's light/temperature control.
- Service will be available 24 hours a day.
- Users will be provided instructions and help on using this service upon request by means of a single command. This help will be context sensitive.

- Access to the light/temperature control system will be within 1 minute after user initiation.
- Users can complete the settings for an average home (7 rooms) within 10 minutes.
- Users will be able to make their initial setup for their house within 30 minutes.

Table 4.2 Sample Measurement Criteria for Effectiveness, Efficiency and Satisfaction

Usability Attribute	Measurement Criteria
Effectiveness	• Percent of task(s) completed • Ratio of successes to failures • Percent completeness of output data • Percent correctness of output data • Percent or number of errors • Ratio of successes to failures finding appropriate information in performance support.
Efficiency	• Time to perform task(s) • Time required to fix errors • Time required in using help system or support documentation • Number of repetitions of failed commands • Number of repeated (regressive) behaviors • Number of times user disrupted from a work task • Time to learn (or relearn) system features
Satisfaction	• Ratings of ease of use • Ratings of the quality of the product • Number of users preferring system over another system • Number of times users express satisfaction or frustration with system • Rating of how easy the system was to learn

It also may be useful to have users and managers rate the importance of usability attributes for their particular system and environment. Figure 4.6 provides an example of a checklist for user ratings of the importance of the different usability attributes. Results of such ratings can help developers put appropriate emphasis on the attributes considered most important by users and managers.

User Checklist for Importance of Usability Attributes

Usability Attribute	Relative Importance Little ← → Great 1 2 3 4 5 (Circle appropriate no.)				

Task Outcome (Effectiveness)

	1	2	3	4	5
• Appropriateness (validity) of data, information, procedure for successful task completion	1	2	3	4	5
• Completeness of data/information	1	2	3	4	5
• Reliability (correctness) of data, information	1	2	3	4	5

Efficiency

	1	2	3	4	5
• Time to perform task	1	2	3	4	5
• Time required to fix errors	1	2	3	4	5
• Time required in using help system, documentation	1	2	3	4	5
• Learning/relearning time	1	2	3	4	5

Acceptance (Satisfaction)

	1	2	3	4	5
• Ease of use	1	2	3	4	5
• Quality of product	1	2	3	4	5
• Learning ease	1	2	3	4	5

Figure 4.6 Sample Checklist for User Ratings of Importance of Usability Attributes

Usability Objectives for Performance Support Products

In addition to developing usability objectives for the system, it is very useful to develop usability objectives for the performance support for that system. It may be appropriate to develop a preliminary version of such objectives and then have management and users review them to ensure that they are appropriate. Examples of a set of performance support usability objectives are:

General:

- Performance Support (PS) System access can be accomplished by means of one user action from anywhere within an application.
- After going through the help tutorial, 90% of first time users of the PS System will be able to navigate through the Performance Support System without mistakes.
- Learn to use the basic features of the PS System within 45 minutes.
- Access and read desired "object help" information within 2 actions and within 15 seconds.
- Users will rate the ease of use of the object help as 4 or more on a 5 point scale.

- Access and read desired "keyboard help" information within 3 actions and within 15 seconds.
- Users will rate the ease of use of keyboard help as 4 or more on a 5 point scale.
- Access and read desired "task help" information within 3 actions and 60 seconds.
- Users will rate the ease of use of task help as 4 or more on a 5 point scale.
- Access desired "tutorial" within 3 actions and within 15 seconds.
- Task tutorials will be completed by 90% of users within 30 minutes or less.
- Access desired "browser" information within 2 actions (plus input query, if needed) and within 15 seconds.
- Users will rate the ease of use of the browser as 4 or more on a 5 point scale.
- Users will rate the ease of use of the PS System as a whole as 4 or more on a 5 point scale.
- Users will rate the ease with which they learned how to use the PS System as 4 or more on a 5 point scale.

Application based:

- Object help will be available on all objects which are not intuitive for the user population.
- Keyboard help will be available on all special function keys and key combinations which are unique to the application.
- Information provided through task help will allow 90% of the user (having gone through initial training) to perform 90% of the tasks without referral to additional information (i.e., the information will be appropriate, complete and reliable).
- 90% of learners will successfully accomplish 90% of tutorial/course objectives.
- After completing a task tutorial, 90% of users will be able to perform system tasks without assistance other than reference to on-line help.
- After completing initial training, no more than 5% of the user's total task time will be spent in obtaining help information.
- 90% of new users will be able to perform 90% of job tasks (and meet usability objective criteria for these tasks) in 2 weeks without assistance from a "live mentor."

Needs Assessment Reporting

After completing a needs assessment, it is important to communicate the results in a form that can be used by both management to support decision making and as a data source for down stream analysis (i.e., task analysis). Figure 4.7 provides a template that can be used to report on the needs assessment study. Often needs assessment reports require the inclusion of a project plan that provides an initial view of the time and effort required to implement the proposed performance support solutions. Such project plans, and any modifications required by the using organization management, serve as the initial planning document for the development of performance support.

Needs Assessment Report

Executive Summary

1. Introduction

2. Initial Indicators of the Need for Performance Support

3. Data Collection Methods/Procedures

4. Findings

- Level 1 Deficiency Analysis (initial sources)
- Level 2 Deficiency Analysis (SMEs, supervisors, Trouble Reports, etc.)
- Level 3 Deficiency Analysis (users/incumbents)

5. Conclusions and Recommendations

- Deficiencies with potential performance aid and/or online help solutions
- Deficiencies with potential advisor and/or prompting solutions
- Deficiencies with potential automation solutions
- Deficiencies with potential documentation solutions
- Deficiencies with potential training solutions
- Deficiencies requiring non-performance support solutions

6. Cost/benefit Analysis

- Estimated costs of current deficiencies
- Estimated costs of potential solutions listed above
- Estimated benefits (both in terms of cost savings and customer satisfaction)

7. User and Management Needs

- User Needs
- Management Needs
- Usability Objectives

8. Proposed Project Scope and Schedule (if appropriate)

- Deliverables
- Resource requirements
- Schedule

Appendix A - Performance Support product(s) objectives

Appendix B - Data collection instruments

Appendix C - Data summaries

Figure 4.7 Sample Template for Reporting Needs Assessments

TASK ANALYSIS FOR PERFORMANCE SUPPORT

There are many good books on task analysis, e.g., *Evaluation of Human Work*, edited by John Wilson and E. Nigel Corlett (1990), *A Guide to Task Analysis*, edited by Kirwan and Ainsworth (1992) and the chapter titled "A Task Analytic Approach to Dialogue Design" (Phillips, Bashinski, Ammerman and Fligg, 1988) in the *Handbook of Human-Computer Interaction* edited by Martin Helander. The purpose of this chapter is not to describe the various methods of task analysis, but to present a method that has been used successfully for analyzing tasks associated with the development of performance support for computer-based systems.

Task Analysis in the context of the development of performance support for new or revised systems includes the design of new performance as well as the analysis of existing performance.

Analyzing and Describing Current Performance

If the system is a revision of an existing system or a new system intended to automate existing manual operations, it is important to analyze and describe the current performance of those individuals who will use and support the new system. Data concerning current performance is important because:

1. The manner in which people are performing current tasks will influence the revisions of tasks and the design of new tasks.
2. Development of effective performance support must take into consideration the backgrounds of the people using the previous system and will likely be using the new system (i.e., entering skills and knowledge).

In addition, if a needs assessment was done, the task analysis team should become completely familiar with the data and conclusions reported. Deficiency analysis and critical incident data will be particularly important in the development and revisions to task procedures for the new system. If workflows for current processes exist, they also will be very useful in the analysis. Often workflow analysis is done by business or system analyst as part of the system requirements derivation stage. Workflow analysis is the analysis of the inputs, outputs and work activities involved in producing a product, or group of products within an organization. This process identifies the external and internal customer requirements and determines the sequence of events currently being used to accomplish them. Typically, both the flows of information and data through the organization and associated systems are analyzed to determine interdependencies, contingencies and decision-making requirements. In addition to providing useful context information for task analysis, workflow analysis data will be very useful in the design of performance support products.

Task analysis for existing performance is essentially a decomposition procedure consisting of the following five steps:

1. Collect available source data.
2. List relevant responsibilities or functions.
3. For each responsibility, list all of the tasks performed.
4. For each task, list all of the steps.
5. For each step requiring further detail, list all cognitive and physical actions performed to accomplish the step.

Collecting Source Data

Data concerning the target population, task characteristics and the environment can be obtained from a number of different sources. Table 4.3 lists the various methods that can be used to obtain task-related information. As noted earlier in this chapter, however, sources and methods may be limited by the performance support development environment. Interviews have the advantage that the interviewer can vary their questions based on the responses obtained from interviewees. Also, the interviewer can provide context to the interviewee when collecting task data. For example, in our Air Force Studies on task analysis (McCormick and Williams, 1961) we found that when incumbent interviewees were provided with concrete definitions for tasks, elements and work activities, they were much more reliably able to provide appropriate levels of detail when describing their jobs.

Another question that is typically raised concerns the number of performers that will need to be interviewed or observed to obtain reliable data. The answer to this question depends on the variability of the work, differences in work locations, and differences in the incumbents. For reasonable reliability, data should be collected for each of the parameters (i.e., work, location, and people) that are expected to vary. In unpublished research done by the author (Williams, 1960), it was noted that the lower the level of detail of the task descriptions required, the more individuals that needed to be interviewed to obtain reasonable completeness. For example, the first interview yielded approximately 60% of the task descriptions, 50% of the elements (steps), and 40% of the work action statements relevant for an Air Force job. It also was discovered that very little new unique task level descriptions were obtained after the first three interviews. On the other hand, information on work actions was still being added by each subsequent incumbent up to the seven incumbents interviewed. Obtaining information from new locations also contributes to information completeness. In the Air Force study, job incumbents were interviewed at three different bases. No unique data were obtained after interviewing three incumbents from the second base and four incumbents from the third base. Pragmatically, the most logical approach is to stop collecting data at each location when no new data are added by subsequent interviews. In our experience, collecting data from three to five individuals for each job type and location seems to provide most of the data.

Table 4.3 Methods for Obtaining Task-related Information

Information Category	Information Type	Method
User Characteristics:	Who	- Existing data - Market surveys - Observation
	Turnover	- Existing data - Interviews
	Description (entering skills and knowledge)	- Existing data - Interviews - Questionnaires - Checklists
	Frequency of use	- Existing data - Interviews - Questionnaires - Checklists
	Needs, Attitudes, Biases	- Interviews - Questionnaires - Checklists - Attitude scales
Task Characteristics:	Requirements	- Existing data - Interviews - Questionnaires - Checklists - Critical Incidents
	Description	- Existing data - Interviews - Questionnaires - Checklists - Task Analysis
	Procedures	- Existing data - Interviews - Questionnaires - Checklists - Task Analysis - Task Design
	Importance, frequency, time, complexity, difficulty	- Existing data - Measurements - User or SME ratings
	Deficiencies	- Existing data - Interviews - Questionnaires - Checklists - Deficiency Analysis
Environment:	Physical	- Existing data - Measurements - User ratings
	Organizational	- Existing data - Interviews - Attitude scales

Listing Responsibilities (or functions)

A responsibility (or function) can be defined as a portion of a job that includes two or more related tasks and is performed to meet a specific goal. Examples of responsibilities include: assigning customer telephone numbers, resolving customer complaints, preparing credit statements, troubleshooting a piece of equipment, installing a new service and producing a report. Typically when asked to describe their major job responsibilities, people will list the things that they believe that management is holding them accountable for. However, when collecting data relevant to a computer-based system development, it is important to limit respondents to report only on responsibilities that entail the use of the system. If data on responsibilities are obtained on the basis of existing documentation, the analyst will need to extract the relevant system responsibilities from this documentation.

Listing Tasks

A task is defined as a discrete, organized sequence of two or more related activities; involving interaction with equipment, environment or other people; that is performed by an individual with a work cycle; has a definite beginning and end; produces a single meaningful product; and is performed for its own sake (i.e., not dependent on another job action for meaningfulness). Tasks will usually have most of the following characteristics (McCormick and Williams, 1961):

- A task is an activity composed of small work units or procedural steps that are closely related to each other and share a common goal, i.e., that defined by the task itself.
- The essence or nature of the task is to produce a meaningful product, service or consequence that is readily observable, consistent from time to time, and highly significant in view of the overall objective of the job. (In a maintenance job, for example, this objective is to keep some piece of equipment in good operating condition.)
- The immediate purpose of a task is to contribute in a direct manner to the objective of the job. It would thus be quite logical and meaningful for a worker to perform a single activity of this type solely for the sake of achieving its outcome, with no regard for its relationship with other activities.
- An activity that does not contribute directly and significantly to the objective of the job should nevertheless be considered a task if it is performed as a "preparation for some responsibility or for a group of tasks." It is not of task scope if it is performed in preparation for only a single task activity. An example of a preparatory task might be to load a database prior to performing database operations.

It is important to note that the complexity of a task will differ depending on the nature of the job. Typically the more cognitive behavior involved in the task the higher the complexity. Tasks for an auto mechanic might include: checks engine emissions, rotates tires, services radiator and replaces exhaust system. More complex tasks associated with service outages might include: monitors and adjusts load balances, upgrades network, prepares load balance reports, troubleshoots customer outages and prepares outage reports. Examples of tasks of medium complexity for a customer service representative might include:

- Processes customer phone orders for equipment.

- Processes customer mail orders for equipment.
- Handles customer complaints.
- Prepares customer activity reports.

If interviewing is the data collection approach used, incumbents are asked to list the tasks involved in accomplishing each of the system related responsibilities described in the previous step. As noted previously, providing the above definition of a task and some examples, prior to obtaining the task list from the incumbent, will improve the reliability of the descriptions. In addition, a useful approach is to use a tape recorder to record a paraphrasing of the descriptions given by the incumbents and then ask incumbents to verify the descriptions before recording the data for the record.

Where direct observation is used to collect task information, the observer should use the above task definition when describing the observed performance. Observation, however, is limited to recording those tasks that are done during the observation period and requires considerably more time than interviews.

If task information must be extracted from existing documentation, the analyst will need to extract the tasks from that documentation. Because work activities at various levels of detail are often defined as tasks, it may be necessary for the analyst to reconstruct some of the activities to ensure that they meet the definition of a task. In addition, where existing documentation is used as a source, the analyst would extract the associated steps and work actions at the same time. If the task analysis is for an existing system that has procedural oriented help, it also may be appropriate to extract task, step and work action information from the help system.

Listing Steps

A step is defined as one or more procedural work steps involved in accomplishing a task. It does NOT produce a meaningful product (i.e., is meaningless to perform for its own sake) and is highly dependent on other steps in the process. Steps (or elements as they were originally called in the Air Force study) will usually have most of the following characteristics (McCormick and Williams, 1961):

- A step is one of the procedural work steps involved in a more general activity, e. g., a task. It is closely related to other work steps that together comprise a fairly standard sequence and share a common goal, that of accomplishing the higher order activity.
- The essence or nature of this activity is to serve as a constituent part of some higher order activity. Its product or end-result, therefore, is more immediately significant to the objective of that higher order activity than to the overall objective of the job.
- The purpose of a step may be thought of as merely to assist in the accomplishment of another activity, thus making the step only indirectly related to the overall objective of the job. It would appear meaningless for a worker to perform a step solely for the sake of achieving its own outcome; it becomes meaningful and derives a reason for its existence only when associated with another activity of which it is a part.
- An activity of a "preparatory" nature should be considered a step if it is performed in preparation for only one higher order activity or one specific kind of higher order activity.

When using the interview technique to collect task details, incumbents are asked to list the steps involved in accomplishing each of the tasks described in the previous step. As noted above, prior to asking the incumbent to list the steps, provide the above definition of a step and some examples. Examples of steps for processing a customer request for service might include:

1. Greet customer
2. Obtain customer information
3. Provide customer with list and benefits of different options available
4. Ask customer to choose between options
5. Enter option choices into system
6. Provide customer with date of service activation

Listing Cognitive and Physical Actions

An action is defined as the smallest meaningful unit or behavior (usually described) and typically is a single stimulus and a single response (but not individual motions). Actions describe *how* the step is performed and include cognitive as well as physical behavior. Work actions will usually have the following characteristics (McCormick and Williams, 1961):

*   A work action is a minute act that typically is a single human response to some specific stimulus. This response nature does not reduce it to an individual motion, however, for the action is usually made up of a collection of motions or a movement pattern that produces a single effect.
*   A work action is usually found to be related to other actions by virtue of being part of a sequence which, in its totality, explains how some higher order activity is performed. Once started, the actions in the sequence may flow automatically, or each one may be consciously directed, but they are so related that the conclusion of one serves as the cue for the second.
*   The purpose of a work action is to explain explicitly how a worker performs a given activity, and its descriptive statement is of such detail that the reader is left with no question whatever on this score.
*   Work actions include mental as well as physical behavior, even though the former is not readily observable and must be determined by studying the outcome of a given activity or by questioning the worker. It is felt that such actions as receiving information, interpreting information, recalling knowledge, making decisions and communicating information by some specific means are fairly inclusive of any mental behavior that might be employed.

If the interview technique is used to collect task details, incumbents are asked to list the work actions involved in accomplishing each of the steps. It is best to have incumbents list the work actions associated with each step immediately after they list the step so as to keep the focus on their recollection of the activity. As noted above, prior to asking the incumbent to list the work actions, provide the above definition of a work action and some examples. For example, work actions for the step of "provide the customer with list and benefits of different options available" might include:

*   Enter request code into system.
*   Review available options identified by the system and associated benefits.
*   Note most favorable options to the customer.
*   Describe available options and their benefits to the customer, one at a time, in order of their benefits (i.e., most favorable options presented first).

Object Oriented Task Analysis

Another approach to analyzing activities in a system is object oriented task analysis. This approach may be particularly useful where the system and user interface is developed by means of an object oriented process. In object oriented development, an object is a physical "thing" requiring analysis or manipulation. Examples include:

- Devices, e.g., telephone, printer, keyboard, mouse.
- Data, e.g., reports, bar charts, a description, a field.
- Containers, e.g., files, folders, desk.

Device objects also can be physical devices (e.g., printer) or logical devices (e.g., out-basket, waste basket). Data objects could include text, graphics, audio, and video. One of the important aspects of objects is that they can be hierarchical and share interrelationships (see Figure 4.8).

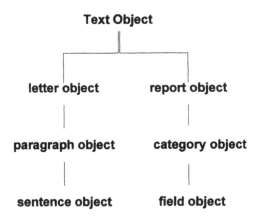

Figure 4.8 Object Interrelationships (Hierarchy)

Object oriented task analysis shares some relationships with object oriented programming, but also has some different characteristics. For example:

- They share some of the same concepts such as hierarchy and inheritance.
- Object oriented task analysis differs in that objects do not typically represent programming objects.
- User objects are more subtle in terms of inheritance and hierarchy.
- User object hierarchies are based more on similarity in appearance and behavior.

As noted above, object oriented task analysis is most appropriate when the system and interface design is accomplished by means of an object oriented approach. For an existing system, the analyst can determine what system objects are utilized by users to perform their work activities by interviewing users following the procedures listed above. Object oriented task analysis has the following steps:

1. Determine characteristics of the product – This activity involves reviewing all of the system requirements, design documentation, operational software (if the system is currently in operation), prototypes, etc.
2. Analyze work flow in terms of objects analyzed or manipulated to produce outcome objects – To accomplish this activity, information about current or planned workflows must be available. These workflows should depict the various user tasks needed to accomplish organizational goals (produce desired outputs) associated with using the system. Utilizing this information, the analyst would determine what system objects are analyzed or manipulated to accomplish each task.

3. Identify characteristics of these objects – After determining the objects involved in each task, the analyst specifies the specific characteristics of each object in terms of its structure and attributes. For example the characteristics of a graphic may be that: each graphic primitive is a singular unit, each graphic primitive remains a unit despite any manipulation, portions of the graphic may not be manipulated independently and portions of one graphic covered by another graphic are not erased or altered. This information should be available in the user interface design specifications for an existing system, or one where the development has progressed to the detailed design level.
4. Identify interrelationships between objects (hierarchy, inheritance)
5. Identify actions taken on objects and results of these actions (in terms of change or creation of new objects)

Designing New Performance

If the system is an entirely new system, or new functions or tasks must be created for using or operating the system, new tasks must be designed. The design of new tasks is much harder than the analysis and description of existing performance and requires considerable knowledge of human behavior. However, experience in analyzing performance for similar systems and environments will be very beneficial in the design of new behavior. For example, experience in analyzing similar types of tasks will provide insight into the design of new tasks requiring the same type of behavior.

Designing new operations, associated tasks and lower level details can be accomplished by performing the following steps:

1. Determine system operations or functions to be performed by users or support personnel.
2. Perform input/output analysis on each operation (or function).
3. Derive human activities needed to produce output(s) for each operation.
4. Perform decision analysis on each activity.
5. Breakdown activities into lower level activities (e.g., steps) until the required behavior are specified to a level appropriate to the target population.
6. Perform a contingency analysis of each of the operations.
7. Organize the activities within an operation into logical task groupings.

It should be noted that the performance design approach described in this chapter also can be used to improve performance on an existing system.

Determining System Operations (or functions)

Information concerning system operations, or functions, should be available in the system description and requirements documentation.

Performing Input/Output Analysis

To perform input/output analysis the following information should be available:

• System objectives, system performance specifications and usability objectives.
• A detailed listing of input/output requirements.
• A description of all manual functions.
• Function dependency flowcharts.

Utilizing the above information, do the following:

1. Identify and list each required output – The process begins with an identification of the required outputs and a description of their characteristics. This identification requires a detailed knowledge of user needs. The analyst should reference the appropriate parts of the system documentation concerning system objective and performance requirements. In addition, if the system is being designed using object oriented design methodology, outputs will be described in terms of objects.

2. Describe characteristics of each output – The purpose of this step is to enable logical derivation of the activities necessary to change inputs to outputs. Certain basic characteristics are normally associated with each output, but these characteristics are not all inclusive, and the efforts of the designer may reveal other characteristics. These characteristics include:

   a) Title or Label – The identifying title or label is a basic summary description of the total set of items forming the output. It may be the name of a record or a name given to a collection of related records. Often, this can be the title of a particular output, the name of a screen, or its identifying number.

   b) Information Content – A listing of the items which constitute each output and the units in which they are expressed. For example, for toll billing, the information might be: Billing telephone number, in ten digits (e.g., 908 345-6766); Called numbers, in ten digits; Duration of each call, in minutes; Amount per call, in dollars and cents; and Total toll amount, in dollars and cents.

   c) Order – Content order concerns the information items are arranged within the group and how the groups arranged relative to each other. A toll ticket, for example, has the following information in the following order: billed telephone number, originating point, and destination point, start time, and disconnect time.

   d) Form and Type of Media – The form in which the information is recorded usually relates to the items as a group rather than as individual items. For example, database records, CRT displays, computer printouts, etc., are all forms or types of media. The results of the analysis can be used as inputs for designing the form of the input and output.

   e) Accuracy of Data – The accuracy associated with an item of information to be collected as well as the accuracy expected on outputs. The level of accuracy must be specified separately for any item of information for which the precision of an output is of concern. Precision is vital if it relates to detectable errors (e.g., it is worthwhile to know that in 20 percent of the cases a name is entered in the date field. However, it may not be necessary to know that in 20 percent of the cases the date in the date field is incorrect).

   f) Volume/Frequency/Time Spread – Comprised of Volume (the number of occurrences of the output that are required or expected, e.g., "1000"); Frequency (the time-base of the expected volume, e.g., "per month"); and Time-spread (the time-spread of the expected occurrences across the frequency interval, e.g., "spread over the 22 working days," or "50% on the first of the month, and 50% on the 15th" or "10 per hour for 8 hours").

   g) Destination – This characteristic involves "who" and "where," since it is almost always necessary to answer these two questions when describing the destination. The level of detail with which this is expressed can vary with the type of system and the functions involved.   Sometimes the question is whether it is the immediate destination, or the ultimate one. In case of doubt, both should be listed, with the differences clearly explained. While it is always important to know the immediate disposal, it is often also desirable to know the ultimate user and to ensure that the output is formatted for ease of interpretation or use by that user.

h) Quality – This refers to the degree of mutilation, illegibility, distortion, etc., which is acceptable in an output. It is usually related to the item as a whole. For example, if a printed bill contains smudges, or the type is not aligned properly, it would not have sufficient quality to send to a customer.

i) Criticality – The output should be stated in terms of the level of criticalness, i.e.: not critical (will not significantly degrade system performance); moderately critical (may downgrade system performance); or very critical and must be performed accurately and within acceptable time limits.

j) Other Characteristics – In addition to the characteristics described above, other characteristics may be recognized as important during the course of the analysis and should be included when necessary. It is better to have more information than might be absolutely required than too little.

An example of outputs and some of their characteristics for the telephone temperature and light service introduced earlier in the section on usability objectives is shown in Table 4.4 below:

Table 4.4 Sample Outputs and Characteristics for Temperature and Lights Service

Output (Label)	Characteristics	
	Content	**Use/Destination**
House location	Telephone number	To identify house location to system
Room designators	Living room (LR) Dining room (DR) Kitchen (K) Den/study (DS) Bedroom 1 (BR1) Bedroom 2 (BR2) Bedroom 3 (BR3) Bedroom 4 (BR4)	Linked to room unit designations in house control system
Days of week designators	Monday, Tuesday, Wednesday, Thursday, Friday, Saturday, Sunday	Input to system clock for initiating setting, or change in setting
Temperature settings	Temperature value (in "F" degrees) On time value (in 24 hr. time) Off time value (in 24 hr. time)	Linked to room temperature control unit Input to system clock for initiating setting, or change in setting
Light Settings	On time value (in 24 hr. time) Off time value (in 24 hr. time)	Input to system clock for initiating setting, or change in setting

3. Identify and list each available input – When listing each required output, the available and required inputs to each function should also be identified and their

characteristics described. Inputs are items of information which are required to be available before the activity occurs. Normally, inputs represent outputs from other functions. This listing activity is performed in the same manner as with outputs, and the same characteristics are examined. However, some modifications may be required. For example, in considering information content, the analyst needs to consider whether the information is always significant or only in the event of change.

4. Describe characteristics of each input - This activity is accomplished by describing the inputs according to the same list of characteristics detailed previously for outputs. However, rather than listing the destination of an output, the analyst is concerned with the source of an input. Table 4.5 provides an example of the temperature and lights service application inputs and their characteristics.

Table 4.5 Sample Inputs and Characteristics for Temperature and Lights Service

Input (Label)	Characteristics	
	Content	Source/Use
Dialup location	Telephone number (nnn-nnn-nnnn)	From caller ID to identify location
Room control unit designators	Location codes for temperature and light control devices	From home control system output
Personal Identification No.	PIN (6 – 9 item alphanumeric value)	From user input
Voice Menu Selection	Options: 1. Initialize, 2. Modify, 3. Help, 4. Quit (user voices option number or keys in)	From user input to identify next step
Rooms Selections	Options: Living room, Dining room, Kitchen, Den/study, Bedroom 1, Bedroom 2, Bedroom 3, Bedroom 4 (voice input by user)	From user to identify rooms to be controlled
Days Selections	Options: All, or Monday, Tuesday, Wednesday, Thursday, Friday, Saturday, Sunday (voice input by user)	From user to assign days that temperature setting applies
Temperature settings	Temperature in "F" degrees (voice input by user)	From user to set temperature values
Temperature time	On time: voice input by user (in 12 hr. AM or PM time) Off time: voice input by user (in 12 hr. AM or PM time)	From user to set on and off time for temperature
Light Settings	On time: voice input by user (in 12 hr. AM or PM time) Off time: voice input by user (in 12 hr. AM or PM time)	From user to set on and off time for lights

5. Determine strategy for categorizing inputs and outputs – At this step, the analyst can begin to impart some order to the information gathered previously. Generally, inputs and outputs are categorized by information content and source/destination. As an alternative, the categorization could be by form or type of media. This is especially

relevant when considering user interface activities. Criticality and source/destination are categories especially useful for activities relating to the question of priorities.

6. Group and categorize outputs according to the above strategy and document results.
7. Group and categorize inputs according to the above strategy and document results.

Deriving Activities

The inputs to this operation represent the output of the previous operation. They are the documented, categorized descriptions of the inputs, and outputs for each manual function. This operation consists of the following activities:

1. Review inputs and outputs and identify differences – The differences between inputs and outputs, in terms of their characteristics, are determined in this step on the basis of information collected and documented previously.
2. Determine data from available inputs necessary to produce required outputs – In this step, the designer must examine each of the inputs to determine exactly what information they will supply. For example, for a listing of information for a motor vehicle operator control system, an individual's driver license could be considered an input and found to supply data on age, height and weight. Cross-checking across inputs to outputs for each function (as shown in Figure 4.9 below) is the basic means of aligning those inputs required to produce a certain output:

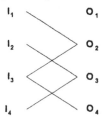

Figure 4.9 Inputs Required to Produce Outputs

3. Is additional input data required? – A negative answer to this question allows the analysis to continue by proceeding to Step 5. A positive answer requires the analyst to determine which additional input data is required but not available. This is done in the following step.
4. Determine input data not available but required to produce output – Continuing with the same example used in the previous step, it could be necessary to determine the color of eyes for each individual covered in the system. This information might not be available from an individual's driver license and must be so specified.
5. Determine activities required to convert inputs to outputs – With the determination of the differences between the inputs and the outputs (as described in step 1), the lower-level activities necessary to meet system objectives (i.e., the logical processing involved) can be derived. The name for an activity should indicate the nature of the behavioral requirements. Each should begin with an "action verb" (e.g., verify, check, determine, transmit, receive, sort, file, etc.). A potential list of action verbs is presented in Figure 4-10. It should be noted that this list is provided as a guide, and it is NOT to be considered all inclusive. The action verbs with an asterisks symbol (*) in the list may imply a decision to be made.

Accumulate	compute	gather	originates	scrutinize
Adapt	conduct	generate	outline	search*
add	confirm	give		secure
adjust*	conform	group*	perform	select*
adopt	construct		plan	sell
advise*	contact	hire	point	send
alert	control	hold	post	separate*
align*	convert		present	sequence*
alter*	copy	identify*	prepare*	set
amend*	correct*	implement	print	show
analyze*	count	indicate	process	solve*
announce	create	inform	produce	sort*
answer*		initiate	program	specify
apply	date	inquire	prove	start
appoint	decide*	insert	provide	stipulate
appraise*	decode	inspect	publish	study
approve	define	interpret*	pull	submit
arrange*	delegate*	interview	punch	substantiate
ascertain*	delete	introduce	purchase	substitute
assemble	deliver	investigate		summarize
assign	demonstrate	issue	query*	supply
associate*	describe		question*	survey
assure	design	limit		synchronize
attach	designate*	listen	read	
attest	determine*	locate	receive	tabulate
authenticate	develop	log	recommend*	teach
authorize	direct*		reconcile*	tell
	discover	maintain	record	title
balance*	distribute*	make	register	trace*
batch	divide*	match*	regulate*	train
	document	merge	release	transcribe
calculate	draft	modify	remember	transform*
cancel		monitor	render	translate*
cause	edit*	move	repeat*	transmit
certify	enter	multiply	report	treat
change*	establish		represent	type
check*	estimate*	name	request*	
choose*	exit	note	require	underline
circle	explain	notice	resolve*	update
circulate	extract	notify	restrict	
classify*		number	review	validate*
code	file		revise	vary*
collect	find	observe	rewrite	verify*
compare*	formulate*	obtain		
compile	forward	operate	scan	write
complete		order	schedule*	
		organize*	screen*	

Figure 4.10 Action Verbs for Use in Activity Naming

An example of the activities required to initialize the telephone service for setting lights and temperature is listed below:

1. Dial up service.
2. Provide PIN.
3. Select action.
4. Select help, if first time use, or if needed.
5. Listen to instructions, repeat if necessary.
6. Set up room designators.
7. Confirm designators.
8. Set temperature for each room.
9. Provide "on" and "off" time.
10. Vary temperatures for each day if desired.
11. When all days completed, confirm settings
12. Modify settings if necessary
13. Set "on time" and "off time" for lights.
14. Vary times by different days if desired.
15. Confirm settings.
16. Redo settings as necessary.
17. After settings confirmed, exit system.

Note that the above activities are listed in a straight linear fashion, as would be the case if the information was collected from a job incumbent. However, there are important advantages to portraying task and step sequences in flowchart form. In the next operation, a linear flowchart is constructed from the activity lists derived in this step.

6. Perform a linear flow analysis of each activity – For this operation, first perform a straight-forward linear flow analysis of each activity. The analyst describes the serial actions required to transform the input to the specified output. In linear processes, the sequence of actions derived is one which does not vary according to conditions. During the performance of this activity, the activities analyzed will break down into those activities which are purely linear and those requiring decisions within the activity. An example of a simple linear flow for the activities for setting up the temperature and lights service application described previously is shown in Figure 4.11:

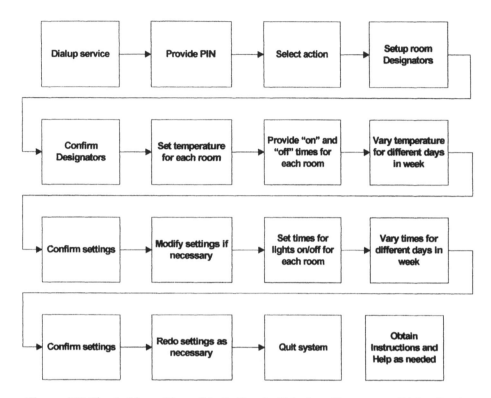

Figure 4.11 Simple Linear Flow of Activities for Telephone Temperature/Lights Service

Performing Decision Analysis

In the previous operation, the activities to produce outputs were depicted in a linear fashion. However, most sequences of activities are not purely linear and involve decisions that require alternate activities. Analyzing such decisions is particularly important for identifying cognitive behavioral requirements and alternative strategies for producing required outputs. Using the linear flow as input:

1. Identify any potential decision points in the flow – This activity requires carefully evaluating each activity in the linear flow to determine if a decision would be involved in performing the activity. The activities required to make decisions usually can be identified by such verbs as "sort," "determine," "compare" or "verify." These verbs serve as clues to the designer that, at these points, the worker must make decisions before the work can proceed. Additional words besides action verbs may also imply a decision (decision-oriented verbs are only a guide to decision points). The actual manual activities themselves must be studied to obtain the most reliable, comprehensive view of the decision points involved. The analyst should go through the activity several times to uncover any decision points not identified in the first examination.

2. Identify alternatives required to make decisions – In a decision analysis, the analyst describes all decisions required for the normal functioning of the system. For each decision, the alternative conditions calling for different actions are identified. The

need for a decision is usually apparent when it is impossible to break down an activity into sequential steps which do not vary. These steps must be described in terms such as:

If A, do X; if B, do Y.

Decision analysis must be applied to activities detailed enough to assure that the behavioral characteristics requiring decision-making can be identified. When a decision point is identified, the alternatives must be expressed as simple "Yes" or "No" decisions. The analyst must then identify all of the information required to make the decisions during the day-to-day operation of the system. It is desirable to examine the alternative actions in relation to other activities and to ensure that subsequent tasks/functions permit the decision to be implemented.

The results of the decision analysis on the steps described above should be documented by means of a flow chart using the decision diamond symbol as shown in Figure 4.12.

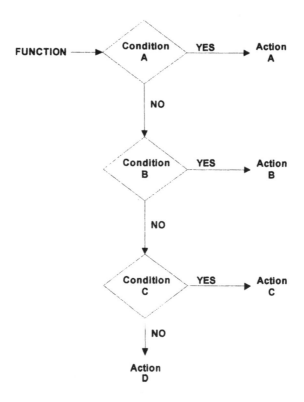

Figure 4.12 Decision Alternatives

Figure 4.13 provides an example of an alternative sequence flowchart explicitly showing decisions. Notice that the sequences of decisions are broken down to provide alternative responses from the customer.

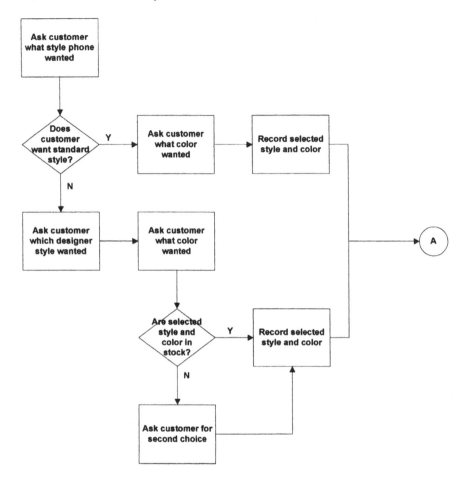

Figure 4.13 Example of an Alternate Sequence Flowchart

Documentation could also be done in the form of a decision table. The decision table is made of four parts:

a) In the Condition Column, list the conditions which form the basis for decision.
b) In the Condition Entry, indicate the presence or absence of each condition. (If the condition is present, enter Y for Yes; if absent, enter N for No. A dash means "Doesn't Matter.")
c) In the Action Column, enter the actions (activities) to be performed for the various conditions.
d) In the Action Entry, indicate whether or not the action (activity) is to be performed depending upon the conditions in the Condition Entry.

If the same information shown in flowchart form in Figure 4.12 were documented in a decision table, the table would appear as follows in Table 4.6:

Table 4.6 Conditional Decision Table

Condition	Condition Entry			
Condition A	Y	N	N	N
Condition B	N	Y	N	N
Condition C	N	N	Y	N
Action	**Action Entry**			
Action A	X			
Action B		X		
Action C			X	
Action D				X

3. Determine conditions that would cause the performer to decide on each alternative within the set – The conditions which determine the choice to be made from among the various alternatives must be detailed by the analyst. Once these conditions have been specified, the next step in the analysis can be performed. Using a time card processing example, the sorter could be directed to sort the cards according to three specific conditions:

    * Regular employees working a regular work week
    * Regular employees who have worked overtime
    * Part-time employees

4. Determine specific information revealing each condition – Each alternative can be identified by specific factors. This information must be derived by the designer and communicated to the worker who must make the decision. It should be noted that the information for making the decision must be obvious to the worker. In the time card sorting case, for example, the environment must permit the worker to comprehend readily the basis for sorting the cards.

    For example, the three types of cards described might be color-coded to start, and the worker only has to sort according to color. This operation should be designed so that there is good lighting which will enable the worker to see the type of card easily and make the appropriate decision. It may become necessary to redesign prior functions which influence or impact upon this particular decision point. For example, a card-gathering function will require transporting the cards from the various employees at their work stations to a central location, i.e., a well-lighted room where the sorting can take place.

5. Determine relationship between triggering conditions and action caused by decision – In designing a decision point, the designer must specify what to do with each set of alternatives. No matter what action results from a decision, the worker must be told what to do in each case. Figure 4.7 below depicts an example of the basic direction needed for the time card sorting case:

Table 4.7 Time Card Sorting Trigger/Actions Table

Conditions	Actions
A two-color card filled out only in the main, white area (regular employees, straight time)	Place in Bin A
A two-color card filled out also in the secondary, blue area (regular employees, with overtime)	Place in Bin B
An all yellow card (part-time employees)	Place in Bin C

If the activities listed for the telephone temperature and lights service in the example under step 5 of Deriving Activities were re-evaluated to include decisions (i.e., conditions and actions), they would include the following additional decision related activities:

1. Dial up service.
2. Provide PIN.
3. Select option choice from the voice menu.
4. If choose "initialization," select help from initialization menu, if first time use, or if needed.
5. Listen to instructions, repeat if necessary.
6. Listen to voice menu.
7. Select "designate rooms" from the voice menu.
8. Provide room designator codes as prompted.
9. Confirm designators OK at prompt.
10. If not OK, select "redo" from voice menu.
11. When room designation completed, select "set temperature" from the voice menu.
12. At prompt for room, indicate temperature to be set.
13. At prompt, provide day.
14. At prompt, provide "on" time.
15. At prompt, provide "off" time.
16. At prompt, select repeat for "all" days, or select will "vary by day."
17. If select "vary by day," at prompt for each day, indicate repeat previous, or change.
18. If change selected, provide "on" time at prompt.
19. If change selected, provide "off" time at prompt.
20. When all days completed, at prompt, select whether confirmation of daily setting desired.
21. If yes, after reviewing each daily setting, at prompt, specify whether change is required.
22. If change required, redo settings at prompts.
23. After settings confirmed, at prompt, select whether lights are to be set for room.
24. If yes, indicate "on time" at prompt.
25. Indicate "off time" at prompt.
26. At prompt, select "repeat" for all days, or select "vary by day."
27. If select "vary by day," at prompt for each day, indicate repeat previous, or change.
28. If change selected, provide "on" time at prompt.
29. If change selected, provide "off" time at prompt.

30. When all days completed, at prompt, select whether confirmation of daily setting desired.
31. If yes, after reviewing each daily setting, at prompt, indicate whether change is required.
32. If change required, redo settings at prompts.
33. At prompt, confirm settings OK, or go back to change.
34. When finished with settings, exit system.

Breaking down Activities into Lower Levels

It typically will take a number of derivation cycles to arrive at the level of detail necessary to depict all of the activities and decisions involved with performing the various human tasks relevant to using and maintaining a system. In addition, the analysis must be driven down to a sufficient level to determine the skill and knowledge required to enable performance. The level of detail is appropriate when:

- The logical end is reached.
- All outputs are produced and all inputs are processed.
- A sequence is established for every condition.
- Discrete tasks can be identified.
- All contingencies can be accounted for.
- The activities are specified at a level appropriate for the target population.

One of the best techniques for breaking down activities is by using successive detailed flowcharting. This technique involves looking at each human activity on a flowchart and, when possible, breaking down that activity into the next lower level activities. For example if the original flow was at a task level, each of the tasks would be broken down into the steps needed to accomplish the tasks. This new level of activities would be then depicted on a lower level flowchart. The detailing would progress until either the activity could not be broken down any further, or it was down to a level of description that could be understood readily by most members of the target population. An example of a lower level flowchart for the telephone temperature and lights service, based on the activities listed above, is shown in Figures 4.14 and 4.15 on the following pages. It should be noted that it would be possible to drive some of the activities on the flowcharts down to at least one additional level of specificity. For example, the activity "Call service to obtain PIN" in Figure 4.14 could be broken down into the lower level actions required to dial the number and request the PIN from the customer service representative. However, most of the decision activities are well represented at the current level depicted on the flowcharts.

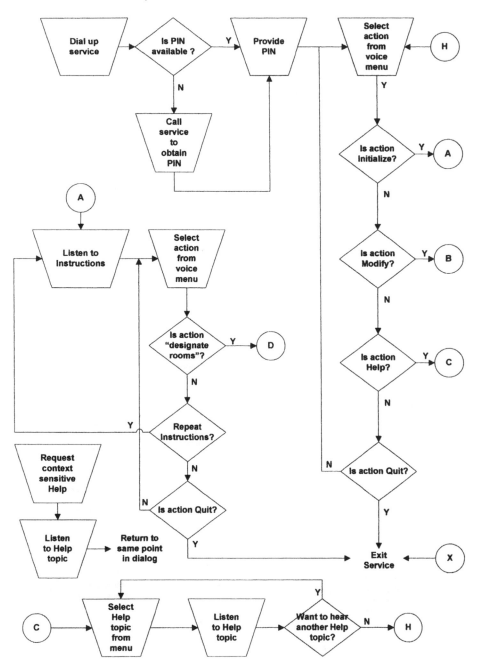

Figure 4.14 Lower Level Flowchart for Temperature/Lights Service – Page 1

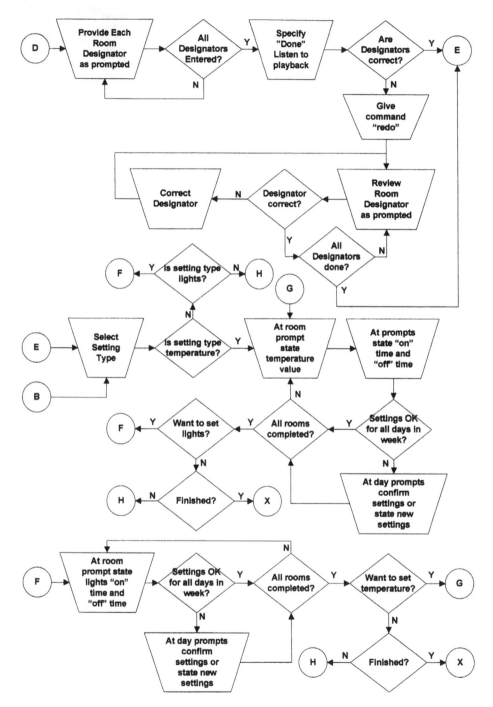

Figure 4.15 Lower Level Flowchart for Temperature/Lights Service – Page 2

Performing Contingency Analysis

Contingency analysis is essentially a "what-if" analysis and is important for both error control and user-friendliness. It is important to note that a contingency analysis can be done only after "normal" activities have been identified. The results of a contingency analysis are useful to the understanding of the kinds of errors likely to occur. Such information can be used to prevent errors by minimizing the likelihood of their occurring, or, if not preventable, providing easy recovery. A contingency analysis for the entire system can be time-consuming since a large number of activities might be derived for each manual function in the system. The designer must remember that mundane problems (such as what to do if an order handler breaks a pencil point) would make the contingency analysis excessively tedious and unnecessarily complicated. The analyst must determine what is important and what is not. Generally, if the contingency does not result in any system degradation or extra work on the part of users and support personnel, it is probably not worth considering.

The basic steps in a contingency analysis are as follows:

1. Determine what errors can occur, how frequently they are likely to occur and how critical they would be if they did occur – As noted above, a contingency analysis is essentially a "what-if" scenario. To determine potential problems, the analyst goes through the flows of all of the activities and for each activity and decision asking the question as to what could go wrong. For each problem identified:

    a) Estimate the frequency of the problem – The frequency with which a potential problem can be encountered increases with the frequency with which the activity is performed. That activity's frequency of performance must be determined by the analyst. This will permit an estimate to be made of how often problems might be encountered.

    b) Estimate the criticality of the problem – The analyst must estimate the extent to which system performance would be degraded if the contingency went uncorrected. The assignment of a criticality value is a relative ranking which requires consideration of the overall system and the system objectives. (See *Performing Input/Output Analysis* step 2.(i) above.)

2. Define potential preventive design actions and/or corrective procedures and their operational implications – In this activity, the analyst identifies and recommends all potential preventive design actions which might eliminate or reduce the possibility of the contingency situation occurring. These may include extensive redesign, such as automating functions previously allocated to humans, or simple actions like color coding forms or providing warnings on screen. If the contingency can be completely eliminated through redesign, the need for corrective action no longer exists. Potential corrective actions which would accommodate the contingency, if it could not be prevented, should be identified. The analyst will determine the activities required for correcting the unavoidable contingencies. In such a case, the decision point remains in the system and must be clearly identified.

    In addition to the above activities, the analyst must determine the operational implications of the preventive/corrective actions which have been identified. This is necessary since the correction of a contingency can result in a requirement for more time, effort, materials and equipment than had been anticipated before the contingency was uncovered. If the implication on system operation is clearly excessive, the contingency should be avoided through redesign.

3. Describe the recommended procedures – The recommendation for a corrective action requires a set of activities composed of a decision point and the actions to be taken.

The analyst will then have to perform a decision analysis on each set of activities not already covered. These activities should then be added to the activity flow diagram at the proper point in the sequence of activities. The recommendation for preventive measures will result in the contingency being completely eliminated through redesign. However, if preventive measures will only result in reducing the frequency of occurrence, corrective actions will still have to be developed.

4. Document problems and corrective actions on contingency tables or narratives – The condition should be documented on a contingency table. This table would include a description of the corrective or preventive actions to be followed. Such recommendations will be based on the frequency of the problem, its criticality and the operational implications of the recommended action.

Deriving Tasks

Often, when breaking down activities into successive layers of detail, unique tasks get lost in the process. This is due to the fact that different types of activities break down into different layers of underlying steps and actions required to accomplish them. The more complex the higher level activity, the more levels of detail necessary to describe it. In our experience, some activities could be described completely by breaking them down two or three levels, while others took five or six levels.

It is important to derive the tasks for an operation because the task level is the most useful level to organize activities in performance support products. This is particularly true if the tasks are based on the definition provided in the section in this chapter on Analyzing and Describing Current Performance. As defined previously:

A task is a discrete, organized sequence of two or more related activities; involving interaction with equipment, environment, or other people; that is performed by an individual with a work cycle; has a definite beginning and end; produces a single meaningful product; and is performed for its own sake (i.e., not dependent on another job action for meaningfulness). A task is discrete in that they differ from one another in relation to the following factors:

- Special conditions or requirements associated with the tasks.
- Nature of the actions performed in each task.
- Nature of the stimuli and inputs that initiate the tasks.
- Nature of the outputs produced.
- Types of materials, media and equipment used to perform the tasks.
- Skill, knowledge and physical requirements.
- Location where the tasks ale performed.
- Destination of the outputs and origin of the inputs.
- Tune of performance.

Using the definition for a task, the higher level activity flows should be evaluated to see if any of the activities fit the definition of a task. If so, use the name of the activity as the task name. For those cases that the higher level activity does not fit the definition for a task, restructure the hierarchy to include placeholder for a group of steps at the lower level that could be considered a task. Provide a task name for that grouping.

Task Characteristics

It is often useful to identify the major characteristics of each of the tasks to facilitate grouping tasks into positions or duties and to aid further analysis (e.g., skill and knowledge requirements). Task characteristics that should be identified include:

- Importance – How important the task to the overall responsibility.
- Frequency – How often the task is (or is expected to be) performed.
- Time – The typical time the task takes (or is expected to take) to perform.
- Complexity – Rating on the relative complexity of the task.
- Difficulty – Rating on the difficulty of the task (it may be appropriate to specify both physical and mental difficulty in some cases).

In our study on Air Force jobs (McCormick and Williams, 1961), we found that judgments on the specificity of job activity statements were highly correlated with ratings of complexity, type of object worked on, time and importance. As one might expect, we also found that mental difficulty (and to some extent physical difficulty) was highly correlated to complexity. However, the most important finding from the study was that subject matter expert raters can reliably rate work activity statements on time, complexity, physical difficulty, mental difficulty and importance (in descending order of the reliability coefficients).

Typically, forms used for recording task details (tasks and associated steps) provide columns for ratings of task characteristics. If rating scales are used for importance, complexity and difficulty, a 5 point scale or a 7 point scale is recommended to allow for rater variability. Raters should be subject matter experts or analysts with considerable experience in task analysis, or (preferably) both.

Potential Performance Support Solutions

At this stage of the analysis (prior to skill and knowledge derivation), enough information may be available to make some preliminary judgments concerning the types of performance support that may be required to enable performance. Management may also require such judgments in order to support planning activities. Information about the task and their characteristics, as well as needs assessment information, can be used for this purpose. One approach that can be used is to review each task and make an initial determination as to whether it could be supported by:

- Performance aids and/or online help
- Advisor and/or prompting or automation
- Documentation
- Instruction
- Non-performance support (e.g., organizational changes)

It should be noted, however, that judgments on performance support methods will be much more accurate after completing the skill and knowledge derivation process described in the next chapter.

Sample Task Analysis Report Template

Figure 4.16 presents a sample template for reporting task analysis results. This template is very general and may need to be modified depending on the nature of the analysis.

Task Analysis Report

Executive Summary

1. Introduction

2. Population descriptions

- Primary target population(s)
- Secondary target population(s)

3. Data Collection Methods/Procedures

- Data sources
- Collection techniques
- Data collection plan

4. Data Summaries

- Overview of work process (including major tasks, primary goals, input and output requirements)
- Summary of task characteristics (e.g., importance, frequency, time, complexity, learning difficulty)
- Environmental considerations (should cover both organizational & physical environments)

5. Conclusions and Recommendations

- Potential performance aid and/or online help requirements
- Potential advisor and/or prompting or automation requirements
- Potential documentation requirements
- Potential training requirements
- Other non-performance support recommendations

Appendix A: Detailed Task/step listings

Appendix B: Task flowcharts

Appendix C: Task characteristics matrix

Figure 4.16 Sample Template for Reporting Task Analysis Results

Needs Assessment and Task Analysis Data Checklist

The procedures in this Chapter require the collection of a large amount of data about performers, performance data (e.g., deficiencies), work activities, support aids and task characteristics. The checklist in Table 4.8 provides a convenient means to record the collection of such data.

Table 4.8 Needs Assessment and Task Analysis Data Checklist

Data Required	Date Acquired	Source
Performance Data		
• Outputs		
• Performance Standards		
• Deficient Outputs		
• Deviations		
• Producer		
• Conditions for occurrence		
• Causes		
• Penalties		
• Value of solving		
Population Characteristics		
• Job title		
• Subgroup (equal opportunity)		
• Entering Skill & Knowledge		
• Attitudes		
• Numbers		
Work Activity Data		
• Responsibilities (functions)		
• Tasks/steps/work activities		
• Terminal events (outputs)		
• Inputs		
• Task relationships		
• Decisions		
• Contingencies		
• Environment		
Task Characteristics		
• Importance		
• Frequency		
• Time		
• Complexity		
• Performance difficulty		
• Learning difficulty		
Support Aids (used)		
• Performance aids/help		
• Guides/manuals		
• Reference documents		
• Tools and materials		
• Rules or policies		

REFERENCES

Flanagan, J.C. (1954) The Critical Incident Technique. *Psychological Bulletin* (July), 51(4), 327-358.

Gilbert, T. (1978) *Human Competence – Engineering Worthy Performance*, New York, McGraw-Hill.

Harless, J. (1970) *An Ounce of Analysis (is worth a pound of objectives)*, McLean, VA, Harless Performance Guild, Inc.

ISO 9241-11 (1998) *Ergonomic requirements for office work with visual display terminals (VDTs), Part 11: Guidance on usability*, Geneva, International Organization for Standardization.

Jackson, S. (1986) Task Analysis, In *Introduction to Performance Technology, Volume 1*, Washington, D.C., National Society for Performance and Instruction.

Kaufman, R. (1986) Assessing Needs, In *Introduction to Performance Technology, Volume 1*, Washington, D.C., National Society for Performance and Instruction.

Kirwan, B. and Ainsworth, L. (1992) Editors, *A Guide to Task Analysis*, London, Taylor and Francis.

McCormick, J. and Williams, J. (1961) *The scaling of job activities on specificity and related variables*, Air Force Systems Command, ASBP-TM-61-21, June.

Phillips, M., Bashinski, H., Ammerman, H. and Fligg, C. (1988) A Task Analytic Approach to Dialogue Design, In *Handbook of Human-Computer Interaction*, M. Helander (ed.) North-Holland, Elsevier Science Publishers.

Praxis (1972) *The Performance Audit* (performance aid), NY, Praxis Corporation.

Stammers, R., Carey, M., and Astley, J. (1990) Task Analysis, In *Evaluation of Human Work*, Wilson, J. and Corlett, E. (eds.), London, Taylor and Francis, pp. 134-160.

Williams, J. (1972), Standardized Task Analysis in Business Information Systems Development, In *Proceedings of the Conference on Uses of Task Analysis in the Bell System*, American Telephone and Telegraph Co. Human Resources Laboratory, Training Research Group, Hopewell, NJ, October 18-20.

CHAPTER FIVE

Matching Performance Support Methods to Task Requirements

INTRODUCTION

In order to determine which performance support methods or enabling strategies are most appropriate for ensuring performance, it is necessary to first determine the skills and knowledge required to perform the various user and support personnel tasks. The purpose of this chapter is to provide a methodology that can be applied to determine the skill and knowledge requirements and use this information to determine the most appropriate methods to enable these skills and knowledge. The process proposed in this chapter builds on the task analysis methodology presented in the previous chapter.

Almost all of the books and papers concerned with performance technology and training indicate that it is important to determine skill and knowledge requirements as a basis for designing performance support interventions. However, very few provide specific information on how to accomplish this. Gagne (1985) identified five types of learning: intellectual skills, cognitive strategies, motor skills, attitudes and verbal information. He proposed different strategies for each of these types of learning. As a result, many instructional designers have simply classified skills and knowledge into these five types and have gone from the classification into instructional design, thereby losing much of the important descriptive information within the skill and knowledge statements.

DETERMINING SKILL AND KNOWLEDGE REQUIREMENTS

In the absence of skill and knowledge (S&K) requirements, performance support developers will tend to develop product and course objectives strictly from work activity statements (primarily tasks). This can result in products that contain more information than is necessary to perform the job or learn the material. Rather than providing only the material necessary to enable the required skills and knowledge that are common across tasks, developers typically repeat material. This repetition is usually due to the fact that the developers are not aware of the underlying skill and knowledge requirements for the tasks. The derivation of skill and knowledge takes on added importance with changing job populations because S&K relate closer (or more directly) to population variables than do work activity statements. In addition, skill and knowledge should be stated in operational terms (i.e., what is actually required) rather than in terms of some classification scheme. However, it may be necessary or helpful to later classify them for particular purposes such as knowledge support or training strategy development.

In general, most of the task detailing and skill and knowledge documentation prepared for computer systems is either too general or not at the level of detail required to develop good performance support. Also, the more specific the skill, the more detail required to describe it. However, it is not necessary to state skill and knowledge that the potential target population obviously already possesses. For example, the skill of "reading" would hardly be necessary to specify for most adult populations. If there is any doubt in anyone's opinion, then it should be stated to be on the safe side.

Defining Skill

A skill is comprised of knowledge components and skill components. Sometimes a knowledge component can be viewed as preceding and separate from the skill component and sometimes knowledge and skill components are too interrelated to justifiably separate. Often both conditions exist. In this book, we will use the following definition for skill:

Skill is the ability to perform an activity at a given level of precision (i.e., to a standard). This includes the ability to use one's knowledge effectively and readily in execution of performance. It requires the interaction and coordination of various physical and mental capabilities and previously required knowledge to produce a given output. Generally, skills are learned and enhanced by practice. Skills can be classified into three categories:

- Basic — those required for activities performed by most people, e.g., reading, walking, and talking. Basic skills are generally acquired through normal maturation and socialization processes or through the typical educational process.
- General — those required for activities performed by large segments of the population, e.g., typing, driving. General skills are acquired through experience or specialized training courses that are typically common to the target population. For example, computer programming for programmers.
- Specific — those required by people performing a specific work activity, e.g., entering data into a particular computer input form.

Following is a description of some of the major types of skills relevant to performance in a system environment:

Skill in performing a specific activity

The overall skill of performing an activity (job, task) as a whole is a critical aspect of the performance. This performance must be:

- At the required accuracy (a kind of quality level),
- At a required rate, quantity, timeliness, and
- To a level of completeness (also a kind of quality level).

Part of the definition of a skill is that it is the ability to perform an activity at a given level of precision. This given level of precision can be expressed as an accuracy requirement, a required rate, quantity or completion within a specific time frame, or merely as a level of completeness. Often, but not always, practice is required to achieve the given level of completeness.

It is often not sufficient to simply practice skills until the various skill/knowledge components become an acquired reaction unless the practice takes place under normal job conditions. For example: people may practice cable splicing in the relatively "clean" environment of a learning center. They practice (until they meet the standards for number of splices done with allowed errors) in an area that is airy, well lighted and grime free. However, when these persons get on the job, they find that the normal working environment is a cable vault which is relatively airless, cramped, poorly lighted and laden with dust. The odds are that they will not splice as many cables as are required with the proper quality until they become acclimated to this normal job environment.

Consequently, practice may have to take place under conditions which most closely approximate those of the job. If people are required to perform jobs under varying normal conditions, they must practice until they have achieved a level of precision under the most difficult of normal conditions. Normal conditions should not be construed to mean "special" conditions (wherein "special" often equates to "bizarre"). It is "normal" to find a cable vault airless, cramped, poorly lighted and dusty; it is "special" to find it burned out, fume-ridden, sooty and water soaked from a fire.

Practice under bizarre conditions should rarely if ever be done when the expense of practice can not be justified by the usefulness of the enhanced level of precision (cold storage learning, diminished level of precision caused by lack of reinforcement).

In most instances, practicing to be able to do a task at a required accuracy level, quantity, time standard or degree of completeness under normal, though simulated, job conditions is sufficient to equal ability to do the task. No "real world" verification is necessary.

Occasionally, however, verification that the practice actually took place, and the skills and knowledge can be applied on the job, might be needed. For example, suppose you were taught or tested on each required skill and knowledge required to fly a plane. Suppose further, these lessons and/or tests were at the S&K level and did not include actual performance of the tasks. Would you be willing to fly a plane on your own at that point? Or, would your performance require that you actually perform under someone's watchful eye first?

Skill in making discriminations and decisions or selecting contingent alternatives

Discriminating between input stimuli and selecting appropriate alternatives is often an important skill needed for task performance. For example, in the case of an operator handling a call from a coin telephone, the operator must first determine (discriminate) which kind of call it is (collect call — charge home phone, collect call — charge another phone, credit card call, etc.). The operator must then, for example, enter certain information on a numeric keyboard and do this at a certain speed (rate) and with perfect accuracy (quality level). This is a skill. While entering the data on the keyboard, the operator must discern (discriminate) where on the keyboard the numerics are and determine (decide) which data must be entered first, second, third, etc.

Obviously, the ability to determine which kind of call it is can be practiced separately from the skill of entering data correctly on the keyboard. However, the skill and knowledge of entering data on the keyboard quickly and accurately can not readily be divorced and must be practiced together. In the "real world" the preceding knowledge component and the skill/knowledge component might have to be practiced together since they occur in a normal sequence and may be best learned in that sequence.

Skill in making generalizations

Since a generalization occurs when two or more stimuli require the same action to be initiated, then one would have to recognize (know) that the stimuli are generic and will require the same action. Recognition that the stimuli are generic can be assured by presenting a person with all generic stimuli and asking him or her to verbalize what action(s) he or she would take or by presenting a person with all generic stimuli and requesting him or her to actually perform the resultant action(s). The ability to recognize all stimuli that require the same action be initiated is the skill. Knowing what each stimuli is (comprised of) is the knowledge.

Defining Knowledge

System users and administrative support people need to have the necessary knowledge to accomplish their various tasks. In some cases the knowledge will have to be learned, but in other cases it can be supplied as it is needed to perform a task.

Knowledge is the factual information required to accomplish an activity. It can be facts, general truths, principles or concepts. In a performance support environment, knowledge is meaningless in itself and is only relevant to the extent it supports (enables) a skill(s) required to accomplish the work activity. Knowledge can be classified into two categories:

* Process related — knowing what to do, when to do it and how to do it.
* "Environment' related — knowing the necessary words, equipment, tools, etc.

Process Related Knowledge

Some of the more common types of process related knowledge are described below:

Knowledge of what

Obviously the most important knowledge related to performing a job is knowing the appropriate tasks and specific steps involved in performing that job successfully. In addition, the performer must know the inputs required to perform an activity and the outputs expected at the completion of the activity. Often when a person knows what to do, a person is able to do it. This is because the person already possesses any other required skills or knowledge. At other times, however, when knowing what to do, the person may not be able to do it because, for example, knowledge about the sequence is not known.

Knowledge of when

Jobs are made up of several responsibilities, e.g., install equipment, add to or delete from equipment, repair equipment, diagnose troubles in equipment. Often when someone sets out to accomplish one responsibility (e.g., install) they find other responsibilities coincident with the first responsibility must be done (e.g., diagnose troubles and correct them). It is usually necessary that the person performing a job know all the stimuli (input/trigger) which cause him or her to perform other activities (at the responsibility, task, sub-task, etc. level).

Knowledge of sequence

Regardless of what level of detail (responsibility, task, sub-task, etc.) data are reflected, there is for every job a sequence in which the activity level(s) take place. "A" must be done before "B," "B" before "C" or "D," "C" or "D" before "E," etc. This sequence must be known and followed in order for the job or task(s) to be successfully completed. If one of two or more activities can be chosen interchangeably, this must also be known (as well as where in the sequence this choice appears). Knowledge of the sequence is particularly important when performing tasks that must be done in sequential order in order for satisfactory conclusions to be drawn (system diagnosis, trouble shooting) or equipment to function properly.

Knowledge of principles (Job Concepts or Theory) related to task accomplishment

This is basically a matter of being able to distinguish between "better" performance and merely adequate performance. It concerns the theory that a person has about the job or, better, the concept of what the job is supposed to accomplish.
Example:
Engineer "A" receives a telephone equipment order (TEO) to be engineered, furnished and installed. Although the TEO contains missing information and shows equipment to be installed in the wrong place or in the wrong sequence, he engineers it exactly as received and sends it on to be placed on Manufacturing. Engineer "B" receives a similar telephone equipment order. She also identifies missing information, wrong or outdated equipment, etc. She engineers only the part of the order that is correct as received, refuses to engineer the incorrect parts and gets on the phone immediately to straighten out the incorrect parts.

The above represents two different theories, approaches or concepts about what the same job is supposed to accomplish. Obviously, engineer "B's" theory is better than engineer "A's" which is at best adequate. Engineer "B's" job will be installed in the field at little or no extra cost to the company and will place no special burden on the Installation force. Engineer "A's" job will threaten service; cost thousands of dollars in terms of premium transportation for delivery of missing equipment, overtime and job delays; and will generate reams of otherwise unnecessary paper.

Knowledge of contingent alternatives

Most jobs and tasks do not proceed serially, in linear fashion (i.e., do A, then B, then C, etc.), but rather reach "crossroads" where contingent alternatives must be known and processed. For example:

Contingency	Course of action
If there are no late registrations	Normal procedure
	Check work area to determine punched in employees are at their work stations.
If there are late time registrations	Alternative procedure
	Record "lates" on Absence Control
	Record on time card.
If all are present	Normal procedure
	Initial time cards and return to rack.
If all are not present	Alternate procedure
	Determine why employee is punched-in but not at work station.

A contingency alternative is an approach that a person must take (and know he or she must take and how) when some thing or person causes a deviation from the normal, the usual or the ideal. Also, the alternative approach itself (when compelled to pursue it) might have its own "normal" course of action and other deviant, contingent alternatives. The presence of the word "if" is a clue that a contingent alternative may be forthcoming. However, "if" is also often used to introduce a generalization (generic stimuli) or discrimination or a decision to be made.

Knowledge of discriminations or decisions

Discriminations and decisions are made on any job. They are akin to contingency alternatives in that they reflect a "cross road" situation.

Discrimination	**Course of action**
Determine if there are unpunched time cards	If yes, do task 3 time cards
Discriminate between punched and unpunched time cards	If no, do task 1

Decision	**Course of action**
Determine if incorrectly punched time card is still usable	If yes, do task 7
Decide if usable or not	If no, do task 8

There are several words which indicate that a discrimination or decision is necessary. Decide, differentiate, distinguish or determine are the most common, with "determine" as the most often used.

Knowledge of generalizations

On most jobs, there are usually several inputs ("triggers," or stimuli) which cause the receiver of them to perform the same activity or activities. These several inputs when causing the same activities are usually referred to as a "generalization." More formally, they are "generic stimuli."
For example:

Generalizations	**Activity**
A) When a primary or secondary trouble lamp lights on the alarm, display and control panel	Take steps specified to locate faulty circuit pack
B) When a major or minor audible alarm sounds	Take steps specified to locate faulty circuit pack
C) When a maintenance output message is printed	Take steps specified to locate faulty circuit pack

Whenever there is more than one trigger or stimulus to an activity, it is important that the person who performs the activity knows all the stimuli so that he or she will react correctly when confronted with either one or all.

Knowledge of policies and rules

Most if not all jobs must conform to company policy or rules. This policy is set down in practices, procedures or company instructions. Successful job performance depends upon following the rules. For example, a purchasing agent would have to know that the company has a prohibition against her accepting gifts or entertainment from vendors (existing or prospective).

Not all policies or rules are promulgated at the corporate level nor are they always set down in writing. When reporting for a new work assignment at a Central Office, you may be told by your boss not to take any piece of equipment out of service until you clear it through him. Your performance depends on your knowing the rules.

In knowing the policy or rule, it is important to know where they are located. Where are the policies and rules (instructions, practices and procedures) spelled out? Where are they maintained (online computer file, file cabinet, at supervisor's desk; available from Personnel, Methods Engineering, etc.)? Are they in the head of an expert or supervisor?

Knowledge of special precautions

The knowledge of special precautions is very important to successful job performance. For example, a precaution such as "Do not interrupt the SAVE operation until it is completed" is important in assuring that the saved data is not corrupted. Such knowledge is usually highlighted (e.g., printed in bold, italic type) in online help, procedural documentation, handbooks, etc. Precautions should be acquired during data collection, whether they are published or not, and they should reflect information that must be known to ensure good job performance.

Environment Related Knowledge

Below is a description of the most common types of environment related knowledge:

Knowledge of why

Often knowing that something has to be done and how it should be done may be sufficient to induce people to do it. Failing to know why and failing to receive feedback regarding why engenders a "so what" attitude. Knowing the "why" can instill a positive attitude. For example, the task to be completed was simple: when the time tickets are reviewed, approved and slipped in an envelope to be mailed to payroll, a five digit code designating the sending location was to be printed in the lower left hand corner of the envelope when addressed. All people responsible for forwarding the time tickets knew the code, knew it should be on the envelope, knew it identified their location as the sender, but did not know why it had to be printed on the envelope. Consequently, only half bothered to record it. In fact what did happen was that their envelope joined thousands of others funnelling into a centralized payroll processing location. Clerks at that location scanned the number and from it identified the part of the country the envelope came from. Those envelopes which codes indicated that they came from a considerable distance were sorted out for immediate processing so that the paychecks would be back at the sending location on the designated payday. Envelopes without codes were thrown into a "Dead Letter" file and processed last. If that codeless envelope had come from two thousand miles away, the employees could have a payless payday. Had the reason why the code had to be put on the envelope been made known, perhaps, it might have been done more often.

Knowledge of effect

Knowing how to do a task, sub-task, etc. affects the person doing it, the organization, or the company. It is important to note that knowledge of effect also affects attitude. Many people labor in relative obscurity because they do not know how their efforts contribute to their own well-being or the well-being of others. In many cases, the impact upon job performance is also a "so what" attitude and a resultant loss in efficiency, productivity and level of quality.

Some jobs are structured on a flat salary rate basis plus group earnings incentive (the higher the group productivity, the higher the bonus pay). Lacking the knowledge that one shares in and contributes to group earnings can have a negative effect upon the salary treatment of oneself and the group.

Knowledge of consequences

Failing to grasp the consequences of correct or incorrect performance also has attitudinal implications. One of the responsibilities of an Installation Supervisor is to insure that when any modifications are made to equipment the pertinent equipment drawings and all other associated drawings are marked and forwarded to engineering to be re-drafted and filed for later use.

However, the prevailing attitude regarding marked drawings was that in light of other duties with a higher priority, this duty had a very low priority indeed. Consequently, drawings were not marked at all, not marked correctly and in many cases not even forwarded to Engineering. The responsible persons did not grasp that at some future date, perhaps months or years out, they, themselves or their peers would be required to do other modifications on the very same equipment and would be working from incorrect or out-of-date drawings. The potential impact upon service (interrupted) is obvious.

Knowledge of overall function

This is the other component of grasping the "big picture" of the equipment or system. For example, when performing an activity (e.g., troubleshooting) on a telecommunications sub-system, the performer may need to know how each component of that sub-system handles and routes a message, how that sub-system fits into the entire system and how the rest of the system handles the message.

Knowledge of basic theory

When performing work on a piece of equipment/apparatus or upon a system, whether that "work" involves installation, modification, troubleshooting or repair, one might require knowledge of the theory of the equipment or system in order to be able to perform.

For example, if one is performing work on a radio system, one might be required to understand the concept of modulation and demodulation since work performed may affect those. Another example is if one is working with a system that supports wireless, that person might be required to know how cells work.

Knowledge of performance aids, tools and resources

Performance aids, tools, resources and forms are part of any job in that they typically facilitate job performance. Without knowledge of their identity (existence) the job either does not get done properly or takes significantly longer to complete. If a task involves locating troubles in an electronic system, the person assigned to diagnose the troubles must know what performance aids are appropriate, what test set or sets are to be used (tools), what local procedure or handbook (resources) to follow and what forms to complete to indicate that diagnosis was done.

Along with knowing what performance aids, tools, resources and forms are to be used for any job or task, a person has to know where to go to get them in order to perform the task properly. Are they available online? If so, how are they accessed? Are they in document form? If so, where are they located? If it is a tool, where is it located?

Knowledge of terminology and special symbols

Most if not all jobs, whether they involve hardware or not, employ specific terms or symbols which the people doing the job must know. These comprise the language of the job. Acronyms, abbreviations and other job specific terms must be known. Special symbols appearing on hardware or set down in handbooks or equipment drawings must also be known.

Knowledge of relationships among various factors that make up job

On any given job, a person may be responsible for maintaining several standards of performance. These can be expressed as:

- maintaining a level of acceptable productivity
- maintaining a level of acceptable quality (expressed as an appearance standard or a minimum number of defects)
- minimizing the usage of new material (by salvaging rather than scrapping existing components)

These standards are usually specified in some handbook or practice. Often they are expressed as a rate or an amount of time. Perhaps the standard is unspecified in handbooks or practices but is a job standard expressed as a degree of completeness or thoroughness. A person doing a job must know what these standards are for his or her job and how they relate to each other. For example, he or she must know when to use new components in an assembly, rather than take time to salvage existing components, in order to speed up production. They will negatively affect material usage variation (new components cost, salvaged components cost nothing). Conversely, if people are more scrupulous about appearance standards than is required, they will lose time and reduce outputs.

Knowledge of the relationships among various factors of the job enables job incumbents to prioritize their activities and, equally important, to re-juggle these priorities when necessary. (On some jobs, by management dictate, production is being stressed this month. Last month quality was stressed and next month minimizing material usage may be stressed.)

The relationship between or among job factors may have nothing to do with a standard. For example, if a supervisor suspends an employee for two days, he or she must know that they have to amend the employees payroll data (code a time ticket, issue a payroll exception reporting form, etc.) so that the employee is not paid. Another example, if a modification is made to existing Central Office equipment, the people doing the modifications have to know or ask themselves when marking the drawings covering the equipment, if there are any associated drawings that are affected so that these too can be marked.

Knowledge of equipment layout or arrangement

A task may require one to locate a circuit pack on a frame. The location information provided as input may state the frame number, bay number, unit or panel designation, mounting bar designation and slot number. In this case, it may be essential that the population expected to perform this task know the equipment layouts.

What Must Be Done before Skill and Knowledge Derivation?

The task detailing (as described in the previous chapter) must be completed to a sufficient level of detail to communicate how the task is performed prior to deriving the skills and knowledge. This level of detail must be that which would be required by either the potential target population (non-SME) or the performance support developer(s) (whichever is the lower!). The level of detail must be sufficient so that once skills and knowledge are derived and specified, either of the two (i.e., member of target population or performance support developer) could do the tasks (except for those skills which they do not possess) using the task details and skill and knowledge statements. In such cases, the user or developer would clearly know what skills would have to be developed. Therefore, the person doing the detailing and derivations should have as much information as possible about the skills and knowledge possessed by the target population.

When the task detailing is specified at the level of detail required above, the specific skills and knowledge for all intents and purposes "fall out", i.e., they are relatively obvious and therefore can be documented readily. Basic and general skills may also "fall out." Frequently it is unnecessary to specify and derive either the basic or general skills. Those that are required tend to be those obviously possessed by most populations. However, care must be taken in those areas in which basic or general skills may not be possessed by the target population. Be particularly careful in those cases where activities must be performed that have never been done. In these cases, the basic skills may actually require working at a level lower than the task detailing statements, e.g., specifying finger dexterity or eye-hand coordination.

Skill and knowledge derivation should be done immediately after the task analysts have finished data collection and have listed all of the tasks, steps and associated dependencies (see Chapter 4). It should not be done in stages as the data collection progresses. Redundancy of data after all variables have been explored is, again, the clue that data gathering should stop.

Assumptions

The following assumptions concerning skill and knowledge derivation are important to understand the framework of the derivation process:

1. Work activities must be described to a sufficient level of detail to communicate (to a person that is not an SME) specifically how the task is performed prior to deriving skills and knowledge requirements.
2. Skills as well as work activities can be described hierarchically.
3. Skills are generalizable (across people and other activities) statements about the abilities required to perform a work activity.
4. Skills can be classified as basic (possessed by most of the population — to a more or less degree, e.g., reading); general (possessed by large numbers of the population, e.g., typing); and specific (possessed by people performing a unique work activity, e.g., filling out a particular form, or a general skill applied to a specific work activity).
5. A given work activity may require all three types or any subset of the skill types.
6. Skills and knowledge should be stated in operational terms (i.e., what is actually required) rather than in terms of some classification scheme. It may be necessary, however, to classify skills and knowledge for a particular purpose, e.g., strategy development or job aid development.
7. The more specific the skill, the more detail required to describe it. Basic skills do not require description unless it is suspected that the job population may be deficient in them, e.g., reading in some minority group population. General skills should be listed only if they are assumed by the analyst as a prerequisite for acquiring the specific skills, e.g., typing skill is a prerequisite to acquiring skill in typing a particular form. All specific skills require listing but only those thought to be deficient or not available in the Job population need be broken down into lower level skill components.
8. Knowledge is meaningful and relevant only to the extent it supports a skill(s) required to accomplish the work activity.
9. Knowledge must be stated in relation to and after the skill has been derived because of its dependency on the skill for relevancy. In addition, the method which is chosen to enable the skill may change the knowledge required (a very important consideration in performance support design).
10. Knowledge can be classified as:

    *   Process related (knowing how to do it)
    *   "Environment" related (knowing necessary words, equipment, tools, etc., being manipulated)

11. Knowledge requirements translate to enabling objectives.
12. Skills translate to terminal objectives, but might require "enabling" by means of enabling objectives.
13. Test items are intended to measure skill and knowledge possession or acquisition.
14. Skill and knowledge derivation is important to ensuring equal opportunity for people with different backgrounds and special needs because S&K related closer (or more directly) to population variables than do work activity statements.
15. Skill and knowledge requirements are also necessary for developing performance support components that address multi-populations and modular development environments because of the need to synthesize skills and knowledge across activities.

Skill and Knowledge Derivation Process

The following procedure is designed to require the listing of skills and knowledge for only those tasks and activities which can not be performed by all members of the target population (including members of any subgroups). If the analyst is confident that members of the target population can perform the activity to the required job standard and others who have knowledge of the capabilities of the population would agree, the skills and knowledge required need not be stated. However, when in doubt, the required skills and knowledge should be determined.

1. Read the description of the first task under study.

    a) Do you have reason to believe that all members of the target population already possess the skills and knowledge required to perform this task?
    b) If yes, skip to the next task and repeat Step 1.
    c) If no, continue with Step 2.

2. Read the description of the first activity within the task.

    a) Do you have reason to believe that all of the target population already possesses the required skills and knowledge to perform the activity?
    b) If yes, skip to the next activity and repeat Step 2.
    c) If no, continue with Step 3.

3. Determine whether the activity requires the use of any basic skills which might not be possessed by the target population.

    a) Use the questions in Check List A as prompts to help you determine whether any basic skills are involved.
    b) Base your judgments on the description of the activity, what you know intuitively about the required performance and the capabilities of the target population (especially subgroups, e.g., physically handicapped).

4. Determine whether the activity requires the use of any general skills which might not be possessed by the target population.

    a) Use the description and examples provided in Check List B to help you determine whether any general skills are involved.
    b) Base your judgments on the description of the activity and the capabilities of the target population (especially in terms of previous training and work experience).

5. Determine whether the activity requires the use of any specific skills not expected to be possessed by the target population.

    a) Use the questions provided in Check List C to determine if specific skills are required.
    b) Is only one specific skill required to perform the activity?
    c) If yes, revise the activity description to more explicitly state the skill involved and document the skill by merely stating "activity skill."
    d) If more than one specific skill is required to perform the activity, perform one of the following steps:

    - breakdown (if practical) your activity description to a lower level of detail so that the resultant activities include only one skill and then indicate that skill by stating "activity skill"

- • leave the activity description as written and separately state each of the specific skills required.

6. For each of the skills identified in Steps 3, 4 and 5, determine the skill components not expected to be possessed by the target population.

   a) Use the questions provided in Check List D to determine the skill components involved.
   b) If only one component is determined to be required, you may wish to rewrite your skill statement (or activity statement) to more explicitly state the skill requirement.
   c) List the skill components not expected to be possessed for each of the basic, general and specific skills identified.

7. For each of the activities and skills identified in Steps 4 through 6, determine the knowledge required to perform the activity.

   a) Use the questions provided in Check List E to determine what knowledge might be appropriate.
   b) Only state knowledge requirements that are not already possessed by the target population.
   c) Only state knowledge that is necessary to perform the activity, not things which might be nice to know.
   d) As each knowledge requirement is identified, either describe the specific knowledge, or identify where it is already specified in your existing documentation.

8. Repeat Steps 2 through 7 for each of the remaining activities within the task.
9. Determine whether additional knowledge is required to perform the entire task which had not been identified in Step 7. Review the questions in Check List E (Table 5.1) to make this determination.
10. Repeat Step 1 through 9 for the remaining tasks.
11. Cross-reference activities, skills and associated knowledge identified in the foregoing steps.

Table 5.2 provides a simple example of the results of the derivation process for the task of creating a new window type for online help. It is important to note that once the above procedure is utilized a few times, the analyst should be able to internalize the procedure and generally not need to refer repeatedly to the procedure or checklists provided in this chapter.

Check List A: Basic Skills Derivation

1. Does the activity require the use of skills which are generally acquired through the typical education process experienced by the expected job population (e.g., reading, basic mathematics, oral communications, written communications)?
2. Does the activity require the use of skills which are generally acquired through normal maturation and socialization processes (e.g., ability to follow directions, coordinated body movements).

Check List B: General Skills Derivation

1. Does the activity require the use of skills which are generally acquired through special training courses, or experience (e.g., typing, driving, using computers,

developing spreadsheets, preparing project plans, preparing engineering drawings, ability to read schematics, using test instruments, programming and solving complex problems)?

2. If the ability to perform the activity can be effectively and efficiently acquired without acquiring the general skill identified, then the general skill cannot truly be considered as required.

Check List C: Specific Skills Derivation

1. Does this activity involve specific applications of general skills required (e.g., develop engineering drawings using a new software tool) that are not likely to have already been learned by experience or be easily performed by transfer from the general skill?

2. Is this an activity where the possession of the general skill may, in fact, make it more difficult for the expected job population to acquire the skill to perform an activity because of changes in the way it is performed (e.g., a change in soldering methods, where soldering by the old method would ruin the equipment)?

3. Are coordinated sets of mental and/or physical actions required to accomplish the activity which are unique to this activity (e.g., adjusting a new piece of equipment, filling out a particular form, or utilizing a stylus to input data) that are not likely to have already been learned by experience or be easily performed by transfer from the general skill? To determine the answer to this question consider the following:

   a) Does the activity require that a number of current sensory and motor skills already possessed be combined into a new efficient integrated stimulus-response system?

   b) Are new combinations of inputs, processes and/or outputs required?

   c) Does the activity require a higher degree of efficiency or precision in a skill possessed by the expected job population than was previously expected?

   d) Are there unique aspects of performing the activity which make it unlike similar activities?

   e) Are new associates to previously learned stimuli or responses required?

Check List D: Specific Skill Components

Table 5.1 Check List D: Specific Skill Components

Check List Questions	Suggested Format of Skill Components Description
1. Does the activity require that the input be covertly or overtly recoded or re- structured before it can be processed?	Recoding (or restructuring) _____from_____ to_____
2. Does the activity require the covert identification and/or recognition of unique conditions or inputs for its accomplishments?	Identification (or recognition) of _____ (features) of _____(inputs or objects).
3. Is it necessary for the individual to continually covertly sample sensory inputs to monitor the status of some condition(s)?	Sampling _____at _____interval(s) to monitor status of _____

Check List Questions	Suggested Format of Skill Components Description
4. Must unique strategies for accomplishing the activity be covertly developed and carried out by the individual in response to different combinations of inputs or conditions?	Development and execution of _____ strategies in response to conditions (or inputs) _____
5. Does the activity require that relationships or characteristics of objects be perceived?	Perception of _____ relationships (or characteristics) of _____
6. Are serial contingencies involved (i.e., as each successive part of a problem is solved, information is obtained which applies to solving later parts)?	Solution of _____ based on solutions of _____
7. Are translations across senses required to perform the activity (e.g., translating a verbal message to a written output)?	Translation of _____ (input) to _____ (output).
8. Is the coordination between sensory and motor activity required (e.g., a (response) to keying response to an auditory signal)?	Production of _____ (response to) _____ (cue).
9. Are mathematical operations required to accomplish the activity?	Performance of _____ (mathematical) operation.
10. Are logical deductive processes required?	Deduction of _____ from _____ (premises).
11. Are inductive processes required?	Induction of _____ (generalization) from _____ (specifics or observations)
12. Is a specific response required on the basis of specific inputs or conditions?	Production of _____ (response) on the basis of _____ (inputs or conditions).
13. Are choices between alternative responses required?	Choosing between _____ _____ alternative responses
14. Are continuous responses required to multiple varying inputs (e.g., as when driving a car)?	Production of _____ (continuous responses) to _____ (varying inputs).
15. Is a chain of coordinated outputs or physical movements required in response to an input or condition?	Production of _____ (coordinated outputs or movements) on the basis of _____ (inputs or conditions).

Check List E: Knowledge Derivation

Process Related Knowledge:

1. Must one know what activities and/or outputs are required to accomplish the task or activities within the task?
2. Must one know any or all of the stimuli (i.e., when the activity should be performed)?
3. Must one know sequence?
4. Must one know principles (job concepts or theory) that relate to accomplishment of the activity (i.e., why it must be performed in a particular manner or sequence)?
5. Must one know contingent alternatives?
6. Must one know which discriminations or decisions to make?
7. Must one know which generalizations to make?
8. Must one know company policy, rules or cause and effect relationships to accomplish the activity?
9. Must one know special precautions? A precaution usually warns the performer not to do something, or not to do if in a certain way.
10. Is knowledge of particular strategies (problem solving, diagnosis or trouble-shooting) required to accomplish the activity?

Environment Related Knowledge

1. Must one know why task, sub-task, etc., has to be done?
2. Must one know how doing it helps self, organization and/or company?
3. Must one know delayed consequences of performing incorrectly?
4. Must one know the theory of the equipment and/or system (hardware) in order to be able to perform?
5. Must one know the function of the equipment and/or system in order to be able to perform?
6. Must one know by name and/or number the tools, equipment components, reports, resources and forms to be used?
7. Must one know the location/source of things such as the tools, equipment resources, forms, etc. to perform the activity?
8. Must one know special terms, codes or vocabulary to perform the activity?
9. Must one know the identity and location of documentation on the company policy and rules?
10. Must one know the relationship among the various factors that make up the job?
11. Must one know the layout or arrangement of equipment, office or building to be able to perform task?
12. Does the performer need to identify the "things" being manipulated as belonging to a class or category of things? If so include in your knowledge description, the attributes of the class or category which are important to performing the activity.
13. Is the knowledge of specific symbols or cues required to perform the activity? If so, what information about the cue or symbol is required? Does the performer need to memorize the symbol or cue or just recognize it?
14. Are there characteristics of the things being manipulated which may be important in acquiring the skill even though they may not be necessary later?

Table 5.2 Sample Skills & Knowledge Derivation for Creating a New Window Type for Online Help

Activities	Basic/General Skills	Specific Skills	Skill Components	Knowledge Required
1. Select "Project Settings" from File menu	Computer literacy; Use of Windows user interfaces	Use of mouse; Windows interface interactions	(possessed); (possessed)	Process for creating new window; Location of File menu and recognition of Project Settings option
2. Click the Windows tab	(Same as 1.)	(Same as 1.)	(possessed)	Recognition of Windows tab and its purpose
3. Click New (Window Properties dialog opens)	(Same as 1.)	(Same as 1.)	(possessed)	Recognition of New option and its purpose
4. Enter name in Window Name field	(Same as 1.)	Keyboard skills; Selecting appropriate window name	(possessed); Production of appropriate window names	(possessed); Relevant window naming conventions for file usages
5. Enter title for window in Caption field	(Same as 1.)	Keyboard skills; Selecting appropriate captions	(possessed); Production of appropriate captions for help windows	(possessed); Relevant window captioning conventions for help windows
6. Determine if Navigation Pane required	Developing online help applications	Determining need for navigation pane	Identifying features of new help window requiring navigation	Navigation requirements and considerations for help windows
7. Set tabs settings for Navigation Pane	(Same as 1.)	Making tab settings for Navigation Panes	Choosing between available tab parameters	Appropriate tab setting parameters for help windows
8. Set functionality settings for Navigation Pane	(Same as 1.)	Making functionality settings	Choosing between available functionality parameters	Appropriate functionality setting parameters for help windows
9. If Navigation Pane not required, clear TOC and Index	(Same as 1.)	Clearing TOC and Index settings	(possessed)	Procedure for clearing TOC and Index settings

PERFORMANCE SUPPORT CONSIDERATIONS AND ALTERNATIVES

As noted in the introduction, there are many different performance support techniques available to support users and system administration personnel in performing their jobs. The question is: which mix of performance support techniques is appropriate to support a given individual? In addition, the time required to produce a particular performance support product, and when it is needed, must be considered.

Techniques for Enabling Immediate Performance

The following are examples of techniques that can be used to enable immediate task performance:

Minimizing reliance on memory

Providing specific information relevant to task performance, rather than rely on the performer's memory, can be an important strategy to enable performance. Quick availability of such information is important particularly when speed and accuracy is required, activities are complex and/or the quantity of the information is too great to be remembered. Task supporting information may concern procedural steps, input requirements, output descriptions, cautions, system and interface component descriptions, etc. Performance aids and online help are two of the usual means of providing such information.

Advising

Advising involves providing the performer with specific advice related to making decisions or taking actions. The advice typically represents "best practice" or strategy and consists of task-specific hints, tips and reasoning support. Applications of this method often allow the performer to obtain additional explanation of the advice upon request. Advice may be provided automatically by the system on the basis of certain conditions occurring, or may be obtained by the user as needed.

Prompting

Prompting provides the performer with the appropriate choices to be made for a given operation. For example, an input form is displayed and the appropriate input choices for a field are listed when the user positions the cursor over that field. In the example, the user interface will likely include the prompts, but such prompts also could be overlaid on the interface by the performance support software. Prompting may be done automatically by the system (e.g., after a certain delay time), or may be provided upon request by the user (by means of the online help system). In addition, prompting is typically used in question-and-answer dialogues associated with wizards.

Automating

Automating portions of the performer's task can be an important method to enhance performance. This is particularly true for activities that the performer finds boring or tedious, or requires skills generally not needed for the rest of the job. Wizards are often used to automate such activities.

Techniques for Enabling Learning

Instructional techniques are the means by which instructional strategies are carried out, or more specifically, the manner by which the instructional content is provided to the learner. Technique should not be confused with media since media are the physical forms of conveyance to the learner (e.g., by an instructor, self-instructional text, computer). The following are examples of instructional techniques that can be used to enable learning:

Lecture

A lecture is the presentation of instructional content to a learner. In the strictest case, learners are not able to actively respond during that presentation.

Tutorial/dialogue

A tutorial, or dialogue, consists of a presentation of instructional content, query for assessment of learning, and re-presentation or remediation, when the learner has not met criteria.

Drill and Practice

Drill and practice involves repeated presentation of the instructional material, followed by testing of acquisition, until the responses meet criteria.

Inquiry or Generative

The inquiry or generative method involved the presentation of data, information, etc. in response to the learner's inquiries. In some cases, the form and order of presentation is adaptive based on previous responses by the learner.

Demonstration

In a demonstration, the learner is shown how something operates, is performed, etc. by being taken through the appropriate steps, actions and/or decisions required.

Role Playing

The learning experience in role playing is primarily interactive, with the participants assuming specific roles in the interaction. Role playing typically attempts to simulate the job environment and particularly is appropriate when people interaction is involved.

Games

Generally, the game uses a model with a set of mathematical relationships built to represent a particular environment. Games can be paper-and-pencil exercises or computerized. They usually closely approximate the real world in that the data used by the learner are the same, but they normally operate in a compressed time frame. However, games also can be used to teach particular enabling skills or knowledge related to the overall job performance (e.g., decision making skills).

Discussion

Discussion can be structured (guided) or unstructured. In guided discussion, questions, prepared in advance, are directed to the learners to guide the discussion along a preconceived path. The discussion is restricted within predetermined boundaries to ensure the group stays on track. In unstructured discussion, the learning experience is controlled by the participants who also provide the subject matter expertise. Participants also provide the direction and effort towards reaching the desired goal.

Simulation

Simulation involves the representation of the work environment (data conditions, etc.) in simulated manner. While the simulation may represent real data and conditions, they are not real-time (actually occurring in a system at that current time). The participants, individually or as teams, represent users or decision makers and perform the same kinds of operations and make the same types of decisions they might make in a real life situation.

Exploration

Exploration is an approach that allows the learner to freely explore the subject matter as a means to learning its content.

Evaluation

Evaluation is a discrete or combined analysis of responses for the purpose of deciding the next portion of instruction to provide.

Hands-on Practice

Hands-on practice makes use of the actual system equipment, or simulated versions, to provide a job-like experience to the learner.

Supervised Practice

Supervised practice is practice done under the direct supervision of an instructor, supervisor, etc.

On-the-job Practice

On-the-job practice is practice that is performed in the job environment with the actual system, equipment and supporting materials (e.g., job aids).

On-the-job Performance

In some cases it is appropriate to actually perform certain activities on the job, instead of a training environment, as a means of learning them.

PERFORMANCE SUPPORT SELECTION AID

This aid is comprised of two decision tables which will assist you in determining: 1) the most appropriate method(s) to support users in both learning to use and using the product; and 2) the mode of delivery most appropriate for these methods.

Using the Tables – Decide which selection factors are relevant for your combination of tasks, users, environment and development and implementation constraints and identify those methods, and delivery modes which are indicated ("checked") as being appropriate for each relevant factor. It may be necessary to make "tradeoffs" between competing methods and modes in some cases.

Support Method – Table 5.3 will help you decide which method (or methods) will provide the user with the support necessary to perform the job to the required level of effectiveness and efficiency within a specified time frame. Examples of such methods are: Performance aids (including online help and coaches), advisors, procedural guides, reference documentation and instruction. Although not represented in Table 5.3, automating tasks (e.g., wizards) to support performance should be considered as a viable option for tasks that are very repetitive or require skills not otherwise utilized on the job.

Delivery Mode – After selecting appropriate support methods, use Table 5.4 to determine the best way to present the material to the user or trainee. Such delivery modes include: Instructor/facilitator delivered, video web delivery (Distance Learning), Paper self-use (job aids or self-instructional text), Video self-use (Video-based self-instructional material), CBT non-embedded (Conventional Computer-based delivery), On-line/Embedded (includes on-line helps, tutorials, embedded CBT), Diagnostic & Advise/Computer (includes computer applications where the computer provides diagnostic evaluation of user inputs and provides advise on courses of action) and EPSS (Electronic Performance Support Systems, where the computer provides all support methods as an integrated system).

Table 5.3 Performance Support Method Options

Selection factors:	Performance Aid/Help	Advisor	Guide	Reference	Instruction
Procedures/information is likely to change	X			X	
Speed or accuracy is: • Important • Critical	X	X X			X X
Sequence of activities is: • Important • Critical	X X		X		X X
Support for on-the-job decisions or discriminations is required: • Immediately • Later	X	X		X	
Speed of finding, retrieving or using information is important	X				X
Quantity of information is too great to be remembered	X			X	
Procedures/activities are: • Very complex • Performed frequently • Performed infrequently	X X	X X	X X X		X X
Visualization of complex information is required		X		X	X
Cross-referencing is required			X	X	
Skills must be learned by guided practice					X
Skills must be acquired prior to performing job					X

Table 5.4 Delivery Mode Options

Selection Factors:	Instructor delivered	Video (web)	Paper Self-use	Video Self-use	CBT / non-Embed	On-line/ Embed	Diagnostic & Advise Computer	EPSS
Technique:								
• Memory reduction			X			X		X
• Advice							X	X
• Prompting						X	X	X
• Automating								X
• Lecture	X	X		X				
• Tutorial/dialogue	X		X		X	X		X
• Drill & practice	X		X		X	X		X
• Inquiry	X					X	X	X
• Demonstration	X	X		X				X
• Role playing	X							X
• Games					X			X
• Discussion	X	X						
• Simulation					X	X	X	X
• Evaluation	X		X	X	X	X	X	X
• Hands-on practice			X			X		X
• Supervised practice	X							
• On-job practice			X			X	X	X
• On-job performance			X			X	X	X
• Exploration						X	X	X
Development constraints:								
• Time short	X	X						
• Cost must be low	X	X	X	X				
Delivery constraints:								
• Facilities		X	X					
• Equipment	X	X	X					
• Lack of instructors		X	X	X	X	X	X	X
Population:								
• Few students/users	X		X	X				
• Large number	X		X	X	X	X	X	X
• Many locations		X	X	X	X	X	X	X
• Diverse skills			X	X	X	X	X	X
• Need time differences			X	X	X	X	X	X
Content required:								
• Local differences	X	X					X	X
• Unknown	X						X	X
differences	X	X						
• Volatile	X	X	X					
• Short life expectancy								
Current mode:								
• Instructor-led	X	X	X	X				
• Self-paced paper			X		X	X		X
• Self-paced video				X				X
• CBT					X	X		X
Control required:								
• Outcome			X		X			X
• Learning					X	X	X	X
• Process							X	X

REFERENCES

Gilbert, T. (1978), *Human Competence,* New York, McGraw-Hill.

Gossman, J. (1972), Driving Skill and Knowledge Requirements for Task Analysis in A System Design Environment, In *Proceedings of the Conference on Uses of Task Analysis in the Bell System,* American Telephone and Telegraph Co. Human Resources Laboratory, Training Research Group, Hopewell, NJ, October 18-20.

Williams, J. (1972), Standardized Task Analysis in Business Information Systems Development, In *Proceedings of the Conference on Uses of Task Analysis in the Bell System,* American Telephone and Telegraph Co. Human Resources Laboratory, Training Research Group, Hopewell, NJ, October 18-20.

Williams, J. (1977), Process for Deriving Skills and Knowledge, Training Skills Workshop, *National Society for Performance and Instruction Annual Conference.*

CHAPTER SIX

General Design Guidance

INTRODUCTION

This chapter provides general design guidance for information presentation, media selection, the use of color, icons, accessibility and internationalization. To be useful to designers and developers, guidelines must be directly applicable to the design context, i.e., the guidelines must support design decisions relevant to the performance support products being developed. The intent of this chapter is to provide guidelines, based on research and best practice that can be directly applied to product design.

Since a basic understanding of user characteristics is important in applying the various guidelines, this chapter also will provide a general description of the physical, information processing capabilities, and the perceptual characteristics of users. The section on information presentation describes categories of information presentation, task/information use dependencies, steps for determining information requirements and data forms. In the section on layout and structuring, display factors such as density, complexity and information arrangement are discussed. The section on media selection includes guidelines on both the use of individual media and the combination of media.

USER CONSIDERATIONS

In order to design effective information presentations, it is necessary to have a basic understanding of human capabilities and limitations. It is important to understand the physical aspects of perception, human information processing capability, perceptual characteristics and individual differences that will affect information presentation and media selection. This section is not intended to provide extensive coverage in this area, but to provide a brief overview of important factors that need to be considered. For an extensive coverage of human perception see the *Handbook of Perception and Human Performance* edited by Boff, Kaufman and Thomas (1986).

Physical Aspects

The physical aspects of perception are essentially the characteristics of the modality (e.g., eyes, ears) itself. Such factors as the modality structure, sensitivity to stimuli and geometry all affect perception. Since performance support products are either seen or heard, or both, we will only discuss vision and audition.

Vision

The human eye is a very capable organ, but it does have characteristics and limitations that affect design. For example:

- As an object departs from being viewed in center of the eye (fovea), visual acuity deteriorates rapidly (by 5 degrees, it has dropped 50%). This means that information not directly in the center of the gaze will not be discerned.

- Normal eye movements (saccadic movements) affect the way people read material. Reading saccades, correction saccades and line saccades have been recorded by means of eye movement cameras. These saccades affect how people discern words and chunk information.
- The size (on the retina) of the object being viewed affects its perceptibility and recognition. This is one of the reasons it is generally recommended that a minimum of 8 point type be used on video displays. It should be noted that the further you get from the display the larger the type must be to be legible (due to its diminished size on the retina).
- The contrast (difference in brightness) between the object being viewed and its background must be sufficient to permit distinguishing between the two. Contrast requirements are very important in the selection of foreground and background color combinations discussed later in the section color.
- Different areas of the retina are differentially sensitive to different colors (see Figure 6.1). This means that colored objects and areas in a display viewed in the peripheral areas of the retina may not be correctly recognized.

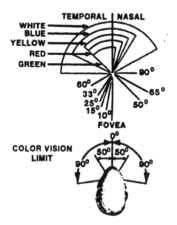

Figure 6.1 Areas of the Retina Sensitive to Different Colors (under normal illumination)

- Movement is better recognized in the peripheral areas of the eye than in the center. As a result, movement is the most appropriate means for drawing attention to peripheral areas of a display.
- Binocular vision (using both eyes) is important to recognizing depth, but also increases image detection and recognition capability.

Audition

The human ear also has some characteristics and limitations that need to be considered in presenting information aurally to users. For example:

- The normal (young) ear detects sounds within the 20 Hz (cycles per second) to 20000 Hz range. However, speech sounds are usually within the 200 Hz to 10000 Hz range, but are predominantly in the lower frequencies below 1000 Hz.
- Pitch (tonal sensation), loudness (sound intensity), volume (size of the tone, big, little) and density (compactness or thinness of the tone) are important perceptual

attributes of sound. Sound codes (earcons) make use of these attributes to create sets of sounds that can be discriminated for information purposes.
- Background noise masks (interferes with) speech and sound perception. This is one of the reasons that users should be allowed to adjust the volume of audio presentations.
- Binaural hearing (two ears) allows the location of sound sources. As is the case with binocular vision, stimuli received by both ears increase detection and recognition.

Information Processing Capability

It is important to understand how humans process information so that the presentation of information aids rather than hinder that process. Human information processing is both time and task dependent.

Time Dependencies

Human information processing is time dependent in that the various processes, from the original detection of the information to the understanding of its content, happen over a period of time. Figure 6.2 shows the various time dependent stages for processing visual information.

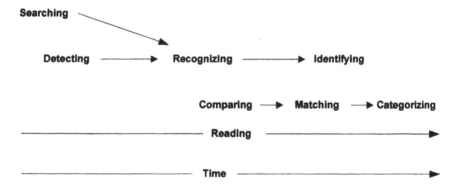

Figure 6.2 Time Dependency of Visual Information Processing

Human information processing is essentially a serial process in that each of stages depicted in Figure 6.2 begins only after the stage preceding it has been completed (although there is some overlap between the stages). It also important to note that memory processes are involved in the later stages of the processing. Comparing and matching two stimuli can be accomplished just using short term (or working) memory, but identifying and categorizing depends on the use of long term memory. Accessing memory takes additional processing time because information must be retrieved and analyzed. This is why performance aids that provide specific inputs to specific conditions speed task completion time.

Task Dependencies

As noted above, human information processing also depends on the task being performed. For task requiring the immediate use of current data, complex item designators can be used. But, if the information must be retained, coding and memory requirements must be considered. Also precise judgments require more information and processing time than relative judgments. Likewise, speed vs. accuracy will affect processing strategies. It also is important to note that comparisons are more accurate than absolute judgments. Complex tasks, i.e., tasks that require many different variables to be processed and require more memory operations, have longer completion times than simple tasks. Williams and Fish (1965) found in a study of immediate memory for number and symbol items that short-term retention decreases as the item length increases or as the number of different elements in the item increases. Table 6.1 shows some processing rates for different tasks.

Table 6.1 Processing Rates for Some Cognitive Tasks

Task	Processing Rate
Matching items against working memory:	(from Cavanaugh, 1972)
• Digits	33 msec/item
• Colors	38 msec/item
• Letters	40 msec/item
• Words	47 msec/item
• Geometric shapes	50 msec/item
• Nonsense syllables	73 msec/item
Perceptual judgment:	92 msec/inspection (Welford, 1973)
Matching:	(from Posner et al., 1969)
• Physical match:	435 msec/match
• Name match:	525 msec/match
Menu item selection:	(from Landauer and Nachbar, 1985)
• 4 items	2500 msec.
• 8 items	3000 msec.
• 16 items	3700 msec.

Perceptual Characteristics

Perception attends to change (but ignores steady states), is selective, attempts to maintain constancy, organizes individual sensations into "configuration" or "form," is interpretive and changes over time.

Attention

In order to perceive a stimulus, one must attend to it. Attention is selective and is directed to sudden changes in stimuli, but attention to non-changing conditions is deemphasized. It also is important to note that people differ in their attentiveness (i.e., how they perceive change in their environment). The stimuli characteristics that affect attention include: intensity, size, position, isolation, change, suddenness of onset, movement and repetition.   In addition, there is the subjective aspect of attention – novelty. That is, if a condition or characteristic of the stimuli is new, it is more likely to get attention.   Wickens and Carswell (1997) conceptualize attention as having three modes: selective attention, focused attention and divided attention.   Selective attention (or selective perception as described below), chooses what to process, focused attention sustains processing of those elements selected and divided attention allows the processing of more than one element or attribute at a time.

Selective Perception

Selective perception (Broadbent, 1958, 1972) is the term describing the phenomena of different individuals perceiving the same physical stimuli differently. It overlaps attention in that it directs attention. A good example of selective perception is an orchestra leader's ability to hear the different instruments in the orchestra when typical members of the audience can only hear the combined instruments. The conductor example is also a good illustration of one of the major reasons for selective perception – experience. Selective perception is often described as an "input filter" and often associated with user mental models in that users typically have developed a model (or schema) of what information to attend to based on their experience with a particular domain. As a result, selective perception is highly individualized.

Selective perception also is affected by focused attention which can be easily demonstrated by giving differential instructions to members of a group on what to attend to in performing a task. For example, a group of people are told that they will be viewing a display comprised of a mixture of alphabetic, numeric and geometric symbols (see Figure 6.3). The group is divided into four subgroups and each subgroup is asked to count a different type of symbol or symbols. The display is presented for a short period of time (just enough to allow the counting task to be completed). Subgroup members are then asked to report their results and indicate what other symbols were on the display. The results will clearly show that individuals having received different instructions will perceive the information displayed differently (demonstrated by the symbols not instructed to count noticed).

Figure 6.3 Figure Counting Task (Differences in Instructions)

Selective perception is a "conservation" technique that is necessary to manage the tremendous number of perceptual inputs available at any one point in time. It also is important to keep in mind that individuals differ in their ability to perceive different stimuli. Such differences will impact the type of mental models and selective perception strategies developed.

Constancy

Constancy is the tendency of humans to judge things as they really are despite varying conditions under which they may be perceived.   This perceptual characteristic has obvious advantages in that people perceive their world according to its fixed physical features instead of its varied sensory representations.   Some examples of constancy include:

- Lightness constancy – where the lightness of an object remains the same under different levels of illumination. For example, if you view a piece of coal under various lighting conditions, it will seem to be the same darkness.
- Color constancy – where the color of an object remains the same under different viewing conditions. For example, when an object moves into the peripheral area of the eye, it is still seen in color although no color preceptors actually perceive it.
- Size constancy – where the size of an object appears to be the same although it is viewed at a different distance (causing the image on the retina to be a different size). An example of size constancy is the apparent size of people when viewed at different distances.

Constancy requires both stable (i.e., reliable) and veridical (accurate) judgments. Stable and veridical judgments occur when sufficient information is available.   When misleading information is available, judgments are stable but not accurate. Figure 6.4 provides an example of the distortion that will result in a stable, but non-veridical stimulus situation. Note that the top of the square in the image appears to be larger than the bottom (although, if measured, they are equal in length).   This illusion is probably due to conflicts between the apparent depth effect caused by the receding lines and the actual size of the square.

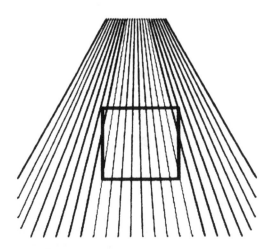

Figure 6.4 Stable Non-veridical Stimuli
(Modified from Rock, 1986, Figure 33.74, pp. 33-43.)

Unstable judgments (or fluctuations) occur when insufficient information is available to make a judgment. The familiar figure-ground reversal problem is an example of the unstable situation (see Figure 6.5).

Figure 6.5 Vase with Faces Background (Modified from Hochberg, 1964)

Visual spatial illusions are typically caused by constancy conflicts. Illusions will occur when stimuli that normally preserve constancy are operating but the image of the object is not varied according to expectations (Day, 1972). For example, if distance stimuli (retinal disparity, convergence-accommodation) are varied but the image is not varied, illusions of size occur. In addition, manipulations that are independent of the observer of stimuli for orientation and movement (orientation and motion of the image at the retina not varied) will produce illusionary orientations and movements of the objects. The waterfall illusion is an example of a movement illusion. This illusion occurs when a pattern in motion appears to move in the opposite direction. For example, if a user rapidly scrolls through a display and then stops abruptly, the display sometimes appears to move in the other direction.

Constancy is so much a part of our perceptual world that we rarely notice its effects, except for the illusions mentioned above. Constancy is one of the reasons that it is so hard to get "true-to-life" color photographs. Although we automatically adjust the color for the lighting conditions (e.g., fluorescent, incandescent, sunlight), the camera doesn't. The important thing to remember about constancy is that it can be either a positive or negative factor in correctly interpreting the performance support information that we provide. On the positive side, the depth effect caused by the receding line in Figure 6.4 is often used in two dimensional displays to effectively simulate depth. On the other hand, data presented on graphs can be distorted due to constancy effects. For example, Poulton (1985) reported that errors in reading line graphs seemed to reflect a perceptual "flattening" of the line as its distance from the y-axis increased.

Organization

The way people tend to organize their perceptions is an important consideration in the way information is presented. While there are a number of different theoretical approaches to perceptual organization (Pomerantz and Kubovy, 1986), the Gestalt approaches provide the broadest set of principles. Since a number of the Gestalt "laws" of perceptual organization have been successfully applied to the design of information displays, we will concentrate on those laws that have the most practical applications. These are: area, proximity, similarity, closure, continuity and symmetry.

Area – The smaller a closed region the more likely it is to be seen as a figure. This principle governs whether an area on a display is seen as an object or background. The tendency of outlined symbols to be more easily perceived than solid symbols (Williams and Falzon, 1963) may be explained by the area principle in that the outline symbols result in more clues for the closed region.

Proximity – Symbols or objects that are close together tend to be grouped together (see Figure 6.6). This principle should be used to group information in a display that is intended to be used together. On the other hand, it is important not to group unrelated information because users will conclude that the grouped items are related.

Similarity – Symbols or objects that are similar (or identical) tend to be grouped together (see Figure 6.7). Similarity may be in terms of shape, color, size and direction. Similarity and proximity used together can be a powerful means of identifying groups of information on a display. For example, the larger groupings may be based on proximity while subgroups may be based on similarity.

Closure – Areas with closed contours are more likely to be seen as figures than those with open contours. Closure involves two components, 1) closed or bonded regions are preferred over open regions, and 2) the perceptual system closes the gaps or fills in open regions to close the form. In Figure 6.8, the symbol is typically perceived as an "R" even though the lower right hand leg of the symbol is not connected. The closure principle relates to our tendency to see symbols made up of dots as solid symbols.

XXX XXX XXX XXX XXX XXX XXX XXX XXX XXX XXX XXX XXX XXX XXX XXX XXX XXX XXX XXX XXX XXX XXX XXX XXX XXX XXX XXX XXX XXX XXX XXX XXX XXX XXX XXX XXX XXX XXX XXX	X X X X X X X X X X X X O O O O O O O O O O O O X X X X X X X X X X X X O O O O O O O O O O O O X X X X X X X X X X X X O O O O O O O O O O O O X X X X X X X X X X X X O O O X X O O O X X X	● ● ● ● ● ● ● ● ● ● ● ● ● ● ●
Figure 6.6 Proximity	**Figure 6.7** Similarity	**Figure 6.8** Closure

Continuity – The arrangement of figure and ground tends to be seen based on the fewest changes or interruptions in straight or smoothly-curved lines or contours. This principle is a powerful principle that can actually override the principles of closure and symmetry. In fact, good continuity with cues for depth can actually lead to closure (Pomerantz and Kubovy, 1986). The continuity principle is very important for the display of graphical information.

Symmetry – The more symmetrical a closed region is, the more likely it will be seen as figure. Preferred forms tend toward symmetry, balance and proportion. Elements in a display are more likely to be grouped if they are arranged symmetrically and the symmetrical regions of the display tend to be perceived as figure. When a display contains alternating symmetric and asymmetric columns, the symmetrical columns tend to be seen as figure and the asymmetrical ones as ground. Generally, displays having symmetrical balance are viewed as more pleasing than those that are not balanced.

Interpretive Perception

As noted above, we do not perceive the world around us on a one-to-one basis with its physical manifestations. Individuals interpret the information they perceive by making judgments as to its content and characteristics. People also organize their perceptions by the use of chunking and categorization. Perceptions are organized into more manageable "chunks" by coding perceptual inputs into units of information that can be handled more efficiently. These chunks can then be categorized into "classes" to simplify their memorization and processing. For example, a "square" is a class of a two-dimensional object. Categorization is often, but not always conceptual. That is, we have category names (based on concepts) for many things, but we still categorize many stimuli without realizing it. As might be expected, learning is an important aspect of categorization.

Chunking and categorization are unique from individual to individual and result in different "mental models" or schemas. Since perceptions are interpreted based on each individuals own mental model, we need to consider the impact of the user's schema when we design information presentations.

Experience Effect

From the preceding discussion, it is easy to see that experience affects schema development and its modification. In the earlier example given about the selective perception of the orchestra leader, it was noted that the conductor's ability to perceive the individual instruments was based on experience. Over the years, the conductor learned to perceive the individual instruments by attending to their individual characteristics. It is also important to note that once something is perceived in a new way, it is difficult to perceive it again in the original form. Essentially, experience builds expectations that we utilize to interpret the stimuli that we perceive. Sometimes, these expectations are incorrect.

Individual Differences

Individual differences in perception are an important consideration in the presentation of information. A number of these differences have been touched upon in the discussion on perception. Some of the more important differences that we need to take into consideration are: physical differences, schema differences and perceptual (or cognitive) styles.

Physical Differences

The most prominent differences between individuals in their physical sensory capabilities are those related to age, sensory organ abnormalities (or disabilities) and the use of correction devices. Age affects both vision and hearing. Visual acuity, particularly dynamic visual acuity (ability to recognize moving objects), begins to decrease after age forty. Static visual acuity at eighty is only about half of the visual acuity at forty. The dynamic visual acuity of a fifty-year-old has decreased by 50 percent for recognizing objects moving at 60 degrees/second and 73 percent for objects moving at 150 degrees/second (Burg, 1966). As a result, care should be exercised when creating animations that will be viewed by older workers. Accommodation (the ability of the eye to focus on close objects) also changes with age, falling steadily until about age 50. As we get older, we also become less sensitive to blue due to yellowing of the lens (blue sensitivity decreases 30% by age 50). We become more sensitive to glare as we get older and we require more background illumination (task contrast). It has been estimated that the amount of light transmitted is reduced by two/thirds in a 60-year-old eye because of decreased pupil size and increased density of the lens (Weale, 1963). In terms of information processing, age seems to affect the motor responses (execution of actions) more than the coding and processing of information (Strayer et al., 1987).

Hearing also diminishes with age and by age 75 almost 40% of us will have hearing impairments. Since hearing losses due to age are typically in the higher tonal ranges, sounds used for feedback or coding purposes should be kept in the lower ranges. Nielsen and Schaefer (1993) found that sound effects used in a paint program made the interface more difficult for users in their 70s. Speech perception also decreases with age, particularly when listening conditions are less than ideal and/or speech is degraded (Bergman, 1971). Also increased speech presentation rates are likely to be detrimental to older listeners.

Visual or hearing abnormalities that may be present in the target population also are important to consider in the presentation of information. For example, color blindness is present in about 8% of the male population to various degrees (about 6% have markedly reduced sensitivity). The major color deficiencies, "red blindness," "green blindness," "red weakness" and "green weakness" can be compensated for by adding more yellow or blue to the color displayed. Astigmatism is also a common problem that will affect the way people view displays. If there are individuals in the target population with special needs (e.g., have low or no vision, have low or no hearing), information must be presented within the sensory capabilities of such individuals.

The use of correction devices by the target population will affect their perceptual ability in various ways. For example, people wearing hearing aids are more affected by background noise. Since corrected vision (e.g., eye glasses) cuts the amount of light entering the eyes, additional illumination may be required for compensation.

Schema Differences

As discussed previously, people differ considerably in their internalized structures (schema) representing the interrelationships between and among various objects, data and procedural elements associated with a particular situation or environment. Knowledge and procedures (or processes) are stored and retrieved in terms of the schema's structure. Schemata (also frequently called mental models) are unique to the individual and are developed over a long period of time on the basis of experience and perceptual (or cognitive) style. Due to schemata differences, it is important to explicitly state any models that are being used in the interface design to represent data, objects, etc. Metaphors (analogies) used in mental models should relate to concepts that are familiar to the user and/or their experiences with the work environment. It is very important to tie the application of the model to the user's experience in that:

- The model objects should be recognizable as its real world counterparts.
- Actions should correspond to activities performed on the real world counterpart objects.
- Changes on the object caused by user actions should reflect the user's real world experiences.
- Instances where the model does not hold should be made clear to the user.

Perceptual (Cognitive) Style

Perceptual or cognitive style is essentially "the characteristic, self-consistent modes of functioning which individuals show in their perceptual and intellectual activities"

(Witkin, Oltman, Raskin, and Karp, 1971, p. 3). One of the more popular cognitive style constructs, field dependence/independence (Witkin, 1964), is based on the extent to which an individual is dependent versus independent of the organization (or structure) of the surrounding perceptual field. Field dependency (also called psychological differentiation) is typically measured by the Rod and Frame Test and the Embedded Figures Test. Field dependency is of particular interest in the presentation of information because it describes the extent to which:

- The surrounding structure (framework) dominates the perception of items within it,
- The surrounding organized field influences the perception of items within it,
- A part of the field is perceived as a discrete form,
- The organization of the prevailing field affects the perception of its components
- Perception is analytical.

Field dependent individuals find it difficult to locate information within a source because other information tends to mask what they are looking for. They also tend to reorganize, restructure or represent information on the basis of their own needs. On the other hand, field independent individuals tend to be able to recognize and select important information from its background. They typically do not need to restructure the information and are more likely to accept and process it as it is.

A considerable amount of research has been done on the relationship of field dependence/independence and various kinds of performance including learning. Citron, Thorton and Cabe (1969) found perceptual style (measured by embedded figures test) to be a predictor for the ability to read non-numeric displays. The author (Williams, 1966) and Thorton, Barrett and Davis (1968) found a significant correlation between perceptual style and the ability to identify targets within aerial photographs. Johassen and Grabowski (1993) noted (p. 93) that Wise found field independence to be important in analyzing and categorizing visual stimuli. They also noted that it represented an analytical approach to problems as well as a perceptual "disembedding" skill. Canelos, Taylor and Gates (1980) found that field dependent learners had more difficulty in abstracting relevant information from instruction supporting more difficult learning tasks.

Johassen and Grabowski (1993) suggest that materials should be organized and presented so that it capitalizes on the preferences of field dependents, but is still usable by field independent learners. For example:

- Including orienting strategies
- Providing extensive feedback
- Providing well-organized and well-structured materials
- Presenting advanced organizers and outlines or graphic organizers of content
- Providing graphic, oral or auditory cues
- Providing prototypic examples
- Embedding questions throughout the learning
- Providing deductive or procedural instructional sequences

I have concentrated on the field dependence-independence cognitive style because of my own experience with it and the number of studies relating it to information processing tasks. However, it is important to note that there are a number of other cognitive styles that have been investigated over the years (see Jonassen and Grabowski, 1993 and Sternberg and Grigorenko, 1997) that may provide useful insight on presenting information and instruction to computer system users.

INFORMATION PRESENTATION

One of the first things to keep in mind in presenting information is that the presentation must match the purpose of the information. For example information may:

- Describe the attributes of an object, characteristics of an event, etc.
- Depict the status of something (e.g., on/off, good/bad).
- Provide a specific value for an object or condition (e.g., 12 pt. Type face).
- Show the difference between two or more things (e.g., temperature is 10 degrees less than specified temperature).
- Provide the steps or procedures for accomplishing an activity.

In addition, the information presentation must take into account the context in which it is being used. Context of use relates to the type of user, the user's intentions, and the using environment. For example, if the user must make a decision quickly from the data, the information must be presented in a form that will allow quick judgments to be made. Also, it is often important for users to understand the context of data presentation model (e.g., users of a database need to understand the database model in order to understand a specific data element).

Categories of Information Presentation

Information can be categorized, based on its purpose, into the following five categories:

- Descriptive information – describes the attributes or characteristics of objects, entities, processes, databases, states, histories, environments, etc. For example, a description of a system component. Descriptive information can also include information describing cause and effect, explanations, concepts, facts and options. Explanations typically answer such questions as: "What is this?", "What is it for?", and "What can I do with this"? Also, descriptive information may relate to physical or non-physical characteristics of objects and events.
- Qualitative information – describes information in terms of relative categorical characteristics or properties. For example, very large, large, medium, small, very small.
- Quantitative information – describes properties of objects, data, etc. in terms of specific numerical values or quantities. For example, the database currently contains 9500 items, or the average system response time is 50 msec. Quantitative information may also describe information concerning rates or movement (e.g., vehicle traveling at 50 miles per hour).
- Comparative information – provides information about the association of two or more characteristics of objects, data, etc. For example, Location A sold 200 units, Location B sold 300 units.
- Procedural information – provides information concerning a sequence of actions related to achieving some specific goal or task. For example, a list of the steps and actions required to accomplish a system task.

In many cases, more than one category can be used to display a particular type of information. Also the qualitative and quantitative categories listed above can be considered dimensions of the descriptive, comparative and procedural categories. Table 6.2 illustrates this relationship.

Table 6.2 Information Categories

	Qualitative	**Quantitative**
Descriptive	Categorical characteristics Nominal Status	Values Frequencies Distributions Population statistics
Comparative	Relative status Relative differences (e.g., more than, less than)	Percentages Correlations Ratios Differences (numeric)
Procedural	Tasks Steps Actions	Computational sequence Precision behaviors (turn screw ¼ turn) Machine instructions

Task/Information Use Dependencies

As noted under context of use, different tasks require different kinds of information. For example, precision (accuracy) must be considered as compared to the need for speed. Other task/information use dependencies include whether the information is needed at the same time that application information is being presented, whether it is needed only briefly or for an extended length of time and how timely (current) the information must be.

Steps for Determining Information Requirements

The following steps (based on task analysis data as discussed in Chapter 4) are typical for determining information requirements:

1. Describe the user(s) in terms of:

   - Education & training
   - Job & job experience (including level)
   - General characteristics (e.g., reading level, age, visual ability)
   - Experience with data forms and display media
   - Knowledge of terms, abbreviations, codes, etc.
   - Use environment, that is:

     — Where is it used
     — When is it used
     — How often is it used

2. Ascertain the tasks to be performed and their purpose.
3. Determine data items required to support the tasks.
4. Determine the form(s) in which the data will (or can) be available.

5. Determine whether the same data will be used to support different users and/or different tasks.
6. Determine the sequence in which the data will be used.
7. Determine the dependencies between data items.

Data Forms

Data form is the basic structural format in which the information or data are presented (i.e., narrative, tabular, graphic or image format). A specific data form is more or less appropriate for presenting the types of information described above (in the discussion of Categories of Information Presentation). In addition, each of the data forms has advantages and limitations and special considerations in its application.

Narrative

The narrative data form is the presentation of information in verbal language format (i.e., words and sentences). Narratives may be visually presented (e.g., text and messages) or may be presented by means of the auditory medium (e.g., human or synthesized speech).

Text – is most appropriate for presenting descriptive and procedural types of information that require prose to provide full meaning.   For additional information on text characteristics such as fonts and line length see "Text Presentation" in the section in this chapter entitled "Layout and Structuring Considerations." When using text consider the following:

- Text should be presented in mixed-case letters and not hyphenated.
- Generally use the active voice for instructions and avoid negatives.
- Provide the level of detail appropriate to the target population's knowledge and experience.
- Keep sentences as short as possible (but not so short that comprehension is compromised) and use short paragraphs (separate paragraphs by blank lines) that cover one idea. The flow of one sentence to another within a paragraph should be clear.
- For longer passages, allow text to fit the width of the display window. For short passages (e.g., instructions) keep text between 26 - 50 characters per line. If the text needs to be broken into columns, separated the columns by at least 5 spaces.
- It is preferable to display text in dark characters on a light background.
- Avoid using codes in text presentation.
- Assure that the vocabulary and terminology used and the reading level of the text matches that of target population. Use terminology consistently.

Messages – are appropriate for informing the user of system status, errors or the need for action.   Messages also are appropriate when the information cannot be coded efficiently and must be presented verbally.   Types of messages include: information messages, attention messages and action messages.   When developing messages consider the following:

- Messages should be brief so that they can be read quickly.
- The information in a message should be specific to the event. Also, if a message is for warning users of a possible future error, it should be displayed prior to the system or user carrying out the action to which it applies (BS 7830: 1996). If the message

will affect the user's decision about an action, it should be provided at the point where the decision is being made (BS 7830: 1996).

- State messages in a positive tone in that it is usually easier to understand positive, affirmative information than information stated negatively (Galitz, 1994). Also messages should be non-threatening and non-anthropomorphic, i.e., not having it appear that the computer is a person (Galitz, 1994).
- Messages should be constructive in that they should state the problem and the available options (if appropriate) and not be critical of what user actions may have led to the problem.
- State messages at a reading level that is comprehendible to the target population.
- Messages should be user-oriented rather than system-oriented in that messages should always be stated in a way that the user feels that they are in control.

Table 6.3 Bad and Good Examples of User Messages

Bad Examples	Good Examples
Enter next request	Ready
Enter next instruction	>
Illegal command	Load or Save?
Syntax error 245	Unmatched left parenthesis
Invalid entry	Months range from 1 to 12
Faclntrpt 00400040000	File must be opened before reading
The processing of the text editor yielded 44 pages of output on the line printer	Output 44 pages

Tabular

The tabular data form characterizes information or data that are presented in linear fashion in one or more columns. Such formats include lists, tables, matrices and decision tables. Tabular data forms are appropriate when the data need to be presented in a specific order, it is quantitative, values need to be compared or the number of data sets is small.

Lists – are appropriate for both qualitative and quantitative information where only a single array of data or information need to be presented. Lists are used to display menu options, procedures, choices, characteristics, attributes, etc. Since users can scan lists quicker than text passages, it is better to display data in a list than to embed the data into text. The following guidelines should be considered when using lists:

- List items should be numbered if order is important and bulleted if not. If list items need to be selected by keyboard entry, they also should be numbered.
- No more than two nested levels of a list should be used (BS 7830: 1996). Horton (1991), however, suggests that sub-lists should be considered for lists with over five items and that lists should not exceed three or four levels.
- Items in a list should be logically similar and be presented in a consistent manner (Horton, 1991).

- Whenever possible, list items should be presented in an order that is meaningful to the user (e.g., procedures in order of accomplishment, from most to least important, best to worse, chronologically).

Tables – are the best way to depict exact numerical values and are preferable to graphics for many small data sets (Tufte, 1983, p. 178). Tables are particularly appropriate when two or more related arrays of data items must be displayed. Also tables are appropriate when the data require many localized comparisons to be made (Tufte, 1983, p. 179). Horton (1991) suggests that tables should be used to: present a large amount of detailed information in a small space, facilitate item-to-item comparisons, depict individual data values precisely and to simply access individual data values. The following guidelines should be considered when using tables:

- All columns in a table should be labeled (see Table 6.4 below).
- Use row headings when information in the rows is unique (See Table 6.4 below).

Table 6.4 Layout of Table with Multiple Column and Row Headings

Column Head 1	Column Head 2		Column Head 3	
Row Head 1	Subhead 1	Subhead 2	Subhead 1	Subhead 2
Subhead 1	Data Item	Data Item	Data Item	Data Item
Subhead 2	Data Item	Data Item	Data Item	Data Item
Row Head 2				
Subhead 1	Data Item	Data Item	Data Item	Data Item
Subhead 2	Data Item	Data Item	Data Item	Data Item

- Order rows and columns using a clear, logical scheme that users can easily follow to locate appropriate column and row headings (Horton, 1991).
- If the table includes multiple levels of column and row headings, the main heading should span the subheadings and subordinate row headings should be indented (Horton, 1991).
- Use lines to separate table features very carefully and only as needed (i.e., white space separation is not adequate). If lines need to be used, use thin lines (Horton, 1991).
- Arrange items in a table in an orderly manner, e.g., alphabetically, chronologically, geographically, by magnitude, by a descriptive classification.
- Information that users need to read together should be in rows, not columns (BS 7830: 1996).
- Items in a table that need to be compared should be in close proximity, e.g., columns should not be separated more than three to five times the distance between lines (Horton, 1991).
- Reduce tables to the simplest number scale to permit reading to the degree of precision required, but no greater.

- When table columns are long, separate numbers into groups of five.
- Display all significant totals.
- If the table will be translated into other languages, consider the length of other language words when designing headings (BS 7830: 1996).
- If the length of a table presented on the screen exceeds the available window space and scrolling is required, the headings should remain fixed (BS 7830: 1996).

Matrices – are appropriate when it is necessary to depict how a group of items has been organized or classified into two or more dimensions according to a set of rules or sorting attributes. Matrices also are useful when relationships for connections (cells) between two sets of data items need to be presented (e.g., conditions and actions) or values within cells are a mathematical function of both dimensions of the matrix.

SYSTEM PERFORMANCE SPECIFICATION

STRATEGY	OUTPUT CONTENT	TIMELINESS	ACCURACY OR QUALITY	RELIABILITY OR DEPENDABILITY	ACCIDENT, INJURY, OR MATERIAL LOSS	COST	PERSONNEL UTILIZATION	EQUIPMENT UTILIZATION	NOTE: Specific performance criteria and weighting factors are dependent upon the specific system under design
1	1	3	5	1	4	2	3	1	
2	2	4	3	2	1	2	4	2	
3	3	1	2	3	3	1	2	3	

Figure 6.9 Example of a Matrix

Decision tables – are appropriate when actions in a decision making process require judgments based on one, two or three factors. Decision tables work best when decision/action information is basically symmetrical and can be divided into roughly parallel lists of decisions and actions. Also, consider using decision tables when a combination of events or equipment is involved. Decision table can simplify complex sets of instructions by summarizing "if-then" conditions (see Table 6.5 for a sample decision table). When decision tables are used consider the following:

- A decision table relative to a step in a procedure should immediately follow the procedure, or in the case of on-screen display, have a hyperlink from the step.
- Decision tables should be designed to portray the conditions and actions related to the decision in a simple, straightforward manner (e.g., conditions should be listed in the order that they would be evaluated logically).
- Keep the statements in the decision table as short as possible and use terminology familiar to the target population.
- If the number of conditions exceeds three factors, consider using a matrix instead of a decision table.

Table 6.5 Sample Decision Matrix for Customer Phone Selection

IF:	AND:	THEN:
Customer selects standard phone	---	Record order for standard phone
Customer wants specific deluxe model	Model is in stock	Record order for deluxe model
	Model is not in stock	Ask customer if willing to wait for reorder
	Customer willing to wait	Reorder deluxe model
	Customer not willing to wait	Inform customer of other models in stock
Customer accepts available model	---	Record order for model
Customer will not accept in-stock model	---	Ask customer if you can help them with anything else

Graphical

Graphics can be used to show what something looks like, clarify information that may be misunderstood, show complex interrelationships and provide the "big picture" (gestalt). Although in common usage the term "graphic" includes pictures and illustrations, this section is limited to "data graphics" (i.e., methods of presenting information and data relationships). Pictures and illustrations will be covered later under "images." A data graphic should be used when a large amount of data needs to be displayed in a small space; it is necessary to depict relationships between and among data points, decisions, or objects; and the shape of the function is important or interpolation is necessary. According to Tufte (1983) a graphical display should:

- Reveal the data.
- Induce the user to think about substance instead of methodology, graphic design, etc.
- Avoid distorting the data.
- Present a large amount of data in a small space.
- Make large data sets coherent.
- Encourage the eye to compare different data. (It should take advantage of human comparative capabilities.)
- Reveal the data at several levels of detail (from an overview to fine detail).
- Serve a clear purpose such as: description, explorations, tabulation or decoration.
- Closely integrate with statistical and verbal descriptions of a data set.

In his course "Presenting Data and Information" (1998), Tufte listed the following principles on designing graphical displays:

1. The graphic should answer the question: "compared to what?" Visual displays should emphasize visual comparisons.
2. The display should show causality whenever possible.
3. Since the world is multivariate, the display should capture these multiple variables.
4. Figures, text, etc. should be integrated into a cohesive whole.
5. A graphical presentation will stand and fall on its content, quality, relevance and integrity of content.
6. Comparisons can be made when the data are within eye span, but not otherwise. Users would rather see information adjacent in space than stacked in time.
7. Use small multiples of data (increases creditability because of more detail). Since small multiples are easy on the viewer, a good design principle is to replicate the architecture.

Graphical presentations include many different approaches to displaying relationships between and among data. However, in this chapter we will cover the use of: line charts, bar graphs, pie charts, nomographs, synthesis charts, process and flow charts, and statistical maps.

Line charts – are appropriate for data where the function is continuous or smoothed, or has many points. Line charts are also good for showing trends (especially if the x-axis is ordered, e.g., time) and when comparing a series with the same x-axis. Consider the following guidelines when designing line charts:

- The shape of the line graph should tend towards the horizontal with greater length than height because the eye is practiced in detecting deviations from the horizon (Tufte, 1983).
- Avoid elaborate encoded shadings, cross-hatching and color (Tufte, 1983). However, consider using high contrast shading to highlight the shape of the function.
- Do not use abbreviations in labels and present horizontally (never vertically).
- Keep labels to single lines (Tufte, 1983).
- Consider starting the vertical axis at the lowest data point rather than at the horizontal axis (Tufte, 1983). This allows the user to immediately see the value of the lowest point on the distribution.

Bar charts – are appropriate when the information has discrete categories and few data points. Bar charts are also useful when there are individual levels of the information (i.e., no order for an x-axis) or there is a need to estimate ratios or differences between adjacent values. When designing bar charts consider the following:

- Width of the bar can be used to code a 2nd variable.
- Color or texture can be used to indicate grouping.
- The shape of the bar graph should tend towards the horizontal with greater length than height (Tufte, 1983).
- Present the bar chart without a frame, vertical axis, or ticks and use a white (or contrasting color) grid to depict the label values (Tufte, 1983). (See Figure 6.10 for an example.)
- As was the case with line charts, keep labels to a single line, avoid abbreviations and present them horizontally (Tufte, 1983).
- If positive and negative values are to be presented, use a bi-level chart (see Figure 6.11 for an example).

For additional information on the use and design of various bar charts, see the *Handbook of Effective Graphic and Tabular Communications* (Enrick, 1980) and *A Compilation of Graphic Methods of Data Presentation* (Davidson and Epstein, 1963).

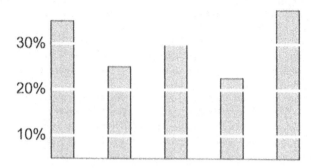

Figure 6.10 Bar Graph Using White Lines for Ticks

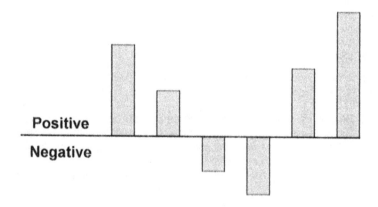

Figure 6.11 Sample Bi-Level Chart

Pie charts – are useful when a rough estimate of difference of similarity between components is needed. They may also be appropriate when there is a need to compare proportions or multiple percentages of different totals or a need to show additional component percentage data on a map. If pie charts are used, consider the following:

- Users should be able to clearly discriminate the different "slices" of the pie (e.g., by color, shading, etc.).
- For fastest and most accurate user interpretation of pie charts, place values clockwise from largest to smallest.
- Place values and labels on "slices" horizontally. If labels do not fit, consider placing adjacent to slices with "callout" line.
- Pie charts can be combined with line graphs (see Figure 6.12) as well as maps.

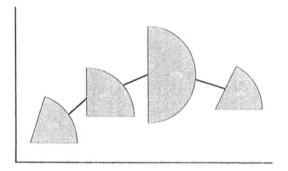

Figure 6.12 Combination Line Graph and Pie Chart

Nomographs – are appropriate when there is a need to provide a simple graphic solution to a numerical problem by interpolation between two scales. They are essentially a paper analog computer that provides a graphic solution to a numerical problem (see Figure 6.13 below for an example). Nomographs may be useful as simple job aids for computing frequently performed calculations.

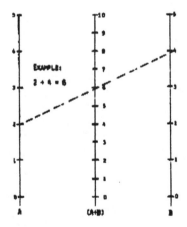

Figure 6.13 Nomograph for Obtaining Sum of Two Numbers

Synthesis charts – can depict conceptual relationships between ideas, objects, procedures, etc. graphically. Synthesis charts may be useful to show hierarchical relationships, dependencies and relative importance or magnitudes. An example of a synthesis chart is shown in Figure 6.14.

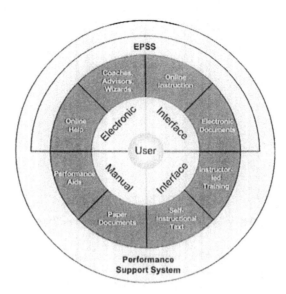

Figure 6.14 Example of a Synthesis Chart for Performance Support Systems

Process and flowcharts – are most appropriate for depicting processes or actions that require decisions to be made based on a number of different factors (see Chapter 4 for the use of flowcharts to depict task decision points). Flowcharts are useful in processes where there are frequent returns, or loops, to previous steps and actions need to be repeated. They can also provide a view of the "whole" process as well as the parts (i.e., individual procedures). Process or flowcharts may be useful to depict hierarchical relationships between objects, activities and events. Horton (1991) suggests the following guidelines for developing flowcharts:

- Keep the flowchart simple by dividing complex procedures into multiple simple flowcharts.
- Minimize the number of decisions in a specific procedure.
- Make the flow easy to follow by making the starting point apparent and the direction of flow obvious.
- Pick flowchart symbols to suit the purpose of the flowchart. For initial learning, consider realistic pictures or visual symbols. (However, conventional usage of symbols by the target population should always be kept in mind.)
- For general audiences (not computer knowledgeable), consider styling the flowchart as a map.
- Make the simplest path of the flow the default case, the most common situation, the recommended path, or the emphasized path, when possible.

Images

Images include photographs, video and illustrations that depict what things looks like. Photographs and video are useful when it is necessary to faithfully represent the natural world (e.g., people, events, actions, natural scenes and equipment). A photograph can be used to show the appearance of the object or component so the user can recognize it. Illustrations are most suited for identifying and depicting locations of screen or physical objects, component parts, etc., particularly in relation to performing actions on such objects. An illustration is intended to show where the object or component is located on the screen or equipment so that user knows where to find it. Images used to depict equipment do not always need to be exact replications of the equipment. In many cases, illustrations, depicting major characteristics, are better than actual photographs because they stress salient features thereby simplifying the image. Consider the following guidelines when using images:

- Use images consistently to minimize possible user orientation confusion.
- When showing solid objects, use photographs or three-dimensional illustrations rather than flat views or engineering drawings (Horton, 1991).
- When presenting illustrations on the screen, the whole image and any associated text should be visible. If the illustration is too large to include the associated text, provide the capability for printing the illustrations and text (BS 7830: 1996).
- If the level of detail needed by the user on an illustration cannot be presented (when presenting the entire image), provide facilities for zooming in to enlarge portions of the illustration (BS 7830: 1996).
- When illustrating procedures, present only the amount of detail relevant to the step being performed (Horton, 1991). However, it may be necessary to show the location of the portion being worked within the whole object (e.g., window, equipment) to orient the user. This can be accomplished by displaying the whole object with an enlarged view of the relevant portion.
- For complex images depicting multiple components, use numbered locator arrows to help the user find the object of interest. If the image is displayed on the computer screen, hyper-links should be provided from the number locator to the detailed image.
- If the part of the object that the user interacts with is small, present two pictures: one to show where the part is located and a second (close-up) to show how to manipulate it (Horton, 1991).
- Emphasize objects of interest by the use of callouts, contrasting highlighting, or contrasting text, but text descriptions should be avoided (Hackos and Stevens, 1997).
- When using text or callouts on pictures or in illustrations, consider translation requirements (BS 7830: 1996). Note that word lengths are different in different languages.
- When illustrating actions, use arrows to show the direction of movement required for an action (Horton, 1991).
- Distinguish between action arrows and attention directing arrows, e.g., make action arrows solid and attention arrows shaded (Horton, 1991).
- For complex systems, use symbolic illustrations of system functioning to represent relationships among components. When selecting picture elements and graphic symbols (e.g., valves and pumps in a process system) for symbolic illustrations, ensure common meaning and use symbols consistently (Tullis, 1988).
- When depicting screen images, reproduce image exactly and reduce size of image to 50 – 75% of the actual size (Horton, 1991).
- If only part of the screen image is important, emphasize it by: showing only a portion of the screen area, print portion in black and white and main screen in gray and white, or use reverse-video and thick lines so as not to dominate other items on the display (Horton, 1991).

Data Form Selection Aid

Table 6.6 summarizes the major uses of the various data forms in the form of a decision table. To use the Data Form Selection Aid, first, look at the "When" column for each of the major Forms (Narrative, Tabular, Data Graphic and Image) and determine whether the data form applies. Then look at the subcategories to see which of them best fits the presentation requirement.

Table 6.6 Data Form Selection Aid

Use:	*When:*
NARRATIVE	**Need to provide verbal information**
Text	Descriptions of events, procedures, objects, etc. that require lengthy prose to provide full meaning is necessary.
Messages	Short descriptions, indications of status, requirement for a single action, simple instructions, etc. need to be presented.
	Information cannot be coded efficiently and information must be presented verbally.
TABULAR	**Need to depict exact numerical values**
Lists	Single array of data items is required.
Tables	Two or more related arrays of data items must be displayed. Many localized comparisons of data are required. Have many small data sets.
Matrices	It is necessary to depict how a group of "things" have been organized (or classified) into two or more dimensions according to rules or sorting attributes.
	Need to present relationships for connections (cells) between two sets of data items (e.g., conditions and actions).
	Values within cells are a mathematical function of both dimensions by which the data are arrayed.
Decision Tables	Action required is decision making and one, two or three factors are required for any one action.
	The decision/action information is basically symmetrical and can be divided into roughly parallel lists of decisions and actions.
DATA GRAPHIC	**Need to present a large amount of data in a small space; depict relationships between and among data points, decisions, objects, etc.; or the shape of the function is important or interpolation is necessary.**
Line Charts	Function is continuous or smoothed, or has many points. Showing trends (especially if x-axis is ordered, e.g., time). Comparing a series with the same x-axis.

Use:	*When:*
Bar Charts	Have discrete categories (especially if few data points).
	Have Individual levels (especially if no order to x-axis).
	Need to estimate ratios or differences between adjacent values.
	Width is used to code the 2nd variable.
	Color or texture is used to indicate grouping.
Pie Charts	Components sum to 100%.
	Need *rough* estimate if differences or similarity between components.
	Need to compare multiple percentages of different totals.
	Need to show additional component percentage data on map.
Nomographs	Need to provide simple graphic solution to numerical problem by interpolation between two scales.
Synthesis Charts	It is important to show conceptual relationships between ideas, objects, procedures, etc. graphically.
Process Charts and Flowcharts	Actions need to be depicted and two or more factors must be considered for any one action.
	There are frequent returns, or loops, to previous steps and actions need to be repeated.
	It is important to view the "whole" process as well as the parts (or individual procedures).
	It is necessary to depict hierarchical relationships between objects, activities, events, etc.
Statistical and Topological Maps	It is important to depict data that varies on the basis of geography or location.
IMAGES	**It is necessary to depict what things looks like, where they are located or interactions with objects.**
Photographs or Video	It is necessary to faithfully represent the natural world (e.g., people, events, actions, natural scenes and equipment).
	It is important to show the actual appearance of the object or component so the user can recognize it.
Illustrations	Images do not need to be exact replications of the objects or equipment.
	It is important to stress salient features to simplify the image.
	Complex processes can be illustrated graphically.

LAYOUT AND STRUCTURING CONSIDERATION

The previous section discussed the various data forms and how they can best be presented. However, it is important to consider the overall layout and structure of the information presentation. This section provides some general guidelines for laying out and structuring information on the screen or window.

Display Density

In general, information presented in a display should not be too densely packed. Most empirical data indicate that, as long as the information relevant to the task is present, performance decreases with increases in display density. Irrelevant items of information on a display are usually described as "clutter" and tend to detract from the location of relevant items. Density has been defined in terms of overall density (the percent of the available screen space filled) and local density (the percent of a specific data area, or field space filled). If density is too low, display utilization will be poor and may result in insufficient data being displayed to the user. On the other hand, if density is too high, clutter will result and the user will take longer to find the desired information. Density effects seem to be a U-shaped function (with mid-ranges of density being best). Recommendations for overall density range from a low of 15% (Danchak, 1976) to a high of 60% (NASA, 1980). Based on our research (Williams and Leaf, 1995), a maximum density of 30% seems to be good general advice. Galitz (1994) also recommends a maximum of 30% density. However, the best rule is to display only the information that is necessary to make decisions or perform actions for a given task.

Complexity

Complexity can be defined in terms of the number of different or unique items on a display. There are also two kinds of complexity, within group complexity (item orderliness) and across group complexity (group orderliness). The overall complexity of a display is directly related to the number of groups, the number of items, the number of choice categories and the number of total elements (words, designators, etc.) on the display. The larger the number of unique items in a display or group, the longer it will take a user to find a particular item. In addition, the more embedded an item is with a display (i.e., similar to other items in the display) the more difficult it will be to recognize. To minimize complexity, information should be presented in limited quantities, in perceptually distinct groups and in a form (or location) that will suggest to the user where specific items of interest can be located. However, all of the information required to perform a task should be provided on the display if possible.

Grouping

Information can be grouped in many different ways on a display. Appropriate grouping of information on a display is one of the most important factors in determining its usability. In our study comparing objective and subjective judgments of screen formats (Williams and Leaf, 1995), we found that perceived uniformity and grouping distinctiveness correlated with expert predictions of "ease of use" for displays.

Group Size

A number of authors (Danchak, 1976; Tullis, 1984; ISO 9241-12, 1998) suggest that data groups within a display should not exceed a 5-degree visual angle circle (which corresponds to about 10 to 14 characters wide and about 5 – 7 lines high, depending on font point size and line interspacing). However, research on human reading indicates that eye fixations do not actually take in information within a visual angle circle. Rayner and colleagues (McConkie & Rayner, 1975; Rayner, 1975; Rayner & Bertera, 1979) demonstrated that the perceptual span (region from which useful information is acquired) is restricted to an area from 3 or 4 spaces to the left of fixation to 14 or 15 letters to the right of fixation (for English). However, information used to identify words is restricted to 7 to 8 letter spaces to the right of fixation. Other gross information (e.g., the length of upcoming words) is acquired out to 15 letters. It also is important to note that the perceptual span is essentially the same regardless of the size of the letters used in the text. Therefore, if search time is important, consider keeping word lengths to 8 characters or less and word combinations (e.g., item descriptions) to 15 characters or less.

Also if data items will consist of long numbers or codes, they need to be partitioned into subgroups of 3 to 4 digits for easier short term memory storage (e.g., telephone number such as 908 456 7890). ISO 9241-12 (1998) suggests the use of a blank as a separator between subgroups unless it conflicts with conventional usage.

Grouping Distinctiveness

It is important to be able to easily distinguish the various groups of information items from each other. Methods for ensuring that information groupings are distinctive include:

- Perceptual grouping – based on the principles of proximity, similarity and closure discussed earlier in this chapter. Essentially information that should be placed in the same group is placed in proximity. Information groups are separated so as not to be considered part of another group. The separation between groups should be such that the distance between groups is at least three times the distance of the item separation within the group (ISO 9241-12, 1998, recommends separating by 3 – 5 spaces). Similar items are placed together and borders are used to provide closure.
- Color – by using different colors, or backgrounds to differentiate different data or data groups.
- Graphical boundaries – by delineating the group or groups by presenting a graphical border around it. In some cases, borders may be very subtle and just be based on shading.
- Highlighting – by increasing the brightness, or reversing the video for an area of the display (mostly used to differentiate selected window from others).

Arranging Information

In order for information to be suitable for the user's task, it must be arranged properly. The following principles can be applied in the placement and sequencing of information on a display:

- Sequence of use – in which information is ordered based on its use in the task sequence. This principle is appropriate for tasks that require a highly structured order of information processing (e.g., transcription tasks).
- Frequency of use – where information is ordered in terms of its probable frequency of use in the task(s) with the most frequent appearing first.

- Functionality – where information is organized into groups based on its semantic meaningfulness to users. In addition, the functionality principle may be appropriate for information that is processed together. Sequencing within the groups would be based on the other principles.
- Importance – where the information is ordered in terms of its importance to the task. In such cases, those items that are critical to task performance would be placed first.
- Conventional (or habitual) use – in which information is arranged on the basis of common conventional formats (e.g., addresses).
- Specificity – where information is presented in order of general through more specific. This approach is useful when data are hierarchical in nature and higher level items establish a context for lower level items (Tullis, 1988).
- Alphabetical or chronological – in which information is arranged in alphabetical (e.g., names) or chronological order (e.g., date) based on the information type.

Consistency is critical to applying the above principles for arranging information on displays, particularly for display elements such as menus, task bars, etc. In general, grouping and sequencing approaches should be used consistently throughout the performance support system. Also, different major display elements (e.g., titles, menu bars, tool bars, prompts, error messages) should be uniformly located across displays within a performance support system.   Teitelbaum and Granda (1983) found that positional constancy yielded clear performance advantages. It also should be noted that more than one principle may fit a particular task environment. In such cases, a tradeoff analysis may be required.   The things to consider during a tradeoff analysis are: the criticalness of the decisions to be made utilizing the data, accuracy requirements and the ability to verify (cost of errors) and timing requirements (how quickly the data needs to be processed).

In the absence of specific knowledge about where information will be located on a display, users will tend to look at specific areas of the display in a particular order. Warren (1981) found different response latencies for different screen positions (see Table 6.7). The numbers in parentheses represent the order of the eye fixations. From this table it can be seen that users will probably look in the middle of display for data if they have no previous information as to where it may appear. The next favored location is the upper left hand portion of the display.

Table 6.7 Response Latencies by Screen Position (in msec.)
(Modified from Warren, 1981)

(2) 1408	**(4) 1528**	**(6.5) 1815**
(3) 1411	**(1) 1316**	**(5) 1715**
(6.5) 1815	**(9) 1976**	**(8) 1926**

Typically, the most important elements should be favored when placing information on the display. Figure 6.15 provides some general recommendations on positioning favored elements on displays with various layouts.

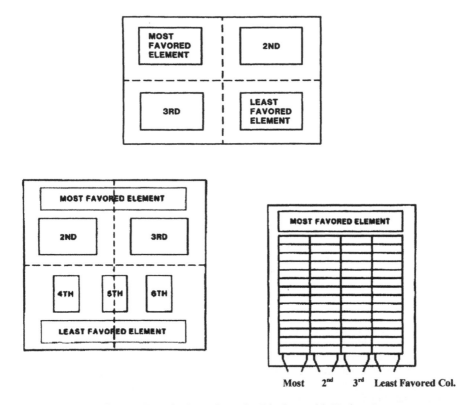

Figure 6.15 Most Favorite Locations for Displays with Various Layouts

There have been a number of methods proposed to consistently structure various kinds of information. One of the most popular methods is "Information Mapping" originally developed by Robert Horn in 1966 which focuses on providing and structuring the information needed by users to perform jobs correctly (Horn, 1974). Information Mapping®[1] provides comprehensive (somewhat rigid) rules for chunking and labeling information in blocks to ensure consistency in information presentation. It provides a modular structure intended to make information easy to access and utilizes methods to enhance and support scanning, including the use of white space, effective labeling, and task-based organization and design (Information Mapping, Inc., 1999). Information Mapping® has been applied to the development of printed materials, job aids, instruction, web pages and other online materials. Whether using the Information Mapping® method or other methods for structuring performance support materials, it is critical to provide a consistent and highly visible structure that meets the needs of both the information to be presented and the needs of users. Also, any structure used should be tested on typical users and modified based on the results of such tests.

---

[1] Information Mapping® is a registered trademark of Information Mapping, Inc.

Windows

When performance support information needs to be displayed in a window within an application, additional layout and structuring considerations need to be applied. For example, if the information is needed only briefly (e.g., field definitions) it should be displayed in a pop-up window adjacent to the subject area (e.g., field). If the information will be needed during the task being performed in the application window, it should be displayed in a secondary window adjacent (but not obscuring) the task window. The relationship between a primary window and its secondary windows should be clearly evident by being contained within the primary window, using consistent styles, or common window titles (ISO 9241-12, 1998). Secondary windows should be clearly labeled and be movable by the user. If multiple windows are required (e.g., when comparisons of data or information is necessary), they should be presented in a tiled format so that the user can view them at the same time. In cases where the number of windows is large, users should be able to switch between a tiled and overlapping window format.

In any case, all windows within the performance support system should have a consistent appearance, consistent navigation elements (menu bars, icons, etc.) and consistent control elements (e.g., scrolling, resizing, closing, etc.).

Labeling

Generally all display elements (e.g., windows, groups, fields, icons) should be labeled unless their meaning is obvious to the user (ISO 9241-12, 1998). Labels should be positioned consistently, should be grammatically consistent and should describe the content of the elements contained in the group or describe the item, or object, itself. Labels need to be positioned within proximity of the element described, but sufficiently distinguishable to denote that it is a label (by spacing, font style, color, etc.).

Text Presentation

There have been various studies on the presentation of text for both paper and computer screens (e.g., Tinker, 1955; Poulton and Brown, 1968; Moskel et al., 1984). Those aspects of text that need to be considered include: upper and mixed-case font, font styles and size, line width and interline separation.

Upper vs. Mixed-case Presentation

Most of the studies on reading text clearly show an advantage of mixed-case text over all upper-case text (e.g., Tinker, 1955) for printed materials. Studies on the presentation of text materials on computer screens (e.g., Moskel et al., 1984) have also shown an advantage of mixed-case for both comprehension and reading. However, there has been some research to indicate that captions and titles with all upper-case letters are more quickly found than those in mixed-case (Vartabedian, 1971). The author (Williams, 1988) also found that upper-case was faster for finding short menu items. Generally, text and messages should be presented in mixed-case. Conventional usage also suggests that menu bars, pull-down menu options and pushbuttons be presented in mixed-case. Upper-case should be considered for titles and section headings in that case differences will aid differentiating these from lower level headings (Galitz, 1994) and improve search time.

For screens displaying labels and data items, Tullis (1988) suggests using mixed-case for labels and upper-case for items to differentiate the two.

Font Styles and Size

Font styles are useful for discriminating between headings, text and emphasized words. Fonts are either serif (i.e., a font with strokes that extend above and below the basic letter shape) or sans serif (non-serif). For extensive text areas, a serif font such as Times Roman is recommended. It is believed that the added contribution of the serifs gives the words "shape" that helps word recognition during reading. For shorter passages that need to be read and understood quickly (e.g., online help), a sans serif type font such as Helvetica or Arial is recommended. Tullis (1995) also found that for type fonts 10 points and smaller, a sans serif type font was more readable than a serif type font. Galitz (1994) recommends not using more than two fonts in the same family (e.g., roman and sans serif) or two weights (i.e., normal and bold).

Type size is an important consideration, particularly for material to be presented on a computer display. Galitz (1994) recommends not using more than three sizes of type fonts. Generally, fonts should be 11 to 12 point for good readability (14 point is even better for older adults; Bernard et al., 2000). Tinker (1955) found that for printed text, 11 point type (followed by 12 point type) was read the fastest and had the highest preference. Since the display resolution (e.g., 600 x 800; 1280 x 1024) will affect the actual size of the various type font point sizes, decisions on point size should be made based on the screen resolution capability of the users' display monitors. Also, many operating systems provide the capability for users to increase font size.

Line Width

Tinker (1955) found that, for printed material in 10 point type, line widths from 17 to 27 picas were equally legible. For 12 point type, line widths having equal legibility ranged from 17 to 37 picas. Some standards (e.g., BS 7830: 1996) recommend that line length for material to be presented on a computer screen not exceed 60 characters. However, some researchers (e.g., Gould and Grischkowsky, 1986) have found that longer line lengths (e.g., 80 – 130 characters) did not result in a reading decrement. Tullis (1995) recommends that line lengths not be shorter than 26 to 56 characters in length. In a windowing environment, it is probably safe to assume that the text line length can fill the available width of the window. For performance support products, line length should be a function of the information to be presented (e.g., text should have long line widths while online help would have short line lengths).

Word and Interline Spacing

Right justification of text presented on computer displays should be avoided because it slows reading time (Trollip and Sales, 1986; BS 7830: 1996). Fully justified text (left and right justified) causes the words in the text to be unequally spaced. Justified text in printed form seems to cause fewer difficulties and is popular because of its more pleasing appearance.

There have been a number of experiments and different recommendations for interline spacing (spacing between two lines of text). Kurt and Muter (1984) compared single spacing (1:1.3) and double spacing (1:2.6) on a computer display and found that the double spaced text was read 11% faster. Williams (1988) also found that double spacing resulted in shorter search times than single spacing for menu items, particularly for menu items displayed in all upper-case. Also, 85% of the participants preferred the double spaced menus. However, there is some evidence that interline spacing of a space-and-a-half is acceptable for mixed-case text.

Aesthetic Factors

In general, displays that are balanced (have some degree of symmetry) are preferred over those that are not. Some authors of screen design guidelines (e.g., Galitz, 1994) have proposed that the spatial relationships among the screen elements have symmetrical balance (i.e., distributed equally across the display). Note that the display layouts shown in Figure 6.15 (page 157) are balanced. Galitz (1994, p. 61) suggests that symmetry should be created by replicating elements left and right of the screen center line. However, there is no data to indicate that symmetrical displays result in better task performance.

The appearance of a display in term of the pleasantness of the shapes, colors, lettering and overall design is another aesthetic factor that should be considered. Taylor (1960) suggests the following visual design principles:

- Balance – The design elements should have equal "weight" comparing the top half to the bottom and the left half to the right. Dark colors, large objects and unusual shapes are perceived as heavier than light colors, small objects and regular shapes.
- Sequence – A plan should be developed for how the eye is expected to move through the display so that important pieces of information can be significantly placed. The eye typically moves from bright colors to uncolored objects, from dark to light regions, from big to little objects and from unusual to usual shapes.
- Emphasis – The most important part of the display should draw attention immediately. As a general rule, there should be only one important object in a display. Otherwise the eye fights for control.
- Grouping – Grouped objects is more pleasing than scattering objects in a display. Groups tend to attract attention. Use similar shapes and close spacing of objects to promote grouping.
- Proportion – Pleasing displays can be created by applying the "golden ratio" of the Greeks (i.e., making the height to width, light to dark areas, and placement of shapes fit a rule of thirds). Marcus (1992) describes the square, square root of two, square root of three and the double square as additional pleasing shapes.
- Unity – Visual design should be coherent (i.e., everything should appear to belong together). Using similar shapes, colors and size will promote unity. Placing borders around a display or using white space at the edges also helps to provide unity.

General Layout Guidelines

On the basis of the material covered above on density, complexity, grouping, arranging information, labeling and aesthetic factors, the following general layout guidelines are recommended:

- Provide only the information that is necessary for the task and try to keep the overall density of displays to 30% or less.
- Minimize complexity by consistently organizing information in distinctive groups and consistently locating information where it can be easily found.

- Group information by using the Gestalt principles of proximity, similarity and closure. Emphasize groups by using color, graphical boundaries or highlighting.
- Keep important words in a display to 8 characters or less and descriptions to 15 characters or less.
- Divide long number items or codes into segments of 3 to 4 digits.
- Arrange information using arrangement principles of sequence of use, frequency of use, functionality, importance, conventional use, specificity or alphabetical or chronological order. Structure and arrange information within and across displays using consistent format and structuring rules.
- Locate important information on the display where it will be mostly likely viewed first (typically the top of the display and upper left hand corner for English).
- Label all display elements such as screens, windows, fields, icons, message areas, etc. Ensure that the label is associated with the information, but distinctive.
- Use mixed-case for menu bars, pull-down menu options, and pushbuttons and upper-case for titles and section headings.
- Use font styles (but limit to two) for discriminating between headings, text and emphasized words. For long text passages use a serif font (e.g., Times Roman), but use a sans serif font (e.g., Arial) for short passages and type fonts below 10 point.
- Type size should be at least 11 point (13 to 14 point for older adults, if not adjustable through the operating system).
- Text displayed electronically should not be right justified and the interline spacing should be at least a space-and-a-half.
- Apply visual screen design principles of balance, sequence, emphasis, grouping, proportion and unity to enhance the pleasantness of the displays.

MEDIA SELECTION

The selection of media is an important decision and should be based on the information to be presented. Media selection is a major means for determining how the performance support will be presented to the user. However, many decisions about the use of media are based on the popularity of a particular media or combination of media (in the case for multimedia). For example, the use of multimedia in instruction, particularly online instruction (i.e., e-learning), has mushroomed in recent years due mostly to the increased capabilities of computers and the availability of multimedia authoring software and presentation tools. Even such presentation tools as Microsoft's PowerPoint have multimedia capabilities. Although multimedia can provide many opportunities for performance support developers, it is often used ineffectively and its use sometimes actually results in decreases in performance. Many claims are made by various authors as to the added effectiveness that multimedia can bring to training programs and presentations. Kalyuga, Chandler and Sweller (2000) suggest that dual-modality presentations are only beneficial under certain well-defined situations and have negative consequences in other situations. The purpose of this section is to provide guidelines for the use of individual media and the combination of media based on available research.

General Design Considerations

It is important to apply well founded design principles in the application of any media or combinations of media in the development of performance support products. The most important variables to consider are: the characteristics of the target population, the task to be supported and the enabling strategies applied. It is especially important to consider the perceptual capabilities as well as preferences of the target population. For example, if some members of the target population have visual disabilities, it may be appropriate to provide alternative media to supplement or complement the visual presentations (see the section on "Accessibility" later in this chapter). Obviously another consideration in selecting media is the development time and cost. Project constraints in regard to time and costs may require media to be selected that is not optimum for delivery of the performance support product. Also, there are situations in which the media have been pre-determined by the customer. In addition to the above variables, some general factors (Williams, 1998) that need to be considered in design include:

- Motivating or attention directing factors, such as: introductory or priming techniques, methods that direct attention to presentation points to follow, organizational outlining and internal structuring of the content, and methods to emphasize or direct attention to important or relevant information.
- Approaches that enhance the user's interaction, by: aiding or replacing mental processes, minimizing passive viewing, increasing active user participation (e.g., eliciting responses) and providing corrective or confirming feedback.
- Techniques that reinforce, such as: combining media when they complement each other, providing feedback, repeating important sequences of information, branching to summaries of material and focusing on critical elements when summarizing.
- The use of color when it: aids in discriminating among objects, is useful for cueing or highlighting relevant information and when its recognition is part of a task to be performed or learned (see "Use of Color" later in this chapter).

Typical use of media

The choice of media always should be based on the performance objective to be achieved and the strategy being applied (i.e., decisions about the content and strategy should proceed decisions about media). Strategies include such things as memory reduction, advise, prompting, lectures, tutorials, inquiries, drill and practice, demonstrations, role playing, modeling/simulation, hands-on practice, etc. A given strategy is comprised of various components (e.g., an inquiry is comprised of the statement(s) of the question(s), response choices by the user, and feedback to the user) which are communicated by means of the media.

In Table 6.8, some typical uses of the various media are shown. However, it is important to note that the typical uses depicted in the table are just that (typical uses) and are not necessarily effective uses of the media. Media effectiveness depends on how well it implements the intended strategy and produces the desired performance outcome. The creditability of the media is also an important consideration in that some media may be seen as more credible than others. For example, text is often seen as the most credible for instruction, while video recreations of events are less credible (Laurel, Oren and Don, 1992). To ensure the credibility of the information, the media use should reflect the goals of the performance support performance product. For example, if cartoon graphics are used with text, viewers may feel that the text is more believable than the graphics. However, they may also feel that the graphics are more fun (Laurel, Oren and Don, 1992).

Table 6.8 Media Use Table*

Media	Typical Use
Text	• Information • Procedures • Guidance • Instructions • Labels, annotation • Clarifications
Sound	• Attention (e.g., input required) • Feedback (e.g., correct or incorrect answer) • Realistic sound effects (e.g., the sound of a failing mechanical component) • Informational ("earcons") • Background music
Speech - narration	• Introductions • Motivation ("power figure") • Explanations • Description of event, process, etc. • Feedback • Multiple persons interaction
Still pictures	• People, places, objects (where realism important) • Actions (e.g., assembly operation) • Backgrounds
Graphics	• Visually illustrate components or relationships (e.g., equipment diagram, flowchart, map, floor plan) • Depict detailed information • Symbolic representation (e.g., icons)
Animation	• Graphic simulation of movement • Illustration of concepts • Sequence of events over time • Continuity in transitions • Changing dimensions • Illustration of 3D structures • Attention
Moving pictures	• Moving events (people, places, activities, operations, etc.) • Computer screen activity sequences • Demonstration of skill to be modeled • Product demonstration

* Modified from Williams (1998)

Use of Individual Media

As noted in the table above, individual media can be used effectively to present various kinds of information. Since performance support information primarily is intended to support the system's functions or user interface, it is typically presented in a textual or graphical form that corresponds to the user interface. Following are some guidelines for the use of individual media:

• Text – should be used for presenting instructions, descriptive information (Booher, 1975) and conceptual information (Booher, 1975, Suttcliffe and Faraday, 1994). It should be noted that speech also can be used for such purposes. However, text is preferred over speech when the user may need to view or review portions of the information.

- Sound – should be used for representing important actual system sounds (e.g., busy signal), for alerting (e.g., warning beep for an error, or response required), for feedback (e.g., correct or incorrect answer) or for coding events that may not be observed visually (informational earcons). Alerting sounds should be used sparingly and all sounds used for information should be used consistently.

- Speech – should be used when the credibility of the speaker is important to the acceptance of the material. As noted above, speech also can be used for presenting instructions, descriptive information and concept information. Speech is particularly useful for representing multiple person interactions. Narrations are typically used in conjunction with another media, e.g., animation.

- Pictures (stills) – should be used for presenting visual-spatial information where movement or changes in perspective is not important (Bieger and Glock, 1984). Pictures are very useful in presenting information where realism is important (e.g., people, computer screen). Still images also should be used when simple or discrete actions need to be presented (Hegerty and Just, 1993).

- Graphics – should be used for the spatial representation of abstract concepts or to represent complex relationships within and between sets of values (e.g., graphs, bar charts, pie charts). Graphics can represent processes and sequences of operations (e.g., flowcharts, process diagrams), particularly those where interactions are present. Also graphic representations (e.g., icons), used to represent objects within a user interface, can enhance performance and minimize translation requirements.

- Animation – should be used to present complex or continuous actions where realism is not critical (Stako, et al, 1993). Animation can better represent complex physical actions than realistic media (i.e., video) because the coordination of discrete motor actions can be inspected.

- Moving Pictures – should be used to represent complex or continuous action where realism is important (e.g., proper golf stroke). Moving pictures also can be used for displaying events captured over time (e.g., sequences of computer screens during a user session).

Combining visual and verbal information

Visual and verbal information combinations generally lead to equal or enhanced comprehension compared to their use alone if they do not conflict and are carefully matched (Wetzel, Radtke and Stern, 1994). However, if users are required to split their attention between (and integrate) two or more related sources of information, strain on limited working memory may result and cause a decrease in performance (Chandler and Sweller, 1991). Visuals provide concrete representations of information that may not be easily conveyed otherwise. The following guidelines should be considered when combining visual and verbal information (Williams, 1998):

- Visuals and narratives should be presented simultaneously or the visual should precede the narrative by up to 7 seconds. If the narrative is presented in advance of the visual it tends to be disruptive.

- While the addition of audio to a text presentation may not improve comprehension, it may increase user satisfaction with the material.

- Only relevant illustrations (i.e., that provide a meaningful supplement to the text information) should be used to aid learning from text. Unrelated illustrations should not be used because they will not facilitate learning. The biggest effect is on long term memory.

- Textual prompting or references to the illustrated information should be used to aid readers in extracting relevant information from complex illustrations.
- Visuals and illustrations should not be more complex than needed to distinguish relevant information or illustrate concepts, devices, etc. Individuals with lower spatial relations ability have more trouble with complex illustrations than those with higher spatial relations ability.
- Greater time should be provided for viewing large or complex visuals.

In some cases, physically integrating diagrams and text is not effective, e.g., some of the information is unnecessary or redundant (Sweller and Chandler, 1994). If the text cannot be integrated into diagrams (i.e., split-source diagrams) and must be presented separately, the following additional guidelines should be considered (Kalyuga, Chandler and Sweller, 2000):

- Textual materials should be presented in auditory instead of written form.
- The same text material should not be presented in both auditory and written form.
- If presented in auditory form, text should be able to be turned off easily or ignored.

Text and narration

Text and narration are often used in combination with other media. For example, an instructional video may have text overlaid on the video picture and also may be narrated. Redundant text and narratives can aid learning if used properly. Including both text and narrative versions of the content also is useful for providing alternative sources of information (particularly important for learners with perceptual difficulties as well as learners with strong media preferences). The following guidelines should be considered when using texts and narratives (Williams, 1998):

- Excessive text on the screen relative to the amount of other visual material should be avoided since it results in decreased comprehension.
- Topic overviews should be used to provide the reader with advance knowledge of the upcoming content.
- If text is to be used in a video, no more than two lines of text should be displayed at any one time and each line should not contain more than 32 characters.
- Video captions should be displayed for more than 6 seconds.
  Note: There is evidence that captions may benefit most viewers, particularly for difficult material and viewers with impairments.
- Text and narration should be consistent with each other and generally should coincide in time. However, a slight asynchrony between the two may avoid simultaneous demands on the viewer.
- Off-screen narration should be used rather than on-screen narration in most cases. In general, off-screen narration is superior to an on-screen narrator unless the narrator is a recognized authority on the topic.
- The speed of narration for an average audience presented with simple content should be approximately 160 words per minute. The speed of narration depends on the complexity of material and other visual and auditory information being presented at the same time. It should be noted that rapid narration can reduce comprehension and should be slowed slightly when used with motion or to introduce new ideas or concepts.
- Reading level of the narrated material should be the same as the reading level of the audience.

- Continuous narration should be avoided, use intermittent pauses to sustain attention.

Use of motion and animation

Dynamic visual presentation has three components: 1) visual appearance, 2) verbal or cognitive meaning, and 3) motion or trajectory characteristics. Motion can be useful when:

1. It enables discriminations to be made,
2. Attention is directed to relevant features that change,
3. It clarifies sequential relations by providing continuity between events,
4. Learning a concept that itself is defined by motion,
5. Learning the motion itself, and
6. The task is unfamiliar or difficult to express verbally.

Graphic animation (combing graphic illustration with simulated motion to present objects, processes or concepts) can be considered a special case of motion. Although animation can be used to present information using the same techniques as video, the degree of realism is controlled by the designer (e.g., time, distance, scale, access or complexity). In addition, animation has been found to be particularly effective when used with a corresponding narration. Mayer, Moreno, Boire and Vagge (1999) also found that presenting animation in small bites was superior to presenting them in large bites. The following guidelines should be considered when using motion and animation (Williams, 1998):

- Dynamic visual displays should be considered for: demonstrating sequential actions in a procedural task; simulating causal models of complex system behaviors; explicitly representing invisible system functions and behaviors; illustrating tasks that are difficult to describe verbally; providing visual analogies for abstract and symbolic concepts; and drawing attention to specific tasks or presentation displays.
- Motion may be useful when discrimination of information is required for: discriminating figure from ground, revealing three-dimensional relations and indicating directionality, speed and velocity.
- Motion also may be useful for its attention value, depicting continuity in sequential temporal-spatial relations, when it is a defining characteristic of a concept to taught, when motion itself must be learned and when it directly represents information that is difficult to describe verbally.
- The portion of the display that will depict moving objects should be placed within a bordered frame to provide a fixed frame of reference for the movement. Divita and Rock (1997) found that the displacement of an object relative to a frame of reference to which it belongs determines its perceived path of motion.
- Animation should be used with caution and only when related to performance objectives. While animation has shown some benefits for some tasks, it has not provided significant advantages over static graphics in others and takes more time.
- If appropriate to the task, animation may be used to attract or direct the viewer's attention to particular portions of the screen or changes among important elements. However, it is important to avoid multiple competing animations.
- When animations are used for attention purposes, users should have the capability to turn them off.
- Animation that provides modeling and feedback can be useful in learning motor skills or to enhance practice (e.g., in interactive simulation).
  It should be noted that adult learning studies have shown only a slight support for the effectiveness of animation (except in those cases where narratives were used to

supplement the animation). When effects are found they are usually related to using the animation to practice an idea or a skill.

- Animation should be incorporated only when its attributes are congruent to the learning task. The attributes are: visualization, motion and trajectory.
- Animations should be used to simulate concepts and events with representations difficult to capture in the real word because of their scale, speed or complexity.
- Animation should avoid unnecessarily detailed backgrounds or distracting techniques designed to dazzle the viewer.
- Learners not familiar with the content should be provided guidance on the purpose of the animation.
- Narratives (speech cues) and labels should be used to reinforce important components (e.g., objects, processes, results) of an animation.

Use of Video

Video has the capability to present either real or simulated still or moving objects, people and events with or without an audio component. It should be noted that viewers recall information from video in terms of visual and action details, while information from audio is seen in the retention of various audio and linguistic details often accompanied by additional verbal embellishments (Wetzel, Radtke and Stern, 1994). In using video, the following guidelines should be considered (Williams, 1998):

- Video's capabilities of motion, sound and color should be employed in selective ways that are critical to meeting the intended performance objectives and are appropriate to the user's current level of skill and knowledge.
- If users are not knowledgeable about the subject, progression through the material should be under program control. Program-controlled interactive video has been found to be more effective than learner-controlled interactive video (primarily for students with little prior knowledge of subject) (Fletcher, 1990; McNeil and Nelson, 1991).
- Avoid overly realistic features of visuals, motion or complex tasks that provide irrelevant detail in excess of those elements that are critical to a performance objective.
- Avoid busy backgrounds, particularly those that detract from the subject matter.
- If the video depicts moving parts, they should move slowly.
- It is preferable to depict light figures on dark backgrounds.
- When devices are depicted, they should take up approximately 2/3rds of the screen.
- Adjust shot length appropriately to show desired detail to be depicted in the image.
- If three-dimensional objects are presented, they should be suspended in space for greater visibility.
- Avoid the use of glazed, reflecting or transparent materials, or treat them, if possible, to appear dull.
- If text is used in videos, it should be printed in large enough letters to be easily read.
- Use dramatization only when the actors' credibility, competence or status is accepted by the viewer as well as the accuracy of the story, setting and intended message.
- Simple forms of presentation should be used whenever possible.
- The length of a single presentation should not exceed 25 - 30 minutes.
- All important points should be made early in the presentation.
- Video presentations should contain introductions (e.g., advanced organizers), as well as reviews and repetition of important sequences and ideas.

- Avoid the use of special visual effects inserted between scenes such as wipes, fades, complex visual patterns because these techniques have no apparent effect on learning retention. However, freeze frames have had some effect on recall.
- Avoid rapid cutting (transitions between shots) because, although rapid cutting increases viewer attention, it tends to confuse viewers by preventing them from processing the information as it is presented. A rapid series of fast moving images on a screen causes viewers to look toward the center of the screen without focusing on any particular object.
- Consider using cueing techniques such as: camera effects; cutting, editing, and composition effects; captions; and accompanying commentary/narration to increase the viewer's attention. However, the common commercial television technique of changing shots frequently does not leave viewers time to analyze and comprehend shots.
- Video presentations should be cut into a series of shots rather than uncut sequences. Viewers seem to prefer edited presentations if they result in understandable presentations that are cut at a rate appropriate to the complexity of the scenes and are not sustained to the point of boredom.

Realism and fidelity

Realism refers to the characteristics of a presentation such as motion, color and image quality which accurately express the real-world object(s) in detail. Fidelity is the degree to which realism is expressed from realistic to abstract.

Attention getting devices

Attention getting devices are those aspects of media that are used to attract the learner's attention or to motivate learners towards the content. Research indicates that learning is not significantly improved by devices that temporarily draw attention, e.g., rapid cutting between shots, sudden noticeable changes, special visual or sound effect, or when these are included merely for realism (Wetzel, Radtke and Stern, 1994). Moreno and Mayer (2000) also found that music or sound added to an animation with concurrent narration decreased performance. Results were consistent with cognitive theory in that auditory adjuncts can overload the performer's auditory working memory. The following guidelines should be considered (Williams, 1998):

- Sound effects used for the purpose of attracting viewer attention generally should be avoided. Although sound effects can increase viewer interest in the presentation, they have shown no effect on learning.
- Music generally should be avoided in instructional and other presentations because music has not been shown to have significant positive effect on instructional effectiveness. In fact, fast-paced music has shown a detrimental effect while slow-paced music has shown no effect.
- The use of humor in instructional presentations generally should be avoided because it has not been effective and can actually decrease learning.
- Use zooming in on a portion of the display to draw attention to details cautiously because zooming tends to aid performers who are unable to isolate the details themselves, but hinder higher ability performers.

Performer involvement and control

As noted earlier, performer or learner involvement is a critical aspect of assimilating material and needs to be fostered wherever possible. In instructional situation, learner control is typically recommended, but research suggests that the learner control should be carefully orchestrated.

- If access is provided to different media representations of the material, a structure of the relationships between the media and guidance for following a predefined path should be provided. It should be noted that most users tend to follow a predefined path and do not explore alternative routes unless instructed to do so.
- In instruction, practice questions should be embedded with the instructional sequence allowing an opportunity to initiate interactivity.
- Combine techniques of lesson organization, path sequencing, diagnosis of progress and remedial branching to optimize learning. Some research indicates that directive approaches are more effective than techniques offering less guidance to learners (such as some simulations, optional reviews or other unguided student decisions). Robinson and Kiewra (1995) found that graphic organizers were more effective than outlines when used with text materials. Also, overviews should be used only to the extent that they supply the user with advanced knowledge about the content (Murray and McGlone, 1997).

Multimedia Use Summary

Table 6.9 provides a general summary of some of the most important points to consider for the use of multimedia.

Table 6.9 General Multimedia Use Considerations*

Combine media:	<ul><li>When they are all relevant to the performance goals.</li><li>When they are carefully matched and do not conflict.</li><li>To provide alternative views of the content, concepts, etc.</li></ul>
Use motion and animation:	<ul><li>When it is relevant to the performance goals.</li><li>For demonstrating sequential actions in a procedural task.</li><li>To simulate causal models of complex behaviors.</li><li>For explicitly representing invisible system functions and behaviors.</li><li>When learning a concept defined by motion, or the motion itself must be learned.</li><li>To illustrate tasks that are difficult to describe verbally.</li><li>For providing visual analogies for abstract and symbolic concepts; and</li><li>To draw attention to specific tasks, relevant features that change, or display elements.</li></ul>
Use video:	<ul><li>When video's capabilities of motion, sound and color are relevant to the performance goals.</li><li>For integration of other media.</li></ul>

- To present screen activity sequences.
- For product demonstrations.
- To present real or simulated moving objects, people and events.

Generally:

- Present media combinations simultaneously (or, in the case of visuals and narratives, the visual should precede the narrative by up to 7 seconds).
- Provide text prompting or references to illustrations and animations to describe relevancy,
- Allow sufficient time to view complex media.
- Use off-screen narration, rather than on-screen narration, when possible.
- Limit video captions to two lines of text and display for at least 6 seconds.
- Use narratives and labels to reinforce important elements in animations.
- Provide the capability to turn-off attention animations.
- Use simple forms of presentation whenever possible.
- Keep presentation lengths to 25 - 30 minutes.
- Make important points early in the presentation.
- Cut video presentations into a series of shots.
- Incorporate realism only to the extent that it is relevant to the intended objectives.
- Use color to aid in discriminating among objects, for cueing or highlighting relevant information, and when its recognition is part of the task to be performed or learned.
- Provide predetermined paths through the media.
- Provide a structure of the media relationships and access instructions when different media representations of the material are available.

Avoid:

- Distractions.
- Excessive visual detail and busy backgrounds.
- Unnecessary complexity.
- Multiple competing animations.
- Visual and sound effect devices to attract viewer attention that do not have any relationship to informational content.
- Special visual effects between scenes (e.g., rapid cuts, wipes, fades, complex visual patterns).
- Humor.
- Pacing that is too fast to allow information to be processed.
- Lengthy presentations without pauses since long presentations tend to fatigue learners or force them to continuously process new information.

* Modified from Williams (1998)

USE OF COLOR

Color can be a very important attribute of information when it is used correctly. However, color is often used more for its esthetic properties than for its information properties. Although color is typically preferred by viewers, it should not be used for unrelated realism or as an attention-getting device.

Color Definitions

To understand the application of color in the presentation of information, it is important to be familiar with typically used definitions for color and its properties. These definitions are often used in various standards and guidelines associated with color.

Achromatic color: A perceived color devoid of hue. The color names *white*, *gray* and *black* are commonly used

Brightness: Attribute of a visual sensation according to which an area appears to emit more or less light (stimulus magnitude).

Chromatic color: A color that has hue and saturation; for example, blue, yellow, brown and magenta, and, therefore cannot be placed in the white-gray-black series.

Color: A characteristic of the appearance of objects as determined by the emitted or reflected wavelengths of visible light coming from the objects. The appearance of color is generally described by three attributes: hue, brightness and saturation.

Complementary colors: Colors that are on the opposite side of the color wheel (see Figure 6.16) that when mixed, produce white or gray. Pairs of complementary colors include: red and blue-green, orange and green-blue, yellow and blue, and yellow-green and violet.

Focal colors: Colors that generally represent the hue name to the intended user population. These include red, green, yellow and blue. In this document, the term includes the set of colors that have names in most languages: red, green, yellow, blue, purple, orange, brown, pink, white, gray and black.

Hue: The visual impression of color as typically determined by the predominant wavelength or wavelengths of the visual stimulus.

Lightness: A perceived quality of color that ranges from white to black. The lightness of a color can be described by comparing it to an achromatic white surface.

Saturation: The homogenity of the wavelengths contributing to a color sensation, or the purity of the color. The narrower the band of wavelengths, the more highly saturated the color sensation. A pure color (or hue) is **completely saturated**, while a mixture in which no single wavelength dominates (or which is complementary to no single wavelength) is **completely unsaturated**.

Spectrally extreme colors: Colors whose chromaticity coordinates are significantly distant (red when u'>0.4 and blue when v'<0.2).

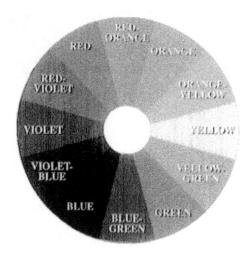

Figure 6.16 Color Wheel depicted in shades of gray.

Color and Information

"Information consists of differences that make a difference." If layers of information are not clearly differentiated, cluttered, incoherent displays filled with disinformation result and lead to the "interactive visual arithmetic of flatland" where "1 + 1 = 3 or more" (Tufte, 1997). Color can be used as: a visual code to identify objects, components, logical structures, and sources and status of information; a formatting aid to differentiate between the same, similar and different objects or information; a highlighting method to call attention to particular information, object or area of a display; and to realistically portray natural objects. In using color for information purposes, consider the following general guidelines:

- If different parts of the screen are focused on separately, color-code the different parts to focus selective attention to each in turn (Galitz, 1994).
- If decisions are made based on the status of information on the screen, color-code the types of status (Galitz, 1994).
- If the task requires searching the screen to locate information of a particular type, color-code the types for contrast (Horton, 1991; Galitz, 1994).
- If the information displayed on the screen has high density (packed or crowded), use color to provide visual groupings (Galitz, 1994).
- To enhance color discrimination, use complementary colors or select distinct bright saturated colors (Horton, 1991).

Choosing Colors to Display

When choosing colors to display, it is important to consider the human visual system, the possible problems that the use of color may cause, contextual effects that may occur, the viewing environment and the user's task. Below, guidelines for the use of color are provided in terms of general design considerations, discrimination, harmony, emphasis, visual search, continuous reading, location objects, comparing objects, common meaning, color ordering, foreground and background colors and combinations, gray scales, and windows and borders.

General Design Considerations

In applying color in the design of information displays, the following general design principles should be kept in mind:

- Design for monochrome first (this is an important principle when designing for: people with color deficiencies, monochrome displays, ambient lighting situations that distort perceived color and cases where color fails); Galitz, 1994.
  Note: The majority of color blindness problems can be compensated by the addition of yellow or blue to the colors used.
- Use colors conservatively and not where other identification techniques (such as location) are available; Galitz, 1994.
- If color is used for coding, combine color with other coding techniques (Horton; 1991; Galitz, 1994; ISO 9241-12: 1998).
- Only enough colors to achieve the design objectives should be used; Galitz, 1994.
  — (Note: More colors increase response times as well as increase the chance of errors due to color confusions.)
  — Minimize the need for additional colors by applying other identification techniques such as position and structure (e.g., a menu bar at the top of the screen).
- Use smallest effective difference principle (Tufte, 1997). Make all visual distinctions as subtle as possible, but still clear and effective.
- Use colors consistently within a screen, set of screens and within an application.

Discrimination

Color discrimination is the ability of the user to discriminate between and among colors. To ensure proper color discrimination, consider the following guidelines:

- For best absolute discrimination, use no more than four or five colors widely spaced on the color spectrum (Galitz, 1994; Geldard, 1953; Smith, 1988; Marcus, 1986b).

  — Good choices are red, yellow, green, blue and brown (Marcus, 1986b).
  — If the meanings for more than five colors are necessary, use a legend to provide a match between the color and the meaning (Galitz, 1994).

- For best comparative discrimination, use six to seven colors (Note: In addition to the colors listed above, add such colors as orange, yellow-green, cyan and violet or magenta; Marcus, 1986b).
- If the task requires the user to recognize pairs of colors with different meanings, choose easily discriminable pairs.
- Select colors that are widely distributed in hue and saturation, or change the luminance difference.
- Use color complements (e.g., red and cyan, blue and yellow, and green and magenta); Thorell and Smith, 1990. Note: Yellow on blue has more contrast than the red on blue.
- Use good opponent pairs such as red/green and yellow/blue. However, do not overuse pairs of opponent colors because opponent colors can leave afterimages and suggest shadows (Horton, 1991).

- To improve discrimination between adjacent colors, separate colors with a thin line of a neutral color (Thorell and Smith, 1990; Horton, 1991).
- Use bright colors for older viewers or extended viewing; Galitz, 1994. (Note: Age related changes in the eye make distinguishing colors more difficult. Also, extended periods of viewing result in the eye adapting to brightness levels for all viewers.)

Harmony

Harmonious colors are those that work well together. To obtain harmonious color combinations:

- Choose harmonious colors (Galitz, 1994). (Best achieved with a monochromatic palette).

  — For each background color, different lightness or values are established by mixing with black and white.
  — Avoid complementary colors – those at opposite sides of the color wheel (Marcus, 1986b).
  — Note: Strong colors that are complementary and equal in value may cause vibration effects (Tufte, 1997).

- Use split complements (one color plus two colors on either side of its complement) or use three colors at equidistant points around the color circle.
- Use colors on opposite sides of the traditional color-harmony circle (Horton, 1991; Thorell and Smith, 1990).
- Pure, bright or very strong colors should not be used, unrelieved, over large adjacent areas because they have loud, unbearable effects. However, such colors can be useful when used sparingly on or between dull background tones (Tufte, 1997).
- Light, bright colors mixed with white should not be placed next to each, particularly for large areas (Tufte, 1997).
- Mute large area base-color backgrounds with gray so that the smaller brighter color areas stand out more vividly (Tufte, 1997).
- In order to maintain picture unity between two or more large enclosed areas of different colors, use the colors from one area repeatedly intermingled in the other (Tufte, 1997).
- Combine images that share a common hue, but do not juxtapose full-color images containing too many different hues (Horton, 1991).
- If colors are repeated frequently or used over wide areas (e.g., ongoing themes and design motifs), use low contrast, desaturated or darker shades of color (Thorell and Smith, 1990).

Emphasis

Emphasis is drawing attention to an object or information. For emphasis:

- Use bright colors (to de-emphasize, use less bright colors).

  — Perceived brightness of colors from most to least are white, yellow, green, blue and red.
  — Danger signals should be brighter or highlighted.
  — At high levels of ambient illumination, colors can appear washed out or unsaturated and, therefore, brightness differences may not be effective.

- Emphasize separation by using contrasting colors (possible pairs are red/green and blue/yellow)
- Use similar colors to convey information or screen element similarity (Horton, 1991; Galitz, 1994). For example, blue and green are more closely related than red and green.

Visual Search

Visual search pertains to looking for and finding an object of interest on a display. Searching on the basis of color is the most efficient of all coding techniques (Thorell and Smith, 1990). However, since approximately 10 percent of the population has some color deficiencies, color-coding should be combined with other coding techniques. To enhance search on the basis of color, consider the following guidelines:

- When a rapid visual search based on color discrimination is required, no more than six colors should be used (ISO 9241-12: 1998).
- Use blue for text, or small symbols, with caution since it may not always be legible.
- Background patterns decrease search performance and should be avoided if possible (Zwaga and Duijnhouwer, 1995).
- If the user must recognize a color displayed alone, use only three or four colors (Silverstein, 1987; Horton, 1991).

Continuous Reading

If the task requires continuous reading of text, medium contrast colors and desaturated colors that are not spectral extremes should be used. (Thorell and Smith, 1990; Galitz, 1994).

Locating Objects

Locating objects pertains to the discrimination of a specific object within a display. To optimize the location of colored objects:

- Objects that need to be discriminated on the basis of color should be presented within the center area of the screen. For example, in an application for monitoring the status of a water cooling system, the user is required to adjust the water temperature when the temperature in a given container reaches a critical point. The temperature changes slowly, and is reflected in changes in hue. The graphic representing the cooling container should be placed in the area of the screen near the central area of the screen.
- For information in the center of the visual field, use red and green. (Note: the eye is most sensitive to red and green in the center of the visual field.)
- For peripheral viewing, use blue, yellow, black or white (Note: the eye is most sensitive to these colors in the periphery.)
- If the user's attention must be directed to an event in the visual periphery, a cue in addition to color should be used. For example, a blinking icon in addition to the color change could be used since a blinking object will be readily observed in the periphery of a user's field of view.
  Note: For peripheral viewing, use area-fill, large images, bright saturated colors and color backgrounds. Avoid depending on color identification and discrimination when images are expected to be in the far periphery (Thorell and Smith, 1990).

- Colors appearing adjacent to each other should differ in hue and lightness for a sharp "edge" and maximum differentiation. (Note: colors differing only in their blue component should not be used since the eye does not discriminate blue differences well.)
- Use brighter colors for objects to be located by older users (Galitz, 1994).

Comparing Objects

Comparing objects relates to the discriminating between various attributes of an object including color, shape and area. When the task requires object comparisons:

- Objects that must be simultaneously viewed to make a relative comparison of their colors should not be separated by a visual angle between them of more than 40 degrees.
- If the areas of two objects need to be compared, red and green should not be used together. This is because red areas appear to be larger than equally sized green areas. Due to chromatic aberration, red colors are focused behind the retina, blue colors are focused in front of it and yellow-green is focused directly on the retina. This effect causes the perception of the size of the object to be distorted.
- If color differences are available, users tend to use color more often than other graphical information to make judgments (Ziets, 1998).

Common Meanings

Colors have many different meanings based on common usage, learned associations, cultural associations and business or industry conventions. In general:

- To indicate actions are necessary, use warm colors (e.g., red, yellow and orange). Note: Warm colors advance, drawing attention.
- To provide background or status, use cool colors (e.g., green, blue, violet and purple). Note: Cool colors recede, thereby drawing less attention.
- Conform to human expectancies concerning color use. For example (modified from Marcus, 1986b):

Red:	Stop, fire, hot, danger, loss (financial)
Yellow:	Caution, warm, slow, test
Green:	Go, OK, clear, vegetation, safety
Blue:	Cold, water, calm, sky, neutrality
Black:	Gain (financial)
Gray:	Neutrality
White:	Neutrality
Warm colors:	Action, response required, spatial closeness
Cool colors:	Status, background information, spatial remoteness

- Implications for dramatic portrayal (also modified from Marcus, 1986b):

High illumination:	Hot, active, comic situations
Low illumination:	Emotional, tense, tragic, melodramatic, romantic situations
High saturation:	Emotional, tense, hot, melodramatic, comic situations
Warm colors:	Active, exciting, leisure, recreation, comic situations
Cool colors:	Efficiency, work, passive, tragic and romantic situations

- If the application will be used in various cultures, consider the different cultural uses of colors. For example, white means death in China, while purple represents death in Brazil. Also, yellow is sacred in China, but signifies sadness in Greece.

Color Ordering

Color ordering pertains to the use of colors to code the order of the information.

- If ordering of colors is required (e.g., high to low, levels of depth), arrange color by their spectral position.
  Note: The spectral order of color appears to be natural (Fromme, 1983).
- The spectral order is red, orange, yellow, green, blue, indigo and violet.
- If ordering is required within a color, order from darkest to lightest or lightest to darkest (Galitz, 1994).

Foreground Colors

The foreground color is the color of the object or character on the display.

- Use colors as different as possible from background colors (most contrast).
- Use warmer, more active colors (see above). Note: Use caution in using more fully saturated red and orange because they may be difficult to distinguish from each other.
- Use colors that possess the same saturation and lightness.
- For text or data, use desaturated or spectrum center colors, e.g., on dark backgrounds use off-white, yellow or green (Marcus, 1986a; Smith, 1988). Note: Desaturated or spectrum center colors do not excessively stimulate the eye and appear brighter.
- To emphasize, highlight in a light value of the foreground color, e.g., on dark backgrounds use pure white or yellow (Marcus, 1986a).

Background Colors

The background color is the color of the area of the display upon which the object or character is displayed.

- Use a background color to organize a group of screen elements into a unified whole
- Use colors that are not competitive with the foreground colors
- Use cool, dark colors (e.g., blue, black) ; Lalomia and Happ, 1987; Pastoor, 1990
- Use colors at the extreme end of the color spectrum; Marcus, 1986a (in order of priority: blue, black, gray, brown, red, green, purple)

Foreground/Background Combinations

Foreground/background combinations refer to the combination of a foreground and background color pair, particularly for presenting text. In general:

- Always choose the background color first.
- Display no more than four colors at one time.
- Ensure sufficient contrast.
- Remember that with adjacent colors, any ground subtracts its own hue from the colors that it carries (Tufte, 1997).
- For dark on light combinations, equalize luminance-contrast ratios (Pastoor, 1990).

- Any foreground color may be acceptable if the background color is chosen properly.
- Any dark, saturated, foreground color is satisfactory. (Note: Increased saturation of the foreground seems to only marginally affected user ratings.)
- Saturated backgrounds should be avoided. (Note: Saturated backgrounds typically are rated unsatisfactory by users.)
- Use less saturated backgrounds with any foreground color. (Note: Less saturated backgrounds generally receive high ratings with any foreground color.)

If light on dark combinations are to be used, equalize luminance-contrast ratios (Pastoor, 1990) and:

- Do not use combinations involving saturated colors.
- Limit color saturation of foreground color. (Note: as foreground color saturation increases, the number of background colors yielding high ratings diminishes.)
- Use desaturated foreground/background color combinations.
- Use short wavelength, cool colors for backgrounds (blue, bluish cyan, cyan).

If text is to be displayed, discernable foreground and background combinations will vary depending on whether the text is presented in bold or normal. Table 6.10 provides recommended foreground and background combinations for normal text and Table 6.11 provides recommendations for bold text.

Table 6.10 Recommended Foreground and Background Combinations*

Foreground	Background							
	Black	Gray	White	Blue	Green	Yellow	Brown	Red
Black		O	O	A	O	O	A	P
Lt. Gray	A		P	A	P	P	A	A
White	O	P		O	P	P	O	O
Blue	P	O	O		A	A	O	A
Green	O	P	P	P		P	O	O
Yellow	O	P	P	O	P		O	O
Brown	P	A	A	P	A	A		P
Red	P	O	O	P	O	O	P	

O=Optimal, A=Acceptable, P=Poor
* Adapted from Thorell and Smith (1990) and Pace (1984)

Table 6.11 Recommended Foreground and Background Combinations with Bold Text

Foreground	Background							
	Black	Gray	White	Blue	Green	Yellow	Brown	Red
Black		O	O	A	O	O	A	A
Lt. Gray	A		P	A	P	P	A	A
White	O	P		O	P	P	O	O
Blue	P	O	O		A	A	O	A
Green	O	P	P	P		P	O	O
Yellow	O	P	P	O	P		O	O
Brown	P	A	A	P	A	A		P
Red	P	O	O	P	O	O	P	

O=Optimal, A=Acceptable, P=Poor
* Adapted from Thorell and Smith (1990) and Pace (1984)

Color Combinations

Smith (1989) recommends the following two and three color combinations:

- For combining two colors, use white with green, gold with cyan/green, green with magenta/lavender, or cyan with red. However, she recommends avoiding red with blue/green/purple/yellow/magenta, white with cyan/yellow, blue with green/purple, green with cyan or cyan with lavender.
- For combining three colors: use white with gold and green/blue/magenta, white with red and cyan, red with cyan and gold, cyan with yellow and lavender, or gold with magenta and blue/green. But avoid red with yellow and green, red with blue and green, white with cyan and yellow, red with magenta and blue, or green with cyan and blue.

Gray Scales

Gray scales pertain to the use of the non-color values of black through white for information coding. When using gray scales:

- For fine discriminations use a black-gray-white scale (recommended values are white, light gray, medium gray, dark gray, black)
- Gray scales can be used for screen design (Marcus, 1986b) as follows:

White:	Screen background
	Text located in any black area
Light Gray:	Pushbutton background area
Medium Gray:	Icon background area
	Menu drop-shadow
	Window drop-shadow
	Inside area of system icons
	Filename bar
Dark gray:	Window border
Black:	Text
	Window title bar
	Icon border
	Icon elements
	Ruled lines

Windows and Borders

Since color displays and a windows style interface are very common, the following guidelines concerning the use of color for windows and borders should be considered:

- Avoid too much color, particular saturated colors, on multi-color windows to prevent the "video game" look that does little for readability (Tufte, 1997).
- For framing windows or fields, the color should be light in value (muting the I + I = 3 effects) and, at the same time, relatively intense and saturated to provide a strong visual signal for the active window (Tufte, 1997). Note: Tufte feels that only yellow satisfies this joint requirement.

Things to avoid in the use of color (modified from Galitz, 1994)

- Relying exclusively on color
- Too many colors at one time
- Highly saturated, spectrally extreme colors together: Red and blue, yellow and purple
- Low-brightness colors for extended viewing or older viewers
- Colors of equal brightness
- Colors lacking contrast (e.g., yellow and white, black and brown, reds, blues and browns against a light background
- Using color in unexpected ways
- Fully saturated colors for text or other frequently read screen components
- Pure blue for text, thin lines and small shapes (Note: blue sensitivity drops 30% from age 20 to 50.)
- Colors in small areas
- Color for fine details
- Red and green in the periphery of large-scale displays
- Yellow on green (due to vibrating effects)
- Adjacent colors only differing in the amount of blue they possess
- Color to improve legibility of densely packed text

ICONS

The use of icons (or pictorial symbols) can be an important aid to identifying performance support controls, features and information. Icons can be used wherever word labels are used (Horton, 1991). Typically, icons are used to label user interface commands and objects because they can aid search and recognition and are easier to internationalize. There are a number of texts concerned with user interface icons, e.g., Horton (1994), Griswold, Jeffery and Townsend (1998) and Ziegler and Greco (2001). In this chapter, only icons used in performance support products such as documentation, online help and instruction will be addressed.

In using icons for performance support applications, consider the following general guidelines:

- If possible, use icons that are already well known to the target population.
- When designing new icons:

   — Exploit the intended user's knowledge and experience.
   — Use clear, simple shapes with the distinctive features made prominent.
   — Use existing pictorial representations that represent objects with high imagery words (e.g., stop sign for stop).
   — Keep icons small, but not so small that the distinctive features become unrecognizable.
   — Keep icons stylistically consistent.

- Icons always should be labeled to ensure that both novice users and users with visual problems can identify their meaning.
- Icons should be used consistently throughout the performance support system.
- Icons used for performance support should be compatible with icons used in the application. If the same icon is used, it should have the same basic meaning and operate in the same manner.
- New icons should be tested on target population members to ensure that they are recognizable and meaningful.

- Consider the cultural meaning of an icon when the application will be used internationally.

Icons for Informational Purposes

One of the major uses of icons in performance support products is to provide information. Table 6.12 lists those icons that are specifically used for relaying safety or risk-related information. More general recommendations for other informational icons that can be usefully applied in performance support products are provided in Table 6.13.

Table 6.12 Safety and Risk-Related Icons*

⚠	**Danger, Warning, Caution (This icon should be used only for safety-related warning messages of the following types)** **Danger:** Use to **warn** of a hazard that the user *will be* exposed to that will likely result in death or serious injury if not avoided. **Warning:** Use to **warn** of a potential hazard that the user *may be* exposed to that *could* result in death or serious injury if not avoided. **Caution:** Use to **warn** of a potential hazard that the user *may be* exposed to that *could* result in minor or moderate injury if not avoided.
🚫	**Alert (Prohibitive):** Use to **alert** the user of an action that must be avoided in order to prevent damage to equipment, software or data, or interruption of service.
❗	**Alert (Imperative):** Use to **alert** user to an action that must be performed to prevent damage to equipment, software or data, or interruption of service.
🔥	**Fire Safety:** Use to **inform** the user of fire safety information and locations of fire-fighting and fire-safety related equipment. Not to be used to warn of specific safety hazards.
❗	**Safety:** Use to inform the user of general safety information. Not to be used for specific safety hazards or for fire-safety information.

*Modified from: TCIF Guideline "Admonishments (Safety-Related Warning Messages)," TCIF-99-021, Issue 1, 12/27/99

Icons for Navigation and Media Control

Table 6.14 provides some examples of icons that can be used for page and structural navigation within an application and Table 6.15 provides some examples of some simple media controls.

Table 6.13 Recommended Non-Safety-Specific Informational Icons

⬤	**Stop:** Use to **inform** the user that corrective action is required before proceeding.
⊘	**Avoid:** Use to **inform** the user of actions that they should not perform or about an error situation (in GUI's). This icon also can be used for non-GUI alert messages (see above).
✖	**Error:** Use to **inform** the user about a critical error situation (in GUI's).
ⓘ!	**Important:** Use to **inform** the user about important information that needs to be considered in performing an activity.
ⓘ	**Note:** Use to **inform** the user about additional relevant information.
💡	**Hint:** Use to **inform** the user about a useful course of action, shortcut, etc. that may help them perform an activity more efficiently. Also use in instruction and tutorials to assist students when they appear to need help.
📝	**Remember:** Use to **inform** the user about information that needs to be remembered for a future action.
✔	**OK:** Use to **inform** the user that a response has been appropriate, an action has been accomplished successfully, etc.
✏	Sometimes used as a substitute for "Note" or "Remember" (however, the above icons are preferred and the "pencil" should not be used in conjunction with either if titled the same).
?	**Help:** Use to **inform** the user on the availability of additional help. The "?" also may be used without the background circle.

Table 6.14 Icons for Page and Structural Navigation

⏮	**First:** Use for navigation to the 1st page of the material.
⏭	**Last:** Use for navigation to the last page of the material.
➡	**Next:** Use for navigation to the next page of the material.
⬅	**Previous:** Use to navigate back to the previous page of the material.
⤴	**Return:** Use for navigation back to the last page of the material visited.
	Search: Use for accessing search dialogs. Note: binoculars may also be used for search.
	Topics: Use for navigation to the Topics List (from Horton, 1994).
	Link Map: Use for navigation to the map depicting the Topic Linkages.
	Index: Use for navigation to the Index (from Horton, 1994).
	Glossary: Use for navigation to the Glossary (from Horton, 1994).
◆	**Exit:** Use for exiting the performance support product.

Table 6.15 Icons for Simple Media Control

☺	**Play Audio:** Use as a control for playing an audio segment.
▦	**Play Animation:** Use as a control for playing an animation segment. May also be used for playing a video segment instead of the icon below.
⊡	**Play Video:** Use as a control for playing a video segment.
◀	**Sound off:** Use as a control for turning the sound "off" when audio is presented.
◀))	**Sound on:** Use as a control for turning the sound "on" when audio is presented.
▲◀))	**Volume up:** Use as a control for turning the volume "up" when audio is presented.
▼◀	**Volume down:** Use as a control for turning the volume "down" when audio is presented.

ACCESSIBILITY

Accessibility is the properties of a product that allows it to be used by a wide range of users with various capabilities and limitations. In the design of performance support systems, accessibility is an important consideration, particularly if any of the intended users will have physical or sensory limitations. Also, there are a number of standards and laws that require computer-based systems to be accessible to people with various kinds of disabilities. For example, electronic and information systems used by United States government organizations must meet Section 508 of the Rehabilitation Act which contains a number of requirements for accessibility. There is also an ISO standard (ISO/TS 16071, *Ergonomics of human-system interaction – Guidance on accessibility for human computer interfaces)* and a W3C recommendation (*Web Content Accessibility Guidelines 1.0*) on accessibility. In addition, HFES 200.2 (*Human Factors Engineering of Software User Interfaces – Accessibility*) has been published as an ANSI Draft Standard for Trial Use by the Human Factors and Ergonomics Society.

Some proponents of accessibility claim that designing for all (or universal design) benefits all users, not just those with disabilities (Vanderheiden, 1997). While there is much truth to this claim (because universal design tends to make products easier to use), designing for the lowest common denominator can decrease the functionality of a product. For example, if color is not used because a small percentage of the population is colorblind, the advantage of color for searching for objects and coding information would be lost. On the other hand, by including color and adding redundant coding for those users that may not be able to perceive color, both functionality and accessibility can be obtained. Therefore, the key is to both provide the functionality to enable optimum performance and provide alternative methods of presenting and retrieving information that will enable the maximum number of users to use the performance support system. The above referenced documents provide standards and guidelines for accessibility for computer systems. Following is a list of guidelines extracted from ISO/TS 16071 (2002), the W3C Recommendation for Content Accessibility (1999) and Vanderheiden (1997) that particularly apply to the development of performance support.

Input and Outputs

- Enable user input/output choice. The system should provide the necessary information to enable users to use as many input and output alternatives as possible (ISO/TS 16071: 2003, 7.2.1.1).
- Use features that enable activation of (web) page elements via a variety of input devices (W3C Content Accessibility 1.0, 1999, 9).
- Enable switching of input/output alternatives. Users should be enabled to switch among input/output alternatives without requiring them to reconfigure or restart the system or applications (ISO/TS 16071: 2003, 7.2.1.2).
- Enable user to perform the task effectively with any single input device. Users should be able to perform tasks effectively using only one input device, such as a pointing device, voice or only a keyboard, or an alternative input device (ISO/TS 16071: 2003, 7.2.2).

User Preferences

- Provide user-preference profiles. Users should be able to easily create, save, edit and recall profiles of preferences, including input and output characteristics. To do this, it should not be necessary to restart the system or applications (ISO/TS 16071: 2003, 7.2.3).
- Enable user setting of timed responses. If a task requires users to make responses (e.g., press a button or type information) within a limited time in order for that response to be valid, the time range should be adjustable by the user, including the option to turn off all timing requirements (ISO/TS 16071: 2003, 7.2.4).
- User preferences should be easily individualized (ISO/TS 16071: 2003, 7.12.1).

Object Descriptions

- Provide object descriptions. Where tasks require access to the visual content of objects beyond what a label provides, software should provide object descriptions that are meaningful to users stored as accessible text, whether those descriptions are visually presented or not. Visual objects that are primarily decorative and contain little or no information need not be described. (ISO/TS 16071: 2003, 7.2.5).
- Provide object labels so that users can access object labels stored as additional text, whether those labels are visually presented or not (ISO/TS 16071: 2003, 7.3.2).

- Provide content that, when presented to the user, conveys essentially the same function or purpose as auditory or visual content. (W3C Content Accessibility 1.0, 1999, Guideline 1).

  — Provide a text equivalent for every non-text element (e.g., via "alt," "longdesc" or in element content), including images, graphical representations of text (including symbols), image map regions, animations (e.g., animated GIFs), applets and programmatic objects, ascii art, frames, scripts, images used as list bullets, spacers, graphical buttons, sounds (played with or without user interaction), stand-alone audio files, audio tracks of video and video (W3C Content Accessibility 1.0, 1999, 1.1).
  — Provide redundant text links for each active region of a server-side image map (W3C Content Accessibility 1.0, 1999, 1.2).
  — Provide an auditory description of the important information of the visual track of a multimedia presentation until user agents can automatically read aloud the text equivalent of a visual track (W3C Content Accessibility 1.0, 1999, 1.3).
  — For any time-based multimedia presentation (e.g., a movie or animation), synchronize equivalent alternatives (e.g., captions or auditory descriptions of the visual track) with the presentation (W3C Content Accessibility 1.0, 1999, 1.4).

- Tables should be created and presented in a way that enables alternative output techniques to communicate the information appropriately (ISO/TS 16071: 2003, 7.7.4). Ensure that tables have necessary markup to be transformed by accessible browsers and other user agents by identifying row and column headers and for data tables that have two or more logical levels of row or column headers, use markup to associate data cells and header cells (W3C Content Accessibility 1.0, 1999, 5).

Presentation

- Make letters and symbols on visual displays as large as possible (Vanderheiden, 1997).
- Provide all important information in both visual and auditory form (Vanderheiden, 1997).
- Mark up (web) documents with the proper structural elements. Control presentation with style sheets rather than with presentation elements and attributes (W3C Content Accessibility 1.0, 1999, 3).
- Use markup that facilitates pronunciation or interpretation of abbreviated or foreign text (W3C Content Accessibility 1.0, 1999, 4).
- The use of blinking/flashing text or graphical elements at frequencies between 10 Hz to 25 Hz should be avoided, as the probability of induced seizure is highest at these rates (ISO/TS 16071: 2003, 7.2.10).
- Clarify natural language usage by providing additional information and/or functionality that facilitates pronunciation or interpretation of abbreviated or foreign text (W3C Content Accessibility 1.0, 1999, 4.1; ISO/TS 16071: 2003, 7.2.1.13).
- Alerts, warnings and other user notifications of critical importance should be consistently located on the screen, labeled clearly as critical user information, and be presented in a manner useful to users of assistive technologies (ISO/TS 16071: 2003, 7.3.5).
- Software should provide the option to display implicit designators (ISO/TS 16071: 2003, 7.4.10). An example of implicit designators is the underlined letter in a drop-down menu option.

- If non-speech audio is used, the fundamental frequency should be in the range between 500 Hz and 3000 Hz or be easily adjustable by the user into that range (ISO/TS 16071: 2003, 7.9.3).
- Provide context and orientation information to help users understand complex pages or elements (W3C Content Accessibility 1.0, 1999, 12). Title each frame to facilitate frame identification and navigation (W3C Content Accessibility 1.0, 1999, 12.1).
- Use client-side image maps instead of server-side image maps except where the regions cannot be defined with an available geometric shape (W3C Content Accessibility 1.0, 1999, 9.1).
- Error or warning information should persist or repeat as long as it is relevant to the performance of the task or until dismissed by the user (ISO/TS 16071: 2003, 7.10.1).

Color

- Provide alternatives to color as the only way to convey information or indicate an action (W3C Content Accessibility 1.0, 1999, 2; ISO/TS 16071: 2003, 7.8.1).
- Ensure that all information conveyed on the basis of color is also available without color, e.g., from context or markup (W3C Content Accessibility 1.0, 1999, 2.1).
- Include default color palettes designed for people who have visual impairments (ISO/TS 16071: 2003, 7.8.2).
- Allow users to customize color coding for selection, process or object state/status, except where warnings or alerts have been standardized for mission-critical systems, e.g., red=network failure (ISO/TS 16071: 2003, 7.8.5).
- Hue should not be the only attribute used to code information (ISO/TS 16071: 2003, 7.8.6).

Accessibility Features

- Accessibility features should be easy to turn on and off. The on/off controls for accessibility features should be easy to activate (ISO/TS 16071: 2003, 7.2.6).
- Safeguard against inadvertent activation or deactivation of accessibility features (ISO/TS 16071: 2003, 7.2.7).
- Current status of accessibility features (on or off) should be available at all times (ISO/TS 16071: 2003, 7.2.8).
- To enable effective use of assistive technologies, the software should use system-provided input and output methods, wherever possible. If system routines must be by-passed, system-state information should be set or obtained using system variables or system routines (ISO/TS 16071: 2003, 7.3.1).
- Provide notification of events to assistive software. Events relevant to user interactions should be available to assistive technologies. Such events include, but are not limited to, changes in object status, such as the creation of new objects, change in selection, change in position, as well as changes in attributes such as size and color (ISO/TS 16071: 2003, 7.3.3).
- Information on individual object attributes should be available to assistive technologies (such as 'listeners"). Such attributes may include, but are not limited to, object name, size, position and current state (ISO/TS 16071: 2003, 7.3.4).
- Text characters only should be used as text, not to draw lines, boxes or other graphical symbols (ISO/TS 16071: 2003, 7.7.2). Due to interference with assistive technologies.

- Ensure that (web) pages are accessible even when newer technologies are not supported or are turned off (W3C Content Accessibility 1.0, 1999, 6).

  — Organize (web) documents so they may be read without style sheets. For example, when an HTML document is rendered without associated style sheets, it must still be possible to read the document (W3C Content Accessibility 1.0, 1999, 6.1).
  — Ensure that equivalents for dynamic content are updated when the dynamic content changes (W3C Content Accessibility 1.0, 1999, 6.2).
  — Ensure that (web) pages are usable when scripts, applets or other programmatic objects are turned off or not supported. If this is not possible, provide equivalent information on an alternative accessible page (W3C Content Accessibility 1.0, 1999, 6.3).

- Programmatic elements such as scripts and applets should be directly accessible or compatible with assistive technologies (W3C Content Accessibility 1.0, 1999, 8.1).
- Use interim accessibility solutions (for browser-based interfaces) so that assistive technologies and older browsers will operate correctly (W3C Content Accessibility 1.0, 1999, 8.1).

User Control

- If it is appropriate to the task, when users can activate a menu, control or other user-interface object to display additional information, that information should persist while the user engages in other tasks until the user chooses to dismiss it (ISO/TS 16071: 2003, 7.2.9).
- Provide a mechanism that enables users to undo the effects of unintended actions and/or require confirmation (ISO/TS 16071: 2003, 7.2.11).
- Enable user control of time-sensitive presentation of information by allowing the user to enable, pause or stop the presentation whenever moving, blinking, scrolling or auto-updating information is presented (W3C Content Accessibility 1.0, 1999, 7; ISO/TS 16071: 2003, 7.2.1.12).
- Keyboard navigation actions should not activate user-interlace objects. An explicit activation key or key sequence should be required for activation (ISO/TS 16071: 2003, 7.4.13).
- To increase the legibility of graphics (bullets, graphics, images, etc.), users should be able to change attributes used to determine data presentation, without changing the meaning of that data (ISO/TS 16071: 2003, 7.7.1). However, be cautious of cases where changing the view will change the meaning.
- If the scale of the display becomes large enough to displace information from the visible portion of the screen, a mechanism for accessing that information should be provided (ISO/TS 16071: 2003, 7.7.1).
- Users should be able to individualize audio output attributes such as frequency, volume, speed and sound content (ISO/TS 16071: 2003, 7.9.2).
- Allow users to choose to have system or application task-critical audio output (including alerts) presented in visual or auditory form, or both together (ISO/TS 16071: 2003, 7.9.5).
- Enable users to individualize the size and color of interface elements including, but not limited to, window-title font sizes, window border colors, window border thickness and window controls, if applicable to the task (ISO/TS 16071: 2003, 7.12.2).

- Users should be able to use the keyboard or other non-pointer input mechanisms to move focus directly to any window currently running (ISO/TS 16071: 2003, 7.13.1).
- Provide user control of multiple "always on top" windows, except where window stacking order has been standardized for task-critical reasons. The user should have the option to choose which window is on top or to turn off "always on top" behavior (ISO/TS 16071: 2003, 7.13.3).
- Allow users to assign input focus to any control via keyboard input (ISO/TS 16071: 2003, 7.14.2).
- Users should be allowed to navigate, using keyboard input, among task-appropriate groups of controls and, within those groups, in an order and direction appropriate for the task and interface layout (ISO/TS 16071: 2003, 7.14.3).

Online Documentation and Help

- Information that is presented in pictures and graphics should also be provided as descriptive text suitable for screen reading, printing or Braille conversion so that it can be read by any of these alternative methods (ISO/TS 16071: 2003, 7.11.1).
- Where the context permits, online help should be sufficiently generic to fit a variety of input/output modalities and user preferences (ISO/TS 16071: 2003, 7.11.2). For example, in a task requiring the user to click on an icon, the step in help would not state "click on the green icon," but instead would specify the location and name of the icon. In another example, the help would provide descriptions of performing tasks using as many different input/output modalities as are available (e.g., mouse, keyboard, voice, etc.).
- Provide general information on the availability of accessibility features and specific information about each feature (ISO/TS 16071: 2003, 7.11.3).
- Provide clear and consistent navigation mechanisms (orientation information, navigation bars, a site map, etc.) to increase the likelihood that a user will find what they are looking for at a (web) site (W3C Content Accessibility 1.0, 1999, 13).
- Ensure that documents are clear and simple so they may be more easily understood (W3C Content Accessibility 1.0, 1999, 14).
- Provide clear, concise descriptions of the product and its initial setup (Vanderheiden, 1997).
- Provide descriptions that do not require pictures for all basic operations (Vanderheiden, 1997).
- Highlight key information using large, bold letters, and putting it near front of text (Vanderheiden, 1997).
- Provide step-by-step instructions in a numbered, bulleted or check box form (Vanderheiden, 1997).
- Use affirmative rather than negative or passive statements (Vanderheiden, 1997).

As noted previously, the above guidelines were selected on the basis of their relevancy to the development of performance support. The reader is encouraged to look at the specific standards, guidelines and recommendations for more information regarding accessibility.

INTERNATIONALIZATION

When performance support products will be used internationally, special considerations need to be kept in mind throughout the design. A few of these have already been mentioned in some of the guidelines in previous sections of this chapter. Although internationalization is often included as part of accessibility, internationalization is primarily concerned with the cultural and linguistic aspects of a product or interface while accessibility is primarily concerned with the perceptual and physical aspects. In fact, there are some tradeoffs in design between translation requirements and accessibility. For example, to optimize ease of translation, it would be tempting to avoid the use of labels on graphics, callouts, etc., but this would diminish accessibility. The cultural aspects of internationalization affect the design of the interface, including the use of color and symbols as well as the choice of words and the structure of the content. Language affects the product development both in terms of translation requirements and word size effects on the interface design. Another term often used in conjunction with internationalization is "localization" which refers to customizing for a specific country or customer. The following general guidelines should be considered when performance support products will be used internationally:

- Provide sufficient space for expanding word lengths for labels, callouts, graphics, etc. due to translation requirements (Horton, 1991; IBM, 2003).
  Note: The amount of expansion space needed decreases with the number of characters in the text. For example, 5 characters in English can expand to 15 when translated (Horton, 1991), 10 characters can expand to 20, 20 characters can expand to 35, 40 characters can expand to 60, but over 70 characters requires only a 30% expansion.
- Leave vertical expansion room for graphical images and buttons (IBM 2003).
- Select graphics that are identifiable to an international audience (Horton, 1991). Use symbols that have been standardized internationally whenever possible.
- Use a separate layer for text on graphics so that the text can be produced independently of the graphic layer (IBM 2003).
- Develop a glossary with different language versions to aid in translation.
- Develop and enforce style guides to keep structure and language consistent.
- Write sentences as short as possible (25 words or less) and keep them simple (IBM, 2003). Consider using Simplified English to make translation easier (see Chapter 7).
- Avoid the use of slang, jargon, humor, sarcasm, colloquialisms and metaphors (IBM, 2003).
- Avoid negative constructs in sentences (IBM, 2003).
- Messages and other information should be complete sentences (IBM, 2003).

REFERENCES

Bernard, M., Liao, C., and Mills, M. (2000), The Effects of Font and Size on the Legibility and Reading Time of Online Text by Older Adults, ACM CHI 2000' Poster Session Paper.

Bieger, G. and Glock, M. (1984), The Information Content of Picture-Text Instructions, *Journal of Experimental Education,* 53, pp. 68-76.

Boff, K., Kaufman L, and Thomas, J. (1986), editors, *Handbook of Perception and Human Performance,* New York, John Wiley & Sons.

Booher, H. (1975), Relative Comprehensibility of Pictorial Information and Printed Word in Proceduralized Instruction, *Human Factors,* 17, 3, pp. 266-277.

Broadbent, D. (1958), *Perception and Communications,* New York, Permagon Press.

Broadbent, D. (1972), *Decision and Stress,* New York, Academic Press.

Bergman, M. (1971), Changes in hearing with age, *Gerontologist,* 11, pp. 148-151.

BS 7830 (1996), *Guide to the design and preparation of on-screen documentation for users of application software*, London: British Standards Institute.

Canelos, J., Taylor, W. and Gates, R. (1980), The effects of three levels of visual stimulus complexity on the information processing of field-dependents and field-independents when acquiring information for performance on three types of instructional objectives, *Journal of Instructional Psychology*, 7, pp. 65-70.

Citron, J., Thorton, C. and Cabe, P. (1969), Perceptual style as a predictor of ability to read a non-numeric readout, *Proceedings Human Factors Society Annual Meeting.*

Danchak, M. (1976), CRT displays for power plants, *Instrumentation Technology*, 23, pp. 29-36.

Davidson and Epstein (1963), *A Compilation of Graphic Methods of Data Presentation*, TM LO-784/001/00, Santa Monica, CA: System Development Corporation.

Day, R. (1972), Visual spatial illusions: A general explanation, *Science*, Vol. 175, pp. 1335-1340.

DiVita, J. C. & Rock, I. (1997), A belongingness principle of motion perception, *Journal of Experimental. Psychology, Human Perception and Performance*, 23, No. 5, pp. 1343-1352.

Enrick, N. (1980), *Handbook of Effective Graphic and Tabular Communication*, Huntington, NY: R. E. Krieger Publishing Co.

Faraday, P. & Sutcliffe, A. (1997), Designing effective multimedia presentations, *Human Factors in Computing Systems, CHI 97, Conference Proceedings*, pp. 272-278,

Galitz, W. O. (1994), *It's Time to Clean Your Windows: Designing GUIs That Work*, New York, John Wiley & Sons.

Geldard, F. A. (1953), *The Human Senses*, New York, John Wiley & Sons.

Gould, J. and Grischkowsky, N. (1986), Does visual angle of a line of characters affect reading speed? *Human Factors*, 28, pp. 165-173.

Griswold, R., Jeffery, C. and Townsend, G. (1998), *Graphics Programming in Icon*, Peer-to-Peer Communications, ISBN 1-57398-009-9.

Hackos, J. and Stevens, D. (1997), *Standards for Online Communications*, New York, John Wiley & Sons.

Hegerty, M. and Just (1993), Constructing mental models of text and diagrams, *Journal of Memory & Language*, 32, pp. 717-742.

Hochberg, J. (1964), *Perception*, Foundations of Modern Psychology Series, Englewood Cliffs, NJ, Prentice-Hall.

Horn, R. (1974), Information Mapping, *Training in Business and Industry*, 11, 3. Online. HTTP: <http://www.stanford.edu/~rhorn/images/artcl/artclInfoMappingTraining.pdf> (accessed 8 May 2003).

Horton, W. (1991), *Illustrating Computer Documentation, The Art of Presenting Information Graphically on Paper and Online*, New York, John Wiley & Sons.

Horton, W. (1994), *The Icon Book, Visual Symbols for Computer Systems and Documentation*, New York, John Wiley & Sons.

IBM (2003), *Globalizing your e-business*, Online. HTTP: <http://www-3.ibm.com/software/globalization/topics/writing/index.jsp> (accessed 25 June, 2003).

Information Mapping, Inc. (1999), *The Information Mapping® Method, 30 Years of Research, Research Paper & Notes*, Waltham, MA: Information Mapping, Inc.

ISO 9241-12 (1998), *Ergonomic requirements for office work with visual display terminals (VDTs) – Part 12: Presentation of information*, Geneva, Switzerland: International Organization for Standardization.

ISO/TS 16071: 2003, *Ergonomics of human-system interaction – Guidance on accessibility for human-computer interfaces*, Geneva, Switzerland: International Organization for Standardization.

Jonassen, D. and Grabowski, B. (1993), *Handbook of Individual Differences Learning & Instruction,* Hillsdale, NJ, Lawrence Erlbaum.

Kalyuga, S., Chandler, P. and Sweller, J. (2000), Incorporating Learner Experience into the Design of Multimedia Instruction, *Journal of Educational Psychology,* Vol. 92, No. 1, pp. 126-136.

Landauer, T. and Nachbar, D. (1985), Selection from alphabetic and numeric menu trees using a touch screen: Breadth, depth and width, *Proceeding CHI'85 Human Factors in Computing Systems,* ACM.

Laurel, B., Oren, T. and Don, A. (1992), Issues in multimedia design: Media integration and interface agents. In Blattner & Dannenberg (Eds.), *Multimedia Interface Design,* ACM Press, pp. 53-64.

McConkie, G. and Rayner, K. (1975), The span of the effective stimulus during a fixation in reading, *Perception & Psychophysics,* 17, pp. 578-586.

Marcus, A. (1986a) Proper color, type use improve instruction, *Computer Graphics Today.*

Marcus, A. (1986b) Ten commandments of color, *Computer Graphics Today.*

Matthews, M. and Mertins, K. (1995) The influence of color on visual search and subjective discomfort using CRT displays, In *Human Factors Perspectives on Human-Computer Interaction,* Perlman, Green, and Wogalter (eds.), Human Factors and Ergonomics Society, pp. 125-129.

Mayer, R., Moreno, R., Boire, M. and Vagge, S. (1999), maximizing constructivist learning from multimedia communications by minimizing cognitive load, *Journal of Educational Psychology,* Vol. 91, No. 4, pp. 638-643.

Moreno, R. and Mayer, R. (2000), A coherence effect in multimedia learning: The case for minimizing irrelevant sounds in the design of multimedia instructional messages, *Journal of Educational Psychology,* Vol. 92, No. 1, pp. 117-125.

Moskel, S., Erno, J. and Shneiderman, B. (1984), Proofreading and comprehension of text on screens and paper, *University of Maryland Computer Science Technical Report,* University of Maryland.

Murray, J. and McGlone, C. (1997), Topic overviews and the processing of topic structure, *Journal of Educational Psychology,* Vol. 89, No. 2, pp. 251-261.

NASA (1980), *Spacelab display design and command usage guidelines* (Report MSFC-PROC-711A), Huntsville, AL, George Marshall Space Flight Center.

Nielsen, J. and Schaefer, L. (1993), Sound effects as an interface element for older users, *Behaviour & Information Technology,* Vol. 12, No. 4, pp. 208-215.

Pastoor, S. (1990), Legibility and subjective preference for color combinations in text, *Human Factors,* 32, (2), pp. 157-171.

Perlman, G. and Swan, J. (1995) Color versus texture coding to improve visual search performance, in Perlman, Green, and Wogalter (eds.), *Human Factors Perspectives on Human-Computer Interaction,* Human Factors & Ergonomics Society, pp. 321-325.

Pomerantz, J. and Kubovy, M. (1986), Theoretical approaches to perceptual organization, in Boff, K., Kaufman L, and Thomas, J. (eds.), *Handbook of Perception and Human Performance, Volume II Cognitive Processes and Performance,* New York, John Wiley & Sons.

Posner, M., Boies, S., Eichelman, W. and Taylor, R. (1969), Retention of visual and name codes of single letters, *Journal of Experimental Psychology,* 79, pp. 1-16.

Poulton, E. and Brown, C. (1968), Rate of comprehension of an existing teleprinter output and of possible alternatives, *Journal of Applied Psychology,* 52, pp. 16-21.

Poulton, E. (1985), Geometric illusions in reading graphs, *Perception and Psychophysics,* 37, pp. 543-548.

Rayner, K. (1975) The perceptual span and peripheral cues in reading, *Cognitive Psychology,* 7, pp. 65-81.

Rayner, K. and Bertera, J. (1979), Reading without a fovea, *Science*, 206, pp. 468-469.

Robinson, D. and Kiewra, K. (1995), Visual argument: Graphic organizers are superior to outlines in improving learning from text, *Journal of Educational Psychology,* Vol. 87, No. 3, pp. 455-467.

Rock, I. (1986), The description and analysis of object and event perception, in Boff, Kaufman and Thomas (eds.), *Handbook of Perception and Human Performance,* New York, John Wiley & Sons, Vol. II, pp. 33-43.

Section 508 of the Rehabilitation Act: Electronic and Information Technology Accessibility Standard (29 U.S.C. '794d). Online. Available HTTP: <www.section508.gov> (accessed 12 June, 2003).

Silverstein, L. (1987), Human factors for color display systems: Concepts, methods, and research, In *Color and the Computer,* Academic Press, Boston, pp. 27-61.

Smith, W. (1988), Standardizing Colors for Computer Screens, *Proceedings of the Human Factors Society – 32nd Annual Meeting,* pp. 1381-1385.

Smith, W. (1989), Brown, J. and Cunningham, S. (eds.) *Programming the User Interface: Principles and Examples,* New York, John Wiley & Sons.

Stasko, J., Badre, A. and Lewis, C. (1993), Do algorithm moving images assist learning? *Proceedings ACM CHI'93,* pp. 61-66.

Sternberg, R. and Grigorenko, E. (1997), Are cognitive styles still in style? *American Psychologist,* pp. 700-712.

Strayer, D., Wickens, C. and Braune, R. (1987), Adult age differences in the speed and capacity of information processing: II. An electrophysiological approach, *Psychology and Aging,* 2, pp. 99-110.

Sutcliffe, A. and Faraday, P. (1994), Designing presentation in multimedia interfaces, *Proceedings ACM CHI'94,* pp. 92-98.

Sweller, J., and Chandler, P. (1994), Why some material is difficult to learn, *Cognition and Instruction,* 12, pp. 185-233.

TCIF Guideline (1999), *Admonishments (Safety-Related Warning Messages),* Telecommunication Industry Forum, TCIF-99-021, Issue 1, 12/27/99.

Teitelbaum, R. and Granda, R. (1983), The effects of positional constancy on searching menus for information, *Proceedings of CHI '83 Conference on Human Factors in Computing Systems,* New York: Association for Computing Machinery, pp. 150-153.

Thorell, L. and Smith, W. (1990), *Using Computer Color Effectively: An Illustrated Reference.* Prentice Hall, Englewood Cliffs, NJ.

Thornton, G., Barrett, G. and Davis, J. (1968), Field dependence and target identification, *Human Factors,* 10, pp. 493-496.

Tinker, M. (1963), *Legibility of Print,* Ames, Iowa: Iowa State University Press.

Trollip, S. and Sales, G. (1986), Readability of computer-generated fill-justified text, *Human Factors,* 28, pp. 159-163.

Tufte, E. (1983), *The Visual Display of Quantitative Information,* Cheshire, CT, Graphics Press.

Tufte, E. (1997), *Visual Explanations, Images and Quantities, Evidence and Narrative,* Cheshire, CT, Graphics Press.

Tufte, E. (1998), *Presenting Data and Information Course,* Double Tree Hilton, Somerset, NJ, March 12, 1998.

Tullis, T. (1984), *Predicting the Usability of Alphanumeric Displays,* Ph.D. Dissertation, Rice University, Lawrence Kansas: The Report Store.

Tullis, T. (1988), Screen Design, in Martin Helander, ed. *Handbook of Human-Computer Interaction,* New York: North-Holland, pp. 377-411.

Tullis, T. (1995), Readability of fonts in the windows environment, *Proceedings ACM SIGCHI '95*, ACM.

Vanderheiden, G. (1988), Designing for people with functional limitations resulting from disability, aging, or circumstance, in *Handbook of Human-Computer Interaction*, Martin Helander (ed.), New York, North-Holland, pp. 2010-2052

Vartabedian, A. (1971), The effects of letter size, case and generation method on CRT display search time, *Human Factors*, 13, 4, pp. 363-368.

W3C Content Accessibility 1.0 (1999) Online. HTTP <www.w3.org/TR/WCAG10/> (accessed 12 June, 2003).

Warren (1981), *Responses Latencies for Various Screen Positions*, TM-59474-1, AT&T Bell Laboratories.

Weale, R. (1963), *The Aging Eye*, London, H. K. Lewis.

Welford, A. (1973), Attention, strategy and reaction time: A tentative metric, in *Attention and Performance IV*, S. Kornblum (ed.), New York, Academic Press, pp. 37-54.

Wetzel, C. D., Radtke, P. H. and Stern, H. W. *Instructional Effectiveness of Video Media*, Lawrence Erlbaum Associates, Hillsdale, NJ & Hove, U. K, 1994.

Williams, J. and Falzon, R. (1963), Comparisons of search time and accuracy among selected outline geometricsymbols, *Journal of Engineering Psychology*, 2, 3, pp. 112-118.

Williams, J. and Fish, D. (1965), Effects of item length and number of different elements on immediate memory, *Psychonomic Science*, Vol. 3, pp. 353-354.

Williams, J. R. (1966), Training and photo-interpretation performance, *Proceedings: The Human in the Photo-Optical System*, Society of Photo-Optical Instrumentation.

Williams, J. R. (1988), The effects of case and spacing on menu option search time, *Proceedings of the Human Factors Society 32nd Annual Meeting*, pp. 341-343.

Williams, J. and Leaf, W. (1995), Subjective and objective judgments of screen formats, in *Human Factors Perspectives on Human-Computer Interaction*, Perlman, Green and Wogalter (eds), Human Factors and Ergonomics Society, pp. 43-47.

Williams, J. R. (1998), Guidelines for the use of multimedia in instruction, *Proceedings of the Human Factors and Ergonomic Society 42nd Annual Meeting*, pp. 1447-1451.

Witkin, H., Oltman, P., Raskin, E. and Karp, S. (1971), *Embedded Figures Test, Children's Embedded Figures Test, Group Embedded Figures Test: Manual*, Palo Alto, CA, Consulting Psychologists Press.

Ziegler, K. and Greco (2001), eds., *The Designer's Guide to Symbol & Icon Fonts Online*, Hearst Books.

Ziets, G. (1998) Effects of display types and color on comparison judgments using wide-range, high-accuracy gauges, *Proceedings of the Human Factors and Ergonomics Society 42nd Annual Meeting*.

Zwaga, H. and Duijnhouwer, F. (1995) The influence of a fixed background in a VDU display on the efficiency of colour and shape coding, *Human Factors Perspectives on Human-Computer Interaction*, Perlman, Green, and Wogalter (eds.), Human Factors and Ergonomics Society, pp. 19-23.

CHAPTER SEVEN

Developing Performance Support Products

INTRODUCTION

This chapter provides detailed development procedures and guidance for the development of the various performance support products. While the development process for individual performance support products presumes that needs assessment and task analysis has been accomplished, many of the processes and guidelines presented can be used in a less structured development environment.

It is important that all performance support products be developed with respect to specific product objectives and usability objectives. Such objectives should guide the development so that the product has the highest probability of meeting user and management needs.

In addition, an iterative approach to evolving individual performance support products into an EPSS will be described as a more practical means towards electronic performance support.

DOCUMENTATION

As noted in Chapter 1, documentation is probably the most common form of support material provided with a system. Documentation is the vehicle by which the development organization communicates information to the using organization about installation, operation, use and maintenance of the system. However, documentation is often based on information received from designers or programmers who understand the system, but have limited knowledge about the characteristics and needs of the intended users.

This section on documentation is not intended to cover the general area of technical writing, but is aimed at providing procedures and guidelines to support the preparation of usable documents. There are a number of books and chapters available on how to write effective computer user documentation (e.g., Brockmann, 1991; Price and Korman, 1993; Wright, 1988). In addition, the British Standard, BS 7830: 1996, provides useful guidance on the design and preparation of on-screen documentation.

The basic objectives of document design and development should be to:

- Ensure that users receive "good" documents. If the using organization personnel who will install, operate, use and maintain the system do not receive the types of documents they need, the system will typically be ineffective.
- Provide appropriate documentation inputs from the system design and development process. Since designers do not like to produce documentation, other than that required by the design process, it is important to provide a means by which "deliverable" documentation "falls-out" of the design process.
- Ensure that specific information is repeated only when necessary. Although a certain amount of redundancy in documentation is necessary, needless information should be avoided. If a user needs a particular kind of information, it is undesirable for that user to search for it within a large body of irrelevant information.

Development Approach

While the development of documentation should be parallel to the software development (BS 7830: 1996), documentation typically lags considerably behind software development. This lag tends to happen due to several reasons. One of the reasons is the volatility of the software during early design. Since the software design keeps changing, many managers are reluctant to have writers capture the design until it has stabilized. Another reason is that resources are generally not assigned for documentation until the software is nearing the delivery stage because of the need to keep budgets as lean as possible.

A strategy for getting around this lag problem is to convince management that the document writers should be part of the design team. This can be accomplished by suggesting that the writers, rather than the designers, should be responsible for producing the design documents. There are several advantages to this approach. First, writers are generally better at communicating than designers. Second, if the writers take over the documentation responsibility, designers have more time to make design decisions. In addition, when writers prepare design documents they need to clarify the design so that they can understand it. This leads to better design documentation.

As was noted in Chapter 5, the decision on what information should be provided in documentation versus other performance support products should be based on the purpose of the information and how it is intended to support performance. Since documentation is less capable of supporting immediate performance than online help or performance aids, it generally should be used to provide descriptive, explanatory or reference information. However, because of user preferences, it may be necessary to provide some or all of the material included in online help in user guides. In such cases, the content of the online help and the guides should be closely coordinated to ensure that they are the same. The requirements for documentation should be developed in conjunction with the requirements for other performance support products early in the design (preferably based on a task analysis).

Another question that usually arises is what documentation should be provided in paper form versus electronic form. While any document could be provided in electronic form, there are a number of situations where a paper document is required. For example, initial installation instructions for a software product need to be provided in paper form because the user cannot access online documents until the system is installed. Sometimes such instructions are placed on the software installation disk with the idea that users will refer to instructions before installing the product. However, users often will install the product without referring to the instructions on the disk. Users are much more likely to look at a paper version, particularly if it is highly visible (e.g., titled "READ ME FIRST"). Another example is information on who to go to for support or help. If the user cannot get the system to run, it would do little good to provide such information only online. Promotional material, e.g., a brochure explaining the benefits of a product, also is more likely to be looked at in paper format.

One of the first steps in documentation development is the preparation of style guides and content outlines for all deliverable documentation. This is particularly necessary in the development of large systems that require a large number of documents developed by a number of different organizations. Documentation users expect all of the documentation coming out of a particular organization to have the same "look and feel." Also, when documents of the same type have the same organization and structure, they are easier to use. Style guides should specify the general structure of the documents, headings, type fonts, paragraph styles, footnotes and referencing conventions, graphics location and captioning, writing style, etc. Content outlines should provide the specific structure and general table of contents to be used for each document type. A content outline also should specify the target population for which the document is intended and provide a general list of objectives for the document.

A design document should be developed for each of the deliverable documents. The design document should include the following major sections:

- Purpose and description of the document (including the name of the document and how it fits into the larger structure of performance support products to be delivered to the customer).
- Description of the intended target population (both primary and secondary populations).
- Specific objectives that the document is expected to fulfill (usability objectives, knowledge to be enabled).
- Criteria for the document's evaluation (feedback forms, usability testing, etc.).
- Document design (description of the organizational structure and basic content design – reference to content outline and style guide, hyperlink requirements for online documents).
- System Test Requirements (document delivery requirements for system test stages).
- Project scope and schedule for the document.

Since the current trend is to provide most, if not all, documents online, it is very important to consider how online documents will be used. If an online document primarily will be printed and used in paper format, then it should be designed to be read as a paper document. However, if an online document will be accessed and used in its online form, it should be designed for easy access and navigation. Dillon (1994) lists the following four elements as important to designing electronic text:

1. A task model relating to the reader's needs and uses for the material.
2. An information model that describes the information representation.
3. Manipulation skills and facilities that support the physical use of the material.
4. The cognitive and perceptual processing involved with reading the material.

The previous chapter covered information presentation as it relates to the user's task and needs for information and cognitive and perceptual processing. However, online documentation does have some unique requirements concerning manipulation of the content. In addition, since systems providing online documentation vary considerably in their navigational structure and interface, users typically have not developed highly developed skills that can be transferred from one system to another. This fact also puts additional importance on the standardization of document structures and navigation facilities within the performance support system. Printed documents usually have a table of contents and an index. The table of contents is typically used to find major content items, while the index is typically used to find a specific item of content. Tables of contents and indexes are also often included with online documentation with the added advantage of being able to directly access the desired content by "clicking" on it.

Hyperlinking

The words or phrases in a document (typically highlighted by underlining and/or different colored text) that can be selected to initiate navigation to information relating to those words or phrases are called hyperlinks. Hyperlinking protocols typically vary considerably between different online documentation implementations. One of the problems users often experience when extensive hyperlinking is available is getting lost in the structure. Because of this, it is very important to provide information to users as to where they are in the document structure at any time. In addition, they should be able to return immediately to where they were previously and to the document content list.

One method for improving the usability of the table of contents is to provide a dynamic table of contents, or "fisheye view" (Landauer, 1995). This approach, widely used in file structure representation, provides a view to the user's position within the content structure. The title of the current section and the titles of all of the sections at the same level under the super-ordinate heading are shown as well as the upper level headings. Headings open as the user progresses through them and collapse as the user moves back up to a higher level. SuperBook developed by Bellcore researchers (Landauer et al., 1993) displayed the dynamic table of contents in a window next to the window displaying the specific selected contents. No matter where the user moves within the content, the position within the table of contents keeps pace. Therefore, the user always knows where they are.

Another method often used is to provide headings and subheadings as part of the document "page" structure (usually at the top of the page or window) so that users can tell where they are in the content. These headings also can have hyperlinks back to the higher level content. In addition, some online documents depict (usually by highlighting the headings in the content list) what sections of the document have been viewed. Regardless of the method used, users should be able to easily determine were they are in the document structure at all times.

Hyperlinks can also be used to provide direct access to terminology definitions, clarifications and notes. Linking to lower levels of detail is particularly useful when readers of the document will vary in their knowledge of the subject. Novices can easily click on the link for more detail, while experienced users are not encumbered by detail that they already are familiar with.

As noted previously, no matter what approach is selected for the use of hyperlinks and methods for determining the position within a document, the approach should be used consistently throughout the performance support products.

Text Searching

In addition to searching by means of an index, text searching is an important means for a user to find content related to a specific subject. Typically text searching tools allow the user to type in a word or phrase and the computer locates the first incidence of this word or phrase within the document. In some cases, the search can be refined by the inclusion of "and," "not" and "or" as part of the search criteria. SuperBook refined the search process by finding all of the paragraphs that contain the word or words typed in by the user. The total number of incidents (paragraphs containing the words) was displayed next to the table of contents heading so that the user could determine which headings most likely covered that topic. In addition, SuperBook used an adaptive indexing system (Furnas, 1985) that kept track of the words that users try for finding information and don't succeed. When the user finally finds the sought information item, SuperBook asks the user to identify the words that didn't work that should be added to the index for that item.

The Bellcore work on indexing evolved into Latent Semantic Indexing (LSI) which is being used by numerous organizations to improve document search capabilities. LSI uses statistical algorithms to retrieve relevant documents even when they do not share any words with a query. This approach uses these statistically derived "concepts" to improve search performance by up to 30% as compared to word matching methods commonly used for retrieval (Deerwester et al., 1990). Telcordia Technology (formerly Bellcore) provides patented "Telcordia Latent Semantic Indexing Software (LSI)" that uses a powerful and fully automatic statistical method (singular value decomposition) to uncover associations among terms in a large collection of texts in order to create a semantic or concept space for improving retrieval (Telcordia, 2003). During an analysis of a collection of texts, LSI will learn terms that occur in many of the same contexts so that queries about one of these terms can retrieve documents about the other. Using a tool such as LSI can significantly improve the user's ability to find the information that they are looking for. However, to use LSI, all of the documents must be accessible to the system.

Modularization and Knowledge Management

Since more and more organizations are using, or planning to use, some type of knowledge management system, it is important to design documents with knowledge management requirements in mind. Knowledge management systems are used to categorize, store and retrieve various kinds of knowledge within an organization. Such systems are intended to capture organizational best practice, share lessons learned and make use of the collective intelligence within the organization about the organization itself, customers and competitors. It is important to note that moving to a knowledge management system is a huge undertaking that requires a comprehensive knowledge content model as well as software that can categorize and retrieve knowledge.

Modularity is a critical aspect of a successful knowledge content model (see Figure 7.1 for an example of a document content model). Essentially, modularity can be defined in terms of the self-containment and independence of a segment of content. If a segment of content has optimum modularity, it will be meaningful on its own and not depend on any other segment of content for clarification. Modules pertaining to the same subject also can be written at various levels of detail. An example of a module is a definition for a term, e.g., performance support. This definition could be written at several levels of detail. In order to be used within a content, or knowledge management system, each of the modules must be uniquely identified and placed within the content structure. Ideally, modules are written at the paragraph level so that every paragraph within a document can be identified. If all the content on a subject was described in modules at different levels, it would be theoretically possible to put together documents for different users by assembling modules that applied to those users. Modularization also can be used to develop different versions of a document based on different configurations of a system aimed at different customers. In addition, modularization is critical to efficient maintenance of documentation.

Most publishing tools that support knowledge and content management are based on XML (Extensible Markup Language) and are intended to provide a "single-sourcing" environment for the development and publication of materials. XML has become the language of choice for most applications because it's written in SGML (the international standard metalanguage for text markup systems) which makes it easy to define document types, easy to author and manage SGML-defined documents and easy to transmit and share them across the Web as well as with other systems that handle XML content (XML FAQ, 2003). XML can be used to store any kind of structured information, and to pass it between different computing systems (by encapsulation) that otherwise would be unable to communicate.

One example of a single-sourcing, XML-based, authoring tool that can be used to produce performance support product such as documentation and online help is AuthorIT (2003). In AuthorIT, authors create pieces of re-usable information that are managed and maintained in one (single-source) database which can be published to different audiences, documents and formats in both printed and online versions. With single-sourcing, the information is written once and changes are made in one place thereby reducing errors and re-work, eliminating duplication, minimizing reviews, reducing translation and localization costs, and maintaining consistency.

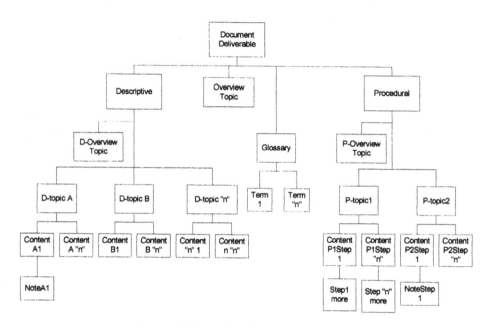

Figure 7.1 Example of a Document Content Model

Performance Aids for Finding and Using Documentation

In very large and complex systems, a considerable amount of documentation may be available concerning various aspects of the system. Often installation people, users and system support people, particularly new ones, do not know what documents are available and what they are for. We were able to solve this problem in one of the large Bellcore Operations Support Systems by providing a "Finder's Guide" that listed all of the documentation available for the system by category of user and purpose of the document. The documentation was listed by number and information on where and how to obtain it was provided. Training courses were also listed so that users and support personnel could quickly tell what training was available to support their functions.

Developing Deliverable Documents

As noted in Chapter 1, three types of documentation are typically supplied with larger software systems: system overviews, user documentation and administrative or support documentation. Development strategies for each of these types of document will be discussed below.

System overviews

System overviews are very important documents since they are often the customer's first exposure to the system. Due to the different types of people (e.g., managers, users, support personnel) that may read system overviews, it is often necessary to develop several different versions. Each version would describe those aspects of the system that are most important to the particular population.

System overviews are often written early in development so that they can be used to give potential users a general understanding of what the system is intended to do and how it works. However, it is easier to produce system overviews after the system has matured and has been described in design and development documents. If system overviews must be developed before the design has stabilized, a good strategy is to use the description of the system specified in the requirements documentation.

A system overview should generally include:

- A high level description of the system.
- What the system accomplishes for the customer (as well as what the system doesn't do).
- What other systems it interacts with.
- How typical users use it.
- What kind of platform it runs on.

User documentation

The most common user documentation included with a system is a user guide. However, in many cases a "Getting Started Guide" is necessary for getting the user started with the system particularly when most of the support material is online. Getting started guides have become very popular and are supplied with many consumer electronic and computer products.

Getting Started Guides should contain sufficient information to get the user started with the system. In some cases, this would include installing the software on their computer. The primary purpose of a Getting Started Guide is to introduce the user to the key features of the system and provide sufficient information so that they can use these features as quickly as possible. In addition, a Getting Started Guide should provide information and instructions on how and where to get more information and support. It is particularly important to acquaint the user with the online help system and any available tutorials. Contents of a Getting Started Guide typically include:

- A brief description of the product/system (including system requirements for software)
- Instructions for installing the hardware and/or software.
- Basic, general instructions on using system menus, buttons, screens/windows (particularly, access and use of key features necessary to initially use the system should be covered, e.g., accessibility features).
- Instructions for using online help, online tutorials.
- Typical task flow using system features (Optional, depending on product).
- Information on where to get support information and help (particularly for problems with hardware or software installation).

User Manuals are intended to support the end-users in all aspects of using a product or system. Therefore, they should contain all of the information that the user will need during any phase of the product or system installation, operation and maintenance (if appropriate). The manual should be designed so that it will accommodate both new users as well as experienced users. Some research (Dillon, 1991) indicates that users tend to prefer a user manual for software products that contain sections such as: contents, getting started, simple tasks, more complex tasks and an index. However, such an organization, progressing from easy to hard in terms of difficulty, may not be appropriate for systems that have many tasks with steps varying in difficulty and complexity. If a Getting Started Guide is provided, the easier tasks can be covered there. In addition, covering material from easy to hard may be more appropriate in instructional material. A software user manual generally should contain the following sections:

- Table of Contents.
- Organization of the Guide (and how to use it).
- Installation procedures (if appropriate).
- Logging onto and accessing the system features.
- Using the system's menus, buttons and screens/windows to perform work tasks (these should be organized by task and not system features).
- Interpreting and resolving errors (information should be organized so that it is easily located by the user based on the error information received).
- Generating and printing output/reports (if appropriate).
- Getting further information, such as other paper documentation.
- Accessing online help and online tutorials.
- Logging off.
- Support (who and where).
- Index.

Administrative/support documentation

Most large software systems require a number of personnel to administer and provide technical support for the system. The larger and more complex a system, the more likely that system administrators and support people will be needed. Large systems may require different administrators for different administrative functions. For example an overall system administrator may be responsible for the day-to-day operation of the system and general support to end users. Where systems have large complex databases, a separate database administrator also may be required. Also, if the system is large and complex, a number of system administrators may be required to handle a variety of end user questions and problems. In a smaller system, or application, only one system administrator may be required to handle all of the system administration tasks.

A System Administrator's Guide should provide all of the information necessary for the system administrator(s) to install and administer day-to-day system operations as well as resolve system and end-user problems. System Administrator's Guides typically contain information on:

- System requirements – hardware and software configuration required to install and operate the system.
- System installation and configuration – how the system is installed and how features are set up for operation and "tuned" for local operation.
- Reference tables (e.g., local information such as account codes, etc.) and how they must be set up for system operation.
- System functional descriptions – how the system uses the user's entries on screens to perform system functions and produce outputs
- Interfaces with other related systems – how the system, or application integrates with systems or applications at the customer's site.
- Error resolution – descriptions of errors that may occur in processing system data and how they can be resolved.

In some cases, it may be necessary to create a separate Installation Guide for systems that have complex installation requirements. The information required to prepare a System Administrator's Guide will need to be obtained from those individuals in the software development organization responsible for the configuration and operation of the system. Information on error resolution can often be obtained from system test personnel.

Database administration involves the entry and maintenance of the system's database. In smaller systems, database administration activities can be included within the System Administrator's Guide. However, for those systems that require one or more additional administrators to handle database administration, a separate Database Administrator's Guide should be prepared. Database Administrators Guides typically contain information on:

- Database structure – what kinds of entities are connected by what kinds of rules.
- Database entities – references material on the types of entities, their data definitions, and how they are entered and maintained.
- Maintenance procedures – online or batch jobs that are used to load and maintain the data in the database.
- Interfaces with other related systems – how the database interacts with other system(s) databases.
- Error resolution – what kinds of errors may occur and how to resolve them.

The information required to prepare the Database Administrator's Guide usually can be obtained from the system development organization responsible for developing the system database. In many cases, the system development organization will want to prepare their own Database Administrator's Guide. However, more usable guides will result if they are prepared by technical writers with experience in developing user-oriented documentation.

Guidelines

Most of the following guidelines have been abstracted from the *Document Design Aid*, available through the FAA (1997), developed for the Office of Aviation Medicine by SUNY-Buffalo and Galaxy Scientific Corporation.

General

- Content should be written with the specific users in mind. The information provided should be flexible and helpful for both novice and experienced users.
- In order to meet the needs of recently practiced as well as less experienced users, provide multiple levels of information. Provide more elaborate information for less experienced users and more concise information for more experienced users performing the same task.
- Utilize a standard framework to distinguish between multiple levels of information (e.g., checklists for experienced users and detailed information for less experienced users).
- Provide current information and information that can be read quickly and is understandable to ensure that it can be used without error.
- Write for the appropriate reading level of the user. Even if the typical user has a high level of reading ability, consider writing information at a 6-8th grade reading level (to decrease errors particularly for complex instructions read under poor conditions).

- Material should have a balance between brevity, elaboration and redundancy of information.
- If possible, verbal material should be complemented by using related pictorial information.
- Primary ideas of long paragraphs in a section should be summarized before the text (aiding learning the content).
- Text should contain the same and standardized syntax.
- Text should be stated as briefly and concisely as possible. State the information as directly as possible without using too many words.
- Keep sentences short and avoid using many subordinate clauses. Avoid negative forms and passive tenses, instead, use definite and affirmative sentences in the active tense. Try to express ideas in positive terms.
- Consider using sentences with personal pronouns.
- Avoid the use of long noun strings in sentences (they are hard to understand).
- Avoid the use of relative clauses without relative pronouns (they create ambiguity and are hard to read).
- Use third person for definitions and limit the use of second person imperative to procedures.
- Consider using Simplified English. Simplified English is a controlled general vocabulary, and a set of writing rules. The vocabulary has sufficient words to express any technical sentence. The words were chosen for their simplicity and ease of recognition. The FAA (1997) *Document Design Aid* provides a tool that allows checking words to see if they are appropriate Simplified English words.

Logical Content

- Title documents to increases comprehensibility.
- Hierarchical relations among the components of procedures should be clearly evident to users.
- Standardize the layout of documents and ensure that the structure is apparent to users.
- Sentences and paragraphs should be structured logically (logically structured material is easier to understand and remember).
- To organize material logically, place general before specific, more important before less important, more frequent first and permanent before temporary.
- Instructions should be written to reflect the logical and temporal order in which the individual task needs to be accomplished.
- In checklists, where many blocks of task steps are not applicable, provide the user with the capability to sign off many steps as (N/A) as one block.
- Provide an outline to show the necessary operations in a step-by-step sequence emphasizing key points of the task.
- Consider using a flow chart in the design of a document (e.g., depicting the sequence of tasks, choice points and alternatives). Number the task steps on the flow chart.
- When designing forms, place reminders of very important procedures on the form itself instead of placing them in the initial instructions.
- Provide appropriate coding for revisions, additions and deletions (e.g., revisions can be identified by a vertical black line or a code letter "R" along the left margin of the page, opposite only that portion of the printed matter that was changed). Also, provide the most recent revision data at the start of a document.

Procedures and Instructions

- Procedures should be written in the natural order in which the task would be done by most users.
- Write clear, simple, accurate and self-explanatory instructions.
- Provide sufficient information in the instruction steps.
- Use action verbs in procedural statements.
- If the task requires movement around the work area, examine the sequence to ensure that the movement is kept to a minimum. To decrease user effort, list physically-adjacent tasks together within the document.
- To prevent "action slip" in directional material, do not include more than two or three related actions per step.
- Work procedures should be broken down into manageable chunks in a logical order.
- Information chunks should be broken down into logical and sensible steps.
- The format of instructions should be adapted to the characteristics of the related task.

Headings and Levels

- Emphasize headings at the same level of the structure of the document in the same way.
- Each step in a process should be numbered.
- Clearly specify the path between task instructions.
- Limit the levels of subordinate (headings and subheadings) within each primary division to three.
- Limit the number of visual properties showing the differences among the headings (each difference implies more structural difference).
- Keep paragraphs, headings and subheadings short when grouping and arranging the text.
- Use subdivisions and heading levels in the text sensibly.
- Ensure that headings and subheadings are clear and understandable.
- Consider developing a topic diagram for the content of the document (topic diagrams are helpful for hierarchical organization).
- If necessary, provide numbers to paragraphs and sections.
- Ensure that the differences among the category responses are clear.

Notes and Warnings

- Provide notes, warnings and comments in the procedures whenever necessary to ensure that the task is performed safely and accurately.
- Warnings, cautions and notes should be used to emphasize important points.
- Directive information, reference information, warnings, cautions, notes, procedures and methods should be easily distinguishable (e.g., use icons to code information category, see Chapter 6).
- The importance of a particular category of information over others should be clear (e.g., warnings, cautions, notes, procedures, methods, directive information and references, in decreasing order of importance).
- Place cautions and warnings directly above, or to the left of, the text to which they apply.
- Place notes after the related text to which they apply.
- Place cautions, warnings and notes on the same page as the text to which they apply.

Typographic Layout

- Single column layout is preferable.
- Keep line lengths to 10 or 12 words (about 6 or 7 inches).
- If 8 ½ X 11 paper is used, provide a left margin of 1.5 inches and permit minimum 1.0 inch for all other margins.
- Place a subject heading at the top of each page.
- Use sequential page numbers that are shown on every page. Place page numbers consistently on all pages and documents (e.g., the lower right corner and 0.5 inches above the bottom edge of the page). Do not extend into the right margin.
- Consider using modified block style paragraphs with 2 spaces indentation for subdivision
- Heading and subheading should be identified sequentially with a label (e.g., 1, 1.1, 1.1.1, etc.).
- Keep paragraphs shorter than a half page in length within a heading.
- Place one blank line between paragraphs and headings.
- If using check boxes in instructions, do not leave a large gap between the check box and the instruction. Use the same check box design throughout.
- If a written response is required, provide sufficient space for the response.
- Leave one space after comma, semi-colon and colons and double space after periods, question marks and exclamation marks.
- Consider use a space ratio 1:2 between sentence spacing (leading space) and paragraph spacing.
- Use equal word spacing, rather than proportional word spacing, among the words.

Pagination

- Limit referencing back to previous text or referencing to other sections of the document. If cross-references must be used, they should be accurate and unmistakable.
- Use the page as a naturally occurring information model (i.e., it should contain an appropriate number of tasks).
- If possible, each task that starts on a page should also stop on that page (try to prevent the carryover of tasks across pages).
- Minimize routing (i.e., do not make the user go from page to page).

Abbreviations, Letters, Words and Numbers

- Only approved acronyms and proper nouns should be used.
- Minimize the use of abbreviations. If they must be used, they should be used consistently and a glossary of abbreviations included in the document. If there is an unavoidable inconsistency for the used abbreviations, a glossary of interchangeable designations also should be included.
- Lower cased letters should be used instead of upper case in the text.
- Mixed-case headings and sub-headings are preferable to all capitals.
- Hyphens for merely showing word division at the end of line should be avoided.
- If a series of words or statements contains mutually exclusive choices, to enhance comprehension, make 'or' explicit throughout the series.
- Avoid the use of Roman numerals.
- If numbers are used in a list (sequence is important), use Arabic numbers followed by a period. If sequence is not important, use a bullet or dash to set off the items.
- In a numbered list, do not contain the number in parentheses.

Lists and Tables

- Present data and information in tables to facilitate understanding and comparison.
- Limit the use of blank spaces to five (about half an inch) in a single row.
- Group lines by content.
- Avoid grouping more than five lines together.
- Separate the groups by controlling the spacing between rows and columns.
- In a list of items, use parallel construction (easier to read and understand).
- A list of a series of items, conditions, etc. is preferable to showing them as a comma-separated series.
- Avoid compound questions and statements.

Graphic Information

- Place illustrations and pictures in the text of a document near the content to which it is related. If this is not possible, put the illustration or picture in an appendix, give it a label and refer to it in the text.
- Place a clear title with a figure number, on the line directly below all illustrations. Use the same title for Illustrations as the title of the text.
- Identify each table or figure with an Arabic numeral label, such as Table 1, Figure 1.
- For ease of reading, consider using either a horizontal-landscape format with the top of the illustration at the binding edge, or a vertical layout to show graphic information.
- Provide sufficient text to make an illustration clear.
- Illustrations should be uncluttered with brief information/learning points, and presented in a self-explanatory way.
- Where ever possible, show all spatial information in a graphical format instead of in a textual format.
- If possible, use simple line drawings (they are generally superior in most cases).
- The same form should be used for figure layout and numbering.
- Consider using illustrations whenever they will simplify, make the text shorter and easier to understand.
- Provide easy reference numbers for figures.
- Avoid the use of perspective part drawings as figures
- Illustrations should provide the same view as seen in reality by the user.
- Incorporate standard and correct technical drawing terminology.
- All tables and figures should be referenced in the text by their numbers.
- Where possible, use bar charts to compare the numerical data accurately.
- Line charts (or graphs) should be considered where it is important to understand trends, and to accurately compare two or more numerical values.

Printing Considerations

- Paper used should have a reflectance (the ratio of reflected light to received light) of minimum 70.
- Matte paper is preferred over medium or glossy paper by most users.
- Use high opacity (the state or degree of not letting light pass through) paper.
- If the user is going to use the document under low illumination levels, use high visual contrast and large type size.
- Black ink on white paper is preferable to white ink on black paper.

PERFORMANCE AIDS

As noted in Chapter 1, a performance aid (or job aid) is a device or document that stores information and makes it available for use on the job. Rossett and Gautier-Downes (1991), in their book *A Handbook of Job Aids,* define a job aid as: "a repository for information, processes, or perspectives that is external to the individual and that supports work and activity by directing, guiding, and enlightening performance." Performance aids (job aids) are intended to help users perform activities by simplifying steps, providing infrequently used or complex information and by providing checklist to help determine whether all required activities have been accomplished. Joe Harless, an early champion of using job aids to reduce training, stated a job aid should meet the following requirements (Harless, 1986):

- Be accessible and used in real time (employed during actual task performance).
- Provide information to the performer on when to perform the task or increments of the task (stimuli).
- Provide sufficient direction on how each task is performed (responses).
- Reduce the quantity of information and or the time the information needs to be recalled (i.e., reduce the reliance on memory).

Performance aids are typically not intended to motivate or provide reasons for performing an activity except in those cases reasons are associated with a decision making process. The following types of tasks are usually good candidates for performance aids:

- Tasks that are performed infrequently.
- Tasks that are highly complex (e.g., contain many steps, have many decision making components).
- Tasks that have specific performance requirements that if not met will result in serious consequences or error.
- Tasks that may change in terms of how it is performed in the future (e.g., use of a different computer system).
- Tasks that require conversions from one unit of measurement to another (e.g., monetary conversions).

Performance Aids vs. Online Help

While online help could be considered a performance aid, in this book we will distinguish between the two in terms of the type of support provided to the user. Performance aids are intended to support a specific task by providing information or knowledge that would otherwise need to be memorized or learned by means of training. They may support job activities that are being performed by means of a computer system, independently of the system, or both. Performance aids may be in the form of paper, plastic or online. An online (or electronic) performance aid for a computer application task is either generated automatically or accessible directly through the application interface when the user is performing the related activity. Online help, on the other hand, is intended to support the user throughout the use of a computer-based application and is accessible by means of a separate command (e.g., F1) or action. It provides procedures, guidance, information and problem resolution assistance relevant to the computer-based application. When electronic performance aids are used to support a computer application, they also may be supported by the online help system.

Development Approach

The need for performance aids will normally be identified during the analysis of skill and knowledge requirements (see Chapter 5). In addition, if the system is a revision to an existing system and a task analysis was done on site, information on what current users have been using as performance aids to support their work will provide very useful insight into the development of new performance aids. It is particularly important to evaluate the type of aids that expert performers have been using on the job.

Performance aid development should include the following seven major activities:

- Identifying needs for performance aids.
- Developing performance aid requirements.
- Preparing the performance aid design document.
- Developing a prototype of the performance aid.
- Testing the prototype.
- Developing the performance aid.
- Testing and revising the performance aid as necessary.

Identifying the Need for Performance Aids

As noted above, the need for performance aids should have been determined during the analysis of skill and knowledge requirements. If skill and knowledge requirements were not developed, or the information is not available, it is important to analyze the task or procedural information to determine the relevancy of performance aids. Each task or procedure should be evaluated in terms of how and when it is performed, who will perform it and the environment in which it is performed.

How and when a task or procedure and its associated steps are performed is important in terms of the order each activity is performed and what initiates its performance. It also is necessary to determine the importance or criticality of the activities, particularly in terms of speed and accuracy requirements. The frequency that the task or procedure will be performed is another important factor that will help in the determination as to whether a performance aid may be appropriate. Also, information concerning the backgrounds and probable skills and knowledge of the person(s) that are expected to perform the task or procedure should be collected. Finally, the work environment in which the potential performance aid would be used needs to be determined.

After the above data are collected and analyzed, the information requirements of the task should be determined (this data should be available if task analysis was performed as described in Chapter 4). Information requirements are the specific information that the performer needs to perform each of the steps in the task or procedure. Information requirements can be classified into directive information or supportive information. Directive information is that information that relates to what to do (i.e., the procedures and steps for the task). Supportive information is that information that supports the performance of the procedures. Such information includes data (e.g., billing rates), reference material (e.g., code explanations) and guidance (e.g., decision making procedures, cues). If skill and knowledge was determined as described in Chapter 5, directive information requirements can be directly derived from the process related knowledge requirements and supportive information requirements can be derived from the environment knowledge requirements. While most performance aids will provide supportive information, it is often useful to provide directive information for infrequently performed or complex tasks.

Once the directive and supportive information requirements are determined for the task and associated steps, the resultant requirements can be analyzed to determine if there is a need for a performance aid. Typically performance aids are useful to support activities that require:

- Skilled use of information or knowledge within the task.
- Directive or supportive information that is not cost-effective to acquire by training.
- Information that is best presented by means of a performance aid (e.g., startup procedures, keyboard mapping).
- Complex decisions or discriminations.
- Calculations or comparisons.
- Infrequent performance.
- Memory of infrequently used information.
- Quick and accurate performance of relatively complex behavior.

In addition, performance aids offer a number of advantages over documentation for on-the-job use, including: unlimited selection of color, size, shape and material, information can be brought into direct physical contact with the source (e.g., keyboard overlay), easier access to the information (i.e., do not need to extract from a large document), easy modification if the information changes.

Each of the tasks and associated steps should be evaluated in terms of the above factors and a decision made as to:

- How essential is it to make the information available for quick and accurate use.
- Whether a special device or document will make the information significantly more useful.
- Whether the information is presented by means of a performance aid it will make it easier to perform the activity.

If the answer to any of the above questions is "yes," than a performance aid is needed.

Developing Performance Aid Requirements

In the previous activity, the need for performance aids was determined. Tasks and steps for which a performance aid would be appropriate were identified and the directive and/or supportive information that an aid should support identified. It is next necessary to determine the user requirements, content requirements, use requirements and environmental requirements relevant to the performance aids.

User requirements include the expected user's reading abilities, previous experience and training, and attitudes. Reading ability concerns the vocabulary, reading speed and comprehension and is normally based on grade level (e.g., eighth grade level, twelfth grade level). Previous experience or training with the particular activity to be supported by the performance aid is also important. Such experience or training may either facilitate or interfere with performing the activity. The performance aid requirements need to take into account the effect of experience or training on the design. Finally, attitudes towards the use of performance aids need to be considered. Individuals that consider themselves experts may be reluctant to use performance aids.

Content requirements include the level of detail and the amount of material to be covered. To determine the level of detail required, the directive or supportive information requirements should be reviewed to ascertain how much detail is required for a typical user to perform the activity being supported by the aid. An example of a content description would be: "The information contained in the aid will be a list of the types of services offered and the rates for each service." The amount of material to be covered can be described in terms of display units. A performance aid display unit can be defined as: a unit of content that includes all of the necessary information to perform a single occurrence of an activity. In the case of a telephone directory, the display unit would be each listing in the directory since the activity would be looking up a particular number. Using the previous content example of services and rates, each service and associated rate would be a display unit.

Use requirements of the performance aid relates to how the aid will be used to support the user's performance. This includes both the informational purpose of the aid and how frequently it would be used. The various informational purposes supported by performance aids are shown in Table 7.1.

Table 7.1 Performance Aid Informational Purposes*

Purpose	Description	Examples
Cue	Direct the user's attention to specific characteristics of the information or provides a signal to proceed in a particular manner.	Arrows in an illustration pointing out important points. A checklist of abbreviated steps as a reminder of the whole activity.
Procedure	Provides step-by-step procedures for accomplishing a task or goal.	A set of directions for installing a system component.
Association	Provides a means for looking up supporting data related to current information. The information can be an elaboration or a conversion (e.g., into different units).	A reference table describing error types in detail. A rate-conversion table.
Relationship	Provides a means of displaying information in other terms (abstract, relational) such as relationships between events in time, space, etc.	A time line chart depicting circuit usage over time. A diagram showing functional relationships between system components.
Example	Provides illustrations, samples, or classes of data, objects, etc.	An example of a properly completed input form. Sample responses of a service representative to a customer's request.

* Modified from *Performance Aid Development,* Table A – Performance Aid Roles, pp. 3-6 & 3-7, Bell Laboratories (1974).

It is important to note that any given performance aid may support more than one of the informational purposes listed above. The frequency that the performance aid will be used also needs to be extracted from the data on how often the task or activity will be performed. Both the purpose served by the performance aid and the frequency of use should be included into a statement of the use of the performance aid. For example: "The aid will cue the user as to the sequence that information should be entered in the service order. This aid is expected to be used 50 times per day. "

The environmental requirements of the performance aid pertain to the characteristics of the work environment that will affect the aid's design. Such characteristics include: location where the aid will be used (e.g., desk, user's site) and work environment (e.g., inside or outside, heat, humidity and lighting). Environmental requirements associated with the performance aid should be stated in the aid's design requirements.

After requirements are listed for performance aids for specific tasks/activities, it is important to determine whether aids can be combined so as to be useful for multiple activities or individuals. While it is beneficial to combine aids so that they can support as many activities as possible, it is critical that the effectiveness on any one aid is not weakened by combining. Generally aids can be combined when:

- Aids have identical or very similar design requirements and essentially provide the same information.
- Activities occur in close sequence to one another or are dependent on one another. Typically, such activities have related information requirements and have similar design requirements.

Performance aids should not be combined if:

- The activities are performed at different workplaces and the requirements of the workplaces (environments) are very different.
- The combined bulk of aid will make it difficult to use or inconvenient to store.

When design requirements are combined across task steps, usually a task-level performance aid results. The content of a task-level aid usually consists of the supportive information required to complete each activity within the task. However, it also may be necessary to develop task-level aids that contain only directive information (e.g., a checklist of task steps).

In those cases where performance aids are combined across jobs, it is important to consider whether the potential users have the same skills or background, and whether the work environment will be the same. If tradeoffs can be made that will not compromise the usefulness of the aid for the different populations and environments, then it will probably be cost-effective to combine the aids. However, if the differences in design requirements are significant, it is better to design separate performance aids.

In summary, the requirements for each activity-level, task-level and combined performance aid should include statements listing:

1. User requirements
2. Content requirements
3. Use requirements
4. Environmental requirements
5. Combination rationale (where appropriate)

The performance aid requirements document also should have sections on assumptions and dependencies, system interfaces (for electronic aids), accessibility and testing considerations.

Preparing the Performance Aid Design Document

After the requirements for the performance aids have been established, design documents for each aid can be prepared. The design document should contain sections such as:

- Product Overview (including purpose, description of target population, usability objectives and product objectives).
- Product Design (including general organization, general formatting, accessibility and a detailed description of each display unit to be included).
- Product Testing (including testing plans and procedures).

The design document specifies the overall physical requirements for each performance aid and defines the specific design of each of the included display units. Physical requirements include size, shape, color, layout and materials for the aid. It is important to note that the design of a performance is a creative process and a number of appropriate design solutions may be possible. The major consideration is to select a design that best matches the performance aid requirements.

While most performance aids will be visual, there are many support situations in which auditory aids may be appropriate. In fact, it is a good idea to provide auditory versions of visual performance aids whenever possible. This is especially the case when it is necessary to ensure maximum usefulness (accessibility) of the application's performance aids for populations with special needs. Where it is not possible or practical to provide an auditory version of the aid, consider developing an electronic version of the aid that can be read by accessibility tools (e.g., a screen reader).

One method for designing a performance aid is the "bottom-up" approach. This approach begins with the design of the display units, then the pages (or windows) and finally the overall configuration of the aid.

Display Unit Design – As noted earlier, the display unit is the information required to support a single occurrence of an activity. In designing a display unit, a decision must be made as to how the information in the display unit can best be presented to the user. To ensure that information is displayed effectively, the information in a display unit should be:

- Arranged in a manner that allows the user to find it when needed.
- Correct to ensure accurate response on the user's part.
- Clear and meaningful so that no judgments or interpretations are required.
- Complete and concise so that it provides all of the information, but only the information needed.
- Legible so that it can be quickly read.

The design of each display unit is based on the content and other requirements for the unit as well as the five effectiveness criteria listed above. Essentially, a judgment must be made on how to best present the content within the context of all of the requirements. Each of the types of design requirements will have different impact on the design. For example, environmental requirements will have the greatest impact on legibility. Factors such as lighting and viewing distance will determine the size of the text, the use of color, etc. However, user characteristics will also need to be taken into account (older users will need larger fonts and better lighting). Guidelines, categorized by effectiveness criteria, are presented later in this section to aid in the design process.

Page (Window) Design – After each of the display units in the aid have been designed, the presentation of the units within the aid's pages (or windows, if electronic) can be determined. A page, or window, can be any size and is essentially the largest display space viewable at any given time. In the case of a printed performance aid, a page relates to the performance aid's page which may be quite small (e.g., a pocket reference guide) or large (a wall chart). The number of pages, or windows, required will depend on the size, layout and amount of information (in display units) that needs to be presented in the performance aid. Generally, a single display unit aid will be presented on a single page, while a multiple display unit aid, containing long units, will be presented on multiple pages. Figure 7.2 provides an example of a one page PHA Profiles performance aid from the U.S. Department of Housing and Urban Development, Housing Authority (HUD, 2003).

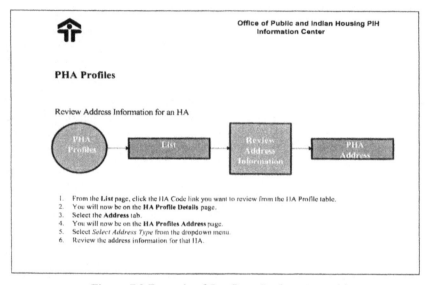

Figure 7.2 Example of One Page Performance Aid

Since it is important that the individual display units are easily found within a page:

1. Present only the information likely to be needed when the aid is used.
2. The layout of the information presented on the page should allow the user to extract the needed information quickly.
3. If multiple display units are presented on a page, the page should be laid out so that the user can focus on one unit at a time (i.e., units do not interfere with each other).
4. Display units should be grouped in a logical order within the page (the order will depend on the type of data and the use). Grouping approaches should be consistent across multiple pages.
5. If keys (symbols or words) are used to find information within the aid, arrange the keys so that they can be easily located (e.g., arrange them alphabetically). In the case of a very large number of keys, consider dividing the keys into groups (e.g., letters of the alphabet in an index).

As noted above, the required size of the aid due to the use and environment requirements will also affect the layout of the display units on the aid's pages. The number of pages may be increased (e.g., pocket guide) or severely limited (wall chart) due to the requirements.

Overall Design Configuration – After the pages, or windows, of the aid have been designed, the overall design configuration for the aid can be specified. On the basis of the previous activity, the aid should have one of the following general configurations: single display unit/single page (window), multiple display units/single page (window), single display unit/multiple pages (windows) and multiple display units/multiple pages (windows). The overall configuration and physical appearance will depend on the use and environment. Particularly, whether the aid will be used on a flat surface, on a device (e.g., computer keyboard), on a wall, or displayed on the computer screen. For example, a multiple display units/multiple pages aid that will need to be placed on a wall could be designed in a calendar style. On the other hand, a multiple display units/multiple pages aid that will be used on a desk could be designed in a flip-chart or handbook style. If the aid is a single display unit/single page, it could be designed as an overlay or a reference card.

The informational purpose of the aid also will affect the over design configuration. For example, if the purpose of the aid is a *cue*, it might be designed as mask, overlay or a template. Where the purpose of the aid is *association*, it may be appropriate to design the aid as a nomograph (or slide rule). Such devices can be more effective than tables because the user is more likely to arrive at the correct solution and they take less space. For further guidance on selecting the most appropriate method to present information in a performance aid, see the section on Data Forms in Chapter 6.

It also is important to consider the modification requirements of the performance aid. When information is likely to change, it is best to design the aid so that only the pages of the information that have changed will need to be replaced (suggesting a loose-leaf type binder). In addition, the requirement for durability should be considered. If the aid is to be handled frequently it may need hard covers or, in the case of a single page, need to be laminated.

Since many different solutions are possible, it may be useful to do a trade-off analysis, based on the requirements, between possible solutions. The trade-off analysis should include the cost of the proposed solutions so that the most cost/effective solution that best meets the requirements can be determined.

Guidelines

The following guidelines are intended to support the performance aid design process by providing examples of solutions and guidance that meet the five different performance aid effectiveness criteria listed in the "Display Unit Design" section above.

Finding Information

- If a checklist is used, place information in the order it will be checked on the job to reduce search time.
- Direct attention to significant information by the position of cue sentences, by using color, or by using arrows.
- Ensure that there is adequate contrast between a cuing device and its background.
- If multiple colors are used for cuing, ensure that the colors used are sufficiently different. Note: see Chapter 6 section on color.
- Use space and borders to differentiate the most important information.
- Use white space as liberally as possible since it is an effective means to set off information.
- Use color coding to separate information into meaningful chunks. However, ensure that the colors can be discriminated if seen in shades of gray.

- If keys or labels are used for designating information groups, ensure that they are easily seen and located. Keys or labels should be consistently located (e.g., to the left of the display unit).
- If a chart is used, place the most significant information in upper-left corner, i.e., for left to right languages.
- If a mathematical table is used, print the base-number column in boldface type since numbers in the base-number column are used to find the data in the table.
- If the user must compare items, place the information in columns.
- Consider grouping information into tables, rather than matrices because matrices are harder to interpret and take longer to use. If space is at a premium, however, a matrix may be preferable.
- Provide sufficient detail to allow the user to tell the difference between similar items or categories.
- Place examples as close to relevant text as possible.
- Place procedural steps last so that they are re-enforced prior to performing.
- If procedures have supporting illustrations, place text beneath illustrations rather than above.
- Arrange the data by: sequence of use, frequency of use, functionality, importance, conventional use, specificity, or alphabetical, numerical or chronological sequence (see Chapter 6, Layout and Structuring Considerations, Arranging Information). Note: use arrangement ordering consistently throughout the aid.
- If lines are used to separate data, limit the number of line widths used to two (hairline width for most purposes and a heavier line for emphasis).

Accuracy

- Review all information (in terms of content requirements) with subject matter experts to ensure accuracy.
- Consider using tables, rather than graphs to minimize information processing.
- If bar graphs will be used, display narrow or widely spaced bars horizontally, rather than vertically (people tend to overestimate percentages represented by vertical bar graphs).
- Items or numerals should be separated into groups of five or six for better accuracy. Note: if the group needs to be larger than 5 or 6, leave extra space between the groups.

Clarity

- Review user requirements and content requirements to determine clarity issues (e.g., the level and type of information that the user will most likely be able to comprehend).
- Use symbols and terminology familiar to the user whenever possible.
- Use symbols and terminology consistently so as to avoid confusion.
- Whenever possible, present a diagram instead of text. Diagrams are typically better than text for relaying procedures, identifying parts, etc.
- Consider using tables or scales instead of graphs for information that does not need to be processed.
- Design procedures and steps to be as straightforward and simple as possible.
- Use headings and labels for item groups and items that are in the user's vocabulary.
- Avoid the use of jargon unless part of the user's language.

Completeness and Conciseness

- Include all of the information necessary to support the performance of the activity, except for information that the user already knows.
- If the aid is designed for speed, include only essential information (minimize unnecessary detail).
- Keep sentences, paragraphs and words as short and concise as possible.
- Avoid adding additional text to fill a page or balance the presentation of an illustration.
- Provide sufficient information (i.e., directive and supportive information) in the aid that it can be used by the typical user without further explanation.

Legibility

The guidelines below address printed material. See Chapter 6 for guidelines on material to be presented on the computer screen (e.g., color, type font) as well as general guidance on the layout and presentation of information.

- Provide sufficient white space to ensure readability (for printed performance aids, leave 20 – 50% white space on a page).
- Use 10 to 12 point type (Times Roman), initial caps, lower case for text (if space permits, however, consider 12 – 14 point to ensure readability for older populations).
- Keep text block lines to approximately 10 to 12 words in length.
- Avoid vertical presentation of text.
- For most reading conditions, use black on white for text (generally avoid colored backgrounds because of decreased legibility).
- If colored ink will be used and the background illumination may vary, use white for the background.
- Ensure that the contrast ratio between the print and the paper is at least 3 to 1.
- When using an additional color with black, use bold face type (other colors will look lighter than the black and using a bold font will compensate for this).
- If a chart type performance aid will be read at a distance, use orange-red tones on bluish-gray backgrounds (these combinations are most visible at long distances).
- Print numbers in Arabic digits instead of words (numbers are much quicker to recognize than words).
- Ensure that the margins on pages are standardized and are at least ½ inch on all sides.
- Ensure adequate spacing between letters, words, paragraphs and display units.

ONLINE HELP

Online help provides the primary guidance and support for the user when interacting with the dialog and user interface. Help should provide information on what can be done, where in the system it can be done, when it is appropriate and how it can be done. Online help should be designed to support the user's goals with regard to using the system, rather than system goals. Different levels of information should be provided by the help system to support users with different skill levels. Some examples of support provided by online help include:

- Command syntax, available keys and data conversions
- Task procedures and steps
- Explanations (e.g., concepts associated with a task)
- Supporting information (e.g., listing of options and actions that can be performed)

- Object descriptions (e.g., icons, buttons, fields, screens)

Development Approach

As was the case with performance aids, the need for online help will normally be identified during the analysis of skill and knowledge requirements (see Chapter 5). If the system is a revision to an existing system and a task analysis was done on site, information on the experiences of users with the current help system should provide useful information for improving the help system for the new release.

Online help development should include the following seven major activities:

- Identifying needs for online help.
- Developing online help requirements.
- Preparing the online help design document.
- Developing a prototype of the help system (for new help systems).
- Testing the prototype.
- Developing the help software.
- Testing and revising the help system as necessary.

Since a well-designed help system is critical to the successful use of a software application, the first five activities should be accomplished by experienced help developers or user interface designers with experience in the design of help systems. In addition, the relevant application software designers and user interface designers need to be stakeholders in the development of the online help requirements and design documents.

Identifying the Need for Online Help

Unless the users are experts or the system is totally self explanatory, it is generally safe to assume that online help will be needed to support any software system. Specific needs for online help should have been determined during the analysis of skill and knowledge requirements. However, if skill and knowledge requirements were not developed, each task should be analyzed to determine what kind of support should be provided by the online help. When analyzing the need for help, analyst should keep in mind who the users are, what they will do with the application, their current skills and knowledge as well as what information they will need to support the task. In general, help is useful to support task activities that require:

- Specific steps or procedures for performing the task (particularly those performed infrequently).
- Information about the user interface, e.g., windows, commands, controls, fields, etc. (i.e., what it is, what it does and how to use it).
- Information about the application, what it does and how it works.
- Memory of infrequently used information.
- Interpretation of results (e.g., description of outputs).
- Quick and accurate performance of relatively complex behavior.

It also is important to determine the information needs for users at different skill and experience levels. Novices will obviously need more information to support using the application than experienced users. Both types of users must be supported by the help system. On the other hand, help is intended to directly support task performance and should not contain tutorial or superfluous information.

Developing Online Help Requirements

The development of online help requirements should be done in cooperation with the application's software developers and in conjunction with the development of software requirements. If possible, the online help requirements developers should participate in the development of the software requirements so that they are aware of how the software is expected to function and can determine what help will be needed to support the user in using the software. The requirements document should contain such sections as:

1. Introduction
2. Assumptions, Dependencies, Constraints
3. Detailed Requirements
4. System Interfaces
5. Testing Considerations
6. Open Issues

It is very important to carefully define the online help detailed requirements because these requirements will drive all of the later design and development activities. In this regard, all help requirements should be numbered to ensure "traceability" later in design, development and testing back to the requirements. The requirements should specify the help format to be used in the application. Help formats include: Microsoft's HTML Help, Java Help, Oracle Help, or multiplatform web-based help such as eHelp's WebHelp and FlashHelp, and Doc-To-Help's Cross-platform HTML 4.0. These help formats have a number of general features in common, including:

* Navigation and organization support (e.g., multi-level indexes and tables of contents).
* Use of a tripane help presentation format (control pane, navigation pane and topic pane).
* Browse sequences allowing users to move forward and backward through a series of topics arranged in a particular order.
* Context-sensitive Help (topics providing information in the context of the user's current window or control element).
* Popup topics (topics that open in a small window positioned on top of the main window).
* Related topics references (lists of other topics related to the subject area).
* Full-text searches (allowing users to search for words related to their content needs).

On the other hand, it is important to note that the different help formats generate output files that support specific viewer requirements, platform requirements and interfaces. For example, for an application running in Microsoft Windows, Microsoft's HTML Help would be the most appropriate solution. However, if the help system will be inside a web-based application and users will use different browsers to access help, a browser-independent, cross-platform help format, such as eHelp's WebHelp or Doc-to-Help's HTML, would be the best selection. In addition, the help format(s) that expected users are currently familiar with should be taken into consideration. The requirements need to clearly state the format that will be used and any variations of that format. An example of a requirements statement for help format would be: "Release 2, HLP-R1: Help will be presented within Microsoft Windows 2000, or XP Professional, using the Microsoft HTML Help format." In addition to the help format to be produced, the requirements should specify the help development tool to be used by help content developers. It is important that all developers use the same development tool so that resultant help files can be merged properly and help system windows and topics look and operate the same.

As noted above, there are a number of help development tools available that can produce a variety of help format outputs. Two of the major tools currently available are RoboHelp Office (2003) and Doc-to-Help (2003). While RoboHelp can produce help files using Microsoft Word or an HTML editor (its own or others), Doc-to-Help relies on Microsoft Word to produce help files. In addition, some of the "single sourcing" software products such as AuthorIT (2003) produce major help formats. It is important to select the tool that best meets the needs of the project. An example of a requirement for the help development tool would be: "All help developers will use RoboHelp Office X4 for developing help projects."

The help structure and content should also be defined in the requirements document. For example: "Release 2, HLP-R2: All help systems will use the standard Microsoft HTML tripane as shown in Figure 7.3." It may also be appropriate to specifically identify the user interface elements in the tripane, such as the top control pane (Hide, Back, Forward and Print buttons), the left navigation pane (Contents, Index and Search Tabs) and the Topic Pane (displaying the help topic text). These elements would be identified as sub-requirements for the main requirement specified for the tripane. Also the initial presentation of the help tripane should be specified. For example: "Release 2, HLP-R3: Initially the help window will be displayed in its complete tripane view with the Table of Contents Tab displayed in the Navigation Pane and the Overview help topic displayed in the Topic Pane." It should be noted that some applications, such as Microsoft Word Help in Office XP, do not provide the TOC as the default initial help display. Instead, the search tab ("Answer Wizard" in Word Help) is the default navigation tab displayed. In fact, users can only access the full help tripane in Office XP by turning off the "Office Assistant" help (an Answer Wizard dialog). This approach assumes that most users prefer to obtain help by direct query which is not necessarily the case. Many users will not know how to word their query and find information much more quickly when they can locate the subject in the TOC or from the index. Also, displaying the TOC initially provides the user with a view of the help system structure which helps them understand where topics are located within the help system. However, the Answer Wizard approach of allowing users to type in the help query in their own words (in response to "what do you want to do?") is a useful improvement to the full search capability in help.

Help structure also includes the help system's hierarchical structure, i.e., the organization of the help topics in terms of detail. A useful approach to develop the hierarchical structure is a "top-down" process built around the concept of progressive disclosure of layered information. This concept involves breaking down information into layers of successively more detail that can be accessed progressively by the user as needed. In this way, information is readily accessible, but information not currently needed does not get in the way or compete for attention with information that is needed to complete the immediate task. Progressive disclosure is particularly useful to support novices as well as experts. A simple example of this approach is a popup description of a window or a control with a button at the bottom for obtaining more detailed information. An example of a requirement for progressive disclosure is: "Release 2, HLP-R4: All help systems will layer help information from basic to detailed to support users of different skill levels. Layers will be accessible progressively by a single click or command."

In order to ensure that all help products related to the application have a uniform structure, the structure of the help contents that will be represented in the TOC needs to be specified in the requirements document. The help system should be organized in a manner that: is logical to the user, provides access to help topics in multiple ways (to meet different user needs and interaction styles) and is consistent with the structure of the application. An example of such a requirement is: "Release 2, HLP-R5: The help

contents of all help products for the application will be organized according to Table X."
Table X would contain a list of sub-requirements specifying each major topic area (e.g., book) and sub-topics with short descriptions of each. For example: "HLP-5.3: How do I... lists individual topics describing procedures, or tasks for the application, grouped under logical headings or functional areas."

Requirements also need to be stated in regard to the information that will be provided in the Topic Pane. For example: "Release 2, HLP-6: All application windows and objects, including menus and buttons, will be described in the help system." Also: "Release 2, HLP-7: All procedures related to accomplishing user tasks with the application will be described in the help system."

The use of popups and secondary windows should be included in the requirements document to ensure consistency across various help products. For example: "Release 2, HLP-8: Popups should be used for showing transient information such as definitions of terms, descriptions of icons and commands, and notes." Also: "Release 2, HLP-9: Secondary windows should be used to present information that the user may want to refer to more than once during their use of the help system (e.g., procedure, sample screen)."

Requirements also should be developed to describe the menu option groupings for the help menu on the application windows. Where applicable, the help menu should provide links to other performance support features such as wizards and training. Requirements for menu options should include the identification of the "key" letter used for keyboard selection as well as whether the option is required, optional or conditional (i.e., based on the application design). The following is an example of requirements for an application help menu:

1st Group – Help Contents and Quick Tour

- Contents (Required)
- Index (Optional)
- Find or Search (Optional)
- Quick Tour (Optional)
- What's This? (Optional) – Not required if right click on object help available

2nd Group – Application/Task Context Sensitive Help

- Window (Required)
- Procedures (Required)
- <Wizard> (Optional)
- <Application Related> Help (Conditional)
- <Application> Frequently Asked Questions (Optional)

3rd Group – Reference and Training

- Glossary (Optional)
- Reference (Optional)
- Tutorials or Training (Conditional) – includes web-based training (submenu to be used for more than one type of course)
- Documentation (Optional)

4th Group – Version/About Information

- About <Application> (Required)
- Help Version (Optional)

The above example represents the help menu for an application having a full range of performance support features. Most applications, however, will only have a few performance support features and would only use a subset of the menu options. The most important point is that all performance support features should be available through the application help menu as well as through appropriate application controls.

Preparing the Online Help Design Document

After the requirements for online help have been established, a design document can be prepared. As was the case for requirements, the design document should be developed in conjunction with the software design documents. It is essential that the online help designers participate in the development of the associated software design documents so that they are fully aware of the system's features, operation, inputs and outputs, and "look and feel." In addition, the participation of online help designers in the software design will often improve the design due to questions that they will bring up concerning the meaning and function of various system features. The online help design document specifies the overall physical requirements for each of the features of the online help specified in the requirements and defines the specific design of each of these features. It should contain sections such as:

1. Help Product Overview (purpose of help, description of target population, usability objectives and help product objectives).
2. Help Design (organization, topic and general text styles, window names, table formatting, alerts and warnings, conformance with standards, table of contents design, related topics design, module design, overview topics design, getting started topics design, common topics design, navigation topics design, windows topics design, menu topics design, dialog topics design, procedural topics design, object/field help topics design, command topics design, "About" topics design, related topics dialogs, glossaries, indexes and file structure and naming).
3. Help Testing (including inspection, usability testing and testing criteria, procedures and material).
4. Issues (outstanding issues that need to be addressed).

In addition to describing the purpose of the help system and identifying the target population, an important part of the Help Product Overview is the statement of the usability objectives that are to be met by the help system. The following list is an example:

*   Less than two errors will occur in seeking a particular piece of information.
*   Total time off the task will be less than five minutes when using help to find information.
*   No more than four "clicks" will be used to find specific information required to resolve a problem.
*   Less than one minute will be required to find a given piece of information.
*   The location within help will be clearly visible.
*   How the Help topics relate to one another will be clearly evident.
*   Users will have complete control and freedom within the help system.
*   Help will support recognition of information rather than recall.

It is also important to list the help product objectives. The following is an example of a help product objectives statement: "This help product is designed to allow users easy access to the information they need to perform their jobs with minimal interruption to their work. However, help is not intended to be a substitute for training, nor is it meant to be a complete reference for the product it supports. For release 'n,' help topics will be provided for following system components:

- Component 1
- Component 2
- Component 3

The Help Design section describes the design that will apply when developing the help system. It should be augmented with templates, job aids and style sheets. Design elements in the design document should correspond to specific requirements in the requirements document and allow easy cross referencing. Such cross referencing is a critical element in ensuring requirements are met during down-stream development and testing.

Organization, i.e., the structure, of the help system as defined in the requirements document should be fully described in the design document so that developers of the various help modules of the system produce consistent products. Help system organization should be clearly evident from the help Table of Contents (TOC) and explained in the introductory topic. The fact that users typically use help to get answers to "what is this?" and "how do I do it?" indicates that these two uses should be clearly represented in the help structure. An example of a help structure, illustrated by the TOC in the Contents Tab, is shown in Figure 7.3. Notice that "Architecture" is listed as one of the topics in the Introduction "book" in the Figure 7.3 example. An architectural topic that provides a graphical hierarchical representation of the system's structure can serve two useful purposes:

1. Provide a "big picture" of the system and its functions.
2. If the graphic contains hyperlinks to "what it is" and procedural topics, users have another means of directly accessing desired information quickly.

Also notice that the help structure illustrated in the Contents Tab in Figure 7.3 contains five major topic areas (or books), i.e., Introduction, Tell me about…, How do I…, Product Descriptions (for help system that pertain to various products) and Glossary.

It is important that the typographical standards for help presentations be stated in the design document so that the various help developers prepare material that looks the same. An example of standards for topic and text styles would be:

- Topic Titles – **H1** = 14 pt. Arial bold.
- Secondary Titles – **H2** = 12 pt. Arial bold
- Tertiary Titles – **H3** = 11 pt. Arial bold
- Procedure Window titles – **H4** = 11 pt. Arial bold, margin top = 4.5pt, Bottom = 0 pt.
- Fifth level Titles - **H5** = 10 pt. Arial bold
- Link Lists – **LL** = 11 pt. Arial regular
- Body Text - **Normal** = 10 pt. Arial regular
- Glossary Terms – **Gterm** – 11 pt. Arial bold
- Glossary Text – **Gtext** – 10 pt. Arial, Bottom 0.5, Margin Left = 10 pt.
- Informatory Notes – **Note** = 10 pt. Arial, Margin Left = 10 pt.
- Warnings – **Warning** = 10 pt. Arial, Margin Left = 10 pt.

For notes and warnings, it is recommended that the international **!** and **i** symbols (as .gifs, not .bmps) be used in the tool bullets and numbers section instead of the words **Note** or **warning** (although the icons also should be labeled "Note" and "Warning" to ensure accessibility). E.g.:

 For updated information about installation see the "readme file."

 Do not run this program with automatic save function turned off.

Although the above icons are not shown in color (due to the limitations of this book), the "Note" icon should be a white symbol on a blue background and the "Warning" icon should be a black symbol on a yellow background.

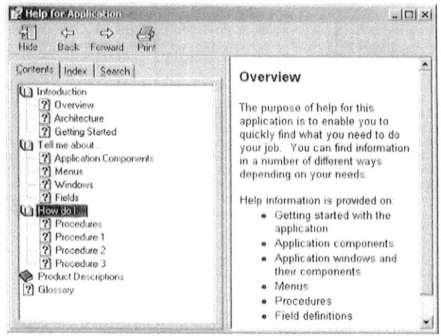

Figure 7.3 Help Topic Structure Example

Window naming conventions need to be clearly stated in the design document. All of the windows displayed in the help system should be identified. Generally the product name should be omitted when specifying application windows in the help system. However, the window name should be spelled exactly as it appears in the application. When describing a window in help, use a capital W in the topic title and lowercase w in the body text.

If tables are used within the help system, their design should be clearly specified. For example:

• Table Widths in Topics: The total width of the table should not exceed the width of the topic window (e.g., 6 inches). It is important to note that the width of a table or graphic defines the word wrap for the window. Therefore, when a user resizes the window to a smaller width than that of the table, the word wrap for the rest of the window will still wrap to the table and not the window.

• Table Properties: The space between margins should be .05 inches and left margin should be 0 inches for all tables.

• Table Column Headings: Headings should be bold and left-aligned.

As mentioned above, the design of the Table of Contents (TOC) reflects the overall structure of the help system. Table 7.2, below, provides an example of a TOC design:

Table 7.2 Sample Table of Contents Design

TOC Heading	Description
\<Application Name\> Introduction	Provide an overview, in a single topic, of the application, what it does, how it functions, and what the user can expect to achieve by using it. In a separate topic, describe what's new in the current release. Also contains the following topics: **Architecture:** Provides a hierarchical graphical representation of the applications architecture (e.g., function, window, window elements). All graphical components provide linkages to relevant descriptions and procedures. **Getting Started:** Provides tips about how to use Help. This topic also includes information on alternative methods of accessing help (accessibility options) within the application.
Tell me about...	These topics are included in a "book" titled: "Tell me about..." and provide descriptive information about the system, its components, application menus, windows and fields. **Application Components:** Provides "what" and "why" information about various system features, functions and processes. **Menus:** Lists all generic (i.e., non-window specific) menu topics in the application or functional area. Menus may be grouped by sub-function. **Windows:** Lists all primary window topics in the application or functional area. Windows may be grouped by sub-function. **Dialogs:** Lists all dialog topics in Application or functional area. Dialogs may be grouped by sub-function. **Text Commands:** Defines, describes and explains (with syntax) all non-GUI text commands.
How do I...	Lists individual topics describing procedures, or tasks, in the application or functional area. Procedures should be grouped under sub-menu headings (or "books") into logical and sub-functional areas. Procedures may also be broken into sub-procedures, or subtasks with mid-topic jumps to the sub-procedure. A separate topic may be included showing the navigation paths to the various windows in the application.
Glossary	Provides terms, definitions, acronyms, etc.

Figure 7.3, discussed previously, provides an example of the TOC design described in Table 7.2.

The next step in developing the design document is to prepare the design specifications for the topic areas listed in the requirements. Each of the topic areas needs to be described to the degree necessary to ensure consistency among content developers. Table 7.3 provides an example of the design specification for a "window" topic.

Table 7.3 Window Topic Design Example

Content Element	Description	Style
Window Title	The name of the specific window for this application.	**H1:** Bold, 14 pt, Arial, name "<Window Title> Window"
Procedures Button	Provides links to procedures for this window. Associated procedures will appear in a pop-up window. Specific procedure can be selected from the list by the user. "Cancel" will return user to the window topic.	Related Topics Button, named "Procedures"
Window Purpose	Each window topic begins with a brief description of the window's purpose.	**Normal:** 10 pt, Arial
Window Components Heading	Heading for the list of all window components including window menu bar, functional groupings, fields, buttons, etc.	**H2:** Bold, 12 pt, Arial, "Window Components"
Menu Links Introduction	The following lead-in sentence introduces the list of menu links: "For information on the menus on this window, select one of the following links:"	**Normal:** 10 pt, Arial
List of Menu Links	Links to descriptions of the menus on the window menu bar. Menu lists are to be ordered horizontally in a table (in the same orientation as displayed on the menu bar). If additional menu groupings are provided on the window, list these menus in a second table (in the same orientation as displayed).	**LL:** 11 pt, Arial (underlined and blue color when linked to topic)
Functional Area Introduction Sentence	The following lead-in sentence is used to introduce the list of functional areas: "This window has the following functional areas."	**Normal:** 10 pt, Arial
Window Group Headings	Headings for window functional group areas, listed in order of appearance on the window.	**Normal:** Bold 11 pt, Arial, named "<Functional Group Name>"

Content Element	Description	Style
Window Group Descriptions	Window Group descriptions for the corresponding headings.	**Normal:** 10 pt, Arial
Procedures Heading	Heading for the list of procedures for current window.	**H2:** Bold, 12 pt, Arial, "Procedures"
List of Procedure Links	List of links (jumps) to the procedures for the current window.	**LL:** 11 pt, Arial (underlined and blue color when linked to topic)
Related Topics Button	Provides related topics links to any other information that relates to this window that isn't covered elsewhere in the topic. A list of related topics will appear in a pop-up window.	Related Topics Button, named "Related Topics"

An example of a help topic created under the Table 7.3 design is shown in Figure 7.4.

The design document should also specify the way procedures are stated so as to ensure consistency across the help design. In general:

- All procedures should have a title. Titles should be consistent (e.g., always start with a gerund such as "modifying," "starting," "creating," etc.).
- Procedures should be stated in generic terms so as not to limit the user's input/output modality preferences (e.g., do not describe procedures only in terms of the visual properties of the interface, such as color, shape, location).
- Procedural and step statements should be as short as possible. Use pop-ups for any instructions that might help a user with less experience.
- Show step number and action for steps that have no significant system response (e.g., selecting an item from a drop-down menu that doesn't change the state of any other objects on a screen).
- Show the result at the end of the procedure and show the result after an interim step in those cases where the system provides a clear response, or at appropriate points for a long set of steps.
- State steps in terms of action verbs, e.g., "Select a report type from the **Report Type** drop-down field." If possible the list of action verbs to be used for typical user interface interactions within the applications should be standardized and listed in the design document.
- Renumber procedural steps for each new window.

To ensure index uniformity across application help products, how indexes are created and presented in the help system needs to be specified in the help requirements document. Indexes should include all meaningful terms in the help system that a user is likely to use to retrieve information in help. The index should include meaningful portions of topic titles and topic text. However, an index should not include entire topic titles or extraneous or repetitious terms, such as "copy," "paste," "dialog," "window," sentence articles, conjunctions, prepositions, etc. For example, index keywords associated with a topic titled "Creating an Output Report" would result in the following associated key words:

Creating output report
Creating reports
Output reports
Outputs
Reports
Creating

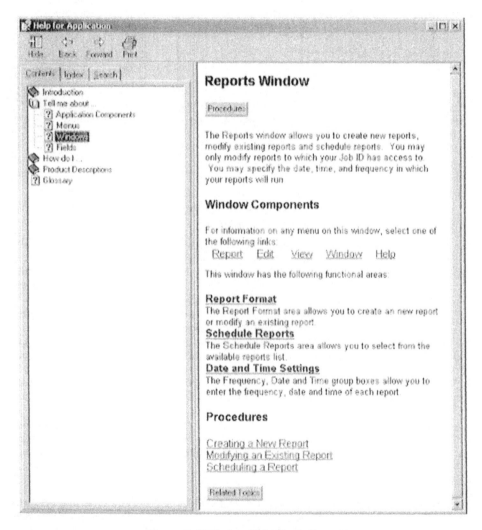

Figure 7.4 Window Help Topic Example

In addition to specifying the appearance and layout of all of the various help topic areas, the design document needs to address file structure and naming conventions to be used by help developers. This is particularly important where help products need to be merged or modified. Help project files should be named in a manner that they can be easily identified with the application, or sub-application that they support. For example:

"hlp_application_subapplication_functionarea.jar." Likewise, topics within the help application need to be named in a consistent manner. It may be appropriate to code the various topic areas used so that the type of topic can be identified easily. For example, for a procedural topic: "File Name: p_newreport.htm." Specific naming conventions may be required for context sensitive help topics, depending on the help format used. In some cases, only the Topic ID is required for topics that are accessed via context-sensitive help. If so, the Topic ID should be the same as the File Name. Also, if possible, both should reflect the actual names used in the user interface.

Developing and Testing the Online Help Prototype

It is very useful to develop a prototype of the help system for a new application before beginning content development. A prototype provides a number of advantages:

1. Allows members of the design team as well as application software developers to view real examples of the help windows and topic formats.
2. Provides a means for evaluating the requirements and design specification for completeness and appropriateness.
3. Can be used to create templates for help content developers.

The help prototype is developed using the help development tool specified in the requirements or the design document. Since the major development tools have "runtime" features, a sample help project can be prepared and run to demonstrate the features and "look and feel" of the help system. Essentially, a help designer familiar with the help development tool will create "dummy" content for all of the help topics types using the specifications in the design document. The resultant help project will be compiled and run to evaluate the output and compare with the design specifications. After everything seems to work properly and represent the design specifications, the prototype help system is demonstrated to various stakeholders for evaluation. Stakeholders would include the help design team, potential help content developers and application interface developers. Changes to the prototype, and potentially to the design document, would be made on the basis of this evaluation.

Developing the Help Software (Content Development)

All help content should be developed using the same help software development tools to ensure the same "look and feel" throughout the help system. If a prototype has been developed using the chosen tool, templates for the various help topic formats can be developed by means of the prototype. Such templates will decrease development time and ensure standardization within different help products associated with an application.

The development of appropriate help content requires considerable knowledge of the application and the context of use (e.g., user tasks, environment, user characteristics), as well as skill in presenting information effectively. If a task analysis and skill and knowledge derivation was done, most of the user's needs for supporting information should be available to the help developer. However, where a task analysis does not exist, the help developer must determine what activities the user will perform using the application and how best to support these activities with help information.

Since "how to" information is one of the most important features of help, the first step in help content development is to list all of the task, or procedures, that will be performed with the applications. If this information is not available from task analysis data, help developers may need to extract it from the application design documents, discussions with designers or end-user representatives, or from the previous application (if one exists). It is very important for help developers to work closely with their corresponding application software developers so that they have full access to information about how the application will look and function. For each of the tasks or procedures identified, the developer needs to list the steps that will be performed to accomplish the procedure. As above, if this information is not available from a task analysis, the developer will need to extract it from other sources.

The steps are then written, clearly delineating the application's user interface components manipulated. As noted in the design document section above, steps should be written as concisely as possible. Steps need to be stated at varying levels of detail so that the help system will be useful for both novices and experts. One strategy for accomplishing this is to initially write the step as a reminder for an experienced user of the application (i.e., assume that the experienced user is familiar with the terminology and has done the procedure before). Then evaluate the step statement and determine what additional information would be needed for a user that has not performed the procedure previously. Provide the additional information in either popups to further describe parts of the step (e.g., control action, field definitions, etc.) or use a "more information" button to go to a lower-level description of the step. The popup approach is preferable for users that need reminders about the content on a particular component of a step rather than all of the detailed information. Where many users with varying levels of experience with the application, consider providing both the popup approach and the "more information" approach. The "more information" layer has an advantage (if presented in a secondary window) in that it can be retained on the screen while performing the task.

In some cases, it is useful to provide a "show me" topic in association with a procedure. A "show me" topic provides a video clip that illustrates the steps performed in accomplishing a procedure. One simple approach for developing such video clips is to use a screen capture program (e.g., RoboHelp's Software Video Camera) that will capture the screen actions and the screens as an expert moves through the steps in the procedure. The resultant AVI file can then be accessed by means of a "show me" button next to the procedure. Video captures also can be useful to demonstrate product features in overview topics. While such topics take additional memory, they can be very useful to novices.

After the procedures are all documented in the help system, the next activity in preparing content is to describe all of the application's components (i.e., windows, menus, controls, etc.). A short description of most, if not all, of these components should be available as context sensitive help (i.e., help that is available when the cursor is within a particular window or area, or is located over a control or other object in the interface). Context sensitive help answers the "what is this?" question and should be available by a single key press (e.g., F1). It is particularly important to provide context sensitive help for editable elements (or their labels), status bar items that do not have text labels, all menu items, all buttons and controls (Microsoft, 2002). The topic IDs of the topics that will be context sensitive need to be provided to the application software developer so that appropriate links from the interface element to the help file can be included within the application software. In addition to being provided through the application software, all of the context sensitive help topics also should be placed within the "Tell me about..." topic area. This supports users that want to browse through the help system to learn about how the application functions. These descriptions should be as short as possible while containing sufficient detail to describe the component. Some of the components may have already been described in conjunction with delineating the procedural steps. If so, links can be provided to the already written topic.

The topics should be organized hierarchically (e.g., window, window area, window elements) so that they represent the applications structure and the manner in which the user would use the application. In addition, application functions and processes should be described and included in the "Tell me about..." topic area. Wherever possible, topics should be described at several levels of detail to provide help information to users with varying experience levels. It is important to provide as many links to other topics within the different topic areas as possible to allow maximum user flexibility in accessing help information. For example, if an application function relates to particular windows, links to those windows should be provided in the application function topic. One way to accomplish this is by use of the "related topics" button at the bottom of the topic window. Clicking on this button would provide a linked list of all of the topics that relate to the current topic. When preparing the list of related topics, the help content developer should list the topics in order of most relevant.

The introductory topics are prepared last because at this point the content developer should have a good understanding of the content of their help product. If multiple help products will be developed for the same application, it is highly recommended that the introductory topic content is coordinated.

Finally, the index should be prepared for the help project. Although the index is finalized after all of the help topics have been developed, it should be developed as the topics are initially created. When developing index keywords, consider: actions that the user may want to take (e.g., copying, routing, saving), subjects that might be related to the problem that help might support (e.g., examples, files and projects), synonyms for the subject and action terms, a related terms that the user may be familiar with (Microsoft, 2002). Many of the help development tools allow the developer to specify the index terms at the same time that the topic title is created. This is an important feature and makes the creation of the index much easier. In any case, all of the index terms need to be reviewed at the end of topic development for completeness and consistency. This step is very important since the completeness and consistency of the index will be very important for those users that rely on the index to find topics.

Testing the Help System

There are essentially five stages to help system testing:

- Initial generation of the help project software and testing links and the appearance of the various topics.
- Reviewing (or inspecting) all help topics by developers and subject matter experts for content accuracy and completeness.
- Running the help system within the application software and checking that all help controls and windows operate correctly.
- Testing the help system using representative members of the target population.
- Testing the final help system for operation and accuracy before deployment.

The initial testing of the help system software involves generating (or compiling) the completed help project and running the output in the help format to be used in the help system. This is done by the individual help content developers. Resultant output help windows and topics are checked to ensure that they appear as expected and meet the relevant format standards. In addition, all help buttons and links are tested to be sure that they work and "jumps" go to the correct topics. All "Broken links" (i.e., links that do not function properly), usually available as a report from the help development tool, would be determined and resolved. In most cases, experienced help developers will not wait until the help project is completed to test the help output. Testing the output as development proceeds minimizes big problems at the completion of the project.

At a minimum, heuristic evaluations (or inspections) of help topics should be done by the developer prior to delivery to the application software designers for review. It is highly recommended that one or more additional inspections be done by knowledgeable peers, or preferably, "double experts" (i.e., people with expertise in both the application area and help design). Inspectors should use a standardized form to record their inspection results. In addition, inspectors should have: a list of the usability objectives relevant to the product, a description of the user population(s), a list of the tasks users are expected to accomplish with the product, and task scenarios for the major or critical tasks for which the product will be used.

Typically, the application software is not completed to the point that the help system can be generated and run within the application until late in development. As a result, the help testing activities mentioned above are done external to the application interface. Therefore, as soon as there is a running version of the application, developers need to run their help system project within the application software to ensure that all of the controls and windows operate correctly and display as expected.

Usability testing of the integrated help system should be done when there is an operational version of the application available. Whenever possible, usability testing of the help system should be done in conjunction with usability testing of the application's user interface because of the interactive nature of user guidance with normal task performance. In addition, if help developers sit-in on the usability testing, they can record user problems that may be eliminated, or minimized, by additions to the help system. Help system usability testing requires: a usability test plan (that includes a list of the usability objectives for the help system, task scenarios or task procedures users are expected to perform, problem scenarios (to determine whether supporting material provides users with correct information and is easily accessed), typical users (a minimum of 3-5 for each user category), an observation room, logging tools and debriefing questionnaires. Chapter 8 will discuss usability testing in much more detail.

Guidelines

The following guidelines for online help were primarily extracted from the ISO standard on User Guidance (ISO 9241-13, 1998) and the User Guidance Section of the Interaction Techniques Part of the HFES Draft Standard for Trial Use (BSR/HFES 200, Part 3, Section 11, 2003). Additional guidelines have been included based on guidelines proposed by the author while at Telcordia Technologies.

General

- Help information should be readily distinguishable from other types of information displayed (ISO 9241-13, 5.2.2).
  a) There should be a clear distinction between application windows and help windows.
  b) Different types of help information should be clearly distinguishable by using such techniques as spacing, highlighting, fonts, etc.
- Any system initiated guidance messages that are no longer applicable to current system state or user actions should be removed from the display (ISO 9241-13, 5.2.3).
- User initiated guidance should be under control of user (ISO 9241-13, 5.2.4).
- Specific task relevant information should be provided by the help system rather than generic messages (ISO 9241-13, 5.2.5).
- Help should not disrupt the user's task or the continuation of the dialog (ISO 9241-13, 5.2.6).

- To gain the user's attention, use distinctive messages or coding. The messages or coding should be used consistently (ISO 9241-13, 5.2.7).
- If interaction varies with user's expertise, users should be able to specify the level of guidance they desire (ISO 9241-13, 5.2.8).
- The result of an action should be stated before how to execute the action is described (ISO 9241-13, 5.3.1).
- Online help should be phrased to enhance the perception of user control rather than system control of the task, e.g., such statements as "the system will ...." should be avoided (ISO 9241-13, 5.3.2).
- Online help should be worded as positive statements. However, negative statements may be used to denote exceptions or to emphasize a point (ISO 9241-13, 5.3.3).
- Online help should be phrased with consistent grammatical construction (ISO 9241-13, 5.3.4).
- Written or spoken text used in help should be stated in short, simple sentences (ISO 9241-13, 5.3.5).
- Help should be stated in an active voice, unless it conflicts with the user's national language (ISO 9241-13, 5.3.6).
- The terminology used in help should be typical of the user population's job and task terminology (ISO 9241-13, 5.3.7).
- User guidance messages should be worded emotionally neutrally (ISO 9241-13, 5.3.8).

System-initiated help

- System-initiated online help is recommended when:
  a) Users are inexperienced, but need to become proficient quickly (ISO 9241-13, 10.2.1; BSR/HFES 200.3-11, 7.1.1).
  b) Access to the system or application is infrequently and users need reminders to enable effective use (ISO 9241-13, 10.2.1; BSR/HFES 200.3-11, 7.1.1).
  c) Users are unaware of available shortcuts in the system (ISO 9241-13, 10.2.1; BSR/HFES 200.3-11, 7.1.1).
  d) Users have repeatedly used incorrect or inefficient procedures (BSR/HFES 200.3-11, 7.1.1).
- System-initiated online help is not recommended if:
  a) If experienced users do not want the help supplied automatically even though inexperienced users may want the system to present it (ISO 9241-13, 10.2.2; BSR/HFES 200.3-11, 7.2.1).
  b) The online help text presentation interferes with the user's interaction on the main task (ISO 9241-13, 10.2.2; BSR/HFES 200.3-11, 7.2.1).
  c) System/application performance is noticeably degraded by the presentation of the online help information (ISO 9241-13, 10.2.2; BSR/HFES 200.3-11, 7.2.1).
  d) Help contains a great deal of detailed information that may not be needed by all users (BSR/HFES 200.3-11, 7.2.1).
- System-initiated help content should be specific to the task context, e.g., screen, procedure, and the most recent user input (or inputs), e.g., selected object, menu selection, command (ISO 9241-13, 10.2.3; BSR/HFES 200.3-11, 7.1.2).
- System-initiated help should be provided is non-intrusive manner (ISO 9241-13, 10.2.4; BSR/HFES 200.3-11, 7.1.3).   That is:
  a) Presented in an area peripheral to the task area or in a non-overlapping window.
  b) Routine help does not distract the user from main task area.
  c) The help text never overwrites the entire task display.

- Users should be able to turn system-initiated help on and off (ISO 9241-13, 10.2.5; BSR/HFES 200.3-11, 7.1.4).

User-initiated help

- User-initiated help should be provided in most cases, particularly when:
  a) Users vary in their experience with the system and level of expertise.
  b) System-initiated presentation of the help text will interfere with the user's interaction in the main task.
  c) The on-line help contains a large amount of detailed information that may not be needed by all users.
- A simple consistent means of requesting help should be provided (ISO 9241-13, 10.3.1; BSR/HFES 200.3-11, 7.2.2). For example: the "?" key; the function key F1; selection of the help icon; verbally stating "help."
- Aids for locating topics such as a table of contents, an index, key word search capability and full text search capability should be provided in the help system (BSR/HFES 200.3-11, 7.2.3).
- Users should be able to specify help topics when appropriate (ISO 9241-13, 10.3.2; BSR/HFES 200.3-11, 7.2.4). Particularly when:
  a) No task context is available for delimiting the type of on-line help to be provided.
  b) Users will be doing other simultaneous tasks and may need flexibility for choosing the type of help to be provided.
- The system should support user help topic selection (ISO 9241-13, 10.3.3; BSR/HFES 200.3-11, 7.2.5). Particularly when:
  a) The task context will delimit the likely set of topics but not the exact topic needed by the user.
  b) Users need flexibility in choosing the help topic but have trouble accurately specifying the topic without assistance.
- If users specify help topics by methods other than selection, synonyms and close spelling matches should be accepted (ISO 9241-13, 10.3.4; BSR/HFES 200.3-11, 7.2.6).
- Ambiguous help requests should be supported by information relevant to the current task or a dialog requesting clarification of the request (ISO 9241-13, 10.3.5; BSR/HFES 200.3-11, 7.2.7).
- Whenever possible, help should be accessible from anywhere in the application.

Presentation of help information

- Only information relevant to the specific topic should be provided (ISO 9241-13, 10.4.1; BSR/HFES 200.3-11, 7.3.1).
- Help should be presented as quickly as possible after the request (ISO 9241-13, 10.4.2; BSR/HFES 200.3-11, 7.3.2).
- Response time for presentation of help should be predictable (ISO 9241-13, 10.4.3; BSR/HFES 200.3-11, 7.3.3).
- Media that is most appropriate to the topic should be used (ISO 9241-13, 10.4.4; BSR/HFES 200.3-11, 7.3.4). For example: text for descriptive and procedural information; graphics to depict abstractions of real world objects and analogies for structures and processes that are not visible; video to provide visualization of operations; animations to show operations that are not directly visible or scenes that do not exist in reality.

Note: Where possible, alternative media should be provided for different user preferences (BSR/HFES 200.3-11, 7.3.4).
- Help should provide task related information about the system and its purpose (ISO 9241-13, 10.4.5; BSR/HFES 200.3-11, 7.3.5).
- Both descriptive and procedural information as required for the task should be provided (ISO 9241-13, 10.4.6; BSR/HFES 200.3-11, 7.3.6).
- If task/procedural help is provided:
  a) The format should be consistent (BSR/HFES 200.3-11, 7.3.7).
  b) The grammatical structure of topic and procedure titles should be coordinated (BSR/HFES 200.3-11, 7.3.7).
  c) All textually formatted steps listed under a procedure should be numbered (BSR/HFES 200.3-11, 7.3.7).
  d) If appropriate to the step and user action, the results of the action should be described (BSR/HFES 200.3-11, 7.3.7).
  e) If possible, all steps in a procedure should be visible without the need for scrolling (BSR/HFES 200.3-11, 7.3.7).
  f) Help should contain all of the steps necessary to complete the activity.
- Help should provide only the information detail relevant to user's task and expertise in subject area (BSR/HFES 200.3-11, 7.3.8).
- Information should be displayed in form and location best suited to user's task (BSR/HFES 200.3-11, 7.3.9). Such as:
  a) Labels indicating the meaning of screen objects should be displayed adjacent to the objects.
  b) Popups should be used to display brief information that is explanatory in nature.
  c) Separate or secondary windows should be used to provide information referenced in conjunction with other help information or the task.
- Links (hyperlinks) to topics and to popups should be distinguishable from text and from each other (BSR/HFES 200.3-11, 7.3.10)
- Help menus should meet the standards for menus (see ISO 9241-14 and BSR/HFES 200.3).
- Help content should be presented in a well-structured manner that is obvious to the users.
- Lists should be presented using bullets, dashes, numbers, etc.
- At least 50% of screen space within a help topic should be white space.
- Screen elements (e.g., navigation buttons) should be consistently located on the help windows.
- Help windows and popups should appear in appropriate screen positions (as expected by the user).
- Color should be used appropriately and sparingly within the help system (see Chapter 6).
- Help should be obtainable in terms of "How do I?", "About" (What's this), etc.
- If command help is provided, syntax information, lists of related commands and usage examples should be provided.
- If appropriate, tips should be provided within the help.
- Terms should be defined or a glossary provided.
- If appropriate to the task, multiple help windows should be viewable at the same time.

Help navigation and controls

- If help takes the user out of the task dialog, a means should be provided to go back and forth between the dialog and help (ISO 9241-13, 10.5.1; BSR/HFES 200.3-11, 7.4.1).
- If online training and/or documentation is available, links to on-line training and documentation should be provided within the help system (ISO 9241-13, 10.5.2; BSR/HFES 200.3-11, 7.4.2).
- If possible, user control of online help should allow users to:
  a) Configure system-initiated help (turn on/off, select level) (ISO 9241-13, 10.5.3; BSR/HFES 200.3-11, 7.4.3).
  b) Initiate help request as desired (ISO 9241-13, 10.5.3; BSR/HFES 200.3-11, 7.4.3).
  c) Select and change help topic (ISO 9241-13, 10.5.3; BSR/HFES 200.3-11, 7.4.3).
  d) Control the type of help information presented (if different types provided) (ISO 9241-13, 10.5.3; BSR/HFES 200.3-11, 7.4.3).
  e) Exit the help system at any time (ISO 9241-13, 10.5.3; BSR/HFES 200.3-11, 7.4.3).
  f) Go back through topics visited (in reverse order) (BSR/HFES 200.3-11, 7.4.3).
  g) Go forward through the subtopic structure of the current topic (BSR/HFES 200.3-11, 7.4.3).
  h) Navigate through the topic hierarchy to find topics at lower levels of the structure (BSR/HFES 200.3-11, 7.4.3).
  i) Bookmark topics for future access.
  j) Print topics if appropriate to the task.
- If the application system has limited capabilities, modular help should be provided that allows users to select the help information they want to keep on their individual systems (ISO 9241-13, 10.5.4; BSR/HFES 200.3-11, 7.4.4).
- If feasible, users should be able to customize help by annotation, by saving context when switching between help and task, and by adding help topics (ISO 9241-13, 10.5.5; BSR/HFES 200.3-11, 7.4.5).
- If the help is modal, cues indicating that the user is in help mode and a method for exiting the mode should be provided (ISO 9241-13, 10.5.6; BSR/HFES 200.3-11, 7.4.6).
- Movement from topic to topic within the help system should be quick (within 2 seconds).
- Quick access within the help system to navigation buttons or commands should be provided.
- The help system should provide the following navigational supports:
  a) Easy recovery if lost (e.g., return to main menu).
  b) A map of help system showing current location.

Browsable help

- Users should be able to browse through help displays provided in order to gain familiarity with system functions and operating procedures (ISO 9241-13, 10.6.1; BSR/HFES 200.3-11, 7.5.1).
- A listing or map of the online help topics should be provided (ISO 9241-13, 10.6.2; BSR/HFES 200.3-11, 7.5.2).
- Support should be provided for locating a topic within a large number of help topics, such as string search, keyword search, hierarchical structuring, topic maps (ISO 9241-13, 10.6.3; BSR/HFES 200.3-11, 7.5.3).

- If applicable, help should provide: direct links to related topics, cues for links, default browsing path, backup through topics, representation of linkage, and user location markers (ISO 9241-13, 10.6.4; BSR/HFES 200.3-11, 7.5.4).
- Quick-access navigation aids should be provided for help (ISO 9241-13, 10.6.5; BSR/HFES 200.3-11, 7.5.5).
- If the help has a hierarchical structure, it should be supported (ISO 9241-13, 10.6.6; BSR/HFES 200.3-11, 7.5.6) by providing users:
  a) the capability to access the information for a help topic at any level in the hierarchical structure, not just the top;
  b) an obvious and consistent method of accessing more detailed on-line help (i.e., lower levels of on-line help structure);
  c) the capability to navigate directly to the parent topic within the hierarchy.
- If help can be randomly accessed, help information should be self-contained, i.e., the system should not assume users have read previous sections of the help (ISO 9241-13, 10.6.7; BSR/HFES 200.3-11, 7.5.7).
- If help extends beyond a single display and help information scrolls, the topic title should remain visible (ISO 9241-13, 10.6.8; BSR/HFES 200.3-11, 7.5.8).
- If users are not familiar with the help system, a topic (e.g., getting started) describing the structure and navigation through the help system should be provided (BSR/HFES 200.3-11, 7.5.9).

Context sensitive help

- Context sensitive help should be provided when the task has specific steps or contextual information that enables the system to accurately predict the help information needed by the user (ISO 9241-13, 10.7.1; BSR/HFES 200.3-11, 7.6.1).
- Context sensitive help should provide task information on:
  a) aspects (e.g., semantic or lexical; descriptive or procedural) of current dialog step (ISO 9241-13, 10.7.2; BSR/HFES 200.3-11, 7.6.2);
  b) current task (ISO 9241-13, 10.7.2; BSR/HFES 200.3-11, 7.6.2);
  c) current application (ISO 9241-13, 10.7.2; BSR/HFES 200.3-11, 7.6.2);
  d) current transaction (ISO 9241-13, 10.7.2; BSR/HFES 200.3-11, 7.6.2);
  e) current window (screen) or dialog box (BSR/HFES 200.3-11, 7.6.2);
  f) object (e.g., field, control) at the current cursor position (BSR/HFES 200.3-11, 7.6.2);
  g) task information presented on the screen (BSR/HFES 200.3-11, 7.6.2).
- If multiple help topics are relevant for the current dialog step, a default topic should be provided while allowing the user to access other topics (ISO 9241-13, 10.7.3; BSR/HFES 200.3-11, 7.6.3)
- Online help specific to user interface objects should provide an explanation of what the object is, what it does and how to use it (ISO 9241-13, 10.7.4; BSR/HFES 200.3-11, 7.6.4)
- If only a subset of interface objects have help, cues should be provided as to those objects that have help (ISO 9241-13, 10.7.5; BSR/HFES 200.3-11, 7.6.5). For example, the mouse pointer appears as a dark "?" when moved over objects that have on-line help available.

Comprehensibility

- The help information should accurately represent what the software can do.
- If metaphors are used, they should be understandable by users.

- Help icons and buttons clearly communicate their functions.
- If graphics are used in the help system:
  a) functional graphics are used (i.e., graphics that clearly support the task);
  b) the graphics are easy to understand by the user population.

Application links

- If possible, relevant information provided by the help system (e.g., command syntax) can be transferred to application program (cut and paste).
- If appropriate, help uses same interface conventions as application.
- Users should be able to work in the application program while help is being displayed.

Window manipulations

- Help windows should be movable by user so as to allow the user to locate the help window to the most advantageous position for using the information while performing the task.
- If appropriate to the task, help windows should be resizable by user.
- If appropriate to the task, users should be able to minimize help windows so that they can retrieve the information as desired.

COACHES, ADVISORS AND WIZARDS

Coaches and advisors can provide additional functionality to a help system or can be provided as separate performance support features of an application. Wizards are typically added as a separate feature of an application and may not be coordinated with other performance support features.

Coaches

Coaches, like a human mentor, provide active guidance to support a novice or infrequent user. They are intended to support task completion and they provide specific 'how to' information to help a user perform an activity or resolve minor problems. Coaches tend to support learning procedural steps because the user is learning while performing the steps initiated by the coach. Some coaches provide a structured interactive walk through the application's procedural steps. Coaching typically consists of basic information, context-sensitive hints or tips, or procedural steps required to complete a specific, complex task. Coaches are often used as a substitute for a human support person. A coach may be presented automatically by the system, in conjunction with performing a procedure or the user may be able to select a coach by choice to aid in performing a procedure. The coach keeps some control when the user is working in the main window to prevent the worker making errors.

"Cue cards" can be considered as a type of coach, but are less sophisticated in that they do *not* keep control when the user is working in the main window. As a result there is a possibility of the cue card getting out of step with the worker's task in the main window. Cue cards can be used to support procedural tasks, troubleshooting and tasks requiring branching. In addition, they are often used to make an existing software application that cannot be changed more performance-centered. Cue cards present procedural guidance, sequenced either by predetermined logic, or by the user's choices. When used in conjunction with help systems, cue cards provide step-by-step instructions while a user is performing a task, without the rest of the help interface appearing.

Advisors

Advisors provide reasoning support and explanations on complicated application features or tasks. They are appropriate when users need to perform complex tasks and need information as to when and why a step needs to be done or why a particular decision was suggested and what information is required to make the decision. Advisors typically provide hints, explanations of complicated concepts and decision aids when a complex task requiring expertise must be performed. Advisors often can help novices perform tasks and make decisions that come close to those made by experts. They can help the user learn to perform complex tasks, acquire relevant domain knowledge and can contribute to continued performance improvement. Advisors may be presented automatically by the application in response to a particular context or input, or the user may be alerted to the availability of an advisor based on a particular context or input.

The difference between advisors and coaches is basically that a coach provides the how-to information on performing the task, while an advisor provides relevant reasoning support to help the user choose the right action or make the right decision. Sometimes the differences between products called coaches or advisors are blurred in that some coaches provide reasoning support in addition to how-to information and some advisors provide how-to information in addition to reasoning support.

Wizards

Wizards provide direct task guidance and execution support by automating a task through a dialog with the user. They help users complete tasks by providing brief, action-oriented assistance in response to the user's need. Rather than simply telling the user how to perform an activity, wizards:

- present choices
- prompt for input
- progress through the task
- provide preview information concerning consequences
- transform data, screens, or states, and automate tasks

Wizards help users accomplish tasks that may be very complex and/or require experience to perform. A wizard can be used to automate almost any highly structured task in a software application (e.g., creating new objects, formatting a table or paragraph). Wizards actually perform a set of actions in the primary window, unlike cue cards and advisors that only *recommend* an action. Since the wizard does it for them, wizards do not help users learn to perform activities. The use of a wizard may be based on its availability as suggested by the application based on context and user actions or may depend on the user's perceived need or awareness of its existence. In those cases where it is desirable to allow expert users to perform, or modify the work done by a wizard, the wizard interface should allow user intervention in the process and/or results. Wizards are particularly appropriate for complex, mundane tasks that users do not enjoy performing or tasks that require highly structured and rigid inputs (e.g., system installation).

Development Approach

Coach, advisor and wizard development should include the following seven major activities:

- Identifying needs for coach, advisor or wizard
- Developing coach, advisor or wizard requirements
- Preparing the design document
- Developing a prototype of the coach, advisor or wizard
- Testing the prototype
- Developing the software
- Testing and revising the coach, advisor or wizard as necessary

As was the case with the previously discussed performance support products, the need for coaches, advisors and wizards will normally be identified during the analysis of skill and knowledge requirements (see Chapter 5). If the system is a revision to an existing system and a task analysis was done on site, information on the experiences of users with any previous versions of coaches, advisors and wizards will provide additional useful information.

Since the requirements and design documents for coaches, advisors and wizards will be very similar to the documents previously described for other performance support products, only the design approach to developing coaches, advisors and wizards will be covered in this section. However, if the coach, advisor or wizard is an independent, or add-on product, a business case may need to be prepared to justify its development. Also, in such cases, "thin requirements" may be acceptable rather than full requirements documentation.

Coaches

A coach is essentially presented as a series of screens displayed in a secondary (overlay) window that provides help and advice to the user for a complex task in the main window one step at a time. The coach also may provide branches according to the user's current context. Cue cards are typically presented in a modeless popup window. Since coaches are very similar to performance aids in terms of the type of information presented, most of the performance aid development procedures discussed earlier in this chapter will apply to developing coaches. In fact, it can be argued that a coach is simply an online performance aid. The first two of five informational purposes (cue and procedure), listed in Table 7.1 for performance aids, will be equally useful in determining the type of information to include in a coach.

Cue cards are one of the most popular means for providing step-by-step procedural support. While there are several tools to produce cue cards as "embedded" applications separated from the help system, secondary windows with all of the features of cue cards also can be produced within most help development tools. These secondary windows can be accessed as context sensitive help through the application interface. An example of a procedure produced in the cue card style is shown in Figure 7.5

```
┌─────────────────────────────────────────────┐ ▲
│                                               │
│  Updating a Report                            │
│  Schedule                                     │
│                                               │
│  To update a Report Schedule:                 │
│                                               │
│  In the Schedule window:                      │
│                                               │
│     1.  Add or remove any reports you wish.   │
│     2.  Update the date, time or frequency if needed. │
│     3.  Select Schedule > Save. The Save Dialog │
│         will display.                         │
│                                               │
│     Show me│                                  │
│                                               │
│  In the Save Dialog:                          │
│                                               │
│     1.  Select a file or type a file name in File Name. │
│     2.  Click OK.                             │
│                                               │
│  In the Scheduler window:                     │
│                                               │
│        Click Schedule > Run.                  │
│                                               │
│  Result: Selected reports will print at the date and time │
│  scheduled.                                   │
│                                               │
│  Related Topics│                              │ ▼
└─────────────────────────────────────────────┘
```

Figure 7.5 Example of a Cue Card Procedure

Advisors

An advisor is typically presented as a series of screens in the main window or in a secondary window designed to support the user by providing tips, relevant decision support information, diagnosing a problem or situation and providing advice. Advice may be based on associated rules or information, simple decision tree logic or on a more complex set of rules using expert system technology. To be effective, an advisor should:

- Support the immediate work activity (i.e., be context sensitive to the step being performed within the application).
- Be based on human expert experience (using knowledge engineering) to ensure continuity of organizational knowledge.
- Integrate organizational policies and procedures.
- Provide consistent rules for interpretation and application.
- Provide detailed explanatory capabilities.
- Simplify decision making by reducing information overload and tedious data analysis.
- Provide an advisory role, an active role or both.

As was the case with coaches, advisors also are very similar to performance aids in terms of the type of information presented. Therefore, many of the performance aid development procedures discussed earlier in this chapter should apply to developing advisors. The last three of the five informational purposes (association, relationship and example), listed in Table 7.1 for performance aids, are also appropriate to the design of advisors. Advisors can be simple (provide descriptive information to support decisions) or complex (require the user to proceed through a dialog to determine the best information or solution to offer).

One example of a simple advisor is "The Fair Labor Standards Act (FLSA) Advisor" (FLSA Advisor, 2003) developed by the Department of Labor. This advisor provides employers and employees with information needed to understand Federal minimum wage, overtime, child labor and recordkeeping requirements. When you start The FLSA Advisor, it provides a brief explanation of what the FLSA does and does not require and then provides an opportunity to review answers to frequently asked questions or to explore information on FLSA coverage, child labor rules, determining hours worked and other FLSA topics. It also provides links to more detailed information (e.g., regulatory text, publications and organizations). Figure 7.6 depicts one of the FLSA Advisor screens.

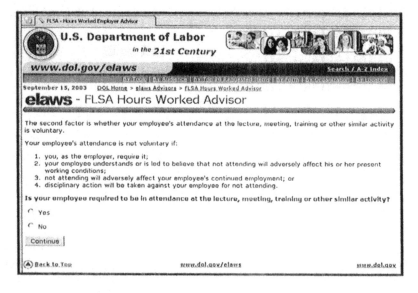

Figure 7.6 FLSA Hours Worked Advisor Screen

Typically, a complex advisor is context-initiated (i.e., on the basis of a user action or step in a task supported by the advisor). If the advisor is system initiated, it should be possible for the user to turn-off the advisor if they do not need or want the advice. Where the advisor is selectable by user, the availability of the advisor should be clearly indicated in the interface (e.g., an "Advisor" button on the task window).

Complex advisors require the design of a series of screens and dialogs. In order to lead the user through the decision process, the screens should proceed in a logical sequence and each screen should be as simple and straightforward as possible. Figure 7.7 shows an example of an advisor screen from the Telcordia Performance Support Project Estimator. This is the first screen in a serious of screens that provides advice on setting the parameters that govern the calculations that determine the outcome of the project estimate. If the user continues using the Set Parameters Advisor, they will be led through the setting of all 14 parameters affecting the deliverable estimate. However, the user can stop using the advisor at any time and set the parameter directly through the user interface. Also, notice that the screen shown in Figure 7.7 specifies the screen that user is on and the number of screens in the advisor dialog.

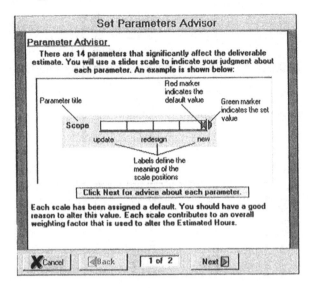

Figure 7.7 Initial Set Parameters Advisor Screen
(Source – Telcordia Performance Support Project Estimator, Copyright © 2000 Telcordia
Technologies, Inc., Produced with Permission.)

The key question to ask in the design of advisor screens is: "what specific information does the user need?" to make the best decision possible in choosing steps or providing input in support of a particular task. Zachary (1986) listed the following six common situations that require support by decision aids:

- Inability to predict processes.
- Difficulty in combining competing attributes or objectives related to the outcome of the decision.
- Inability to manage the information needed to make the decision.
- Difficulty in analyzing or reasoning about the decision problem.
- Difficulty in visualizing the decision problem.
- Difficulty in making quantitative heuristic judgments.

To aid novices, provide a default solution for the various user inputs required by the advisor (see Figure 7.7). By providing default values based on expert judgments, new users will be able to quickly use the advisor; and, as they become more experienced, will be able to experiment with these default values.

In many cases, products called advisors are more like wizards in that they automate many of the steps in the task as well as provide advice.

Wizards

A wizard is a task-oriented interface displayed in a secondary window to perform some task in the main window. A wizard should be designed so only the information necessary to complete a task is gathered from the user. Typically, wizards are presented as a series of steps or pages (dialogues) that help the user accomplish a specific task. The pages or dialogues include the controls needed to gather input from the user and navigate through the wizard's steps. If the wizard will handle a complex task and consist of more than a few pages, it will require an introductory (e.g., "welcome") page and a completion page.

Since wizards are secondary windows, they also require a clear title on each of the wizard windows. Figure 7.8 depicts a wizard initial page with a title.

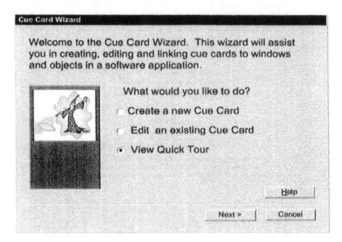

Figure 7.8 Example of a Wizard Welcome Screen

In addition to having a title, it is useful to provide a graphic on the wizard pages that signifies what the wizard does (see Figure 7.8 example). The tool used to prepare the sample wizard pages in this book was Microsoft Visio which allows you to easily develop wizard page examples (including text boxes and control buttons). Such examples should be included in the wizard design document to depict the wizard page layout and design. Visio allows the insertion of standard Windows dialog box controls (e.g., single-click buttons, check boxes or list boxes; or custom controls that provide more complex functionality, such as animation). The controls also can be programmed by writing an "event procedure" in the drawing's Microsoft Visual Basic for Applications (VBA) project. With the use of Visual Basic, a prototype of the wizard (pages and controls) can be developed to demonstrate the wizard's functionality.

The following commands for navigating through a wizard should be provided as buttons at the bottom of the wizard window (Microsoft, 2002):

- < Back – Returns to previous page (not used on initial page).
- Next> – Moves to next page in the dialog sequence.
- Cancel – Discards any user entries and terminates the process.
- Finish – Completes task and applies any user-selected or default settings from all of the pages (used on last page).

In addition to the above commands, it is a good idea to add a help button on pages of wizards that may contain complex operations or require explanation. Also, for a complex wizard it is useful to provide a "quick tour" selection on the beginning page (see Figure 7.8) so that users can get a quick overview of the wizards function and operation.

A flow chart depicting the navigation through the pages of the wizard is an important aid in both designing the wizard and in describing it in the design document. Such a flow chart should clearly depict the linking to other pages and information processing resulting from the selection of the various options available on each of the wizard's pages.

As noted above, wizards should not cause the user to provide any more information than absolutely necessary. If the information to be provided is available from an existing file, the user should be able to identify the file so that the information can be "pasted-in" by the wizard. Wherever existing information may be available, the wizard dialog should ask the user if they would like to enter it in place of creating new information. This would be accomplished by a dialog enabling the user to locate and select the file to be used. Figure 7.9 shows an example of such a dialog.

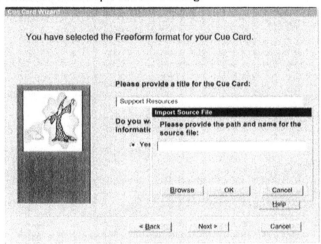

Figure 7.9 Sample Wizard Page with Source File Dialog

The wizard should simplify the users input task by providing as much structure as possible. Also, the wizard should provide any standard or repetitive information rather than have the user provide it. Figure 7.10 provides an example of a table creation dialog.

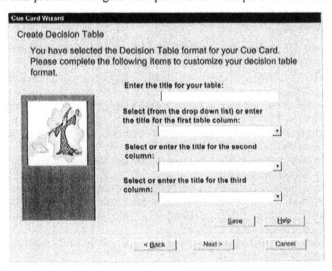

Figure 7.10 Sample Wizard Page for Creating a Table

Where there are sections (or operations) within a wizard, it may be useful to create subtitles for each operation and place them at the top of the wizard pages involving that operation (see sample subtitle in Figure 7.10). If the operation is not self-explanatory, a short description of the operation also should be included under the subtitle.

When designing wizard pages, it is important to make the actions of the wizard and the requirements for user's inputs as simple and self-explanatory as possible. It is better to have a large number of simple pages with few choices than a small number of complex pages with many choices or a great deal of text (Microsoft, 2002).

Guidelines

The following list provides some guidelines for design of coaches, advisors and wizards:

General

- Coaches, advisors and wizards should be tied closely to the work context or task on hand (McGraw, 1997).
- The size and location of the coach, advisor or wizard window should not impede the view of the application window (McGraw, 1997).
- Coaches, advisors and wizards should reflect a consistent, identifiable design (McGraw, 1997).
- Names (or titles) of coaches, advisors and wizards should be short and consistent (McGraw, 1997).
- A statement of purpose (Microsoft, 2002), a brief description or an introduction should be provided on the first page (McGraw, 1997).
- The steps provided in a coach, advisor or wizard should be clear (McGraw, 1997).
- Descriptive text should be clearly distinguishable from text prompting input (McGraw, 1997).

Coaches and Advisors

- The content of a coach or advisor should consist of task-specific hints, tips and reasoning support (McGraw, 1997).
- The content of coaches or advisors should represent "best practice" or strategy (McGraw, 1997).
- Coach or advisor content should be complete enough to act upon without being too wordy (McGraw, 1997).
- If the coaching or advice is triggered by the system, users should be able to turn it off when desired (McGraw, 1997).
- If triggered by the user, it should be clear to the user on how to activate a coaching or advice feature (McGraw, 1997).
- Coaches and advisors should provide the capability to send back data to the application screen to help the user to complete a task (McGraw, 1997).
- Users should be able to add comments or annotations to coaches and advisors (McGraw, 1997).
- Advisors should enable users to ask "why?" and receive explanations of the tip, rule or suggestion offered (McGraw, 1997).

Wizards

- Wizards should enable novice users to complete critical tasks quickly (McGraw, 1997).
- Unless the task is simple or done infrequently, wizards should be used to supplement rather than replace the user's direct ability to perform a specific task (Microsoft, 2002).
- Wizards should help users interactively complete a specific objective or goal, performing a task for the user, based on user inputs (McGraw, 1997).
- Alternatives available from the wizard should provide the user with positive results (Microsoft, 2002).
- Wizards should be designed to hide many of the steps and much of the complexity of a given task (Microsoft, 2002).
- The manner in which the system suggests or presents an option to access a wizard should not detract the user from the task at hand (McGraw, 1997).
- The display of the wizard window should allow the user to recognize it as the primary point of input (Microsoft, 2002).
- The wizard should not require a user to leave the wizard to complete a task (Microsoft, 2002).
- Wizards should clearly indicate how the user either proceeds or quits (McGraw, 1997).
- It should be obvious to the user how to proceed when the wizard has been completed (Microsoft, 2002).
- The Wizard should prompt the user through a clear succession of steps (McGraw, 1997).
- Pages should not be advanced automatically because users may not be able to read the information before the page advances (Microsoft, 2002).
- The user should always remain in control of the wizard, e.g., go back and change a previous response, go forward, clear all, complete (McGraw, 1997; Microsoft, 2002).
- Wizard text should be short, concise and simple and displayed in an uncluttered manner (McGraw, 1997; Microsoft, 2002), but not condescending (Microsoft, 2002).
- Minimize the number of pages that require the use of a secondary window (Microsoft, 2002).
- Ensure that users know that graphic illustrations on wizard pages are not interactive by providing suitable visual differentiation (Microsoft, 2002).
- Provide default values or settings for all controls where possible (Microsoft, 2002).
- Use words like "you" and "your" and start most questions with phrases like "Which option do you want..." (Microsoft, 2002).
- Avoid the use of technical terminology that may confuse novice users (Microsoft, 2002).

INSTRUCTION

As noted in Chapter 1, instruction can be provided by an instructor, by a paper self-instructional text or by a computer. In addition, the instructional media may be very simple (e.g., text) or highly complex (interactive graphics and video). The major goal of instruction in an application performance support system is to enable the user to learn to use the application as quickly as possible so that they can successfully accomplish their work tasks.

Development Approach

The need for instruction (or training) should have been identified during the analysis of skill and knowledge requirements (see Chapter 5). If the system is a revision to an existing system and any follow-up evaluation was done on the current training, such evaluations will provide very useful insights on the modification of existing training and the development of any new instruction. Most instructional development processes are based on the Instructional System Development (ISD) model popularized by Branson et al (1975) and Gagne (1988). The ISD model has many variations but all involve five basic phases: analysis, design, development, implementation and evaluation. It should be noted that these five phases are quite similar to the phases for developing a performance support system. Since in the development of a PSS the analysis phase (as described in Chapter 4 and 5) is intended to support the development of all of the performance support products, in this section we will concentrate on those activities specifically relevant to instructional develop, i.e.:

• Identifying needs for instruction.
• Developing instructional requirements requirements.
• Designing instruction.
• Developing a prototype of online instruction designs.
• Testing the prototype.
• Developing the instruction.
• Testing and revising the instruction as necessary.

Identifying Needs

As was the case with other performance support products, the need for instruction should have been determined during the analysis of skill and knowledge requirements. Skill and knowledge requirements are particularly important for determining both the need for instruction and the type of instruction required. If skill and knowledge requirements were not derived, application functions and associated user task requirements must be analyzed to determine the needs for instruction. Each task or procedure should be evaluated in terms of how and when it is performed, who will perform it, the environment in which it is performed, and the skill and knowledge needed to perform it. In addition, it is important for the development of instruction to obtain information concerning the backgrounds and probable skills and knowledge of the person(s) that are expected to perform the task or procedure. Also, the environment in which the instruction is likely to be administered needs to be determined.

If possible, instructional designers should derive skills and knowledge on the basis of the process described in Chapter 5. If time is not available to perform a complete analysis, however, at least every user task should be reviewed to assess the need for instruction. This can be done by reviewing the steps being performed and making a decision on each step as to whether it can be done just by following the description of the step or requires additional skill, knowledge or practice to perform. Assumptions about the additional knowledge required should be listed to aid in instructional development.

It is important to keep in mind that any user support tools, e.g., online help and advisors, may also require instruction (or diminish the need for instruction) and their use within the application should be included as part of the analysis of task instructional needs.

Instructional Requirements

Objectives provide the major basis for instructional requirements. Designing instruction or training on the basis of objectives was popularized by Mager (1975) and his approach to specifying objectives is still one of the most widely used. Mager states that a correctly stated instructional objective will: identify the performance, the conditions, and the criterion of acceptable performance. It is easy to see that instructional objectives and requirements have a great deal of similarity. Mager further clarifies the characteristics of these three components of an objective as follows:

Performance – An objective always states what a learner is expected to be able to do.

Conditions – An objective always includes the major conditions (if any) under which the performance is to be accomplished.

Criterion – An objective (when possible) states the criterion of acceptable performance by describing how well it must be performed in order to be considered acceptable.

An example of an objective including the above three components would be: "Prepare a cue card for the tasks and steps listed in handout A, using the cue card wizard, with 100% accuracy in 10 minutes." In some cases, objectives are stated with the condition first, for example: "Using the cue card wizard and the list of tasks and steps listed in handout A, prepare a cue card in 10 minutes with 100% accuracy." It really doesn't matter which format is used as long as it is used consistently.

Instructional objectives are typically classified as either terminal objectives or enabling (interim) objectives. Terminal objectives are those objectives that specify what the learner is expected to accomplish at the end of an entire course (e.g., perform a series of tasks comprising a job function) or part of a course (e.g., perform a single task). Enabling objectives, on the other hand, specifies what is to be accomplished after completing portions of the course (e.g., lessons) and is intended to impart perquisite knowledge or skills necessary to enable the performance of terminal objectives. There is also another kind of terminal objective, "post-course objective," that is often stated within training requirements documents. Post-course objectives are those objectives that state what the individual that has successfully met the course objectives is expected to accomplish after a specified time on the job. The post-course objectives take into account learning on the job and guidance from supervisors and co-workers.

However, instructional objectives can also be defined multi-dimensionally in terms of: behavior, use, source/specificity and time. Each of these has the following characteristics:

- Behavior – relates to the *type of behavior* required and its fidelity to actual job behavior. For example:
  a) Real job behavior
  b) Simulated job behavior
  c) Mediating (covert) behavior

- Use – relates to *how* the objectives are used in the instructional development or instructional process, including:
  a) Strategy development
  b) Content development
  c) Criterion test item derivation
  d) Learner motivation or guidance

- Source/Specificity – relates to *where* the objectives are derived and their level of specificity. Sources include:
  a) Job activity statement (job, position or duty, task, step, etc.)

b) Behavioral requirements (overt as well as covert) delineated from task analysis (usually in the form of skill and knowledge requirements).

- Time – relates to *when* the objective is used and interacts with the use dimension. The following points in time are relevant:
  a) Post-course (after)
  b) End-of-course (end)
  c) End-of-unit/lesson (intermediate end)
  d) Within unit or lesson (during)

Using the above dimensions a terminal objective can be defined as: 1) requiring real or simulated job behavior, 2) used for criterion test item derivation, content development and (possibly) strategy development, 3) derived from job performance statements (task, subtask, steps) and 4) met at the end of the course, unit or lesson. Likewise, enabling or interim objectives can be defined as: 1) requiring mediating behavior, 2) used for strategy and content development, 3) derived from skill and knowledge requirements and 4) met within the lesson context.

From the above discussion, it is evident that instructional requirements are essentially based on terminal objectives while enabling objectives are a product of the instructional design process.   Also, it is important to note that a terminal objective requires the accomplishment of either real or simulated job behavior.   If skills and knowledge were derived using the process presented in Chapter 5, the specific activity skill statements can be used to develop terminal objectives.   Since specific activity skill statements list the behavior and provide accuracy, rate and level of completion information, they can be easily converted into terminal objective statements.   The only thing that needs to be added is the degree to which the required performance is to be demonstrated after instruction (accuracy, rate, level), how it is to be demonstrated (actual or at some level of simulation) and the conditional information. Conditional information will typically include the context in which the learner will demonstrate proficiency (e.g., equipment used, aids provided, etc.). For example, the objective may include the use of the help system in accomplishing the task.

In those cases where skill and knowledge data are not available, the easiest method for deriving terminal objectives is to take each of the task statements and write an objective for it based on the criteria stated above and the information collected during needs analysis. It is very important to realistically state the performance expected of the learner upon completing the instruction to be provided on the task. After completing the terminal objectives for each task, terminal objectives can be completed for the higher-level procedures (or task groupings). Again, these can be stated in terms of being able to accomplish the procedure at a particular criterion level under a set of conditions.

After developing the terminal objectives for the procedures, the procedures can be grouped into tentative courses based on their relevancy to intended end-users and support people. However, it is important to keep each of the task or procedures as specific modules to ensure reuse as performance support components. In addition to the list of terminal objectives for each of the procedures and tasks to be accomplished using the application, instructional requirements need to address some additional aspects of the instruction. The instructional requirements should clearly specify the target population for each of the identified courses. If the format of the instruction has been established (e.g., instructor-led, web-based), this format and associated requirements need to be stated in the requirements document. Also, if there are time limitations (i.e., the length for instructional segments), these limitations should be stated in the requirements.

Designing Instruction

Instructional design approaches based on learning theory (Gagne, 1985) assume that there are different kinds of instructional goals and that different instructional strategies are required to effectively and efficiently attain a given goal. Instructional design theories based on this assumption include three components: a descriptive theory of knowledge and skills to be learned, a descriptive theory of the required instructional strategies to promote learning and a prescriptive theory that correlates skills and knowledge with appropriate strategies (Merrill, 1996). Gagne (1985) suggested that the learning tasks for intellectual skills should be organized into a hierarchy based on complexity, i.e., stimulus recognition, response generation, procedure following, use of terminology, discriminations, concept formation, rule application and problem solving. The purpose of the hierarchy is to identify prerequisites that need to be completed to facilitate learning at each level.

There are a number of excellent books on instructional design, e.g., *Instructional Design Theory* (Merrill, 1994), *Designs for Instructional Designers* (Markle, 1983), *Designing Effective Instruction* (Morrison et al, 2001), *Multimedia-based Instructional Design* (Lee and Owens, 2000). The design approach presented in this chapter represents an integration of methods proposed by Gagne, Merrill and others with modifications based on the author's experience in developing instruction for computer system applications. However, a major difference in the design approach proposed here is the emphasis on the task (or procedure) as the major module of instruction. The reason for the emphasis on the task is that carefully designed task instructional modules are better able to support immediate job performance and can be integrated more easily into a full performance support system.

In terms of the objectives model discussed in the section above, instructional design involves the analysis of each terminal objective to determine the enabling objectives and associated instructional strategies necessary to provide mastery of the terminal objective. To accomplish this, sufficient information must be available from task analysis data to derive enabling objectives. If skills and knowledge were derived using the procedures provided in Chapter 5, enabling objectives can be extracted from the skill and knowledge requirements. If not, each terminal objective (as derived in the requirements step above) should be analyzed to determine the associated skills and knowledge needed to accomplish it. Using the skill and knowledge derivation process described in Chapter 5 will make this easier.

The resultant enabling objectives can then be sequenced into the "instructional steps" required to accomplish the terminal objectives. The first step in sequencing is to analyze the skills and knowledge associated with each enabling object to determine their commonalities and dependencies. Those skills and knowledge that are common to a number of enabling objectives and terminal objectives need to be learned first and would, therefore, come first in the sequence.

When all of the instructional steps are identified, learning maps (Gagne, 1985) can be prepared. Learning maps are essentially a flow chart of the hierarchical and linear relationships of the instructional steps (or their associated skills and knowledge). It is important to note that intellectual skills, such as problem solving or learning rules and concepts, are hierarchical while procedural skills are essentially linear. However, procedural skills may require the use of intellectual skills for accomplishment. By using learning maps, the dependencies and commonalities of various enabling skills and knowledge will become more obvious. Figure 7.11 depicts a simplified version of a learning map for designing a screen. Note that the learning map is a bottom-up structure with the enabling skill and knowledge depicted below the higher-level skill. At the top of the learning map is the terminal objective to be met (in this case, the design of a screen).

A more complete version of the learning map for designing a screen would show the steps in the design with the associated skills and knowledge required for each step.

Figure 7. 11 Example of Learning Map for Designing a Screen

The next activity in the design process is to identify the most appropriate instructional strategy for each instructional step. This can be accomplished by first determining the "instructional function" to be served by the objective and then determining strategies that support that function. Instructional functions are similar to the events of instruction proposed by Gagne (1985). The "Instructional Strategy Selection Aid" provided in Annex A can be used to determine relevant instructional strategies that support the identified instructional steps.

After the instructional strategies have been determined, the technique for carrying each strategy needs to be determined. In Chapter 5, instructional techniques were listed in conjunction with the Performance Support Selection Aid to help in the preliminary selection of appropriate methods to enable performance. However, this was just an initial judgment and actual decisions about instructional techniques (i.e., the manner by which the instructional content is to be provided to the learner) must be based on the enabling objectives instructional strategies as determined above. Each of the instructional strategies can be evaluated in terms of the use of the following instructional techniques (see Chapter 5 for descriptions):

- Lecture
- Tutorial/dialogue
- Drill and Practice
- Inquiry or Generative
- Demonstration
- Role Playing
- Games
- Discussion
- Simulation
- Exploration
- Evaluation
- Hands-on Practice
- Supervised Practice
- On-the-job Practice
- On-the-job Performance

Since most computer system tasks involve interacting with the system, the most desirable performance-based approach is to provide instruction using the system itself or a simulation of the system. Therefore, lecture, role-playing or discussion would be less desirable techniques. In addition, games or exploration are fine for learning outside of the job environment, but are generally not very efficient for learning to perform system activities.

Upon completing the selection of the most appropriate techniques for delivering the various instructional components, a decision needs to be made as to how the instruction will be delivered, i.e.: instructor-led, an online tutorial, computer-based instruction or a task tutorial.

Instructor-led training is appropriate for material that is quite complex and the instructor is an application expert; when the system delivery time is too short to develop online training; and when the instructor is a subject matter expert that was involved in the development of the system. Since an online tutorial can be delivered by means of various media (CDs, downloaded from a server to the users desktop computer or via the web), it is a good candidate for delivery of instruction associated with computer system applications. Computer Based Training (CBT), while similar to an on-line tutorial, typically includes testing and tracking of student performance. Therefore, CBT should be used for instruction that requires the demonstration of competency to perform in the job environment. The task tutor provides the most performance-based approach to delivering instruction because it is an interactive dialog that simulates the task or function to be learned. Task tutors are particularly useful for tasks that are extremely difficult to learn, complex or critical. Task tutors also can be assembled together into larger CBT components that can be used for training new users of an application. A useful design approach is to determine the skills and knowledge (enabling objectives) that are common to the various tasks (the learning maps described above will facilitate this activity) and use online tutorials for delivering this material. Then use task tutors as the means of delivering all of the task-related instruction.

As a result of the previous activities, a description of each of the instructional modules that are to be included in the course is developed. The description includes the terminal and enabling objectives to be accomplished, the instructional steps and strategies, and the method of delivery. These descriptions are assembled together into a course description and included in the design document for that course. The course description also should describe the course's target population and contain a list of the required enabling objectives (as prerequisites) that are to be provided by other instruction (e.g., instruction for the common enabling objectives mentioned above).

Prototypes

If instruction is to be delivered electronically by means of a new or revised online delivery interface or tool, a prototype of the instructional interface and delivery mechanism should be developed and tested prior to the development of the instruction istelf. As was the case with the help prototype discussed earlier in this chapter, the instructional delivery prototype should be developed using the development tool specified in the requirements or the design document. A sample instructional lesson, or lessons, should be prepared and run to demonstrate the features and "look and feel" of the online delivery system. After determining that the prototype instruction displays and functions as expected and represent the design specifications, the prototype should be demonstrated to various stakeholders for evaluation. Changes to the prototype, and potentially to the design document, would be made on the basis of this evaluation.

Criterion Tests

If possible, criterion test items should be developed prior to the instructional content. This is also an important development strategy for instruction that will not require test items to be completed by learners. Criterion tests provide a means for evaluating a course in terms of whether it meets its stated objectives. A criterion reference test measures what an individual can do or knows, compared to what he/she must be able to do or must know in order to successfully perform a task (Swezey and Pearlstein, 1975). Although criterion tests can be very useful for measuring learner performance, they are essential for ensuring that the course accomplishes what it is intended to. In such cases, the criterion test is measuring the course, not the learners. At the very least, criterion test items should be developed for each of the terminal objectives included in a course. A criterion test item is essentially a restatement of an objective in terms of the specific conditions and the manner in which it is to be measured after the instruction. The specific conditions include the test environment (e.g., simulated computer input screen) and the material provided (e.g., description of a task scenario, multiple choice statements to be evaluated as correct) to the learner to support the test. The most useful criterion test items are those that require the learner to perform a task activity (terminal objective) that is a reasonable sample of the performance expected on the job.

Developing Instruction

Instructional development is the preparation of the content required to support each of the instructional steps and associated strategies described in the design document. It is highly recommended that the development of a particular course or module be done linearly (i.e., from the beginning of the sequence to the end) to minimize repetition and ensure logical progression. To develop instructional content, developers need to obtain as much familiarity with the subject area as possible. This is usually accomplished by reading all of the available reference materials, talking to application experts and performing the relevant user tasks using the application software (if possible). If an operational version of the application software is not available, instructional developers should simulate the task activities by going through the task steps and referring to the design specification of screens, inputs, etc. Of course, content prepared on the basis of the simulation method will need to be verified once an operational version of the application is available.

There are a number of excellent books available on developing various kinds of instruction, e.g., *The ASTD Handbook of Training Design and Development* (ASTD, 1999), *Computer-Based Instruction: Methods and Development* (Alessi and Trollip, 1991), *Computer-Based Instruction: Design and Development* (Gibbons and Fairweather, 1998), *Designing Web-based Training* (Horton, 2000) and *The Design, Development and Evaluation of Instructional Software* (Hannafin and Peck, 1997). The reader is encouraged to look at these books for more detailed information about the development of specific types of instructional content. This chapter is not intended to provide detailed methodology for producing instructional materials. Instead, a simple practical process that includes the following steps will be discussed:

1. Develop a storyboard (or lesson plan for instructor-led instruction) for the instructional sequence, including each instructional step.
2. Develop the information required to support each instructional step (enabling objective) utilizing the designated strategy.
3. Develop an exercise to reinforce the learner's understanding of that information (e.g., a multiple choice exercise with feedback).
4. Develop a test, or exercise, to test the learner's ability to utilize the material learned to perform a subtask, or task step (terminal objective).
5. Repeat the above for each of the terminal objectives and then develop a performance test (or use the criterion test) to test the learner's ability to meet the course terminal objectives (e.g., perform a task or procedure).

Storyboarding is a useful method for depicting how the instructional material will be presented. It is particularly useful for computer presentation (by the web or a stand-alone computer) because a storyboard includes the layout of the information on the screen. While the learning maps, or instructional step flowcharts, depict the lesson sequence, storyboards depict the content and presentation of the material. The storyboard contains a sketch of the visual aspect of the screen, information to be present, descriptions of animations, interactions, sounds and any other media. Storyboards are typically a series of forms that represent the screens (or windows) in which instruction is to be presented. A different form may be utilized for different presentation windows (e.g., text, exercise, review). Each form type should include the standard controls that will be provided (e.g., back, next, beginning, menu). In addition, branching as a result of user response should be clearly indicated on each storyboard form. Storyboard forms should provide areas to describe all of the various media used to present information. The form also should contain a remarks column so that special situations can be addressed. Figure 7.12 provides a sample of a general storyboard form that includes the elements listed above. The text (or description of the text) to be presented would be shown in the screen area (outlined in bold) as well as the location of other elements such as buttons and graphics.

Title		Screen No.	Date
		Remarks	
		_____	
		_____	
		_____	
		_____	
		_____	
		_____	
		_____	
		_____	
		_____	
		_____	
		_____	
Control	**Description/Action**	**Media**	

Figure 7.12 Example of a Storyboard Form

In the case of instructor-led instruction, a lesson plan should be developed to describe the training content. A lesson plan is similar to a storyboard in that it describes the content to be presented, but it does not cover the layout of the content. It does, however, specify the format of the instructional media (e.g., slides, video, hands-on-exercises) and the student materials (e.g., performance aids, handouts) to be used. The lesson plan is intended to provide as much detail as needed to allow any new instructor to use this lesson plan to present the instruction and with minimum preparation time. As was noted earlier, instructor-led training is often the most cost-effective approach for instruction on new applications where the instructor is also an application expert. Since the instructor knows the material well, typically less specific instructional content needs to be developed.

After the storyboard, or lesson plan, has been developed, the content to be presented is prepared. A statement of the objective to be met should always be stated before the content to ensure that the learner is focused on what is to be learned. This is true of both the course and the lessons, or topics. Learner objectives are simply a restatement of the terminal and enabling objectives in learner terms (e.g., "At the completion of this topic, you should be able to - - - "). It is very important when developing instructional material to only present the material necessary to support the specific objectives to be met. If initial testing indicates that more material needs to be added, it can be added on the basis of test results. However, if a course contains unnecessary material, it is difficult to determine that it is unnecessary during testing. If skills and knowledge were derived using the approach described in Chapter 5, the content to be provided can be directly derived from the skill and knowledge statements associated with each of the enabling objectives. Providing content only to enable those specific skills and knowledge will help minimize the inclusion of unnecessary material.

The development of appropriate exercises is a critical component of instructional development. Exercises are an informal check to determine if learners are learning. They can be as simple as asking one or two review questions or as complex as asking learners to demonstrate performance. Many forms of exercises can be developed such as true-false questions, multiple choice questions, matching, fill-in items, and completing a series of steps using the application (or a simulated version). Figure 7.13 shows an example of a matching exercise developed using ToolBook Instructor. It should be noted that the topic objectives are provided in conjunction with the quiz items in this example. In fact, it is worthwhile to provide topic objectives on every page of the topic to reinforce what is to be learned if space is available.

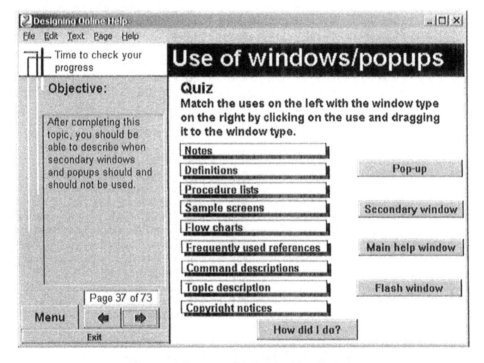

Figure 7.13 Example of a Matching Exercise

Exercises are important in instruction delivered either by an instructor or by computer. In our experience, the most successful instructor-led computer application courses included many hands-on exercises using the system. These exercises usually consisted of a scenario, relevant data and instructions to the learner. The learner uses these materials to perform specific activities on the system and the instructor critiques the results. Typically a training database is developed so that learners can perform simulated application tasks on the system, but not the live operational system (i.e., not with the real operational database). Often test case materials (see Chapter 8) can be used to develop learner exercises. Computer-based instruction also may utilize a training database for exercises. However, in the case of computer delivery, the exercises are built into the self-instructional format of the lesson and the computer evaluates the results.

Depending on the nature of the instruction, it may be necessary to provide remedial instruction for incorrect responses to exercises or test questions. Remedial instruction is essentially instruction provided to remedy a deficiency (incorrect response) by providing additional instruction. If the instruction is to be developed and delivered by computer, many development tools provide mechanisms for creating remedial branching. In the case of task tutors, remedial instruction is very important because the purpose of the task tutor is to ensure that the learner can perform the task correctly.

Performance tests also are very important components of a task tutor as well as other performance-based instruction. A performance test differs from a performance exercise in that it is intended to require the utilization of all of the skill and knowledge related to performing the task or procedure. On the other hand, an exercise requires the utilization of the subset of skills and knowledge involved with performing a portion of the task or procedure. In other words, a performance exercise is *part task* performance, while a performance test is *whole task* performance.

If a help system will be available to assist users while using the computer application, the use of the help system should be built into the instruction. For example, a module in the introductory course, or prerequisite instruction, should describe the help system and provide exercises for finding various materials within help. In addition, task specific instruction should contain exercises that include the use of the help system in performing task activities.

Instructional Development Tools

There are a number of tools available to develop computer-based instruction (e.g., web and CBT). At the simplest level, Microsoft PowerPoint or similar presentation tools can be used to author an instructional presentation. While a PowerPoint slideshow is usually linear, it can include hyperlinks to jump to other sections allowing learners to get more detail or to branch to another section of the instruction. PowerPoint presentations also can include audio and video clips. However, the development of exercises, tests and test scoring is very difficult when using PowerPoint. Resultant presentations can be distributed as a CBT or as Web-Based Training (WBT). Generally, PowerPoint would be a good choice for the development of instructor-led training, but not CBT or WBT. Macromedia's Breeze Presentation Platform (Macromedia, 2003) provides a means to use PowerPoint to create content and media and to publish the content to an on-demand web-based content library that can be viewed, searched and repurposed. Quizzes and surveys also can be added to measure knowledge transfer. Additional Breeze modules extend the Breeze Presentation platform, i.e., the Breeze Training module enables delivery and tracking of training, while Breeze Live adds live meeting and presentation delivery. Since the quiz development feature of Breeze is somewhat limited, it is not ideal for developing full featured online instruction.

Several other Macromedia products, such as Director and Dreamweaver, have been used for the development of WBT and CBT. Director supports the creation of interactive content utilizing long video streams, photo-quality images, audio, animation, 3D models, text and Macromedia Flash content. The resultant material can be deployed on CD, DVD, kiosks or the web. Dreamweaver has become a very popular tool for the development of websites and web-based applications as well as the management of websites. It provides a combination of visual layout tools, application development features and code editing support. In addition, it includes Cascading Style Sheet (CSS) based design and integration. Both tools support the creation of accessible content for people with disabilities. While great for creating multimedia content, Director and Dreamweaver do not contain any of the specialized features for the development of instructional content such as templates, exercises, tests, test scoring, etc.

Two of the most popular authoring tools for producing CBT and WBT are Macromedia's Authorware and Click2Learn's ToolBook. Authorware contains the functionality of Director, but also has special features specifically aimed at developing instructional software. Authorware 7 (Macromedia, 2003) utilizes a visual interface for the development of media-rich learning applications without the use of scripting. Icons are dragged and dropped to create the application's logical outline, and then menus are used to add content. Authorware provides templates and wizards that address common learning functionality (e.g., student logons, course frameworks, questions, and quizzes). Interactivity is provided by 11 different response types. Knowledge Objects (pre-built templates with wizards) are used to accelerate the creation of content by dragging and dropping them from the Knowledge Object gallery and then fill in the content. Developers also can create their own reusable models or Knowledge Objects. Authorware provides facilities for button creation, such as interactive graphical buttons, check boxes, radio buttons and other user interface elements. In addition, interface controls (e.g., buttons, check boxes, radio buttons, combo boxes, list boxes, masked text fields and tab sets) can be used to create user interfaces and simulate other software applications. Authorware also can automatically track student results with built-in tracking functions and variables. It handles a variety of media types, including Macromedia Flash MX and Microsoft Windows Media Player. Data-driven applications can be created by importing external data stored in web-standard XML files.

ToolBook, on the other hand, incorporates a book metaphor (i.e., a book consisting of various pages) with drag and drop authoring for developing instruction rather than the icon approach used by Authorware. There are two versions of ToolBook, ToolBook Instructor and ToolBook Assistant. Both versions use the drag and drop authoring and content created with Instructor and Assistant is cross compatible. Instructor is a full-featured solution for instructional developers of complex and powerful training courses that are highly interactive, are media-rich and contain software simulations. ToolBook Instructor 8.5 (Click2Learn, 2003) provides such interactive features as software simulations, scenario-based instruction, conditional branching, hyperlinks and custom feedback. It supports various media such as Windows Media, RealMedia, QuickTime and Flash. Question types such as true/false, multiple choice, drag and drop, match item, text entry, essay and hot spots are supported. Authors can create robust software simulations using simulation widgets and editors, feedback and instruction text objects, and evaluation objects. While ToolBook Instructor does not use the icon approach, it does provide visual programming using an Actions Editor. Course creation is aided by the use of a course creation wizard; page, course and custom templates; a catalog of smart objects; and a web publishing wizard. The built-in customization capabilities of ActiveX "OpenScript" support scripting and the scripting environment can be used to tailor and extend the software to meet specific authoring requirements. However, features added by scripting may not work when delivered over the web.

ToolBook Assistant is a wizard-driven solution for subject matter experts who need to capture and distribute their knowledge, but who have no experience with course design or programming. Custom catalogs, tools and other authoring productivity aids created with ToolBook Instructor can be used in ToolBook Assistant to provide a standardized development environment for subject matter experts. However, ToolBook Assistant does not contain many of the key features and functionality of ToolBook Instructor such as: the Simulation Editor, Actions Event creation, access to server side databases or application extensibility (scripting capability).

Allen Communication's Quest (Allen Communications, 2003) is probably the third most popular authoring tool used by CBT and WBT developers. Quest 7 provides a visual authoring environment intended for use by both novice and expert training developers. It also integrates with other Allen Communication Learning Services development tools or independently, to create interactive courseware that can be delivered via web, LAN or CD-ROM. Course shells are created from QuickStart templates and course structures and then populated with content and available motifs. Authoring is done using drag and drop tools to provide quick development and interactivity. It provides C support and ActiveX support. Developers can embed training inside ActiveX compliant documents such as word processing files, electronic workbooks, presentation, and other training applications. Quest provides a library of ActiveX objects such as 3-D controls, calendar objects, combo boxes, virtual reality objects, HTML objects, Java Objects, etc. that can be implemented and integrated directly inside Quest Reusable ActiveX components. An object list shows all content piece which has been created from drag and drop tooltab. It is important to note that the Quest Internet Player must be used to deliver courses on the internet.

The three authoring tools listed above all claim to meet the current standards (i.e., SCORM and/or AICC) for assessing and recording user performance. The Advanced Distributing Learning Sharable Content Object Reference Model (ADL SCORM, 2003) provides standards for objects that are passed to a Learning Management System (LMS). Guidelines for the aviation industry for the development, delivery and evaluation of CBT and other training are provided by Aviation Industry CBT Committee (AICC, 2003). ToolBook Instructor claims that they comply with both SCORM and AICC requirements and Click2Learn provides direct links to SCORM and AICC websites. Authorware 7 supports ADL SCORM API Adapter Objects and the Learning Object Packager can create SCORM-compliant learning objects from Authorware files. LMS KOs Professional are used with Authorware to generate both AICC and SCORM-compliant courseware. Quest 7.0 primarily supports the AICC's protocol for communicating data to any AICC-compliant Learning Management System.

A number of the authoring tools also claim conformity with accessibility requirements. ToolBook provides a self-report for compliance to Section 508 and Click2Learn states that its authoring tools will allow the development of accessible instructional software. Macromedia states that Authorware has the capability to support the Web Content Accessibility Guideline (W3C) and Section 508 compliance when designed properly. In addition, Macromedia provides the Authorware Application Accessibility Kit for use by developers to make learning applications accessible to all end users.

Another authoring tool available for producing web training is ReadyGo Web Course Builder. ReadyGo WCB (ReadyGo, 2003) runs on Windows-based systems, resides on a web server and is accessed by any web browser. It provides course generation, templates and automatic generation of navigation elements, chapter and course indexes. Courses created with ReadyGo Web Course Builder are built in HTML and Javascript. Authoring is done by a subject matter expert entering data through a series of dialog boxes, including those for content pages, links and graphics (JPEG, GIF, streaming media and Java applets). Dialog boxes also are used to create quizzes, tests and interactive exercises. Tests can be developed to evaluate knowledge retention (up to 100 questions per test) including such items as: multiple-choice, true/false, fill-in-the-blank, numeric range and per answer feedback. ReadyGo WCB does not use plug-ins for the delivery of content. An additional module (ReadyGo Server Side Testing) is required to allow course creators to register students and save their test scores and survey results.

The choice of which authoring tool to use depends on client requirements, development organization standards and personal preferences. Authorware, ToolBook and Quest are all powerful authoring tools. Many developers with programming experience prefer Authorware because of its icon development approach. Also, developers moving from Macromedia Director typically find Authorware intuitive. On the other hand, many instructional technologist and non-programmers prefer ToolBook because of its more conventional book and page development metaphor. While I have used both Authorware and ToolBook Instructor to develop courses, I personally prefer ToolBook Instructor because it better matches my content development model. The use of ToolBook Instructor and Assistant provides the capability for the development of instruction by both experienced and non-experienced developers. Also, I have found that ToolBook Instructor's exercise item widgets allow the easy creation of exercises and tests.

Testing and Revising Instruction

After the initial version of the instructional content is completed, it is important to have it evaluated for content accuracy by one or more subject matter experts. Even if the developer is a subject matter expert, it is useful to have an additional expert review the material. In addition to the content accuracy review, the content and structure should be reviewed in terms of conformance with existing guidelines (e.g., the guidelines provided in this chapter) and good design practices. Such a review is often called a heuristic evaluation (see Chapter 8). This review can be done by peers, but if possible, at least one expert instructional designer also should review the material. If the instruction is computer-based (web or CBT), each of the learner interactions such as branching, exercise or test item responses, etc. also needs to be checked for proper operation. Any changes determined by the review would then be made by the developer in the content and structure of the course.

Once the changes are made, the course should be tried out on a small sample of typical target population learners to ensure that it works as intended. Participating learners need to be informed that it is a try-out and encouraged to provide as much feedback about the course as possible. It is important to stress to the try-out participants that the course is being evaluated and not their performance on the course. Changes are then made based on the try-out results. All changes in content should be reviewed by subject matter experts to ensure accuracy.

If potential users of the application will be invited to try the application before it is released, it may be possible to have these users take the training before using the application and obtain additional feedback.

Prior to the release of the instruction, a final content accuracy check should be performed by subject matter experts. In the case of computer-based instruction, an operational check of all of the interface elements also should be done to ensure that everything works as expected. Instructional developers and managers should read Chapter 8 for more details on planning and conducting tests.

Guidelines

The following list provides some useful guidelines for the design and development of instruction:

Language and Grammar

- The reading level should be appropriate for the learner and the content and be consistent throughout (Alessi and Trollip, 1991).
- Culture biased language and references should be avoided (Alessi and Trollip, 1991).
- Patronizing language or style should be avoided.
- Grammar, punctuation and spelling should be consistent with local standards.
- Short words and sentences should be used whenever possible.
- Transitions between sentences and paragraphs should be clear and adequate.
- Technical terms, acronyms and jargon should be used only when necessary to the content. When acronyms or technical terms are used, they should be defined.

Layout

- Content organization (e.g., course title, objectives, prerequisites, lessons, exercises, summaries, etc.) should be clear and consistent.
- Graphics and text should flow left to right and top to bottom (Western languages). Information generally should be displayed so that the scan pattern follows the general scan pattern of the learner's native language (Gibbon and Fairweather, 1998).
- Line lengths generally should be limited to provide sufficient "white space" in the margins of the page or window.
- Left margins should be justified and right margins not justified (see Chapter 6).
- Paragraphs should be single-spaced and separated with a blank line. Where possible, test messages should be broken at a phrase or idea boundary (Gibbon and Fairweather, 1998).
- Sentence and paragraph styles should be consistent throughout the course (Alessi and Trollip, 1991).
- Page breaks should be at appropriate points in the presentation (Alessi and Trollip, 1991).
- Text density should be less than 30% to create a clutter-free appearance.
- Navigation controls (e.g., back, forward, menu) should be clear and consistently located in all windows and screens.
- Directions (e.g., Press Forward to continue) should be placed in a consistent location on the window or screen (preferably at the end of the test).
- Input fields should be clearly titled and consistently placed within the content.
- Consistent headings should be used for content summaries and as navigational aids.
- Instructional presentation windows used in conjunction with application screens should not cover up screen fields or information needed by the learner.

Presentation

- Text and graphics should be used appropriately to describe the instructional content (see Chapter 6).
- Accessibility requirements should be considered in the presentation of instructional content (see Chapter 6, Accessibility Section).

- Goals and objectives should be stated clearly in the content prior to the lesson material and should be relevant to the learner (Alessi and Trollip, 1991).
- The content presented should be relevant to the objectives, accurate and complete, at the appropriate level of detail and at the appropriate level of realism (Alessi and Trollip, 1991).
- More difficult topics should be emphasized in the content presentation (Alessi and Trollip, 1991).
- In general, the lesson organization should conform to the subject-matter organization (Alessi and Trollip, 1991).
- For computer delivered instruction, paragraphs should be short (6 – 8 lines).
- Content windows or screens generally should cover only one major concept or instructional step. Words should be picked carefully and displayed on the screen in idea units corresponding to the instructional strategy (Gibbon and Fairweather, 1998).
- The need for scrolling in windows and screens to view content should be minimized.
- Text attributes (e.g., font style, color, underlining, highlighting and reverse video) should be used only to aid comprehension of the material.
- The pace of presenting new information should be reasonable and more or less consistent (Gibbon and Fairweather, 1998).
- Emphasis techniques (e.g., capitalization, italics, motion, blinking, color, etc.) should be used sparingly to draw attention to key parts of the presentation (Gibbon and Fairweather, 1998).
- Fonts used for computer delivered instruction should be a minimum of 11 points.
- When overlaid text is used, it should be easily located on the display (consistent overlay boarders should be used for differentiation).
- If incremental additions are made to a growing graphic, it should be clear as to what part of the graphic is new and what is old (Gibbon and Fairweather, 1998).
- Adequate detail should be provided to fully illustrate the thing being described (Gibbon and Fairweather, 1998).
- Animation and graphics should be relevant, provide important information, at the appropriate level of detail, should be aesthetic and have the appropriate speed of display and motion (Alessi and Trollip, 1991).
- Unnecessary or irrelevant graphics should be avoided, particularly the trivial use of animation and distracting scenes (Gibbon and Fairweather, 1998).
- Motion video should be used only when appropriate (Gibbon and Fairweather, 1998).
- When presenting audio: keep messages short and crisp, pace the introduction of new ideas and the density of technical terms carefully, provide a repeat control, avoid a page turning approach, avoid echoing text with audio (Gibbon and Fairweather, 1998).

Navigation (Computer-based or Web Delivery)

- All windows or screens should have appropriate navigation buttons and keys to progress forward or backward through the content and to return to the beginning of both the lesson and the course.
- Navigation buttons (and keys) should work correctly and same button and key should be used for the same function.
- Accessibility requirements should be considered in the availability of input methods to navigate through the instructional content (see Chapter 6, Accessibility Section).
- Unless a particular lesson sequence is required, a lesson menu should be provided to allow learners to access various lessons within the instructions.

- Learners should be able to exit a window, screen or the instruction whenever they wish without penalty.
- When a learner exits a window or screen, they should be returned to a logical point upon re-entering.

Questions, Exercises and Tests

- Questions should be relevant, well spaced, promote response economy, emphasize comprehension, have variety and be placed appropriately, i.e., before or after the content (Alessi and Trollip, 1991).
- In question answering, it should be clear how to respond, how to correct an answer, the number of tries allowed and whether the question can be left without answering (Alessi and Trollip, 1991).
- The results of the learner's choice should be displayed (Gibbon and Fairweather, 1998).
- Exercises should relate clearly to the lesson objectives and tests should relate clearly to the end-of-course objectives.
- The capability should be provided to review the goals and data related to an exercise (Gibbon and Fairweather, 1998).
- Feedback should be provided in terms of the correctness of all question, exercise item, and test item responses made by the learner.
- Feedback should be supportive, corrective, clear and identify discrimination errors (Alessi and Trollip, 1991).
- Feedback should be of an appropriate type (text, graphic, markup, sound), attract attention and be erasable when no longer needed (Alessi and Trollip, 1991).
- Prompt and feedback messages should be designed so that they blend with, but do not complete with, the exercise (Gibbon and Fairweather, 1998).
- Replies should be varied with no disparaging feedback provided and praise should be used sparingly.

Learner Control and Interaction

- Unless it is inappropriate to the instructional strategy, the learner should control the pace of the instruction and should be able to return to material previously visited.
- Temporary terminations and bookmarks should be available (Alessi and Trollip, 1991).
- If possible, learners should be able to enter comments in the lesson material (Alessi and Trollip, 1991).
- Learner interaction should be frequent, be comprehension enhanced, memory enhanced, transfer enhanced and provided by means of a variety of methods (Alessi and Trollip, 1991).
- Learner interactions should be designed to avoid creating false habits, i.e., not to teach misconceptions about the real world (Gibbon and Fairweather, 1998).
- Modes of learner control should be selected that are easy to use, intuitive and have as much in common as possible with the work environment (Gibbon and Fairweather, 1998).
- Directions should be provided on how to take the course (Alessi and Trollip, 1991).
- Clear instructions and adequate warm-up practice on the interactions learners will engage in should be provided (Gibbon and Fairweather, 1998).
- A review of interactions, controls and their operations should be available during an interactive exercise (Gibbon and Fairweather, 1998).

ELECTRONIC PERFORMANCE SUPPORT

As noted in Chapter 1, a Performance Support System (PSS) contains several, interrelated pieces of more traditional performance support such as online help, online tutorials, online reference material and computer-based training, as well as coaches and wizards. In addition, a PSS may contain features that automate repetitive, simple tasks without user intervention (e.g., automatically fill in spreadsheets, auto-correct spelling). The combination of the electronic components of a PSS that are designed and developed as a system and supported by an integrated, sophisticated user interface is generally called an Electronic Performance Support System (EPSS). While the goal of a PSS is to ensure that all of the performance support components (both computer-based and non-computer-based) are designed and developed as an integrated whole, in some case an EPSS may be developed to support a specific function or user task. The purpose of this section is to provide guidance on the development of such stand-alone electronic performance support applications.

It also was noted in Chapter 1 that an EPSS typically contains the following components:

- Guidance component – provides immediate help on accomplishing tasks and making decisions (e.g., online help, cue cards, advisors, performance and decision aids).
- Knowledge component – provides information relevant to performing the job or task (e.g., descriptions of system components and functions, best practices, supporting information and reference material).
- Instructional component – provides instruction on performing job tasks and system functions, including overviews, tutorials, computer or web-based instruction, task specific instruction and simulation exercises.
- Automation component – provides automation to tasks or task activities that may be tedious or can be performed better or more efficiency by the computer (e.g., wizards).
- User interface component – provides the underlying, integrating user interface that ties all of the EPSS components together.

Development Approach

Since the development of an EPSS is really the development of a software system, many of the development procedures and issues are the same. Also, many books are available specifically dealing with the design and development of Electronic Performance Support Systems, such as *Electronic Performance Support Systems* (Gery, 1991), *Designing Electronic Performance Support Tools* (Stevens and Stevens, 1995) and *Designing and Developing Electronic Performance Support Systems* (Brown, 1996). The reader is encouraged to consult these books for additional design guidance. In the previous sections of this chapter, design and development guidance was provided for most of the individual performance support products that make up an EPSS. Therefore, this section will cover only the unique aspects of developing requirements for designing, developing and testing the integrated system. In addition, the approach discussed in this section is based on the process used by the author and other team members to develop the Telcordia Performance Support Project Estimator (Telcordia, 2000). The following process was used in the development of Estimator:

- Develop project plan.
- Develop requirements.

- Prepare the design document.
- Develop the software and the user interface.
- Perform developmental (alpha) testing.
- Perform usability testing
- Perform customer testing (beta) and product testing

Identifying Needs and Developing the Project Plan

In the case of a new EPSS product, the need for the product would be determined and justified to management by the development of a business case. The business case document typically contains such sections as: a product description, a description of the development activities including an estimated cost for each phase, a market assessment for the product (if it is to be sold), benefits and risks, preliminary assessment of cost vs. revenues (or saving in the case of an internal product) and proposed next steps for the project. Since Estimator was to be an extensive revision of an initial version of the software (called Estimagic), management did not require us to develop a business case. A project plan, however, did need to be developed and circulated for review and approval by the various stakeholders in the project prior to developing requirements (see Chapter 3 for more details about EPSS product planning).

Developing Requirements

A requirements document is essential for both design guidance and as a primary source on what the product is expected to produce and how the product is expected to perform (test criteria). The requirements for an EPSS typically should be sufficiently detailed to ensure that the design is well specified. However, in the case of Estimator the requirements were fairly brief ("thin" requirements) because of the existence of the early version of the product that could be referred to in the thin requirements document. In effect, the earlier version of the product was considered to be a prototype.

The thin requirements document included a general section that contained such topics as opportunities and challenges, product description and features, benefits and value, and assumptions, contingencies and constraints. The Opportunities and Challenges topic describes the potential market for the product or the potential to save cost or provide efficiencies for the organization. Also the potential challenges in building and deploying the product are discussed. In the case of Estimator, this section pointed out that there were currently no available tools that performance support and training product managers could use to develop consistent and reliable estimates of the time and costs associated with the development of the various types of performance support deliverables. It also was noted that it was important to develop Estimator and make it commercially available as soon as possible before any competing product could be marketed.

In the Product Description and Features topic, the basic purpose of the product and its major features is described. Since Estimator was a revision of Estimagic, the product description included those features of Estimagic that were to be retained or enhanced in Estimator as well as new features (the details of the new features and enhancements are described in a later section). The major benefits of the product and value to the organization are described in the benefits and values topic. Some of the benefits stated for estimator included:

- Provides estimates of the cost of producing any type of performance support/training product and projects consisting of multiple products.
- Provides easy retrieval of information concerning projects and deliverable estimates.

- Information supporting the estimation tasks can be quickly accessed by means of advisors and online help.
- Easy to use; an estimate can be produced by a first time user of Estimator in less than forty-five minutes.
- Default values used to make the estimates can be easily changed by users based on their own criteria or experience.

The Assumptions, Dependencies and Constraints topic cover such areas as the type of platform the product is expected to run under, the type of database to be used, the programming to be used in developing the software, etc. In the case of Estimator, it was assumed that it would run on an individual workstation running Windows, be developed in Visual Basic, use Access as the back-end database and use Crystal Reports for report production.

Another important section of the thin requirements document is the Processing and Flows Section. This section describes the major processing activities that will take place within the product in terms of structure and functionality. In the case of Estimator, this section contained a description of the tree structure that was to serve as the model for the hierarchy of projects created in Estimator. It also described the functionality in terms of the logical flow for using the various features of Estimator, e.g., creating a new project.

In the System Architecture Section, an initial view of the system architecture is provided. In the case of Estimator, the system architecture was illustrated by using a flow chart to depict the system components and interrelationships. Typically the system architecture is more fully defined in a Technical Operating Environment Document Addendum.

The Detailed Requirements Section is the most important section in the thin requirements document. This section lists all of the detailed requirements to be met by the EPSS product. In the case of Estimator, the first part of the detailed requirements listed those features of the predecessor product (Estimagic) that were to be included in the new version. These features included:

- "Quick Tour" option to orient new users to the features of Estimator.
- "Advisor" mode that walks users through the various estimation steps by means of a question and answer dialog.
- Estimation project window utilizing a three tab interface (Project Information tab, Deliverables tab and Reports tab).
- "Quick Estimate" option to provide the capability for developing "quick" estimates for any Learning Support deliverable.
- Default Values window (a four tabbed window) that allows users to change the parameters for Delivery Types, Parameters, Staff Levels and Miscellaneous.
- Data Query option that provides the capability to query the database for projects in terms of start-date, end-date and estimate date.
- Online help at both the window level and contents level to support all of the Estimator features and tasks.

In the second part of the Detailed Requirements Section for Estimator, the new and changed requirements were listed. These requirements specified the "capabilities" that were to be included or modified. One of the major modifications to be made for Estimator was the capability to change the default values to values relevant for the using organization. Since the original product (Estimagic) was developed for in-house use only, many of the default values such as personnel levels and salaries were fixed based on the internal organization's values. To be usable by any organization, Estimator's default values needed to be easily modified by the using organization. The addition of this feature also affected the initial use of the product since the default values needed to be specified prior to doing an estimate.

Several other sections, such as System Interfaces and Impacts, Availability and Reliability Requirements, and Testing Considerations, also are included as part of the thin requirements document. Since Estimator was a stand-alone product, the System Interfaces and Impacts Sections were not relevant. The Availability and Reliability Requirements Section specified when the product was expected to be completed and available for shipment and the level of reliability acceptable for the software. For Estimator, the reliability was specified by stating that it will operate without any detectable runtime errors at the time of release. The section on Testing Considerations referred to the Test Plan which was a separate document.

Designing the EPSS

In design, the detailed specifications for the product are developed. Typically a design document (or a number of design documents depending on the complexity of the product) is developed, reviewed by stakeholders and baselined. The design documents should have sufficient detail on the design so that screens can be developed and the software coded. As noted in Chapter 3, the EPSS design document describes the general product (or system) structure, requirements to design traceability approach, functional descriptions, system architecture and impacts, data administration, format and style requirements, accessibility, module design, user interface and interface objects (e.g., screens and fields) and associated attributes, process, module relationships and troubleshooting.

The specification of the interface screens, fields and content is one of the most important parts of the EPSS design. If possible, screens and interface objects should be depicted in the design document utilizing realistic "screen shots" that have the same appearance as the screens and objects to be built. For Estimator, however, we found that we could provide the necessary detail without resorting to simulating the actual screens (see Figure 7.14 for an example). This approach worked well because the basic screen design layouts already were established and the programmer was very familiar with them.

In Chapter 1, it was noted that an EPSS should help performers: grasp the big picture, set goals and understand consequences, get definitions, understand concepts, carry out job tasks, know where they are in the process, get feedback, interpret results, get coaching or guidance when needed, learn, get help geared to their actions and knowledge, access a knowledge base, make decisions and solve problems. Estimator was designed to accomplish as many of the above attributes as possible. For example, the Estimator Deliverables Tab screen shown in Figure 7.15 provides a grasp of the big picture in that it graphically depicts the operations being performed and the position within the operations (activities already accomplished are highlighted). In addition, consequences are shown immediately in the estimation values fields when the Estimation Calculation values are changed.

"Complexity (subject matter)" Advisor

Screen 1

The "Complexity (subject matter)" parameter addresses the impact of the subject matter or content complexity on development time.

Is the complexity of the subject matter being covered by this deliverable very high (e.g., many complicated steps and contingencies involved, many rules and interrelationships need to be explained, highly complex equipment or software needs to be explained)?

        O Yes   O No

Note: "Yes" to Done (slider to high, "No" to next (slider in "medium")

Screen 2

Is the subject matter being covered by this deliverable very simple (e.g., no complicated steps and contingencies involved, simple presentation of factual information, simple equipment or software needs to be explained)?

        O Yes   O No

Note: "Yes" Done (slider to low), "No" to next screen

Screen 3

Estimate the degree of complexity of your subject matter:

      O Medium-low   (Slider to between low & medium)
      O Average complexity (Slider to medium)
      O Medium-high   (Slider to between medium & high)

  DONE

Figure 7.14 Screen Samples used for Estimator Design

The Estimator Parameter Advisor Menu screen shown in Figure 7.16 also demonstrates the progress indication feature. This screen is one of the screens in Estimator's Advisor (one of the guidance components of the EPSS) that steps new users through the process. If a user wishes to use the Advisor, they are taken through a series of question and answer dialog screens (such as depicted in the design sample shown in Figure 7.14) that set the actual parameters. Experienced users can do this directly through the use of the Parameters Values screen depicted in Chapter 3 (Figure 3.1). The Advisor serves as a learning device (instructional component of the EPSS) and after using it a few times, users will typically use the normal input screens instead of the Advisor.

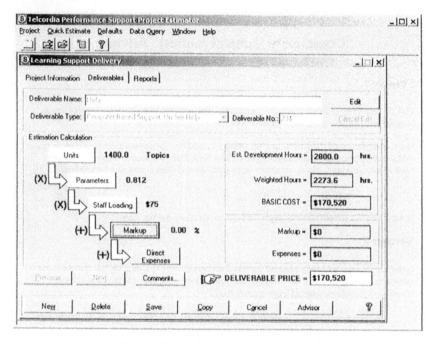

Figure 7.15 Estimator Deliverables Tab
(Source – Telcordia Performance Support Project Estimator, Copyright © 2000 Telcordia
Technologies, Inc., Produced with Permission.)

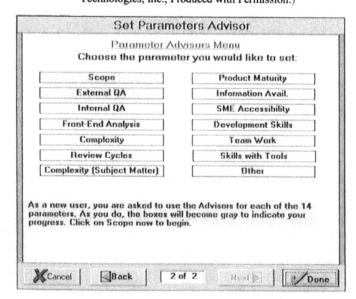

Figure 7.16 Estimator Parameter Advisors Menu
(Source – Telcordia Performance Support Project Estimator, Copyright © 2000 Telcordia
Technologies, Inc., Produced with Permission.)

Performance systems should be designed to provide effective feedback to users. Feedback is important for both correct and incorrect user responses. In many systems, it is particularly important to know what can be accomplished at a particular point in the dialog. Figure 7.17 shows one of the Estimator feedback dialogs that provides information on what has been done and what can be done next.

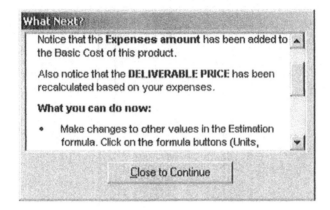

Figure 7.17 Example of an Estimator Feedback Screen
(Source – Telcordia Performance Support Project Estimator, Copyright © 2000 Telcordia Technologies, Inc., Produced with Permission.)

Providing help, based on the user's actions and knowledge, is another important attribute of an EPSS (serving as both a guidance and knowledge component). Estimator's help system was designed to provide knowledge about the estimation process and procedures for performing all of the estimation tasks (see Figure 7.18 for an example of one of Estimator's help screens). As can be seen in Figure 7.18, Estimator's help system was designed to provide content in four major topic areas: an introduction to the product, information about the application and processes, procedures and descriptions of the deliverables.

The combination of the Quick Tour, Advisor mode and online help system was intended to provide full support to the application without the need of external documentation or training. A major design goal of an EPSS is, in fact, to provide full performance support without the need of any additional external supporting material. In addition, Estimator's database of typical estimating factors and values provided an expert knowledge base (knowledge component) that could be used by less experienced estimators. Finally, Estimator automated the calculations needed to develop the estimated cost of a project. The Quick Tour, Advisor, online help, knowledge base and automated calculation features of Estimator comprised the instructional, guidance, knowledge and automation components of the EPSS. It is worth noting that the combination of the Quick Tour, Advisor and logical structure of the interface negated the need for any additional instruction.

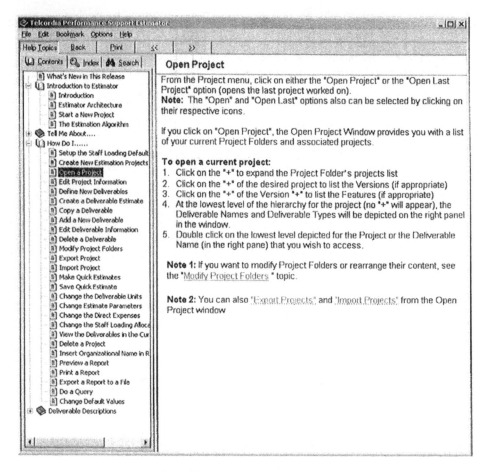

Figure 7.18 Estimator Help Screen
(Source – Telcordia Performance Support Project Estimator, Copyright © 2000 Telcordia
Technologies, Inc., Produced with Permission.)

Developing the EPSS

During the development phase, the databases, screens, screen objects and interfaces are developed according to the design document(s) and the software is coded and initially tested. Embedded support components such as tutorials and online help also would be developed during this phase, but somewhat later due to their dependency on the development of the user interface objects.

In the case of Estimator, the performance technologist (the author) and the programmer worked very closely together during development. The author provided the content, layout and sequence of the screens, dialogs and interactions, and the programmer transformed them into appropriate application code (using visual basic). In many cases, content was provided to the programmer in RTF to minimize the need for re-entering data. The programmer did all of the database design and development according to the requirements specified in the design document. While the programmer was developing the database, the author used RoboHelp to develop the help system content to the extent possible (final help development depends on the availability of operational software to verify the application's response to user inputs).

As soon as the programmer had obtained a stable build (no runtime errors) for an application feature, both the programmer and the author tested it to ensure that it worked as planned. When all of the features were stable, the performance technologist simulated user actions to test all of the features and completed the help content. Any runtime errors encountered during this simulation testing were fixed by the programmer and Estimator was deemed to be ready for alpha testing. The author also prepared storyboards for the Quick Tour and provided them to the instructional developer who prepared the Quick Tour program using Macromedia Authorware.

Alpha Testing

In the alpha test phase, the initial version of the EPSS application is tested according to the test plan to ensure that it functions as expected. Test cases are developed against each of the application's requirements and these test cases are run by project team members and others to determine that all processes and interface elements function according to the requirements. Most of the major software "bugs" are discovered during this phase. Problems and bugs are fixed, based on their severity, and a new "build" of the software is produced.

While both the author and the programmer tested the stable version of Estimator, quality assurance requirements necessitated a formal alpha test be accomplished to verify that it worked correctly. This was accomplished according to the test plan prepared by the author. At least one test case was developed to test each of the Estimator features and associated requirements. These test cases were essentially use scenarios that required the input of specific data and the observation of system responses. An example of an Estimator Alpha Test case is shown in Figure 7.19.

TEST CASE 1

Purpose: To ensure that a new project folder can be created in the "open" dialog window.

Method: Click on the "Open" project icon in the initial dialog box. Select "New" folder and provide folder name.

Results: Estimator displays the "Open" project window. Clicking on the "New" option results in New Folder dialog. New folder is created and name displays properly.

Figure 7.19 Example of Estimator Alpha Test Case

Usability Testing

The major purpose of a usability test is to determine if the usability objectives stated for the EPSS application are met. In addition, since usability testing requires testing the application with representative users, issues regarding difficulties in understanding and using the application and interface elements are more likely to surface during this test.

Estimator usability testing involved the testing of the Estimator software by Telcordia performance support developers with various levels of experience in developing various performance support products. Ideally it would have been desirable to include performance support developers from various organizations in the usability test. However, we felt that it was acceptable to use all internal developers for the usability test for the following reasons:

- It was very difficult to obtain usability testers from other organizations.
- A beta test involving outside organizations was to be done later.
- The fairly large number of Telcordia performance support developers with various levels of experience and backgrounds.
- Estimator was to be used as an internal product as well as a commercial product.

In the Estimator usability test, each participant completed the Quick Tour, did a project description and one deliverable type using the Advisor, completed a project description and two deliverables without the Advisor, used the "Quick Estimate" option to complete an estimate for a deliverable, previewed and printed a report, did a "Query" based on project parameters and accessed Window and Help Contents to find specific help topics. A number of participants also modified one of the default values in the "Defaults" window. Data was collected for each of the test sessions concerning successful completions, errors, user difficulty, completion time and keystrokes (for the online help sessions only). After the test sessions were finished, participants completed a general questionnaire and several checklists concerning their opinions and satisfaction with Estimator.

Beta Testing

When all of the significant user problems and additional software bugs are corrected, the EPSS application is sent out to typical customers for beta testing. Beta testing may vary from simply making the product available and asking users to comment if they have a problem, to user instructions and feedback forms. The problems and suggestions resulting from the beta testing are evaluated for importance and cost-effectiveness and the EPSS application is modified accordingly.

In the Estimator beta test, participants were asked to install Estimator on their computers and try out the various features. While using Estimator, participants were asked to record any problems they encountered and the circumstances under which they occurred. After using the various features of Estimator, they were asked to rate Estimator on a 7 point scale in terms of: ease of use, confidence in estimates, estimating parameters, help structure, help content, and Estimator overall. In addition, they were asked to list what they liked about Estimator, what they didn't like about Estimator, and any other comments that they might have. Only 13 specific problems were reported on using estimator. However, participants provided a number of comments about what they liked and didn't like about the Estimator and made many suggestions for improving the product. Therefore, the beta test was a very important step before releasing the product.

Product Testing

After the modifications based on the beta test are completed, the EPSS application is tested again prior to release. The purpose of this test is primarily to ensure that all of the changes work properly and that the product functions according to requirements and is reliable (has no known faults). As was the case in the alpha test, test cases are developed against each of the application's requirements and these test cases are run by project team members to determine that all processes and interface elements function according to the requirements. In many cases, it is possible to use most of the same test cases used in the alpha test in the product test. Changed or additional test cases may be necessary where features have been changed due to early testing. See Chapter 8 for more details on test planning and conduct.

Guidelines

In addition to the guidelines provided earlier in this chapter for the various individual performance support components, the following guidelines are particularly relevant for EPSS applications:

General

- The application should provide the overall context for the process or work by creating a "big picture" that includes explicit and complete representation of the context (e.g., process, equipment, facilities, etc.) necessary to complete the work (Gery, 1995 & 2003).
- Business or organizational strategy and goals should be reinforced through advice, options or underlying logic that incorporates business rules (Gery, 1995 & 2003).
- The application should aid in goal establishment by presenting explicit goal options (e.g., presents "what do you want to do" dialogs). When appropriate, a means also should be provided to compare goal options and consequences (Gery, 1995 & 2003). It should help users establish what they can do or want to do, or where to go (Raybould, 2000).
- A work context should be established and maintained that is task centered (employs task language and metaphors) and is work oriented rather than software oriented (Gery, 1995 & 2003, Raybould, 2000).
- Support for task progression or cognitive processing should reflect the most current and best known approach or content (Gery, 1995 & 2003, Raybould 2000).
- The behavior, options, process, sequences and deliverables should reflect the natural work situations and work flow (language, metaphors and actions) (Gery, 1995 & 2003, Raybould, 2000).
- The application should provide an interpretation of results, "Why did that happen?" "How did that happen?" (Raybould, 2000).
- The application should rely on recognition, rather than recall, knowledge (Raybould, 2000).

Guidance Component

- Ongoing, dynamic, rich and explicit system or performer initiated advice should be provided based on data, time, options or performer behavior. Advice may be conditional, rule-based or "learned" and may be informational or directive (Gery, 1995 & 2003).
- Content-sensitive access to support resources should be provided that do not break the task context (Gery, 1995 & 2003).
- Whenever possible, support resources should be embedded within or immediately accessible from the primary displays (Gery, 1995 & 2003).
- Information on the system, procedures, etc. should be tightly coupled to task context and available by context-sensitive access (Gery, 1995 & 2003).
- Rich, dynamic and context sensitive access should be provided on business logic and rationale (Gery, 1995 & 2003).

- Resources should be available concerning obvious options and next steps (e.g., "Show me" or "Tell me about" or "Do it" buttons) (Gery, 1995 & 2003).
- Answers should be provided to descriptive questions, such as "What is this?" "What are the differences," functional questions such as "What does this do?" and procedural questions, such as "How do I?" (Raybould, 2000).
- Support (coaching or guidance) should be provided when needed based on proactive monitoring of user actions by the system (Raybould, 2000).
- Guidance should be provided to help users make decisions and solve problems.
- Users should be able to get help that is geared to their actions and knowledge.

Knowledge Component

- Alternative search and navigation mechanisms should be provided to optimize the user's ability to find appropriate information (Gery, 1995 & 2003). The user should be able to search for answers to questions (Raybould, 2000).
- Information should be layered to support performer diversity in prior knowledge, goals, motivation, available time and style (Gery, 1995 & 2003, Raybould 2000).
- Access should be provided to underlying logic (Gery, 1995 & 2003)
- Only relevant information should be provided (Raybould, 2000).
- Users should be able to access a knowledge base relevant to their job tasks.
- Users should be able to obtain definitions for terms, objects and system components.
- Information should be provided to allow users to understand concepts.

Instructional Component

- Instruction should be provided as necessary for users to learn to perform job tasks supported by the application that are difficult or rarely done.
- The instruction should be interactive and specifically aimed at supporting job tasks and improving performance. In order to minimize time away from the job, the inclusion of unnecessary content should be avoided.
- The instruction should provide practice on the task (using real or simulated system components) and provide appropriate feedback on performance.
- Available instruction should be accessible on demand by the user. In some cases, it may be appropriate for the system to offer instruction on the basis of apparent user difficulties.
- The instruction should include the use of the guidance and knowledge components when appropriate.

Automation Component

- Where possible, data, cognitive and judgment tasks should be automated (Gery, 1995 & 2003, Raybould, 2000).
- Consider automating tasks that the intended users either do not like to perform (e.g., are tedious and repetitive) or perform poorly.
- Consider automating tasks that require forms-processing or document generation, require repetitive distribution of standard information or require calculations (Stevens and Stevens, 1995).

User Interface Component

- The user interface should provide access to all of the EPSS components in a straightforward and consistent manner (Gery, 1995 & 2003, Raybould, 2000).
- Elements of the EPSS should be integrated in the interface to provide a meaningful and whole context for the user to work within (Gery, 1995 & 2003).
- The interface should provide direct access to the overall work process, such as definition, process steps, milestones, etc. (Gery, 1995 & 2003).
- A structure should be provided for the work process and progression through tasks and logic based on the proper or best known task or process sequence (Gery, 1995 & 2003). Directly show the structure of the task or process (Raybould, 2000).
- Metaphors and direct manipulation of variables should be used to capitalize on previous learning and physical reality (Gery, 1995 & 2003).
- If appropriate to the task, the interface should observe performer context, prior decisions and physical interactions with the system (Gery, 1995 & 2003).
- Alternative views of the interface and support resources should be provided to present a broad range of structure and freedom to the user (Gery, 1995 & 2003).
- The interface should provide evidence of task progression or conditions, or evidence of accumulated choices and system-generated outcomes (Gery, 1995 & 2003). User should be able to tell where they are in the process.
- Rich, varied, explicit and continuous feedback should be provided related to performer actions, data, task requirements, performer attributes, etc. (Gery, 1995 & 2003). It should give feedback on what you have done or where you have been Raybould, 2000).
- The primary displays should contain embedded knowledge (e.g., obvious options, next steps, content displayed in multiple forms) (Gery, 1995 & 2003).
- Business knowledge and rules should be incorporated into the displays, underlying system or programming logic (Gery, 1995 & 2003).
- Where possible, customization of displays, task sequences, language and system behavior should be allowed according to individual differences and needs (Gery, 1995 & 2003).
- The interface should employ consistent interface conventions, language, visual positioning, navigation and other system behavior (Gery, 1995 & 2003).
- The interface should be forgiving in that it lets the user make a mistake and go back to a previous state (Raybould, 2000).
- The visual appearance of the interface should suggest its use (Raybould, 2000).

In addition to the interface guidelines presented above, the reader is strongly encouraged to consult the guidelines presented in *Interaction Techniques* (BSR/HFES 200.3, 2003).

ITERATIVE APPROACH TO ELECTRONIC PERFORMANCE SUPPORT

As noted in Chapter 1, it is typically very difficult to build a complex, multi-job, EPSS during the initial releases of a large computer system application because of the tremendous investment in resources and the high level of cooperation required between the developers of the EPSS and the developers of the application. Usually, in such environments, online help is developed late in development and instruction is done initially by means of instructor-led training (typically by subject matter experts). As the system matures, online help improves and becomes more extensive and training migrates to computer-based delivery. In addition, documentation that originally may have been delivered on paper is provided online. While the trend to moving the performance support materials online is beneficial (delivery is typically cheaper), the resultant performance support components are rarely integrated.   As a result, there are redundancies and often inconsistencies in the performance support products. In addition, there is no underlying interface to tie them together.

One solution, of course, would be to redo the whole system as an EPSS. However, as noted above, that is not a practical solution. A more practical approach is to start with the available performance support components and iteratively migrate them into a EPSS. This process has the following steps:

- Move any performance support products online that are still delivered off-line.
- Restructure existing performance support products.
- Revamp the online help system into an integrator of existing support products.
- Test the integrated performance support system with typical users.
- Add relevant new performance support components to the system.

Moving Performance Support Products Online

Since many of the performance support products provided with a large system are typically in paper form or delivered by an instructor, the first step is to convert these products to an online form of delivery. Initially, this may be accomplished by simply providing online copies of documents (e.g., pdf versions) and video taping instructor-led training sessions. If the instructor-led training is supported by PowerPoint presentations, these presentations can be directly captured and voice overlays can be added.

Restructuring Existing Performance Support Products

A common look-and-feel is a critical aspect of any performance support system. This can be accomplished for existing performance support products by developing a style guide that specifies the rules for formatting and presenting materials. It is suggested that the style guide be jointly developed by a team of experienced designers representing the various performance support product categories. After the style guide is agreed to by the team and management, existing products can be reviewed and reformatted and restructured according to style guide.

During the reformatting and restructuring, all of the current performance support products should be reviewed for content inconsistencies and unneeded redundancies. This review will require a team of the developers responsible for the various performance products relevant to the application or application feature (e.g., online help developer, instructional developer and technical writer). Since the developers will know their own content, they will be much more likely to uncover and resolve inconsistencies and unneeded redundancies than external reviewers.

Revamping the Online Help System into an Integrator

An existing online help system offers a convenient vehicle to tie all of the online performance support products together. This is due to the fact that most current help system development tools and help engines provide the means to link from the help system to external sources as well as permitting help files to be directly accessed by the application. For example, a task tutorial can be directly accessed from the help window listing the procedures for the task. In another example, the task procedures can be directly presented by means of a pop-up window when the user clicks on a button or invokes a key from the application window. It is also important to note that the help system already supports two of the five components of an EPSS (i.e., the guidance and knowledge components).

As noted earlier in this chapter (in the section on online help), the help menu can be used as one means to access other performance support components. This is accomplished by dividing the help menu into groups, listing the various available support products or product group, with links to the products or group. However, links to other supporting components also should be provided directly from the help system content, particularly from the procedures topics. These links can be included as buttons (e.g., "teach me") or as hyperlinked text (e.g., "also see instruction on performing this task"). Links also can be provided to supplemental documentation by using the "related topics" button or hyperlinks that can be added to a help topic screen. The approach suggested above has the advantage of providing performance support, first via the help screen (which is intended to immediately support performance), and then by instruction or supporting documentation.

To effectively integrate existing computer-based instruction into the help system, it may be necessary to redesign the CBT so that it is modularized by tasks or procedures. This is because the instructional component of an EPSS should directly support task performance. The user should be able to directly receive instruction on performing a specific task without needing to go through a course covering a multitude of procedures or tasks. New computer-based instruction can, of course, be designed modularly so that it can be used either as an integrated course or as modules to support learning specific tasks.

Testing the Integrated System

After the individual performance support products are integrated through the help system, the system should be tested using a sample of typical users. The test should include various use scenarios that require users to use all of the integrated products and features.

Adding New Performance Support Components

The addition of certain performance support components (e.g., cue cards, "show me" videos, performance and decision aids, quick tours and tutorials) can be done by the performance support development staff using existing tools. Other performance support components such as advisors, wizards and task automation will need programming and application interface designer support. The addition of a knowledge base will require additional development and system resources.

In his article on interactive assistance (Marion, 2000), Craig Marion suggests moving from traditional explanatory interactive assistance, through suggestive or guiding interactive assistance, to interactive performance support. Marion defines suggestive or guiding interactive assistance as assistance that either demonstrates how to perform a task or presents possibilities to users they may not be aware of. Microsoft's Show Me Help is one example of guiding interactive assistance in that it enables the user to have the system perform a step or sequence of steps in a task for which assistance was requested. In suggestive assistance, assistance is offered based on the user's probable goal determined from antecedent actions. An example of this type of help is the Microsoft's IntelliSense technology used in Microsoft Publisher. Marion also includes corrective guidance in this category in that corrective guidance provides intelligent feedback to enable a user to meet established criteria or achieve a declared goal. Enhancing the performance support system by adding suggestive or guidance assistance and then adding the more difficult to develop performance support components (e.g., advisors, coaches, wizards and automation) is a reasonable and cost effective approach to evolving into an EPSS. However, all modifications and additions should be based on performance analysis data.

After the above components are in place, the next logical move would be to develop a knowledge base to support all of the EPSS components (see *Knowledge and Content Management* earlier in this Chapter).

REFERENCES

Alessi, S. and Trollip, S. (1991), *Computer-Based Instruction: Methods and Development,* 2nd Edition, Englewood Cliffs, NJ: Prentice Hall.

ADL SCORM (2003), Advanced Distributed Learning, Sharable Content Object Reference Model. Online. Available HTTP: <http://www.adlnet.org> (accessed October 22, 2003).

AICC (2003), Aviation Industry CBT Committee Guidelines. Online. Available HTTP: <http://www.aicc.org> (accessed October 22, 2003).

ASTD (1999), *The ASTD Handbook of Training Design and Development: A Comprehensive Guide to Ccreating and Delivering Training Programs – Instructor-led, Computer-based, or Self-directed,* 2nd Edition, George Piskurich, Peter Beckschi and Brandon Hall (eds.), McGraw-Hill Trade.

AuthorIT (2003), *Features and Benefits,* Online. Available HTTP: <http://www.author-it.com/features.mv> (accessed July 21, 2003).

Bell Laboratories (1974), *Performance Aid Development,* Personnel Subsystem Development Technology Group, Systems Training Department, Business Information Systems Program Area.

Branson, R., Rayner, G., Lamarr Cox, J. Furman, J., King, F. and Hannum, W. (1975), *Interservice Procedures for Instructional Systems Development: Executive Summary and Model,* AD-A019 486, National Technical Information Service, U.S. Department of Commerce.

Brockmann, R. (1991), *Writing Better Computer User Documentation: From Paper to Online,* New York: Wiley & Sons.

Brown, L. (1996) *Designing and Developing Electronic Performance Support Systems,* MA: Digital Press.

BS 7830 (1996), *Guide to The Design and Preparation of On-screen Documentation for Users of Application Software,* London: British Standards Institute.

Click2Learn (2003), ToolBook Instructor and ToolBook Assistant, Click2Learn, Inc. Online. Available HTTP: <home.click2learn.com/en/toolbook/index.asp> (accessed October 21, 2003).

Deerwester S., Dumais, S., Landauer T., Furnas, G. and Harshman, R. (1990), Indexing by latent semantic analysis, *Journal of the Society for Information Science,* 41(6), pg. 391-407.

Dillon, A. (1991), Requirements analysis for hypertext applications: The why, what and how approach. *Applied Ergonomics,* 22, pp. 458-462.

Dillon, A. (1994), *Designing Usable Electronic Text, Ergonomic Aspects of Human Information Usage,* London: Taylor & Francis.

Doc-to-Help (2003), Doc-to-Help 6.5, ComponentOne, Online. Available HTTP: <http://www.componentone.com/helptools.aspx?helptoolscode=1> (Accessed September 5, 2003).

FAA (1997), *Documentation Design Aid,* FAA Human Factors in Aviation Maintenance and Inspection, Online. Available HTTP: <http://hfskyway.faa.gov/jobaids.htm> (accessed August 6, 2003).

FLSA Advisor (2003), elaws Fair Labor Standard Act Advisor, U.S. Department of Labor. Online. Available HTTP: <http://www.dol.gov/elaws/flsa.htm> (Accessed September 15, 2003).

Gagne, R. (1985), *The conditions of Learning and Theory of Instruction,* 4th Edition, New York: Holt, Rinehart and Winston.

Gagne, R., Briggs, L., and Wager, W. (1988), *Principles of Instructional Design,* 3rd Edition, New York: Holt, Rinehart and Winston.

Gery, G. (1991) *Electronic Performance Support Systems,* Tolland, MA: Gery Associates

Gery, G. (1995) Attributes and Behaviors of Performance Centered Systems, *Performance Improvement Quarterly,* 8, No. 1, pp 47-93.

Gery, G. (2003) Attributes and behaviors of performance centered systems, Online. Available HTTP: <www.pcd-innovations.com/key-concepts.htm> (Accessed October 16, 2003).

Gibbons, A. and Fairweather, P. (1998), *Computer-Based Instruction: Design and Development,* Englewood Cliffs, NJ: Educational Technology Publications.

Hannafin, M. and Peck, K. (1997), *The Design, Development and Evaluation of Instructional Software,* Macmillan Publishing Co.

Harless, J. (1986) Guiding Performance with Job Aids, In *Introduction to Performance Technology, Volume 1,* Washington, D.C., National Society for Performance and Instruction.

BSR/HFES 200.3 (2003), Human Factors Engineering of Software User Interfaces, Part 3: Interaction Techniques: Draft Standard for Trial Use, Santa Monica, CA, Human Factors and Ergonomics Society.

Horton, W. (2000), *Designing Web-based Training: How to Teach Anyone Anything Anywhere Anytime,* New York: John Wiley & Sons.

HUD (2003), PHA Profiles job aid, Housing Authority, the Department of Housing and Urban Development. Online. Available HTTP: <http://www.hud.gov/offices/pih/systems/pic/haprofiles/address-jobaid.pdf> (Accessed September 10, 2003).

ISO 9241-13, (1998) Ergonomic requirements for office work with visual display terminals (VDTs), Part 13: User guidance, Geneva, International Organization for Standardization.

Landauer, T. (1995), *The Trouble with Computers, Usefulness, Usability, and Productivity,* Cambridge, MA: MIT Press, Massachusetts Institute of Technology.

Landauer, T., Egan, D., Remde, J., Lesk, M., Lochbaum, C. and Ketchum, D. (1993), Enhancing the usability of text through computer delivery and formative evaluation: The SuperBook project, In C. McKnight, A. Dillon, and J. Richardson (eds.), *Hypertext: A Psychological Perspective,* New York: Ellis Horwood.

Lee, W.W. & Owens, D.L. (2000) *Multimedia-based Instructional Design.* San Francisco CA: Jossey-Bass/Pfeiffer.

Macromedia (2003), Macromedia Authorware 7, Macromedia, Inc.. Online. Available HTTP: <www.macromedia.com/software/authorware/> (accessed October 21, 2003).

Mager, R. (1975), Preparing Instructional Objectives, 2nd Edition, Belmont, California: Fearon-Pitman Publishers, Inc.

Marion, C. (2000), Make Way for Interactive Assistance, Part 2 of What is Interaction Design and What Does It Mean to Information Designers? Online. Available HTTP: <http://www.chesco.com/~cmarion/PCD/MakeWayforInteractiveAsst.html> (Accessed May 15, 2000).

Markle, S. (1983), *Designs for Instructional Designers*, 2nd Edition, New York: John Wiley & Sons, pp. 191-209.

McGraw, K. L. and McGraw, B. A. (1997), Wizards, Coaches, Advisors, & More: A Performance Support Primer, ACM CHI 97 Tutorial.

Merrill, M.D. (1994). *Instructional Design Theory.* Englewood Cliffs, NJ: Educational Technology Publications.

Merrill, M. (1996), Instructional transaction theory: Instructional design based on knowledge objects, *Educational Technology, 36*, pp. 30-37.

Merrill, M. and Boutwell, R. (1973), Instructional development: Methodology and research, in F. N. Kolinger (ed), *Review of Research in Education,* Vol. 1, Itasca, Ill. F.E. Peacock, pp. 53-131.

Microsoft (2002), User Assistance, Microsoft Library, Online. Available HTTP: <http://msdn.mirosoft.com/library/default,asp?url=/library/en-us/d> (Accessed October 26, 2002).

Morrison, G.R., Ross, S.M., & Kemp, J. E. (2001). *Designing Effective Instruction.* (3rd ed.). New York: John Wiley & Sons.

Price, J. and Korman, H. (1993), *How to Communicate Technical Information,* Menlo Park, CA: Benjamin/Cummings.

Raybould, B. (2000) Building Performance-Centered Web-Based Systems, Information Systems, and Knowledge Management Systems in the 21st Century, *Performance Improvement,* July.

RoboHelp Office (2003), RoboHelp Office X4, eHelp Corporation, Online. Available HTTP: <http://www.ehelp.com/products/robohelp/ehelp.asp> (Accessed September 3, 2003)

Rossett,A. and Gautier-Downes, J. (1991), *A Handbook of Job Aids,* San Francisco, CA: Jossey-Bass/Pfeiffer.

Swezey, R. and Pearlstein, R. (1975), *Guidebook for Developing Criterion-Referenced Tests,* U. S. Army Research Institute for the Behavioral and Social Sciences, AD A01-4987.

Telcordia (2000), Telcordia Performance Support Project Estimator, Guided Tour Online. Available: HTTP: <http//www.800teachme.com/tools/estimator.html> (accessed 20 February 2003).

Telcordia (2003), Telcordia Latent Semantic Indexing (LSI) Demo Machine. Online. Available HTTP: <http://lsi.research.telcordia.com> (accessed July 15, 2003).

Wright, P. (1988), Issues of Content and Presentation in Document Design, in Martin Helander, ed. *Handbook of Human-Computer Interaction,* New York: North-Holland, pp. 629-652.

XML FAQ (2003), Online. Available HTTP: <http://www.ucc.ie:8080/cocoon/xmlfaq> (accessed July 22, 2003).

CHAPTER EIGHT

Testing Performance Support Products

INTRODUCTION

This chapter provides a systematic approach to testing performance support products both individually and as an integrated performance support system. While the title of this chapter emphasizes testing (i.e., performance testing), evaluation also will be covered as part of the process. Both tests and evaluations are assessments of a product in terms of some criteria. However, evaluation can be differentiated from testing in that evaluation is essentially subjective (based on judgments) while testing is primarily objective (based on measurements of time, errors, etc.). This chapter will cover five levels of assessment:

- Developmental testing, including heuristic evaluation and alpha testing, using designers, peers or experts to evaluate a product as soon as the first version is completed. Heuristic evaluation is based on a set of criteria (or heuristics), while alpha testing is done to determine whether the product functions as expected.
- Usability testing, using representatives of the target population, of a product, or performance support system in terms of a set of usability objectives.
- Beta testing, using volunteer potential users of the completed product (typically a stand-alone software product) in a real use environment.
- Product testing, using individuals knowledgeable about the application, prior to the release of the product or system.
- Follow-up Evaluation, using on the job incumbents who have been using the product.

Evaluation Methods

In conducting assessments, the following methods can be applied: documentation analysis, documented evidence, observation, analytical evaluation, measurement and empirical evaluation. The choice of method depends on what attributes of a product are being evaluated or tested and how those attributes can best be determined.

Documentation analysis

Documentation analysis is an evaluation method based on the analysis of documents which may describe the general and specific properties or attributes of the product. Such documents may include design documents containing system and user requirements, manuals, user guides, etc. Analysis of such documents by the evaluator provides information as to what attributes of the product should be present. For example, the system requirements for a particular application may specify that only user-initiated help will be used in the help system. This method may be used in preparation for a heuristic evaluation.

Documented evidence

Documented evidence refers to the analysis of any relevant documented information about the task requirements or characteristics, flow of work, user skills, user aptitudes, existing user conventions or biases, test data from the design of similar systems, etc. Such information may be used to determine whether a given guideline is applicable when performing heuristic evaluations. For example, task analysis data may have indicated that rapid response time was an important consideration in the use of a performance aid within a particular task environment.

Documented evidence can also pertain to any documented information relating to the product meeting applicable guidelines during heuristic evaluation. Such evidence may include existing user conventions or biases, prototype test data, test data from the design of similar systems, etc. For example, test data from a similar system may have indicated that the help system navigation structure used was appropriate for the types of users and tasks relevant to the application. In this case, whether the guideline was met is essentially determined on the basis of documented evidence relevant to that guideline for the similar system.

Observation

Observation means simply to examine or inspect the product for the presence of a particular observable property, e.g., the correct output is produced and properly formatted, a given guideline is applicable because the system includes features addressed by the guideline, etc. Observation is the major method used during alpha, usability and product testing. Observations can be made by anyone who has the necessary skill to systematically check the product and determine if it has the particular properties associated with a system requirement or a specified guideline. Due to their obvious nature, such observations readily can be confirmed by another person.

In heuristic evaluation, observation also can be used to confirm that a particular observable condition has been met, e.g., that no more than four colors are used, titles are the correct type font and consistently placed, defined default values are visually indicated, etc. The observed property is compared with the stated guideline to determine if the guideline has been met.

Analytical evaluation

Analytical evaluation pertains to "informed" judgments concerning the properties of a product by a relevant expert (i.e., of those properties). This method is typically used for the evaluation of properties which can be judged only in the context of other information or knowledge. Analytical evaluation can be applied when the system exists only in terms of design documents, user populations are not available for empirical evaluation or time and resources are constrained. In heuristic evaluation, it can be used to determine whether a particular guideline is applicable, e.g., to determine if system-initiated help is likely to distract users, if rapid search time is important, etc. In determining whether the guideline for placing information in columns in a performance aid is applicable, for example, the analytical evaluation would be based upon the knowledge of the expert concerning whether typical users are likely to compare information in performing the task.

Analytical evaluation also can be applied in determining whether a system requirement or guideline has been met. The evaluator needs to have the skills and knowledge necessary to reliably judge the appropriateness and usability of the design solution. For example, analytical evaluation is applied when a relevant expert makes a judgment as to whether the information in a document is current, can be read quickly and is understandable. In the above cases, "read quickly" and "understandable" are the judgmental aspects. It should be noted that analytical evaluation can verify the tenability of a design, but cannot validate the design.   Validation can be accomplished only by using empirical evaluation.

Measurements

Measurement refers to measuring or calculating a variable concerning properties of a product. Examples of such properties are response time, font size, line width, etc. The obtained value from the measurement is compared with the value stated in the requirement or guideline. The measurement method can only be applied when a version of the product exists, i.e., prototype, alpha test version, usability test version, beta test version, product test version.

Empirical evaluation

Empirical evaluation, using representative end users, can be used to determine the relevancy and appropriateness of particular design approaches as well as whether a product meets its requirements and is "usable." This method is most appropriate when a prototype or the actual system is available and potential or actual user population representatives are available. Many kinds of test procedures could be used, but in each case the test subjects need to be representative of the end user population and be of sufficient number that the results can be generalized to the user population as a whole. For example, empirical evaluation to determine whether rapid search time is important can involve a study of users using the product to perform a number of representative job tasks. In another example, empirical evaluation might be used to determine whether users will frequently request help on a topic by having typical users perform a number of representative job tasks using only the on-line help for user guidance.

   Empirical evaluation (in the form of usability testing) is often the only appropriate method to determine whether certain requirements and guidelines have actually been met. In such cases, the task performance of end users using the performance support product is analyzed to determine conformance with the requirements and applicable guidelines. For example, by analyzing the time it takes users to find a help topic, it would be possible to determine if the topic descriptors and navigation processes are appropriate. Such tests could (and should) be performed both during the development process (e.g., by rapid prototyping) and after the design and implementation of the system (e.g., usability testing). Empirical evaluation is used to determine whether the product is usable and is generally based on both objective and subjective user data. It is important to note that it is often necessary to also evaluate test results in terms of effectiveness (e.g., the product supports the user in his/her task in a manner which leads to improved performance, results in a difficult task being performed with less difficulty or enables the user to accomplish a task that he/she would not have been able to otherwise).

WHEN TO TEST

   Heuristic evaluation is typically performed early in the development process when initial versions of a product are available. On the other hand, alpha testing can only be accomplished when a product has reached the stage of development where a testable version is available. Since both heuristic evaluation and alpha testing are done during the development phase, they often are called developmental testing.

   Usability testing should be performed after deficiencies found during developmental testing are eliminated and the "final" version of product is available. Beta testing is often performed on products that are intended for commercial use after usability testing to obtain feedback from intended users before releasing the product. When ever possible, beta testing should be done to minimize problems that may later arise during actual use of the product in its intended context of use and environment. Final testing is accomplished by product testing prior to the release of the product and follow-up evaluation should be done after the product has been in use for six months or more.

TEST PLANNING

A well-developed test plan is essential. It is particularly important to specify usability objectives within the plan because these objectives should be the major criteria for the acceptability of the product. A test plan needs to be prepared for each performance support product and an integration of products in the case of a performance support system. Typically a test plan will have the following sections:

- Introduction – including a description of the product, the product objectives and the usability objectives.
- Overview of test levels (a brief description of the levels being included).
- Heuristic Evaluation – including description, data to be collected, evaluation procedures and resource requirements (personnel, evaluation materials).
- Alpha Test – including description, test cases, traceability, data to be collected, test procedures, test resources requirements (personnel, facility requirements, testing materials).
- Usability Test – including description, test cases, traceability, data to be collected, test procedures, test resources requirements (personnel, facility requirements, testing materials).
- Beta Test – including description of data to be collected, instructions to the users, evaluation procedures and resource requirements (users, evaluation materials, analysis personnel).
- Product Test – including description, test cases, traceability, data to be collected, test procedures, test resources requirements (personnel, facility requirements, testing materials).

Test Cases (Alpha, Usability and Product Tests)

This section describes the test cases to be written and run for each of the detailed requirements as well as all of the features of the product. Test cases are essentially scenarios for testing each of the product's features to determine whether the appropriate output is produced and to ensure that it has no detectable software faults. Typically, at least one test case should be developed for each of the product's features and requirements.

Traceability (Alpha, Usability and Product Tests)

Traceability is the ability to tie each test case, or use scenario, to a requirement or requirements. This is often accomplished by means of a checklist of the requirements with associated test cases so that any problem found can be associated with the affected requirement. In the case of a software product, traceability is often required by the organization's software quality assurance process.

Data to Be Collected

This section describes the specific data to be collected during the test. In the case of an alpha or product test, data for each test case would include: start time of test, end time of test, number of errors discovered, type of error, severity of error, probable cause of error (if known) and repeatability of the error. Usability tests may include additional data such as: time to complete each of the features, number and types of errors made in accessing options and navigating through the product's windows and dialogues, number of times help is used to support each of the user tasks, number of keystrokes and time taken to find appropriate help topic when help is accessed at user's discretion, number of times appropriate help topic was not found when help is accessed at user's discretion, time to access a specified help topic within the help content, number of keystrokes required to access specified help topic within the help content. Ratings and user comments concerning confidence in using the product, overall ease of use of the product and features of the product also may be collected in a usability test. In addition, observer data about test participant's difficulties in using the product are typically collected.

The methods used to collect the data also would be specified in this section. For example, whether the data would be collected by the observer or the test participant and how the data would be recorded.

Test Procedures

The test procedures section specifies the step-by-step process to be followed in conducting the test. It includes briefing participants, instructions to participants, steps in the test sessions and de-briefing participants at the end (including the use of rating forms, questionnaires, etc.). If both observed and unobserved test sessions are being conducted, separate procedures for each type of test session should be included.

Testing Resources

Personnel

Specifies the number of test personnel that will be required to observe participants and summarize the results as well as the minimum number and types of test participants needed.

Facility Requirements

This section describes the location of the test (e.g., at the tester's workstation or at the user's location), the type of equipment (e.g., 400 MHz PC or better running Windows 98, 2000 or XP) and any other facility requirements necessary to conduct the test.

Test Materials

The test materials section describes the specific materials to be used in the test sessions. For example:

- Test Procedure Overview (to be provided in written form to unobserved users and verbally to users by Test Observers)
- Test Log form

- Test scenarios for each of test sessions
- Questionnaires/checklists

DEVELOPMENTAL TESTING – HEURISTIC EVALUATION

As noted above, heuristic evaluation should be done early in development after the first complete draft, or version, of the product is finished. There are various forms of heuristic evaluation. In simplest approach, the product is rated on the basis of a short list of questions, typically concerned with observed quality (e.g., spelling, grammar, appearance, consistency, apparent clearness of the content, etc.). A more involved process (often called "usability inspection") utilizes experts or peers to inspect the product and to evaluate it in terms of a list of general heuristics (a set of usability principles). These general heuristics (Molich and Nielsen, 1990; Nielsen 1994) include such criteria as:

- Visibility of system state
- Using simple and natural dialogue
- Providing user control and freedom
- Consistency and standards
- Speaking the user's language
- Minimizing the user's memory load (using recognition rather than recall)
- Providing feedback
- Providing flexibility and efficiency of use (e.g., shortcuts)
- Helping users recognize, diagnose and recover from errors
- Providing help and documentation

In its typical form, a small number of usability inspectors examine an interactive product and judge its compliance to the list of heuristics. Usually, inspectors also will make judgments as to the severity of each of the problems identified (i.e., the degree to which the problem would tend to impede user performance).

It is important to note that usability inspections and empirical end-user testing lead to the identification of different usability problems (Nielsen, 1993; Desurvire, 1994; Catani and Biers, 1998). Therefore, one is not a substitute for the other and both should be used to optimize the evaluation and testing process. In a comparison of four evaluation techniques, Jeffries et al., (1991) found that each had advantages and disadvantages and identified different types of problems. Also, it should be noted that when the evaluators are both subject matter experts and usability experts, more potential usability problems typically are found during the evaluation.

A number of different heuristics have been proposed for use in evaluating user interfaces (Molich and Nielsen, 1990; Nielsen, 1994; Gerhardt-Powals, 1996). While these heuristics have been widely used, particularly those proposed by Nielsen, they have not been validated. However, there is an ISO standard (ISO 9241-10, 1995) that provides 7 dialogue design principles that can be used for heuristic evaluation at the general level. These principles are:

- Suitability for the task – A dialogue is suitable for a task when it supports the user in the effective and efficient completion of the task and the user is able to focus on the task itself rather than the technology supporting the task.
- Self-descriptiveness – A dialogue is self-descriptive to the extent that at any time it is obvious to the users which dialogue they are in, where they are within the dialog, which actions can be taken and how they can be performed.

- Conformity with user expectations – A dialogue conforms with user expectations if it corresponds to predictable contextual needs of the user and to commonly accepted conventions.
- Suitability for learning – A dialogue is suitable for learning when it supports and guides the user in learning to use the system.
- Controllability – A dialogue is controllable when the user is able to initiate and control the direction and pace of the interaction until the goal has been met.
- Error tolerance – A dialogue is error-tolerant if, despite evident errors in input, the intended result may be achieved with either no or minimal corrective action by the user. Error tolerance is achieved by means of damage control, error correction or error management.
- Suitability for individualization – A dialogue is suitable for individualization when users can modify the interaction and the presentation of information to suit their individual capabilities and needs

Six of the dialog principles used in the ISO standard originated from a factor analysis done in Germany to determine what aspects of a software system interface had the most impact on users (Dzida et al., 1978) and these principles were included in a German standard (DIN 66 234-8, 1988). An additional principle was added by the experts that developed the ISO standard. These principles have been used to support the summative and formative evaluation of software systems in Europe (Gediga et al., 1999) and we included the 7 principles in a checklist (see Figure 8.1), used by both designers and users at Bellcore and Telcordia Technologies, to evaluate performance support product interfaces.

Interactive Dialogues*								Evaluator	Date
Dialogues used in _____ are:								Comments**	
Suitable for the task	Disagree 1	2	3	4	5	6	Agree 7		
Self-descriptive	1	2	3	4	5	6	7		
Controllable by the user	1	2	3	4	5	6	7		
In conformity with user expectations	1	2	3	4	5	6	7		
Error tolerant	1	2	3	4	5	6	7		
Suitable for individualization	1	2	3	4	5	6	7		
Easy to learn	1	2	3	4	5	6	7		

* See ISO 9241-10 for definintions and examples of dialogue principles
** For ratings of 4 or less, please state specific problems in the comments column (attach additional pages as necessary)

Figure 8.1 ISO 9241-10 Checklist

The advantage in using the ISO 9241-10 dialogue principles for heuristic evaluation is that they are an ISO standard and widely accepted by experts in many countries. It also is worth noting that the revision to Part 10 currently underway in the ISO will include a number of guidelines for each of the 7 principles. The result revision should be available as an ISO standard sometime during 2004.

In a more stringent approach, the evaluation is done according to a specific set of criteria such as meeting a list of relevant standards or guidelines. Christie and Gardiner (1990) refer to this walkthrough method as an "audit." The audit approach has the advantage of driving the evaluation down to a more specific set of criteria that require less subjective judgments. It is a well known principle in the psychology of testing and measurement that the more specific the criterion is for making a judgment, the more reliable the results will be. One of the major purposes of this book is to provide criteria for the design and evaluation of the various performance support products. In addition to the general design guidance provided in Chapter 5, specific guidelines for each of the performance support products are provided in Chapter 7. These guidelines have been extracted and are provided in product checklists in the appendices as follows:

* Documentation – Appendix B.
* Performance Aids – Appendix C.
* Online Help – Appendix D.
* Coaches, Advisors and Wizards – Appendix E.
* Instruction – Appendix F.
* Electronic Performance Support Systems – Appendix G.

The product checklists are intended to be used to support evaluation by both designers and experts during the performance support development process. These checklists are essentially a variation of the checklists that the author developed for the ISO software ergonomic standards (ISO 9241-12 through 17). All of the checklists have the same basic layout and are designed to be used in a two step process. The first step is to determine the applicability of the guideline and the second step is to check-off whether the product conforms to those guidelines that were determined to be applicable. Applicability of a particular guideline depends on:

1. Whether the conditional statement, if included as part of the guideline, is true. A particular recommendation is (or is not) applicable when the conditional if-statement is (or is not) true.
2. How the design environment pertains to the guideline. A particular guideline may (or may not) be applicable because of user, task, environment and technology features.

The methods that are appropriate to determine applicability of a particular guideline include: documentation analysis, documented evidence (e.g., prior studies), observation (the feature is included in the performance aid), analytical evaluation and empirical evaluation (see the description of these methods earlier in this chapter).

If a guideline is applicable on the basis of the criteria described above, the next step is to determine whether or not the guideline has been met. This can be determined by using one or more of the following methods: measurements (e.g., line width), observation, documented evidence, analytical evaluation or empirical evaluation.

It is highly recommended that the checklist evaluation be done by the product developer, at least one other developer (preferably an expert) and a performance technologist (or human factors professional). Also, the evaluation will be much more effective if the evaluators simulate the use of the product by going through a number of representative use scenarios during the evaluation. This approach employs the "walkthrough" method as popularized in the "cognitive walkthrough" method. However, the cognitive walkthrough method is primarily an analytical evaluation of the ease of learning a design with reference to attributes correlated with ease of learning. The focus of cognitive walkthrough evaluations is to identify mismatches between the designer's and user's view of the task by simulating the user's problem solving process and determining the probable actions that a user should be able to take without problems imposed by the design (Lewis et al., 1990; Rieman et al., 1991; Wharton et al., 1994).

The walkthrough method proposed in this chapter (sometimes called an expert walkthrough) differs from the typical cognitive walkthrough in that it is not limited to ease of learning considerations. Walking through the task scenarios are primarily intended to establish the context of use for the evaluators so that they can determine better both the applicability of and conformance to the various guidelines. In addition, the walkthroughs provide an opportunity for the evaluators to discover additional problems (including learning) not represented in the guidelines.

Task scenarios for use in heuristic evaluation can be developed by either the product designer, developer or the test administrator. Wherever possible, the scenarios should relate directly to the product's objectives and requirements. Since test cases (e.g., scenarios) will be used later in alpha, usability and product testing, a cost-effective approach is for the test administrator to develop a set of scenarios that can be used through out the evaluation and testing process.

Methods used during heuristic evaluation may include any of the methods discussed earlier in this chapter, but typically should include at least observation and analytical evaluation. Other methods may be required depending on the nature of the attribute being evaluated.

DEVELOPMENTAL TESTING – ALPHA TESTING

Alpha testing is intended to determine whether a software product functions as expected prior to testing it with users. Test cases are developed to verify that the product meets its stated objectives and that the software produces reliable results without failures. Alpha tests are particularly appropriate for online help and EPSS products, but also can be done on any other performance support product that is to be delivered electronically. In the case of large software products having a number of separate software modules, alpha tests are typically done on each of the modules independently.

While alpha testing is often done by only one individual (the developer), it will be more effective if at least one, and preferably two, other members of the development team participate. Since developers know their product so well, they may miss things during the test that a less familiar individual would not. If a separate programmer developed the software, he or she should serve as one of the alpha testers. Even though a programmer typically checks and rechecks everything in the software, a formal alpha test typically uncovers problems that the programmer missed.

The first task to be accomplished in preparing for an alpha test is the preparation of the test cases. As suggested above, these test cases can be "reusable" during subsequent test stages. To develop test cases, each of the product's features and associated requirements must be examined to determine what user actions are required (or may take place) and what outputs should result or changes in system states should occur. A test case (or cases) is then written to test each of these interactions with the product. The cases should be developed in a standardized format to maximize consistency and minimize learning time. Figure 8.2 depicts a standardized format that can be used for developing and presenting test cases.

Figure 8.3 shows an example a completed test case specification for a test having two test cases. While this example relates to an EPSS product, similar test cases can be developed for any performance support product that has a user interface component. For example, a test case for a computer-based instruction module might describe the test procedure to check that all of the options in a quiz work properly and that the appropriate feedback is produced. In the case of an online help product, a test case might describe the test procedure to check all of the links in a particular topic screen to ensure that they work and go to the correct help topic. For the help topic link test, it would be possible to write a generic test case that could apply to all help topic screens that had links. Since this approach minimizes the test case development time and reduces the complexity of the material used by the testers, it is highly recommended where ever applicable.

It is important to be able to tie the test cases to the specific requirements established for the product. This can be done in a number of ways, e.g., listing the related requirement(s) or providing a separate table showing the relationship of test cases to requirements. Probably, the use of a separate table is the easiest approach since the table can be readily modified when new cases are added.

TEST CASE SPECIFICATIONS

TEST 1

Test Case ID: Test Name: author:

Introduction to test 1

TESTCASE 1

   Purpose of test case (e.g., show that ...)

   Method action(s)

   Test Result(s)

TESTCASE 2

   Purpose of test case (e.g., show that ...)

   Method action(s)

   Test Result(s)

Figure 8.2 Sample Test Cases Format Specification

Test 3

Test ID: SL1 **Test Name:** Setup Staff Loadings   **Author:** J. Williams

The Setup Staff Loadings Test is to test the feature allowing all default staff loading values to be modified by the using organization. It requires that the application be installed and a new project selected before initiation.

TEST CASE 1

Purpose: To ensure that entry of staff loading values are echoed correctly and accepted by Estimator.

Method: Enter new values for all staff loading categories.

Results: Estimator accepts and displays new values correctly.

TEST CASE 2

Purpose: To ensure that entry of staff loading values are saved and displayed correctly in Staff Loading Parameter dialog.

Method: Create New Project, click on Deliverables Tab, complete information for a new deliverable, click on Staff Loading, check values against changes made in Test Case 1 above.

Results: Estimator displays new values correctly.

Figure 8.3 Example of a Completed Test Case Specification

In addition to developing the test case specifications, a standard method of reporting test results should be developed. Standardized reporting forms will aid in the analysis of test data and can provide an audit trail on the disposition of errors and problems. Figure 8.4 shows an example of a reporting form that can be used for any test phase involving the use of test cases. The first column of the form would be completed by the individual tester during the test sessions. It should be noted that the steps done by the tester prior to the error also should be listed on the form. The severity column would be completed, either by the individual tester, or as a team consensus after reviewing the problem descriptions. Severity ratings may be in simple terms such as low (small potential impact on performance, but requirements met), medium (some impact on performance, slight deviation from requirements) and high (definite impact on performance, e.g., a system "crash") or may be based on a 5 or 7 point scale (low – high). A more comprehensive approach to severity would be to rate a problem with respect to its frequency and probability of occurrence, as well as its impact on user performance. Corrective action taken would be entered in the action column with the date that it was accomplished. In some cases, the decision on what corrective action to be taken is also made by the team rather than the developer. However, the entry in the action column would be done by the developer when the correction action was completed.

Test Report

Test: **Tester:**   **Date:**

Test Case 1   **Start time:**   **End Time:**

Errors/problems/causes Noted	Severity	Action

Test Case 2   **Start time:**   **End Time:**

Errors/problems/causes Noted	Severity	Action

Figure 8.4 Sample Test Case Reporting Form

Often, a decision is made by the team as to the cost effectiveness of correcting low severity problems noted during the testing. Those low severity problems that pertain to correctness of information or data, no matter how trivial, should be corrected. In any case, all medium and high-level severity problems must be corrected prior to performing a usability test.

USABILITY TESTING

Since usability testing is empirical and based on data collected from representative users, its importance cannot be overstated. Usability testing provides direct information about how users interact with the performance support product and the problems they experience. It is important to note that usability testing provides information on the usability of the product, but not necessarily the usefulness of the product. The usefulness (or utility) of the product is based on needs analysis and can only be verified later by beta testing and follow-up evaluation. The four major goals of usability testing are:

- Quality control – To ensure the product meets its specified objectives and requirements.
- User performance and acceptance – To ensure that the intended users of the product can effectively and efficiently perform the tasks for which the product was designed and find the experience of using the product acceptable (so that it will get used).
- Deficiency correction – To ensure that deficiencies are identified and corrected through appropriate design changes.
- Deficiency prevention – To ensure that potential performance problems in using the product on the job are prevented.

Usability testing is often described as observational testing or evaluation because it is typically accomplished by an observer recording the activities of a user while performing a series of tasks using the product. It also has been called "user trials" by McClelland (1990) who defines user trials as "a series of controlled observations undertaken in an artificial situation with the deliberate manipulation of some variables to answer one or more specific questions about the effectiveness of the product." Setting up a user trial (usability test) involves creating an environment enabling the interaction between the product and the user to be measured and examined in a systematic manner (McClelland, 1990).

Typically, a usability test consists of a number of representative users completing a series of typical (and critical) tasks using the product or application. During the test, an observer (preferably a usability specialist) observes the process and records results, problems, mistakes, the use of resources, time, etc. It is important to note that usability testing also can be done on early prototypes of the product. However, usability tests of prototypes generally are done with fewer test participants due to the expenses involved and the difficulty of obtaining representative users several times during development.

Usability Criteria

The term usability now appears frequently in conjunction with software products and associated user support materials such as online help and documentation. In order to measure usability, developers of usability tests need to know what usability is. Usability has been defined differently by various practitioners and even within different International Standards. As noted above, usability often gets confused with "usefulness" (whether a product helps the user achieve their goals) and "utility" (whether the product has the functionality that the user needs to attain their goals). In fact, Rubin (1994) states that the four goals of usability are: usefulness, effectiveness, learnability, and likeability. Branaghan (1997) defined usability in terms of five qualities (learnability, efficiency, memorability, error minimization and satisfaction). However, the most accepted definition for usability is found in the ergonomics standard: Ergonomic requirements for office work with visual display terminals (VDTs) – Guidance on usability (ISO 9241-11, 1998).

The following definitions are taken from ISO 9241-11. Examples have been added to aid in the development of specific metrics for the components.

Usability

A concept comprising the effectiveness, efficiency and satisfaction with which specific users can achieve specified goals in a particular environment. The inclusion of "in a particular environment" in this definition is very important because it stresses the need to keep in mind (and state) the context of use of the product when designing usability tests. ISO 9241-11 also defines "usability attributes" in terms of the "features and characteristics of a product that influence the effectiveness, efficiency and satisfaction by which specified users can achieve specified goals in a particular environment."

Effectiveness

Measures of the accuracy and completeness of the goals achieved. Examples of effectiveness include:
- Appropriateness (validity) of data/information for successful task performance (e.g., the information provided allowed user to complete the task successfully).
- Completeness of data/information (e.g., the information was complete in that the user did not need to go to secondary source).
- Reliability (correctness) of data/information (e.g., the information was correct and did not lead to user errors).

Efficiency

Measures the accuracy and completeness of the goals achieved relative to the resources (e.g., time, human effort) used to achieve the specified goals. Examples of efficiency measurements include:
- Time to perform task (e.g., user is able to complete the task within specified time or less).
- Fixing time for errors (e.g., user is able to diagnose and fix error in specified time or less).
- Help/documentation time (e.g., user is able to find appropriate help information in a specified time and number of keystrokes, or less).
- Learning/relearning time (e.g., user is able to learn the help system structure and contents within a specified time or less).

Satisfaction

Measures of user's (and other affected people's) comfort with and acceptability for the product. Examples of measurements for satisfaction include:
- Ease of use ratings by user (e.g., user rates the product on an ease of use scale).
- Quality of output ratings (e.g., user rates the product on scales for appropriateness, completeness and correctness of information).
- Ease of learning ratings by user (e.g., user rates the performance support product on an ease of learning scale).
- Standardized usability rating scales (e.g., QUIS).

Usability criteria, therefore, are essentially the required levels of measures of usability (i.e., effectiveness, efficiency and satisfaction) that are to be verified by the usability test. To apply the above examples to evaluating a performance support product, it is necessary to specify the measurable criteria to be met (very similarly to instructional objectives). For example, within a specified time would need to be changed to a specific objective time (e.g., less than 1 minute, 90% of the time).

Participant Requirements

While all authors of usability testing books and articles state that usability test participants should be representative of the members of the target population for the product or application, there are wide discrepancies in opinions on how many users need to be tested. Jakob Nielsen (2000) suggests that 5 users are sufficient and that tests with more than 5 users are a waste of resources. It should be noted, however, that Nielsen suggests running a number of different usability tests (iterative design) until (most) deficiencies are eliminated. He also states that 15 users would be needed to discover all of the usability problems in a design if a single test is used. If using only a few participants, Nielsen suggests that the users selected should be "average" users.

Caulton (2001) argues that the studies showing that only a small number of participants are required for a usability test are based on the assumption that all types of users have the same probability of encountering all usability problems. He further asserts that if the homogeneity assumption is violated, then the number of users required increases with the number of heterogeneous groups. In a model of a hypothetical usability test, Caulton generates three curves; one for common problems, one for rare problems and an overall curve that averaged the common and rare curves. His data suggest that while only two users are needed to find 80% of the common problems, six are required to find 80% of all problems, and eight are required to find 80% of the rare problems. It is interesting to note that the standard for reporting usability test results (ANSI/INCITS-354, 2001) suggests that at least eight users should be included in a usability test.

If statistical sampling techniques are used to determine sample size, much larger numbers of users will be required (generally 30 – 100). However, statistical sampling estimates are based on the assumption that nothing is known about the population and variables being studied which is not typically the case in user testing situations. McClelland (1990) points out that the determination of the number of users required should be guided by practical experience and the constraints imposed by local circumstances. In my experience, 3 – 5 users representing each of the user types (e.g., level of experience in the subject domain, different job specialties that will use the system, different age groups, etc.) provide sufficient data. However, if the application is complex, more users may be required due to the fact that a single user will not be able to test all the available functionality within an acceptable time frame. It is important to note that sample sizes can be minimized by using individuals that fall into more than one category (e.g., age and job specialty) and then analyzing the data using multivariate techniques to see if there are any interactions between the categories.

Determining the categories of users that need to be included in the usability test is, therefore, a very important part of the testing strategy. It has already been stated that users should be representative of the product's intended target population. But the question is, how representative? Organizations developing performance support for computer systems will rarely have sufficient access to potential users to randomly select individuals to be included in the user testing. Since users representatives obtained from outside the developing organization are generally volunteers, it is difficult to systematically select individuals on the basis of the relevant user categories. In such cases, the use of questionnaires for obtaining biographical data on the users is essential to interpreting test results. We have found that it is often possible to obtain people to participate in user testing within the organization that have similar characteristics as the expected target population. When such individuals are available within the organization, much more control is possible in the selection process and it is more likely that participants can be selected on the basis of the relevant user characteristics. However, when in-house people are used for usability testing, it is essential that beta testing be done to verify the results with outside users before the product is released.

Task Scenarios

As noted previously, task scenarios may be developed for use in all of the evaluation and testing phases. However, task scenarios for user testing need to be written specifically for the user representatives that will participate in the test. As a result, more descriptive information about the task and associated procedures may be necessary than was required for heuristic evaluation and alpha testing. Tasks chosen for usability testing should include tasks that are representative of the tasks that users are expected to be able to do with the product and tasks that are of critical importance. These tasks can be extracted from task analysis data (if it exists) or from the requirements stating the intended use of the product. Tasks should be selected that are reasonably short, but still represent the type of user interaction required. Selected tasks also should produce a reasonable product or outcome so that participants feel that performing the task was worthwhile.

Modifying Defaults

The purpose of this task is to change the defaults initially set up in the product to those that best represent your operating environment. Inputs to this task are the specific default values assigned by the test administrator (in your *Test Participant Notice*). The outputs from this task are the modified default values that will be used in the estimation process.

1. Read the following steps before proceeding with the test.
2. Determine what defaults you are to modify from your *Test Participant Notice.*
3. Tell the test administrator when you are ready to start the task.
4. Select the "Defaults" option from the menu bar and select the "Deliverable Types" Tab.
5. Add new Deliverable Type (assigned) and enter "reasonable" values for "Unit Type", "Hrs/Unit" and "Units" for the new Deliverable Type.
6. Deselect types assigned and save the new values.
7. Tell the test administrator that you have completed this part of the task.
8. Click on the appropriate tab for the other defaults that you have been assigned to change.
9. Change the values as specified in your *Test Participant Notice,* save the new values, and return to the main screen.
10. Inform the test administrator when you are done.
11. Record any problems that you experienced while changing the defaults on the Test Log in the Section marked "Problems"
12. Record any additional comments that you may have on changing default values in the "Comments" Section of the Test Log.

Figure 8.5 Example of a Test Task Scenario

Each task scenario should start with a brief summary stating the purpose of the task, the major inputs required and the resulting outputs. Task procedures should be listed in a step-by-step format so that participants can easily follow them. In addition, the task scenarios need to identify the inputs to the task that the participants will be expected to provide during the test. I have found that this can best be done by referencing a separate form that has the specific data for individual participants (see Figure 8.5).

Test Sessions

A test session is essentially a test task or group of tasks that logically constitute a major portion of the user test. The outputs of a test session should relate to one or more specific product requirements or features for which usability determinations are to be made. A test session should be reasonably independent in that it can begin and end without requiring special preparation. However, a test session may depend on a previous test session being performed where a process is accumulative.

Observed vs. Non-observed Tests

While observed user testing (particularly by a trained test observer) is always the preferred method, additional non-observed user testing can extend the test population and enhance the reliability of the usability test data. In our usability testing of Release 2.0 of the Telcordia Performance Support Estimator, we doubled our sample by using non-observed participants as well as observed participants. The data collected from the non-observed participants on task time, serious problems encountered, frequency and time using help, and satisfaction with the product was equivalent (not significantly different) to data collected from observed users. However, data on errors (not recognized by the participant) and minor problems were only reliably reported by observers.

In addition to increasing sample size, the use of non-observed participants in usability testing has a number of advantages, such as:

- Participants can perform the different test sessions at times that fit into their schedules rather than dedicate a single block of time to devote to the entire test.
- The test is performed at the participant's work location, using the participant's own equipment. For software products, this has the advantage of ensuring that the software installs properly and works on the various platforms that are expected to be used.
- Participants tend to provide more comments and suggestions.

On the other hand, the use of non-observed participants has certain disadvantages, such as:

- Non-observed participants are more likely not to perform the test sessions or to perform only some of them. As a result, a good strategy is to select more non-observed participants than is needed.
- Since the test is being performed at the participant's work location, more interruptions are likely. This problem can be partially handled by asking participants to close their office door and not answer calls during a test session.
- Certain data (as noted above) cannot be obtained directly from non-observed participants. In addition, other forms of collecting data (e.g., video taping) cannot be used unless special tools are installed on the user's computer (see *Capturing Tools* and *Test Support Software* later in this chapter).

• Instructions and task scenarios need to be self explanatory and deal with potential contingencies.

If non-observed participants are used in the usability tests, the task scenarios and data collection forms need to be designed to include self recording. Figure 8.6 shows an example of the task scenario written for a non-observed participant (contrast with Figure 8.5).

Modifying Defaults

The purpose of this task is to change the defaults initially set up in the product to those that best represent your operating environment. Inputs to this task are the specific default values assigned by the test administrator (in your *Test Participant Notice*). The outputs from this task are the modified default values that will be used in the estimation process.

1. Read the following steps before proceeding with the test.
2. Determine what defaults you are to modify from your *Test Participant Notice*.
3. Find the **Defaults Test Log** and enter your assigned Deliverable Type to add and those types to be de-selected. Also enter you start time.
4. Select the "Defaults" option from the menu bar and select the "Deliverable Types" Tab.
5. Add new Deliverable Type (assigned) and enter "reasonable" values for "Unit Type", "Hrs/Unit" and "Units" for the new Deliverable Type.
6. Deselect types assigned and save the new values.
7. Record the end time on the Log
8. Click on the appropriate tab for the other defaults that you have been assigned to change.
9. Change the values as specified in your *Test Participant Notice*, save the new values, and return to the main screen.
10. Record the end time on the Log when you have completed.
11. Record any problems that you experienced while changing the defaults on the Test Log in the Section marked "Problems"
12. Record any additional comments that you may have on changing default values in the "Comments" Section of the Test Log.

Figure 8.6 Example of a Task Scenario for Non-observed Participants

During observed tests, physical recording of the test sessions can be used (e.g., video taping or keystroke capturing). In addition, test participants can be asked to "think aloud" and their comments captured by either the videotape or a separate audio tape. The use of recording devices generally requires a usability testing facility, or, at least, a dedicated space (e.g., office) and the appropriate equipment. Because of this, some organizations have outside testing organizations that have their own usability testing labs, do their usability testing. Also, observed testing done in a dedicated facility can include the use of separate observer stations where observers can use special software to record their observations.

Observed usability testing does not require the collection of data using physical recording devices. Good data can be collected by a trained observer using only data collection forms and a stop watch (or even a wrist watch). It is important that observers have a very good working knowledge of the application so that they know what correct task performance looks like and how the application is supposed to work. Additionally, it takes knowledge about the application to observe that test participants are having problems, making errors or not following expected procedures. Expertise concerning the application also is important in situations where there are application failures (e.g., runtime errors) that need to be corrected in order to complete a test session.

Test Data

As noted earlier in this chapter, data collected during a test session should include metrics relevant to the effectiveness, efficiency and satisfaction of the application or product. The test data are summarized across all of the test participants and used to determine whether the application or product met its objectives and where changes need to be made. Examples of the data relevant to testing a performance support product include:

Effectiveness

- Correct completion of the task(s) in the test session.
- Number and types of errors made during the session.
- Number and types of assistance provided (if any) by the observer.
- Type and nature of participant difficulties observed during the session.

Efficiency

- Time to accomplish task(s) and test session.
- Time to find support information (e.g., online help topic, document paragraph) if appropriate.
- Number of keystrokes required to accomplish task or find information.

Satisfaction

- Rating of the overall ease of use of the product.
- Rating of the interface characteristics of the product.
- Rating of the confidence in the product's outputs.
- Listing of major likes and dislikes about the product.
- General comments.

If the application or product contains software, it is very useful to collect data on software problems in addition to the above data, for example, the condition causing the software problem to occur, the impact of the problem, and what (if anything) was done to rectify it.

Test Materials

Materials needed for conducting a usability test include both materials for the test participants and materials for the test observers. I have found that it is a very good idea to place all of the test participant materials together into a "test participant package." This package consists of the following:

- Description of the application or product being tested
- Purpose of the test
- General instructions
- Preparation (e.g., installation instructions)
- Test sessions (including descriptions and procedures)

- Test session logs (for unobserved tests)
- Questionnaires (debriefing materials)
- Instructions for return of test materials (for unobserved tests)

In addition to the above material, individual participants will require a form that specifies the specific data that they are to input and/or features of the product that they are to test. The test observers will need a set of the forms that they will use to record the data to be collected during the test (see Figure 8.7 for an example test log). In some cases, it also may be necessary to provide instructions on how the data should be recorded.

Help Test Log

Participant Name: _____

Window: _____ & Topic (assigned): _____

Start Time (to access Window Help): _____

End Time (topic found): _____

Keystrokes required (if known): _____

Problems:
_____
_____
_____
_____
_____
_____

Comments:
_____
_____
_____
_____
_____

Help Content Topic (assigned): _____

Start Time (Help option): _____

End Time (topic found): _____

Keystrokes required (if known): _____

Problems:
_____
_____
_____
_____
_____

Comments:
_____
_____
_____
_____

Figure 8.7 Sample Test Log Form

Various questionnaires have been used to collect data concerning the user's satisfaction with a product or application. Three of the most popular questionnaires are the SUS, SUMI and QUIS. The SUS (System Usability Scale) is a 10-item questionnaire that gives an overview of satisfaction with a software product. Developed by John Brooke (1996) at Digital in 1986, the SUS was intended to: provide an easy test for subjects to complete (minimal number of questions), be easy to score and allow comparisons across product. It has been used extensively in evaluations of projects at Digital, such as office systems, technical tools and hardware systems and is freely available for use providing acknowledgement is made of the source. The SUS is a 5 point Likert scale that provides a single number representing a composite measure of the overall usability of the system, or product, being studied. It includes questions related to liking the system, ease of use, need for support, integration, consistency, ease of learning and confidence in using the system.

The Software Usability Measurement Inventory (SUMI) is a more extensive questionnaire developed by the Human Factors Research Group (HFRG) of University College Cork, as part of the ESPRIT project (Kirakowski, 1996). SUMI is a 50 item questionnaire that measures five aspects of user satisfaction (Likability, Efficiency, Helpfulness, Control and Learnability). SUMI provides software for scoring as well as a standardized reference database to support the evaluation. As a result, scores of an individual measurement can be related to the SUMI database to obtain an overall judgment of the usability of a product.

The QUIS (Questionnaire for User Interaction Satisfaction) (Shneiderman, 1998) is somewhat like the SUMI, but measures attitude towards eleven user interface factors (screen factors, terminology and system feedback, learning factors, system capabilities, technical manuals, on-line tutorials, multimedia, voice recognition, virtual environments, internet access and software installation). A 9 point Likert scale (for each factor) measures the users' overall satisfaction with that facet of the interface, as well as the factors that make up that facet. The QUIS can be configured for the interface to be analyzed by including only the sections that are relevant. It is important to note that many of the items in QUIS resemble items from an expert evaluation checklist rather than questions measuring user satisfaction. QUIS supposes concrete beliefs to determine the user's satisfaction. As a result, QUIS is less likely to be adaptable to interactive devices other than software interfaces utilizing visual display terminals. The QUIS can be purchased from the University of Maryland (QUIS, 2003).

Lewis (1995) developed a set of questionnaires for the following different stages of usability evaluation:

- Immediate user response after a task in a usability test – After Scenario Questionnaire (ASQ)
- During the post-study evaluation of a usability test – Post Study System Usability Questionnaire (PSSUQ)
- For use in field studies – Computer System Usability Questionnaire (CSUQ)

The ASQ, PSSUQ and CSUQ are all 7-point Likert scales and apply the same items in three subscales (system usefulness, information quality and interface quality). In the ASQ, interactions are rated immediately after the task in terms of ease of completion, perception of temporal efficiency of task completion and the adequacy of support information. The PSSUQ, on the other hand, addresses the specific tasks done during a usability test after the test has been completed, while CSUQ rates the use of the system in general after it has been used in the field. Lewis (2002) describes five years of use of the PSSUQ at IBM.

While the use of standardized questionnaires can be very useful, we have found that good data on user satisfaction can be obtained by combining scales and questions with participant biographical data in a single questionnaire, administered after the test sessions have been completed. An example of the type of test participant questionnaire that we have used in a number of usability tests is shown in Figure 8.8.

Test Participant Questionnaire

Participant Name: _____   *Level:* _____

How long have you been in your present organization? _____

Experience in *subject area*:   □ 1 year   □ 2 – 3 years   □ 4+ years

How many of the types of products produced by the application have you developed? _____

Application Ratings
Please rate the application that you have tested on the following criteria using the 7 point scales below (note – ratings on the right side of the scale are positive):

	Hard						Easy
• **Ease of use**	□	□	□	□	□	□	□
	None						**Very**
• **Confidence in results**	□	□	□	□	□	□	□
	Inappropriate						**Appropriate**
• **Process used in application**	□	□	□	□	□	□	□
	Poor						**Good**
• **Help structure**	□	□	□	□	□	□	□
	Not useful						**Useful**
• **Help content**	□	□	□	□	□	□	□
	Don't like						**Great**
• **Product overall**	□	□	□	□	□	□	□

What did you particularly like about the application?
_____
_____
_____
_____

What did you particularly dislike about the application?
_____
_____
_____
_____

Additional Comments:
_____
_____
_____
_____

Figure 8.8 Sample Test Participant Questionnaire

For products presenting information on the computer screen, another rating scale could be included to determine user satisfaction with the screens (see Figure 8.9 for an example). We also asked participants to complete the ISO 9241-10 Checklist (see Figure 8.1) for products that had interactive dialogs. Participant ratings of items on this checklist were compared with ratings made by experts and developers during heuristic evaluation.

Screen Layouts		Comments**
Screens used in the product:		
Are compatible with software style (e.g., Windows)	Disagree 1 2 3 4 5 6 7 Agree	
Are organized so that the information structure is clear	1 2 3 4 5 6 7	
Contain the appropriate amount of information	1 2 3 4 5 6 7	
Provide appropriate navigation cues to users	1 2 3 4 5 6 7	
Are sequenced properly	1 2 3 4 5 6 7	

** For ratings of 4 or less, please state specific problems in the comments column.

Figure 8.9 Sample Screen Layout Rating Scale

In addition to the materials described above, specific information should be provided to non-observed test participants on whom to contact in case of trouble installing and using the application (e.g., runtime errors) and where to send their completed test logs (e.g., email address). Such information will be particularly important if participants run into trouble and do not know what to do.

Procedures

The test procedures list the step-by-step process to be followed by test administrators (observers) and instructions to non-observed participants. Test procedures should include the following steps:

1. Setup of the testing environment – The first step (if required) is to set up the hardware and software environment for the test and any recording tools that will be used.
2. Briefing participants – Prior to conducting the first test session, participants should be briefed about the purpose of the test and the confidentiality of the test data (i.e., participants should be assured that their individual performance or comments will not be identified in any reports of the test). If participants are from outside the

organization, nondisclosure agreements and release forms (if video recording is to be used) may need to be signed.

3. Installing software (if appropriate) – For software products that will be installed by users, instructions need to be provided for installing the software. Such instructions may be just to follow the information on the package, or more detailed for complex installations.

4. Reviewing test session instructions – As noted previously, detailed instructions for each of the test sessions should be provided to participants. Each participant should be requested to read all the instructions before the test session so that any questions can be answered. Non-observed participants should be able to call a test administrator if they have any questions.

5. Conducting individual test sessions – After the test session instructions have been read and all questions answered, participants are asked to perform the activities listed in the test session instructions. The observer records the data to be collected during the session. In the case of non-observed participants, data are recorded directly by the participant at the start of the session (begin time) and at the end of the session (end time, problems, etc.). While some usability experts (Nielsen, 1997) suggest that having participants "thinking aloud" is a valuable data collection method, I do not recommend it because in my experience it distorts the results since some participants are better at it than others. In addition, it may cause participants to behave differently, and makes task timing difficult to interpret (ANSI/INCITS – 354, 2001). Test participants also should not be provided any hints or assistance (other than what is expected to be available with the application, e.g., online help, documentation) during the test session.

6. Debriefing participants – At the end of all of the test sessions, participants are debriefed using the type of instruments specified in the test plan (e.g., rating forms, questionnaires, etc.). In some cases, the observer may ask participants planned questions and record the answers. During the debriefing, it is very important to thank the participant for their participation in the test and stress that their data will be used to improve the product.

Recording Tools

In addition to using paper forms for recording data, many usability testing organizations utilize video recording, audio recording, logging software and keyboard capturing tools to record data.

Video Recording

Video recording has the advantage of capturing the screen, user actions and comments during the test session. It also can be played back and analyzed a number of times, whereas observer-only data is a one time occurrence. Participants of a test session also could view the video recording during a debriefing session and comment on their actions. Showing video recordings to design team members can be a very useful method to promote understanding about the usability of the product. Video recording generally takes place in usability laboratories, and when several cameras are used, may capture and synchronize data about the screen display, hand movements and other participant behavior during the test session. However, a single camera, if well placed, can be used in a normal work environment to capture screen data and user comments. In addition, video and audio recording can be accomplished by directly taping the video from the participant's monitor and using a microphone. On the negative side, some participants are not comfortable with being recorded and act differently than they would if not being recorded. Also, the analysis of video recordings is very time consuming and expensive.

Audio Recording

Audio recording can be used without video to record observer or participant comments during a test session. If the "think aloud" method is used, audio recording is essential. In addition, audio recording can be a useful method for the observer to summarize observations after a test session and for recording participant comments during debriefing.

Capturing Tools

Capturing tools can record screen displays and input device use during usability test sessions. There are a number of video capturing tools that can be used to record a participant's interaction with a software system in terms of information on the screen and the position of the cursor as they progress through the task scenario. RoboHelp's Software Video Camera (2003), available in RoboHelp Office, is a utility that can record videos of screen actions and save them as standard AVI files (Windows Operating Systems, only). If the computer is equipped with a sound card and a microphone, participant comments can be recorded at the same time. SnagIt 7 (2003) from TechSmith Corporation can capture both rectangular and nonrectangular portions of a screen, freeze and capture, snag an image from an MPEG-4 video stream and also record screen action in AVI format. CamStudio 2.0 (2003) is a free utility from Rendersoft Software that captures on-screen actions in the AVI format, but can also convert movies to Flash (SWF) files. It allows the choice from a number of codecs and offers an auto-adjust setting for the frame rate and frames can be set to capture from every 5 milliseconds up to once per minute. CamStudio also provides sound recording with interleave capability, and an auto-pan feature makes video recording follow the mouse cursor.

There are also a large number of utilities that can capture keystroke information. For example, KEYKEY (2003) is a keystroke recording utility that captures and records in detail everything typed into a computer. Along with the keystrokes, it also can record the task and windows captions at the time the key was pressed. The program records all of the computer activity and securely stores them into a password protected area. KEYKEY works undetected in the background and is able to record PC startup/shutdown time, program launch and any keystroke typed into a computer.

Logging Software

Logging software is used by the test observer to record information during the test session. Such software allows the observer to record on a time track, and, in some applications, code various user actions and make comments via a PC. The Simple Usability Test Logger (Bender, 2003) is an example of simple logging tool created for usability testing (available free). Since log data are saved in Comma Separated Values (CSV), they can be imported into spreadsheet applications. Another free test logger application is the OvoLogger (Butler, 2003). This simple logging interface is used to track user comments and team observations during a usability test. It provides the capability to: automatically generate sorted log outputs, track scenario resolution and time, generate usability findings and associated log observations, save scenario materials in HTML format and output an HTML-based report.

Test Support Software

In addition to software for logging, software is available that is intended to support the entire testing process. Usability Systems (2003) states that UsabilityWare™ is a "beginning-to-end" tool that provides support for preparing, recruiting, conducting, analyzing and delivering usability projects. The preparation portion of the program provides a foundation for defining product information, study objectives and processes. In addition, testing schedules, team member roles, testing protocols and event categories can be created. Recruiting is supported by test subject profiling, session scheduling, and the provision of forms (e.g., consent forms, questionnaires). The UsabilityWare Event Logger provides the capability to record observations during each participant session and evaluation. Observations can be tracked categorically and individual tasks and events can be timed. Test session data can be analyzed using internal templates supplied by UsabilityWare. Calculations provide metrics such as time on task, task success rate, and event frequencies. Finally, selective reports can be generated based on the analysis.

Some organizations have used web observing software to view the user's screen, mouse movements and user comments on the test observer's computer during a usability test. Microsoft NetMeeting® software (Microsoft, 2003) can be used for such remote observations and is typically bundled with the Microsoft operating system. Remote usability testing has the advantage of obtaining data from a wider range of users and may be more acceptable to users that may be uncomfortable in a usability laboratory environment.

BETA TESTING

Since beta testing is based on the participation of volunteer potential users of the product, it is often more difficult to conduct as rigorously as the previously described evaluations and tests. However, beta testing is highly recommended for software products that will be used in various environments by various types of users. Products to be beta tested need to be "stand-alone" products that can be used in the typical user's environment and support the user's current job tasks or provide new functionality to support the user's job.

Beta testing has some similarity to un-observed usability testing, but is less controlled since the user will use the product as they wish rather than follow specific task scenarios. In addition, the recording of user interactions in beta testing is limited to what the user may record as significant (usually aspects of the product that they really like or dislike). Therefore, data obtained in beta testing will be much more subjective than that obtained during usability testing. Objective task performance data such as time to accomplish the tasks and errors will not be available. However, software problems encountered during beta testing are usually reported accurately.

Call for Participants

It is difficult to obtain a wide range of typical users for a beta test due to the volunteer aspect as well as due to the limitations in reaching potential participants. If the product is a revision of an existing product, it is often possible to recruit beta testers of the revised product from users of the existing product. However, if the product is new, beta testers will need to be recruited from potential users of the product. We have found that a good way to accomplish this is to locate web interest groups that contain intended users (e.g., tech writers, online help developers, trainers) and send email to the group with a request for volunteers. If time permits, ads also could be placed in appropriate professional organization bulletins and newsletters. The email request or ad should contain the following information:

- A description of the product.
- The purpose of the test and how the results will be used.
- Types of users desired and that a non-disclosure agreement will be required (if appropriate).
- How much time is expected to be devoted to the test.
- What is to be reported by the participant.
- What the participant will get out of the testing (e.g., a free beta version of the product).

Respondents to the call for volunteers should be asked to indicate their job responsibility and organizational affiliation. If the number of volunteers exceeds the number of beta testers needed, equal numbers of intended user types and environments can be selected from the volunteers. This will make the interpretation of beta test data more meaningful. In many cases, however, beta testing is accomplished by using anyone that volunteers and the results are based on the test population as a whole.

Participant Agreement

Since the product or application to be beta tested is typically proprietary, it is usually necessary to have beta test participants sign a non-disclosure agreement prior to sending them the product to be tested. The agreement would identify the product and the nature of the test and would specify the limitations on the use of the product and disclosure of its features. This document is normally prepared by the organization's legal department.

Data Collection Forms

Many beta tests are conducted without the use of any data collection forms. Such tests rely completely on the type and quality of the information provided by the participants. As noted above, reliable data can be obtained in this way concerning software problems and irritations. Data on usability (mostly related to satisfaction), however, are more reliably obtained by the use of data collection forms.

We have found that by using the same participant questionnaire used in usability testing (see Figure 8.8), we could obtain useful data concerning satisfaction with the product from beta test participants. In addition, the data from the beta test can be compared easily with the data from the usability test.

It is also very useful to provide a form for recording data concerning specific problems encountered when using the product. The form should provide columns for listing the specific problem, the circumstances under which it occurred, what was done to resolve it and what could be done to prevent it.

More intensive data collection can be accomplished during beta testing by using the remote web observing software described earlier in the section on usability testing tools. However, the use of such tools requires a considerable amount of preparation as well as the consent of the participants. Another approach that can be used is to set up data collection forms on a beta test website that test participants can access and write to.

PRODUCT TESTING

The purpose of the product test is to ensure that the completed product meets its stated objectives and requirements, provides correct information (and/or data), and performs correctly and reliably prior to its release. Product testing may be done by the development organization, or a separate integration and testing organization responsible for the integrity of the product before its release. When accomplished by the developing organization, product testing is often done by only one individual (the developer). However, it will be more effective if several additional testers that are not part of the development team also perform the product test. If a subject matter expert was involved in the product development, he or she should participate in the product test. At a minimum, product testing requires a review of the product to ensure that its content is correct and that it functions as expected.

For software applications, product testing is similar to alpha testing and the same test cases typically are used. However, some test cases may need to be modified and others created due to changes made as a result of previous testing. As suggested for alpha testing, if a separate programmer developed the software, he or she should serve as one of the product testers. It is also important to have test cases run by individuals that are not familiar with the product since members of the development team may miss problems due to their knowledge about the application.

Heuristic evaluation also may be done as part of product testing where conformance to specific standards or guidelines is required. For example, the checklists provided in Appendix D might be used to evaluate an online help product before release. If all of the applicable guidelines were met, the organization could claim that the product conformed to ISO 9241-13 and BSR/HFES 200.3.

FOLLOW-UP EVALUATION

Whenever possible, a follow-up evaluation should be done to ensure that the deployed product is meeting its objectives and the needs of its users. It is important to note that a follow-up evaluation will not provide data for improving the current version of the product, but will provide important data towards the development of the next release of the product. However, follow-up evaluations have a number of advantages because the user experience and environment are real. A follow-up evaluation may be as simple as a survey sent to users or as complex as a repeat of a usability test at the using organization location. Follow-up evaluations are obviously easier to perform where the users are part of the same organization as the developers than where the users are customers from many different organizations. Surveys are often done as the first level of follow-up evaluation and more robust data collection methods are used where problems are reported in the surveys.

Surveys typically consist of a number of questions concerning the product that are sent out to all, or a sample of, registered users of the product. One simple method would be to send out the same questionnaire that was used for collecting satisfaction data from participants in the usability test (see Figure 8.8). Using the same questionnaire would allow the comparison of data from people using the product in their normal work environment with the data obtained during usability tests and beta tests. Some organizations include a questionnaire or a form with the product and request that users send it back after using the product for a certain length of time. This approach is particularly prevalent for support materials such as user guides and other system documentation. It should be remembered that surveys are essentially the collection of subjective information and the accuracy of the data (particularly user comments) will be affected by respondent biases and memory. Since respondents are reporting observations about the product after the fact, they may miss, or misrepresent, important information.

If visits to customer sites are required, the problems associated with conducting usability tests at using organizations will apply. These problems include obtaining the customer organization's agreement to the study, obtaining representative participants, scheduling interviews and test sessions, and setting up testing facilities. Also, the same sampling considerations (e.g., number and types of participants, number and types of different organizations) discussed for usability tests will need to be addressed. Follow-up evaluations at customer sites may be limited to interviews with users or may include observations of users using the product to perform typical tasks.

Interviews

Interviewing users is a good method for determining how they use the product, what problems they have had with it and their overall satisfaction with it. When interviews are conducted, structured data collection forms should be used to assure uniformity in the questions asked. Generally, interviews should be around two hours in length because it will be difficult to obtain management permission for longer time commitments and shorter interview lengths tend not to provide sufficient data. Biographical data, such as organization, job title, job responsibilities and time on current assignment, should be collected from each interviewee. The types of questions to be asked include:

- How long the product has been used.
- How they have been using the product.
- How frequently they use the product.
- Whether the product was easy to set up and learn.
- Whether productivity and effectiveness was increased.
- Whether the product met their expectations (and if not, why not?).
- What they particularly like about the product.
- What they particularly do not like about the product.
- Changes that would make the product more useful.
- Any other comments.

All of the follow-up evaluation interviews I have conducted have included the use of critical incident questions in addition to the types of questions listed above. The critical incident technique is a very powerful tool to obtain information about positive and negative experiences with the product. In Chapter 4, the critical incident technique was described as a method for obtaining information on task performance. It also can be used to obtain information on the effectiveness of a performance support product. For product evaluation, the questions would be:

1. What significant incident do you recall where the use of the product led to particularly effective or ineffective performance?
2. What were the circumstances leading up to the significant incident in using the product?
3. Why was the use of the product especially effective or ineffective?
4. What would the normally effective use be under these circumstances?

The advantage of the critical incident type questions over other questions is that respondents do not generalize their overall attitudes about the product in their responses to the questions. In addition, when respondents are asked to provide the details about the significant event, more useful and accurate information is obtained about the nature of problems using the product.

Performance Observations

As noted above, in some cases observations of user performance is done during a follow-up evaluation. Such observations may be a repeat of a usability test or may entail observations of actual job performance. The advantage of repeating the usability test is that the resultant data can be directly compared to the data collected during usability testing. In addition, the time required for a participant to go through the usability test is well known. However, observing users using the product in their real job environment will yield much more useful information.

Real-use observations need to be carefully planned and arranged due to the impact on the user's time and job responsibilities. If the product is used for a particular type of user task performed periodically, participating users would need to inform the observer as to when the task will take place so that the observation session can be scheduled for that time. Where the use of the product might take place at any time during the day, the observer would need to observe the user the entire day and record the user actions when the product was in use. Obviously, this latter situation will require a significant amount of observer resources and is unlikely to be acceptable to users. If acceptable to the customer organization management, it may be possible to use some of the software data collection tools (discussed previously) to collect user data related to the use of the product.

TEST REPORTING

Except for usability tests, data and conclusions resulting from the evaluations and tests described above will be used exclusively by the developing organization. Reporting formats for the various tests may be prescribed by the organization. However, any test report should contain the following basic elements:

- Description of the test (or evaluation) and its purpose.
- Procedures used in the test.
- Summary of results.
- Conclusions (including design change recommendations).
- Exhibits containing data collection forms.
- Exhibits containing data summaries.

When the usability test results need to be furnished to customer organizations, it is important to furnish such test results in a format that is both understandable and usable by the customer. While there are a number of formats for reporting usability test results, it is advantageous to use a standard format for test reporting for the following reasons:

1. Customers will be familiar with the layout of information in the reports.
2. The report's structure acts as a checklist to ensure everything necessary is included.
3. Reports from different organizations or testing labs are comparable.
4. A standardized format is based on a common consensus as to what should appear in a report.
5. Test reporting is more efficient because the report format is reusable for all usability tests.

The Common Industry Format (CIF) for usability test reports (ANSI/INCITS–354, 2001) is a standard method for reporting usability test findings. This format is focused on reports of formal usability tests in which quantitative measurements were collected (particularly summative/comparative testing). The CIF makes a distinction between formative usability evaluation (i.e., evaluation aimed at fixing problems during development) and summative evaluation (i.e., evaluation of the usability of a product at the end of a development). The purposes of summative tests are to: measure or validate the usability of a product; answer the question of how usable the product is; compare against competitor products or usability metrics; and generate data to support marketing claims about usability. The CIF is intended primarily for usability professionals and organizational stakeholders. Stakeholders are the people who can use usability data in the decision making process involved in releasing a software product or procuring such products. It should be noted that the CIF assumes that a usability test was designed and conducted according to best practice and does not specify how a test is conducted, but does specify how to report what was done and the results.

The CIF was a product of the Industry USability Reporting (IUSR) project, started in 1997 by the National Institute of Standards and Technology (NIST). IUSR project members consisted of usability experts from various organizations (including the author) involved with both the development and purchase of software products. Organizations involved included such companies as IBM, Microsoft, Hewlett-Packard, Boeing, US West, Telcordia Technologies, Kodak and a number of consulting organizations. It was based on collating good practice from the different companies, and aligning this with ISO 9241-11. Motivation for developing the CIF originally came from the usability staff in purchasing companies (e.g., Boeing) who were frustrated at purchase decisions made exclusively on the basis of functionality that resulted in large uncontrolled overhead costs from supporting difficult to use software. Members of the IUSR project worked through several workshops to develop the format, ran a number of trials and then ran several pilot studies to show the utility of using the format. In December 2001, the American National Standards Institute (ANSI) approved the CIF as an ANSI standard and the CIF is now in the process of becoming an international standard. It is important to note that in the past few years the number of firms involved with the CIF has grown from about 50 firms to more than 150.

The CIF is based on the usability definitions of ISO 9241-11 (i.e., the extent to which a product can be used by specified users to achieve specified goals with effectiveness, efficiency and satisfaction in a specified context of use).

A CIF report is intended to ensure that:

- Good usability evaluation practice had been followed.
- Sufficient information is provided so that a usability specialist can judge the validity of the results (e.g., whether the evaluation context adequately reproduces the intended context of use).
- Tests replicated on the basis of the information given in the CIF would produce essentially the same results.
- Specific effectiveness and efficiency metrics are used, including the unassisted completion rate and the mean time on task.
- Satisfaction is measured.

The CIF contains an Executive Summary, an Introduction section, a Methods section and a Results section. Since the Method and Results sections provide usability test professionals with a good framework for the report, they are particularly important towards the successful use of the CIF. The Method section prescribes the inclusion of details concerning the participants and their profile, the details of the context of use employed in the test, technical aspects of the testing facility and apparatus and finally all the test procedures. The Results section includes sub-sections for the presentation of performance data (e.g., times or error rates, etc.) and a sub-section for the presentation of satisfaction results.

The following guidelines are provided in the CIF to ensure that test procedures are as close to real world usage as possible:

1. Items to be included in the report format are specified as either required or recommended (a check list is provided).
2. The test report should clearly specify the users, tasks and working environments the product is intended for, and the extent to which these characteristics were actually simulated in the test.
3. Task instructions should inform participants as to what they need to achieve, but not provide any clues about which product features to use.
4. The test situation should be as natural as possible which may require simulating distracters and other working conditions. Evaluators should be as unobtrusive as possible (preferably observing remotely in another room). During the testing, test participants:

   • Should not be asked to think aloud. (Thinking aloud may cause participants to behave differently, and makes task timing difficult to interpret.)
   • Should not be given any hints or assistance, other than by the means normally available to real users (such as documentation or a telephone help desk). (If assistance is provided by the observer, it is difficult to know how usable the product would be if no assists were available.)

5. Data should be obtained from a sufficient number of users in each category for the sample of users to be representative of the intended user group. (The CIF suggests that for consistent results it is best to test at least 8 participants from each user group.)
6. Recorded measures should be usable to establish acceptance criteria or to make comparisons between products (i.e., the measures should be counting items of equal value).
7. The following three basic usability-related measures are useful to the purchaser:

   • Can users complete their tasks satisfactorily? [Effectiveness]
   • How long do users take? [Efficiency]
   • Are users satisfied? [Satisfaction]   The CIF suggests that industry standard measures for satisfaction be used wherever possible.

Note: The CIF also recommends checking on whether major customers have preferred metrics for usability.

The CIF Checklist specifies the required and recommended elements for the following sections and contents of the usability report:

• Title Page (identify report as CIF, name of product, who conducted test, when the test was done, when the report was prepared, company name and contacts, etc.).
• Executive Summary (high level overview of the test, summary of methods and results).
• Introduction (product description, test objectives)
• Method (participants, context of use, tasks, test facility, participant's computing environment, display devices, audio devices, manual input devices, test administer

tools, experimental design, procedures, participant general instructions, participant task instructions, usability metrics).
• Results (data analysis, presentation of results, appendices).

While ANSI/INCITS–354 proposes the use of CIF primarily for usability testing of software systems, we have found that it works equally well for reporting the results of usability testing of performance support products. However, some minor modifications may be required, depending on the type of performance support product tested. I used it to report the results of the usability testing on the Telcordia Performance Support Project Estimator and had no difficulty fitting the test method information and results into the CIF report format.

REFERENCES

ANSI/INCITS–354 (2001), *Common Industry Format,* Online. Available HTTP: <http://www.techstreet.com/cgi-bin/detail?product id=918375> Copies can also be obtained by joining the IUSR project: HTTP: <http://www.nist.gov/iusr> (Accessed October 25, 2003).

Bender, G. (2003), Simple Usability Test Logger. Online. Available HTTP: <http://www.thisoldtractor.com/gtbender/software.html#SIMPLE> (Accessed November 8, 2003).

Branaghan, R. (1997), What is usability, exactly? *By Design,* Vol. 2, Issue 1, Westerville, OH: The Branaghan Group.

Brooke, J. (1996). SUS: A 'quick and dirty' usability scale. In Jordan, P., Thomas, B. and Weerdmeester, B. (eds.), *Usability Evaluation in Industry,* London: Taylor & Francis. Available HTTP: <http://www.cee.hw.ac.uk/~ph/sus.html> (Accessed November 19, 2003).

Butler, S. (2003) OvoLogger Freeware, Ovo Studios. Online. Available HTTP: <http://www.ovostudios.com/OvoLogger.htm> (Accessed December 1, 2003).

CamStudio 2.0 (2003), CamStudio, Rendersoft Software. Online. Available HTTP: <http://www.rendersoft.com> (Accessed November 25, 2003).

Caulton, D. (2001), Relaxing the homogeneity assumption in usability testing, *Behaviour & Information Technology,* Vol. 20, No. 1, pp. 1- 7.

Christie, B. and Gardiner, M. (1990) Evaluation of the human-computer interface. In Wilson, J. and Corlett, E., (eds.), *Evaluation of Human Work, A Practical Ergonomics Methodology,* London: Taylor & Francis, p. 292.

Desurvire, H. (1994), Faster, cheaper!! Are usability inspection methods as effective as empirical testing? In Nielsen, J. and Mack, R. (eds.)., *Usability Inspection Methods,* New York: John Wiley, pp. 173-199.

DIN 66 2234-8 (1988), *VDU work stations – Part 8: Principles of ergonomic dialogue design.*

Dzida, W., Herda, S. & Itzfeld, W. (1978), User-perceived quality of interactive systems, *IEEE Transactions in Software Engineering,* SE4.

Gediga, G., Hamborg, K., Duentsch, I. (1999), The ISOMetrics usability inventory: An operationalization of ISO 9241-10 supporting summative and formative evaluation of software systems, *Behavior and Information Technology,* Vol. 18, Issue 3, pp. 151-164.

ISO 9241-10 (1996) *Ergonomic requirements for office work with visual display terminals (VDTs), Part 10: Dialogue principles*, Geneva, International Organization for Standardization.

Jeffries, R., Miller, J., Wharton, C. & Uyeda, K. (1991), User Interface Evaluation in the Real World: A Comparison of Four Techniques, *CHI'91 Conference Proceedigs, Reaching through Technology*, ACM, pp. 119-124.

KEYKEY (2003), KEYKEY, Cyber 007. Online. Available HTTP: <http://www.cyber-007.com/key_key/> (Accessed November 25, 2003).

Kirakowski, J. (1996). The software usability measurement inventory: Background and usage. In Jordan, P., Thomas, B. and Weerdmeester, B. (eds.), *Usability Evaluation in Industry*. London: Taylor and Frances. Available HTTP: <http://www.ucc.ie/hfrg/questionnaires/sumi/index.html> (Accessed November, 19, 2003).

Lewis, E., Polson, P., Wharton, C. & Rieman, J. (1990), Testing a walkthrough methodology for theory-based design of walk-up-and-use interfaces. In Chew, J. and Whiteside, J. (eds.), *CHI'90 Conference Proceedings; Empowering People*, ACM, pp. 235-241.

Lewis, J.R. (1995). IBM computer usability satisfaction questionnaires: Psychometric evaluation and instructions for use. *International Journal of Human-Computer Interaction*, 7, 57-78.

Lewis, J. R. (2002), Psychometric evaluation of the PSSUQ using data from five years of usability studies, *International Journal of Human-Computer Interaction*, 14, 3 & 4, pp. 463-488.

Microsoft (2003), Microsoft NetMeeting. Online. Available HTTP: <http://microsoft.com/netmeeting/> (Accessed November 25, 2003).

McClelland, I. (1990), Product assessment and user trials, In Wilson, J. and Corlett, E. (eds.), *Evaluation of Human Work: A Practical Ergonomics Methodology*, London: Taylor & Francis, pp. 218-247.

Nielsen, J. (1993), *Usability Engineering*, New York: Academic Press.

QUIS (2003), Questionnaire for User Interaction Satisfaction. Online. Available HTTP: <http://www.lap.umd.edu/QUIS/index.html> (Accessed November 25, 2003).

Rieman, J., Davies, S., Hair, C., Esemplare, M., Polson, P. and Lewis, C. (1991), An automated cognitive walkthrough. In Robertson, S., Olsen, G. and Olsen, J., (eds.), *CHI'91 Conference Proceedings, Reaching through Technology*, ACM, pp. 427-428.

Rubin, J. (1994), *Handbook of Usability Testing*. New York: John Wiley & Sons, Inc.

Shneiderman, B. (1998). *Designing the User Interface*. Reading, MA: Addison-Wesley Publishing Co.

Software Video Camera (2003), RoboHelp Office Software Video Camera, Online. Available HTTP: <http://www.ehelp.com/products/robohelp/demos/tools.asp> (Accessed November 25, 2003).

SnagIt 7 (2003), SnagIt, TechSmith Corporation. Online. Available HTTP: <http://www.techsmith.com> (Accessed November 25, 2003).

Usability Systems (2003), Solutions – Software, UsabilityWare. Online. Available HTTP: <http://www.usabilitysystems.com/products/software.htm> (Accessed November 8, 2003).

Wharton, C., Rieman, J., Lewis, C. and Polson, P. (1994), The cognitive walkthrough method: A practitioner's guide. In Nielson, J. and Mack, R. (eds.), *Usability Inspection Methods*, New York: John Wiley.

Instructional Strategy Selection Aid

INTRODUCTION

Selecting appropriate instructional strategies for the various enabling objectives (or instructional steps) can be accomplished by first determining the "instructional function" to be served by the objective and then determining strategies that support that function. Instructional functions are similar to the events of instruction proposed by Gagne (1985). Table A.1 lists some primary instructional functions and associated strategies. These strategies are briefly described in Table A.2. For a more extensive list of instructional strategies see the Glossary of Instructional Strategies by PlasmaLink Web Services (Plasmalink, 2003).

PROCEDURE

The procedure for using these tables is as follows:
1. For each instructional step, or enabling objective, pick the appropriate instructional function being served from the Function column of Table A.1.
2. Check the appropriate column under "Instructional Function" on the Worksheet. If the function can be broken down further, note the sub-function (by using a second order breakdown, e.g., a., b., c.) in the Function column.
3. Review the list of strategies associated with that function (sub-function) shown in the "Strategy" column in Table A.1. See Table A.2 for descriptions of each of the strategies.
4. List the strategy (or strategies) appropriate for carrying out the enabling objective (instructional step) in the "Strategy" column of the Worksheet.

Table A.1 Instructional Strategies for Various Instructional Functions

Function	Strategy
Preview	
a) Motivating	• Show how it is important to learner: consequences, rationale
b) Orienting	• Show how it fits in: purposes, goals, objectives, "advanced organizers"
	• Show why prior learning is required, how required
c) Providing Inputs, Describing conditions	• Show, tell or demonstrate the starting point (the "givens")
Acquisition of skills and knowledge (Presenting material and providing learning guidance)	(All strategies require providing feedback)
a) Information/knowledge learning	• Mediation (e.g., mnemonic, stimulus-response chaining, drill/over learning

Function	**Strategy**
b) Discriminations	• Shaping (successive approximations) • Divergent Instances • Mediation • Compare/contrast
c) Concepts/generalizations	• Relevant Attributes • Irrelevant Attributes • Divergent Instances • Matched Instances • Negative Instances • Defined Concepts
d) Rules	• Deductive (also ruleg) • Inductive (also egrul and discovery) • Algorithm • Heuristic • Chaining • Shaping
e) Task performance	• Shaping • Drill (repeated practice) • Analogous sequence • Inductive sequence
f) Exercise	• Exercise model (e.g., prime, prompt, perform)
Practice for Proficiency	• Isolated practice (part) with feedback • Integrated practice (whole) with feedback • Practice in job-like environment
Assessing Performance	• Self-testing • Mastery testing • Job simulation
Providing Means for Retention	• Performance aids • Review guides • Practice-distributed over time

Table A.2 Instructional Strategy Descriptions

Strategy	**Description**
Advanced organizers	An overview of new material presented in advance so as to counteract the effects of proactive inhibition; the term originated from Ausubel's theory of meaningful verbal learning (Ausubel, 1963).
Algorithm	A particular procedure specifying a sequence of operations for solving a problem of a given type (Merrill and Boutwell, 1973); or a rule for analyzing a given instance in order to identify its class membership or to set it up for applying the operation. Also may be a rule for synthesizing an answer or product by applying an operation. (Contrast with heuristic.)
Analogous sequence	In the analogous sequence, ideas proceed from like or similar instances (similar or relevant attributes) to generalizations.
Chaining	The linking together of a series of responses in a particular order; the completion of the first responses provides the

Strategy	Description
	stimulus for the second response, etc. with reinforcement provided at the end of the chain of responses (e.g., in the solution of a long division problem; each step in the procedure could be separately taught, even in a random order, but the final performance requires a prescribed order to achieve the solution; to provide a student knowledge of results at the end of the solution).
Compare/contrast	The learner is instructed to describe how two or more concepts, ideas, objects, etc. are similar or different.
Deductive (see also ruleg)	A method of instruction, study or argument which proceeds from general or universally applicable principles to particular applications of these principles and demonstrates the validity of the conclusions.
Deductive sequence	In the deductive sequence, ideas proceed from generalizations, principles, rules, laws, propositions or theories to specific applications. The deductive sequence involves presenting a generalization and then seeking or providing examples.
Defined Concepts	A defined concept is learned when the learner can demonstrate the "meaning" of some particular class of objects, events or relations. The demonstration may involve verbal reference to the definition, and this is an adequate demonstration when one assumes that the learner knows the meaning of the words involved in the definition. If that knowledge cannot be assumed, it might be necessary to ask for the demonstration in other terms. Demonstration of the meaning is emphasized in order to establish a distinction between this kind of mental processing and the kind involved in memorized verbal information.
Divergent Instances	A group of instances of a concept in which the irrelevant attributes are as different as possible (Merrill and Boutwell, 1973).
Drill	Practicing an activity over and over (stimulus – response cycle) until it is correctly performed.
egrul	An inductive approach, leading the student through a series of examples (eg's) before having him/her formulate the rule (ru) him/herself (Markle, 1983). (Also see inductive method.)
Fading/vanishing	Fading is the gradual removal of the prompts in a sequence of items teaching a particular topic. Sequences typically begin with highly prompted items and end with unprompted terminal items. The word is sometimes used as a synonym of vanishing (Markle, 1983). Vanishing involves the removal of more and more of the components of a specific chain of responses. Although often used synonymously with fading, in vanishing the process of withdrawing prompts is not strictly parallel to fading (Markle, 1983).
Feedback	The information received by the learner immediately after the learner's response to a question or questions indicating to the learner the correctness of his/her response. Feedback is not necessarily synonymous with reinforcement, since it is

Strategy	Description
	redefined by its effect on the recurrence of the response. A distinction is made between providing the learner the correct answer, and providing a more extensive discussion of why the answer is correct. Discussion is the feedback (Markle, 1983).
Generality	An abstraction referring to a whole class or relating several classes of specific instances (similar to "rule" in ruleg system) (Merrill and Boutwell, 1973).
Heuristic	The solution of a problem by trial and error, evaluating each step towards a final result. Also "heuristic approach" which is an exploratory approach to a problem using successive evaluations of trial and error to arrive at a final result.
Inductive (see also egrul and discovery)	A method of instruction based on the presentation to the learner of a sufficient number of specific examples to enable him/her to arrive at a definite rule, principle or fact. (Contrast with deductive method.)
Inductive sequence	In the inductive sequence, learners are encouraged to analyze information or data and hypothesize, discover a pattern or draw a conclusion. The inductive sequence moves from examples to discovery or presentation of the generalization.
Irrelevant Attributes	Those characteristics which do not determine class membership of a given instance of a concept (Merrill and Boutwell, 1973).
Matched Instances	A group of instances of a concept in which the irrelevant attributes are as similar as possible (Merrill & Boutwell, 1973).
Mnemonic	The use of a memory device to foster learning a stimulus – response connection.
Negative Instances	Any specific example that is not a member of a class (similar to eg in the ruleg system) (Merrill and Boutwell, 1973).
Prompt	A stimulus added to the terminal stimulus to make the correct response more likely while being learned. It may be pictorial or verbal. Prompts vary in strength, i.e., in the probability with which they will evoke the correct response from a given population. The term is used synonymously with cue and is generally synonymous with the non-technical term hint. Prompts were classified by Skinner into two major types: formal prompts provide knowledge about the form of the expected response, such as the number of letters, the initial letter or the sound pattern (prompted by a rhyme); thematic prompts depend on meaningful associations which make the student likely to give the expected response (Markle, 1983).
Relevant Attributes	Those characteristics that determine class membership of a given instance of a concept (Merrill and Boutwell, 1973).
ruleg	The systematic technique for construction of instructional sequences developed by Evans, Glaser and Homme (1960): All verbal subject matter is classified into (1) ru's, a class including definitions, formulae, laws, etc.; and (2) eg's, a class including descriptions of physical events, theorems, statements of relationships between specific objects, etc. The latter provide examples (eg's) of the former class of

Strategy	Description
	statements. The authors recommend that instructional designers introduce new information according to the formula "ru, eg, incomplete eg," the learner's response being the completion of the incomplete example (Markle, 1983). (See deductive method. Contrast with egrul.)
Shaping	An instruction sequence which begins with copying behavior and moves through highly prompted items through fading to the final criterion performance (Markle, 1983).

WORKSHEET

Instructional Step (Enabling Objective)	Instructional Function	Strategy	Technique

REFERENCES

Ausubel, D. (1963), *The Psychology of Meaningful Verbal Learning*, NewYork: Grune & Stratton.

Gagne, R. (1985), *The Conditions of Learning and Theory of Instruction*, 4th ed., New York: Holt, Rinehart and Winston.

Markle, S. (1983), *Designs for Instructional Designers*, 2nd ed., New York: John Wiley & Sons, pp. 191-209.

Merrill, M. and Boutwell, R. (1973), Instructional development: Methodology and research. In Kolinger, F. N. (ed.), *Review of Research in Education*, Vol. 1, Itasca, IL: F.E. Peacock, pp. 53-131.

PlasmaLink (2003), Glossary of Instructional Strategies, PlasmaLink Web Services, Online. Available HTTP: <http://glossary.plasmalink.com/glossary.html> (Accessed September 30, 2003).

Appendix B

Documentation Evaluation Checklist

INTRODUCTION

The Documentation Evaluation Checklist provided in this appendix contains a shortened version of the guidelines for documentation described in Chapter 7. It is highly recommended that users of the checklist read and become familiar with the guidelines as stated in Chapter 7 before applying the checklist in the evaluation of a document. This checklist format is based on the checklist designed by the author for ISO 9241-14 (Menu dialogues) and used in ISO 9241, Part 12 through 17. The procedure for using the checklist is essentially a two stage process (i.e., determining which guidelines are applicable; and then whether those applicable guidelines have been met). The evaluation procedure should be based on an analysis of typical users, their typical and critical tasks, and their typical usage environments. Evaluations generally fall into the two following categories:

1. When users and user tasks are known, evaluators evaluate the document in the context of users accomplishing typical and critical tasks in a typical usage environment.
2. When specific users and user tasks are not known, evaluators evaluate the document in terms of meeting all of the guidelines that are expected to be relevant.

PROCESS

As noted above, the evaluation process is a two step process:

1. The first step in the evaluation process is to determine which guidelines are applicable. The applicability of a guideline is based on:

    a) Whether the conditional statement, if included as part of the guideline, is true. A particular recommendation is (or is not) applicable when the conditional if-statement is (or is not) true. For example, if a checklist with many blocks was not used (guideline 2.7), guideline 2.7 would not be applicable.
    b) How the design environment pertains to the guideline. A particular guideline may (or may not) be applicable because of user, task, environment and technology features. For example, if procedures and instructions were not included, guidelines in "3 Procedures and Instructions" would not be applicable.

    The methods that are appropriate to determine applicability of a particular guideline include: system documentation analysis, documented evidence (e.g., prior studies), observation (the feature is included in the performance aid), analytical evaluation and empirical evaluation (see Chapter 8 for description of methods).

2. If a guideline is applicable on the basis of the criteria described above, the next step is to determine whether or not the guideline has been met. This can be determined by using one or more of the following methods: measurements (e.g., line width), observation, documented evidence, analytical evaluation or empirical evaluation.

Guidelines	Applicable	Met	Comments
1 General			
1.1 Content written with the specific users in mind and helpful for both novice and experienced users.			
1.2 Multiple levels of information provided.			
1.3 Standard framework utilized to distinguish between multiple levels of information.			
1.4 Information is current information, can be read quickly and is understandable.			
1.5 Written for the appropriate reading level of the user.			
1.6 Material balanced between brevity, elaboration and redundancy of information.			
1.7 If possible, verbal material complemented by related pictorial information.			
1.8 Primary ideas of long paragraphs in a section summarized before the text.			
1.9 Text contains the same and standardized syntax.			
1.10 Text stated as briefly and concisely as possible.			
1.11 Sentences short and the use of many subordinate clauses avoided.			
1.12 Negative forms and passive tenses avoided (definite and affirmative sentences in the active tense used).			
1.13 Sentences with personal pronouns used if appropriate.			
1.14 The use of long noun strings in sentences avoided.			
1.15 Relative clauses without relative pronouns are avoided.			
1.16 Third person used for definitions and the use of second person imperative limited to procedures.			
1.17 Simplified English used.			
2 Logical Content			
2.1 Documents titled to increase comprehensibility.			
2.2 Hierarchical relations among the components of procedures clearly evident.			

Guidelines	Applicable	Met	Comments
2.3 Layout of documents standardized and structure apparent to users.			
2.4 Sentences and paragraphs structured logically.			
2.5 General placed before specific, more important placed before less important, more frequent placed first and permanent placed before temporary.			
2.6 Instructions written to reflect logical and temporal order of task accomplishment.			
2.7 If many blocks of task steps are not applicable in a check list, user provided with the capability to sign off many steps as (N/A) as one block.			
2.8 Outline provided to show the necessary operations in a step-by-step sequence (emphasizing key points of the task).			
2.9 Flow chart used to depict task sequence, choice points and alternatives (task steps numbered).			
2.10 For forms, reminders of very important procedures put on the form itself instead of in the initial instructions.			
2.11 Appropriate coding used for revisions, additions and deletions.			
3 Procedures and Instructions			
3.1 Procedures written in the natural order in which the task would be done by most users.			
3.2 Instructions are clear, simple, accurate and self-explanatory.		.	
3.3 Sufficient information is provided in the instruction steps.			
3.4 Action verbs used in procedural statements.			
3.5 If task requires movement around work area, sequence keeps movement to a minimum.			
3.6 Physically adjacent tasks are listed together within the document.			
3.7 Directional material does not include more than two or three related actions per step.			
3.8 Work procedures broken down into manageable chunks and presented in a logical order.			
3.9 Information chunks broken down into logical and sensible steps.			

Guidelines	Applicable	Met	Comments
3.10 The format of instructions adapted to the characteristics of the related task.			
4 Headings and Levels			
4.1 Headings emphasized at the same level of the structure in the same way.			
4.2 Each step in a process numbered.			
4.3 Path between task instructions clearly specified.			
4.4 Levels of subordinate (headings and subheadings) within each primary division limited to three.			
4.5 Number of visual properties showing the differences among the headings limited.			
4.6 Paragraphs, headings and subheadings kept short (when grouping and arranging the text).			
4.7 Subdivisions and heading levels in the text are used sensibly.			
4.8 Headings and subheadings are clear and understandable.			
4.9 Topic diagram for the content of the document used when appropriate (topic diagrams are helpful for hierarchical organization).			
4.10 If appropriate, numbers used for paragraphs and sections.			
4.11 Differences among category responses are clear.			
5 Notes and Warnings			
5.1 Notes, warnings and comments in the procedures provided as necessary to ensure task performed safely and accurately.			
5.2 Warnings, cautions and notes used to emphasize important points.			
5.3 Directive information, reference information, warnings, cautions, notes, procedures and methods easily distinguishable.			
5.4 Importance of a particular category of information over others is clear (e.g., warnings, cautions, notes, procedures, methods, directive information and references, in decreasing order of importance).			
5.5 Cautions and warnings placed directly above, or to the left of, the text to which they apply.			

Guidelines	Applicable	Met	Comments
5.6 Notes placed after the related text to which they apply.			
5.7 Cautions, warnings and notes placed on the same page as the text to which they apply.			
6 Typographic Layout			
6.1 Single column layout used whenever possible.			
6.2 Line lengths kept to 10 or 12 words (about 6 or 7 inches).			
6.3 If 8 ½ X 11 paper used, left margin of 1.5 inches provided and minimum 1.0 inch for all other margins used.			
6.4 Subject heading placed at the top of each page.			
6.5 Sequential page numbers provided on every page.			
6.6 Page numbers placed consistently on all pages and documents (e.g., the lower right corner and 0.5 inches above the bottom edge of the page). But not extended into the right margin.			
6.7 Modified block style paragraphs with 2 spaces indentation for subdivision used when appropriate.			
6.8 Heading and subheading identified sequentially with a label (e.g., 1, 1.1, 1.1.1, etc.).			
6.9 Paragraphs shorter than a half page in length within a heading.			
6.10 One blank line placed between paragraphs and headings.			
6.11 If check boxes used in instructions, the check box is in close proximity to the instruction. The same check box design used throughout.			
6.12 If a written response is required, sufficient space provided for the response			
6.13 One space left after comma, semi-colon and colons and double space left after periods, question marks and exclamation marks.			
6.14 A space ratio of 1:2 between sentence spacing (leading space) and paragraph spacing used if appropriate.			
6.15 Equal word spacing used, rather than proportional word spacing.			

Guidelines	Applicable	Met	Comments
7 Pagination			
7.1 Referencing back to previous text or referencing to other sections of the document limited. (If cross-references must be used, they are accurate and unmistakable.)			
7.2 Page used as a naturally occurring information model (i.e., it should contain an appropriate number of tasks).			
7.3 If possible, each task that starts on a page stops on that page (try to prevent the carryover of tasks across pages).			
7.4 Minimize routing (i.e., do not make the user go from page to page).			
8 Abbreviations, Letters, Words and Numbers			
8.1 Only approved acronyms and proper nouns used.			
8.2 Use of abbreviations minimized. If used, they are used consistently and a glossary of abbreviations included in the document.			
8.3 If there is an unavoidable inconsistency for the used abbreviations, a Glossary of interchangeable designations included.			
8.4 Lower cased letters used instead of upper case in the text.			
8.5 Mixed-case headings and sub-headings used instead of all capitals when possible.			
8.6 Hyphens not used for merely showing word division at the end of line.			
8.7 If a series of words or statements contains mutually exclusive choices, 'or' used explicitly throughout the series.			
8.8 Roman numerals not used.			
8.9 If sequence is important in a list, Arabic numbers are used followed by a period.			
8.10 If sequence is not important in a list, bullets or dashes used to set off the items.			
8.11 In a numbered list, the number is not contained within parentheses.			
9 Lists and Tables			
9.1 Data and information presented in tables to facilitate understanding and comparison.			
9.2 Blank spaces use limited to five (about half an inch) in a single row.			
9.3 Lines grouped by content.			

Guidelines	Applicable	Met	Comments
9.4 Grouping more than five lines together avoided.			
9.5 Groups separated by controlling the spacing between rows and columns.			
9.6 In a list of items, parallel construction is used (easier to read and understand when the construction is the same).			
9.7 In a series of items, conditions, etc., a list is used instead of showing them as a comma-separated series.			
9.8 Compound questions and statements are avoided.			
10 Graphic Information			
10.1 Illustrations and pictures placed in the text of a document near the content to which it is related. (If not possible, illustration or picture placed in an appendix, given a label and refer to it in the text.)			
10.2 A clear title with a figure number, placed on the line directly below all illustrations. Same title used for illustrations as the title of the text.			
10.3 Each table or figure identified with an Arabic numeral label, such as Table 1, Figure 1.			
10.4 If appropriate, either a horizontal-landscape format with the top of the illustration at the binding edge, or a vertical layout to show graphic information is used.			
10.5 Sufficient text is provided to make an illustration clear.			
10.6 Illustrations are uncluttered with brief information/learning points, and presented in a self-explanatory way.			
10.7 Where possible, all spatial information shown in a graphical format instead of in a textual format.			
10.8 Where possible, simple line drawings are used.			
10.9 The same form used for figure layout and numbering.			
10.10 Illustrations used whenever they will simplify, make the text shorter and easier to understand.			
10.11 Easy reference numbers provided for figures.			
10.12 Perspective part drawings as figures avoided.			

Guidelines	Applicable	Met	Comments
10.13 Illustrations provide the same view as seen in reality by the user.			
10.14 Standard and correct technical drawing terminology incorporated.			
10.15 All tables and figures referenced in the text by their numbers.			
10.16 Where possible, bar charts used for comparing numerical data accurately.			
10.17 Line charts (or graphs) used where important to understand trends, and to accurately compare two or more numerical values.			
11 Printing Considerations			
11.1 Paper used has a reflectance of minimum 70.			
11.2 Matte paper used instead of medium or glossy paper.			
11.3 High opacity paper used.			
11.4 If the user will use the document under low illumination levels, high visual contrast and large type size is used.			

Appendix C

Performance Aid Evaluation Checklist

INTRODUCTION

The Performance Aid Evaluation Checklist provided in this appendix contains a shortened version of the guidelines for performance aids described in Chapter 7. It is highly recommended that users of the checklist read and become familiar with the guidelines as stated in Chapter 7 before applying the checklist in the evaluation of a performance aid. This checklist format is based on the checklist designed by the author for ISO 9241-14 (Menu dialogues) and used in ISO 9241, Part 12 through 17. The procedure for using the checklist is essentially a two stage process (i.e., determining which guidelines are relevant; and then whether those relevant guidelines have been met).

The evaluation procedure should be based on an analysis of typical users, their typical and critical tasks, and their typical usage environments. Performance aid evaluations generally fall into the two following categories:

1. When users and user tasks are known, evaluators evaluate the performance aid in the context of users accomplishing typical and critical tasks in a typical usage environment.
2. When specific users and user tasks are not known, evaluators evaluate the performance aid in terms of meeting relevant requirements and guidelines.

PROCEDURE

As noted above, the evaluation process is a two step process:

1. The first step in the evaluation process is to determine which guidelines are applicable. The applicability of a guideline is based on:

   a) Whether the conditional statement, if included as part of the guideline, is true. A particular recommendation is (or is not) applicable when the conditional if-statement is (or is not) true. For example, if users do not need to compare items guideline 1.11 would not be applicable.

   b) How the design environment pertains to the guideline. A particular guideline may (or may not) be applicable because of user, task, environment and technology features. For example, if a chart was not used (guideline 1.9) then guideline 1.9 would not be applicable.

   The methods that are appropriate to determine applicability of a particular guideline include: system documentation analysis, documented evidence (e.g., prior studies), observation (the feature is included in the performance aid), analytical evaluation and empirical evaluation (see Chapter 8 for description of methods).

2. If a guideline is applicable on the basis of the criteria described above, the next step is to determine whether or not the guideline has been met. This can be determined by using one or more of the following methods: measurements (e.g., line width), observation, documented evidence, analytical evaluation, or empirical evaluation.

Guidelines	Applicable	Met	Comments
1 Finding Information			
1.1 If a checklist is used, information placed in the order it will be checked on the job.			
1.2 Attention is directed to significant information by: **a) the position of cue sentences; or** **b) using color; or** **c) using arrows.**			
1.3 Adequate contrast between a cuing device and its background.			
1.4 If multiple colors are used for cuing, the colors used are sufficiently different.			
1.5 Space and borders are used to differentiate the most important information.			
1.6 White space is used as liberally as possible to set off information.			
1.7 Color coding used to separate information into meaningful chunks. (Colors used are also discriminated if seen in shades of gray.)			
1.8 If keys or labels are used for designating information groups, they are easily seen and located. Keys or labels are consistently located.			
1.9 If a chart is used, the most significant information is placed in upper-left corner (for left to right languages).			
1.10 If a mathematical table is used, the base-number column is in boldface type (since numbers in the base-number column are used to find the data in the table).			
1.11 If the user must compare items, information is placed in columns.			
1.12 Where possible, information is grouped into tables, rather than matrices. (If space is at a premium, however, a matrix may be preferable).			
1.13 Sufficient detail is provided to allow the user to tell the difference between similar items or categories.			
1.14 Examples are placed as close to relevant text as possible.			
1.15 Procedural steps are placed last to re-enforce prior to performing.			

Guidelines	Applicable	Met	Comments
1.16 If procedures have supporting illustrations, text is placed beneath illustrations rather than above.			
1.17 Data are arranged consistently by: sequence of use, frequency of use, functionality, importance, conventional use, specificity or alphabetical, numerical or chronological sequence.			
1.18 If lines are used to separate data, the number of line widths used is limited to two (hairline width for most purposes and a heavier line for emphasis).			
2 Accuracy			
2.1 Information (in terms of content requirements) verified by subject matter experts.			
2.2 Where possible tables used, rather than graphs to minimize information processing			
2.3 If bar graphs used, narrow or widely spaced bars are displayed horizontally, rather than vertically (people tend to overestimate percentages represented by vertical bar graphs).			
2.4 Items or numerals separated into groups of five or six for better accuracy.			
2.5 If the group needs to be larger than 5 or 6, extra space provided between groups.			
3 Clarity			
3.1 User requirements and content requirements reviewed to determine clarity issues (e.g., the level and type of information that the user will most likely be able to comprehend).			
3.2 Symbols and terminology familiar to the user are used.			
3.3 Symbols and terminology are used consistently so as to avoid confusion.			
3.4 Whenever possible, diagrams are used instead of text. (Diagrams are typically better than text for relaying procedures, identifying parts, etc.).			
3.5 If information does not need to be processed, tables or scales are used instead of graphs.			
3.6 Procedures and steps are as straightforward and simple as possible.			

Guidelines	Applicable	Met	Comments
3.7 Headings and labels are used for item groups and items that are in the user's vocabulary.			
3.8 Only jargon that is part of the user's language is used.			
4 Completeness and Conciseness			
4.1 All of the information necessary to support the performance of the activity, except for information that the user already knows, is included.			
4.2 If the aid is designed for speed, only essential information is included (minimize unnecessary detail).			
4.3 Sentences, paragraphs and words are as short and concise as possible.			
4.4 Additional text to fill a page or balance the presentation of an illustration is avoided.			
4.5 Sufficient directive and supportive information is provided in the aid so that it can be used by the typical user without further explanation.			
5 Legibility			
5.1 Sufficient white space provided to ensure readability (for printed performance aids, leave 20 – 50% white space on a page).			
5.2 For text, 10 to 12 point type (Times Roman), initial caps and lower case used (if space permits, however, consider 12 – 14 point to ensure readability for older populations).			
5.3 Text block lines are approximately 10 to 12 words in length.			
5.4 Vertical presentation of text is avoided.			
5.5 Black on white is used for text (generally avoid colored backgrounds because of decreased legibility).			
5.6 For paper aids, if colored ink is used and the background illumination may vary, white is used for the background.			
5.7 For paper aids, the contrast ratio between the print and the paper is at least 3 to 1.			
5.8 If an additional color is used with black, bold face type is used (other colors will look lighter than the black and using a bold font will compensate for this).			
5.9 If a chart type performance aid will be			

Guidelines	Applicable	Met	Comments
read at a distance, orange-red tones on bluish-gray backgrounds are used (these combinations are most visible at long distances).			
5.10 Numbers are presented in Arabic digits instead of words (numbers are much quicker to recognize than words).			
5.11 Margins on pages are standardized and are at least ½ inch on all sides.			
5.12 Adequate spacing between letters, words, paragraphs and display units.			

Online Help Evaluation Checklist

INTRODUCTION

The Online Help Evaluation Checklist provided in this appendix contains a shortened version of the guidelines for online help described in Chapter 7. It is highly recommended that users of the checklist read and become familiar with the guidelines as stated in Chapter 7 before applying the checklist in the evaluation of online help. This checklist format is based on the checklist designed by the author for ISO 9241-14 (Menu dialogues) and used in ISO 9241, Part 12 through 17. The procedure for using the checklist is essentially a two stage process (i.e., determining which guidelines are applicable; and then whether those applicable guidelines have been met). The evaluation procedure should be based on an analysis of typical users, their typical and critical tasks, and their typical usage environments. Evaluations generally fall into the two following categories:

1. When users and user tasks are known, evaluators evaluate the online help in the context of users accomplishing typical and critical tasks in a typical usage environment.
2. When specific users and user tasks are not known, evaluators evaluate the online help in terms of meeting all of the guidelines that are expected to be relevant.

PROCESS

As noted above, the evaluation process is a two step process:

1. The first step in the evaluation process is to determine which guidelines are applicable. The applicability of a guideline is based on:

   a) Whether the conditional statement, if included as part of the guideline, is true. A particular recommendation is (or is not) applicable when the conditional if-statement is (or is not) true. For example, if users only use selection to specify help topics (guideline 3.5), guideline 3.5 would not be applicable.
   b) How the design environment pertains to the guideline. A particular guideline may (or may not) be applicable because of user, task, environment and technology features. For example, if system-initiated help was not utilized, guidelines in "2 System-initiated help" would not be applicable.

   The methods that are appropriate to determine applicability of a particular guideline include: system documentation analysis, documented evidence (e.g., prior studies), observation (the feature is included in the performance aid), analytical evaluation and empirical evaluation (see Chapter 8 for description of methods).

2. If a guideline is applicable on the basis of the criteria described above, the next step is to determine whether or not the guideline has been met. This can be determined by using one or more of the following methods: measurements (e.g., line width), observation, documented evidence, analytical evaluation or empirical evaluation.

Guidelines	Applicable	Met	Comments
1 Common guidance			
1.1 General guidance recommendations			
1.1.1 Recommendations in other relevant Sections			
1.1.2 Readily distinguishable from others displayed			
a) Clear distinction between application windows and help windows			
b) Different types of help information clearly distinguishable by spacing, highlighting, fonts, etc.			
1.1.3 System initiated guidance messages no longer applicable to current system state or user actions removed from display			
1.1.4 User initiated guidance stays under control of user			
1.1.5 Provide specific task relevant information rather than generic messages			
1.1.6 Not disruptive of user's task and continuation of dialogue			
1.1.7 Distinctive message or coding consistently used for attention			
1.1.8 If interaction varies with user expertise, user able to specify the level of guidance they want			
1.2 Phrasing of user guidance			
1.2.1 The result of action stated before describing how to execute the action			
1.2.2 Phrased to enhance the perception of user control rather than system control of the task (e.g., do not use statements such as "the system will --")			
1.2.3 Worded as positive statements. However, negative statements used to denote exceptions or to emphasize a point			
1.2.4 Phrased using consistent grammatical construction			
1.2.5 Written or spoken text stated in short, simple sentences			
1.2.6 Stated in active voice (unless it conflicts with the user's national language)			
1.2.7 Uses terminology typical to the user population's tasks			

Guidelines	Applicable	Met	Comments
1.2.8 User guidance messages should be worded emotionally neutrally			
On-line help - Specific			
2 System-initiated help			
2.1 System-initiated on-line help provided when users: a) are inexperienced and need to become proficient quickly; b) access the system or application infrequently and need reminders to enable effective use; c) are unaware of available shortcuts in the system; d) have repeatedly used incorrect or inefficient procedures			
2.2 System-initiated on-line help not provided when: a) inexperienced users want the on-line help information presented, while the experienced do not; b) presentation of the on-line help text interferes with the user's interaction in the main task; c) system/application performance is noticeably degraded by the presentation of the on-line help information; d) the on-line help contains a great deal of detailed information that may not be needed by all users			
2.3 Task specific content provided for system initiated help			
2.4 System-initiated help provided is non-intrusive			
a) presented in area peripheral to task area or non-overlapping window			
b) routine help does not distract user from main task area			
c) help text never overwrites the entire task display			
2.5 User able to turn system-initiated help on and off			
3 User-initiated help			
3.1 Simple consistent means of requesting help provided			
3.2 Provide aids for locating topics: a) Table of contents, b) An index, c) Key word search capability, d) Full text search capability			
3.3 User can specify on-line topics when appropriate			
3.4 System support for topic selection provided when appropriate			
3.5 If user specifies help topics by methods			

Guidelines	Applicable	Met	Comments
other than selection, synonyms and close spelling matches allowed			
3.6 Ambiguous help requests supported by current task context information or a clarification dialogue			
3.7 If appropriate, help is accessible from anywhere in the application			
4 Presentation of help information			
4.1 Only information relevant to the specific topic provided			
4.2 Help presented as quickly as possible after request			
4.3 Response time for presentation of help predictable			
4.4 Media most appropriate to the topic used Note: Where possible, provide alternative media for different user preferences			
4.5 Task related information about the system and its purpose provided			
4.6 Both descriptive and procedural information provided as required for the task			
4.7 If task/procedural help provided:			
a) Format consistent			
b) Grammatical structure of topic and procedure titles coordinated			
c) All textually formatted steps listed under a procedure numbered			
d) If appropriate to step and user action, results of action described			
e) If possible, all steps in procedure visible without scrolling			
f) Help contains all steps necessary to complete activity			
4.8 Only information detail relevant to user's task and expertise in subject area presented			
4.9 Information displayed in form and location best suited to user's task			
a) Labels indicating meaning of screen objects displayed adjacent to object			
b) Popups used to display brief information, explanatory in nature			
c) Separate or secondary windows used to provide information referenced in conjunction with other help information or the task			
4.10 Links to topics and to popups distinguishable from text and each other			

Guidelines	Applicable	Met	Comments
4.11 Help menus should meet menu standard (see ISO 9241-14)			
4.12 Content presented in well-structured manner obvious to users			
4.13 Lists presented using bullets, dashes, numbers, etc.			
4.14 At least 50% of screen space within a help topic is white space			
4.15 Screen elements (e.g., navigation buttons) consistently located on help window			
4.16 Help windows and popups appear in appropriate screen positions			
4.17 Color used appropriately and sparingly			
4.18 Help obtainable in terms of "How do I?", "About" (What's this), etc.			
4.19 If command help provided, syntax information, lists of related commands and usage examples provided			
4.20 If appropriate, tips provided			
4.21 If appropriate, terms defined or glossary provided			
4.22 If appropriate, multiple help windows viewable at the same time			
5 Help navigation and controls			
5.1 If help takes the user out of the task dialogue, a means is provided to go back and forth between the dialogue and help			
5.2 Links to on-line training and documentation provided			
5.3 If possible, user control of on-line help provided so that users can:			
a) Configure system-initiated help (turn on/off, select level)			
b) Initiate help request whenever wanted			
c) Select and change help topic			
d) Control type of help information (if different types provided)			
e) Exit help system at any time			
f) Go back through topics visited (in reverse order)			
g) Go forward through the subtopic structure of the current topic			
h) Navigate through topic hierarchy to find topics at lower levels of structure			
i) Bookmark topics for future access			

Guidelines	Applicable	Met	Comments
j) Print topic if appropriate to the task			
5.4 If user system limited, modular help provided allowing user to select information to keep on their system			
5.5 If feasible, user able to customize help by annotation, save context when switching between help and task, and add help topics			
5.6 If help modal, cues indicating in help mode and method for exiting			
5.7 Movement from topic to topic quick (within 2 seconds)			
5.8 Quick access provided to navigation buttons or commands			
5.9 Help system provides navigation supports:			
a) easy recovery if lost (e.g., return to main menu)			
b) map of help system showing current location			
6 Browsable help			
6.1 Ability to browse through help displays provided			
6.2 A listing or map of on-line help topics provided			
6.3 Support for locating topic within large number of help topics provided (e.g., string search, keyword search, hierarchical structuring, map of topics)			
6.4 If applicable, help provides: direct links to related topics, cues for links, default browsing path, backup through topics, representation of linkage, user location markers			
6.5 Quick-access navigation aids for help provided			
6.6 Hierarchical help structure supported appropriately			
6.7 If help randomly accessed, information self-contained (i.e., the system should not assume users have read previous sections)			
6.8 Help extending beyond a single display supported			
6.9 If users not familiar with help system, topic describing structure and navigation through help system provided			

Guidelines	Applicable	Met	Comments
7 Context sensitive help			
7.1 Provided when task has specific steps or contextual information that enable the system to accurately predict the on-line help information needed			
7.2 Provides access to task information on: **a) aspects (e.g., semantic or lexical; descriptive or procedural) of current dialogue step** **b) current task** **c) current application** **d) current transaction** **e) current window or dialogue box** **f) object) at current cursor position** **g) task information presented on the screen**			
7.3 If multiple help topics are relevant at the current dialogue step, default provided while allowing the user to access other topics			
7.4 On-line help specific to user interface objects provides an explanation of what the object is, what it does and how to use it			
7.5 Cues when only a subset of interface objects have help			
8 Comprehensibility			
8.1 The help information accurately represents what the software can do			
8.2 If metaphors used, they are understandable by users			
8.3 Icons and buttons clearly communicate functions			
8.4 If graphics are used in the help system:			
a) functional graphics are used			
b) graphics are easy to understand			
9 Application links			
9.1 If possible, information can be transferred to application program (cut and paste)			
9.2 If appropriate, help uses same interface conventions as application			
9.3 User able to work in application program while help displayed			
10 Window manipulations			
10.1 Help windows can be moved by user			
10.2 If appropriate, help windows can be resized by user			

Guidelines	Applicable	Met	Comments
10.3 If appropriate, help windows can be minimized			

Appendix E

Coaches, Advisors, Wizards Evaluation Checklist

INTRODUCTION

The Coaches, Advisors, Wizards Evaluation Checklist provided in this appendix contains a shortened version of the guidelines for coaches, advisors and wizards described in Chapter 7. It is highly recommended that users of the checklist read and become familiar with the guidelines as stated in Chapter 7 before applying the checklist in the evaluation of one of these products. This checklist format is based on the checklist designed by the author for ISO 9241-14 (Menu dialogues) and used in ISO 9241, Part 12 through 17. The procedure for using the checklist is essentially a two stage process (i.e., determining which guidelines are applicable; and then whether those applicable guidelines have been met). The evaluation procedure should be based on an analysis of typical users, their typical and critical tasks, and their typical usage environments. Evaluations generally fall into the two following categories:

1. When users and user tasks are known, evaluators evaluate the document in the context of users accomplishing typical and critical tasks in a typical usage environment.
2. When specific users and user tasks are not known, evaluators evaluate the document in terms of meeting all of the guidelines that are expected to be relevant.

PROCESS

As noted above, the evaluation process is a two step process:

1. The first step in the evaluation process is to determine which guidelines are applicable. The applicability of a guideline is based on:

   a) Whether the conditional statement, if included as part of the guideline, is true. A particular recommendation is (or is not) applicable when the conditional if-statement is (or is not) true. For example, if the coaching or advice was not triggered by the system (guideline 2.4), guideline 2.4 would not be applicable.
   b) How the design environment pertains to the guideline. A particular guideline may (or may not) be applicable because of user, task, environment and technology features. For example, if a wizard was not being developed, guidelines in "3 Wizards" would not be applicable.

   The methods that are appropriate to determine applicability of a particular guideline include: system documentation analysis, documented evidence (e.g., prior studies), observation (the feature is included in the performance aid), analytical evaluation and empirical evaluation (see Chapter 8 for description of methods).

2. If a guideline is applicable on the basis of the criteria described above, the next step is to determine whether or not the guideline has been met. This can be determined

by using one or more of the following methods: measurements (e.g., line width), observation, documented evidence, analytical evaluation or empirical evaluation.

Guidelines	Applicable	Met	Comments
1 General			
1.1 Coaches, advisors and wizards tied closely to the work context or task on hand.			
1.2 The size and location of the coach, advisor or wizard window does not impede the view of the application window.			
1.3 Coaches, advisors and wizards reflect a consistent, identifiable design.			
1.4 Names (or titles) of coaches, advisors and wizards are short and consistent.			
1.5 A statement of purpose, a brief description or an introduction provided on the first page.			
1.6 The steps provided in a coach, advisor or wizard are clear.			
1.7 Descriptive text is clearly distinguishable from text prompting input.			
2 Coaches and Advisors			
2.1 Content of a coach or advisor consists of task-specific hints, tips and reasoning support.			
2.2 Content of coaches or advisors represents "best practice" or strategy.			
2.3 Coach or advisor content complete enough to act upon without being too wordy.			
2.4 If the coaching or advice is triggered by the system, users able to turn it off when desired.			
2.5 If triggered by the user, it is clear to the user how to activate a coaching or advice feature.			
2.6 Coaches and advisors provide the capability to send back data to the application screen to help user to complete task.			
2.7 Users able to add comments or annotations to coach and advisors.			
2.8 Advisors enable users to ask "why?" and receive explanations of the tip, rule or suggestion offered.			

Guidelines	Applicable	Met	Comments
3 Wizards			
3.1 Wizards enable novice users to complete critical tasks quickly.			
3.2 Unless the task is simple or done infrequently, wizards supplement rather than replace the user's direct ability to perform specific task.			
3.3 Wizards help users interactively complete a specific objective or goal, performing a task for user, based on user inputs.			
3.4 Alternatives available from the wizard provide user with positive results.			
3.5 Wizards designed to hide many of the steps and much of the complexity of a given task.			
3.6 The manner in which the system suggests or presents an option to access a wizard does not detract the user from the task at hand.			
3.7 The display of the wizard window allows the user to recognize it as the primary point of input.			
3.8 The wizard does not require a user to leave the wizard to complete task.			
3.9 Wizards clearly indicate how the user either proceeds or quits.			
3.10 It is obvious to the user how to proceed when the wizard has been completed.			
3.11 The wizard prompts the user through a clear succession of steps.			
3.12 Pages do not advance automatically (because users may not be able to read the information before the page advances).			
3.13 The user always remains in control of the wizard, (e.g., go back and change a previous response, go forward, clear all, complete).			
3.14 Wizard text is short, concise and simple and displayed in an uncluttered manner, but not condescending.			
3.15 Number of pages minimized that require the use of a secondary window.			
3.16 Visual differentiation provided so that users know that graphic illustrations on wizard pages are not interactive.			
3.17 Default values or setting provided for all controls where possible.			

Guidelines	Applicable	Met	Comments
3.18 Words like "you" and "your" used and most questions start with phrases like "Which option do you want…".			
3.19 Technical terminology that may confuse novice users is avoided.			

Appendix F

Instruction Evaluation Checklist

INTRODUCTION

The Instruction Evaluation Checklist provided in this appendix contains a shortened version of the guidelines for instruction described in Chapter 7. It is highly recommended that users of the checklist read and become familiar with the guidelines as stated in Chapter 7 before applying the checklist in the evaluation of instruction. This checklist format is based on the checklist designed by the author for ISO 9241-14 (Menu dialogues) and used in ISO 9241, Part 12 through 17. The procedure for using the checklist is essentially a two stage process (i.e., determining which guidelines are applicable; and then whether those applicable guidelines have been met). The evaluation procedure should be based on an analysis of typical users, their typical and critical tasks, and their typical usage environments. Evaluations generally fall into the two following categories:

1. When users and user tasks are known, evaluators evaluate the document in the context of users accomplishing typical and critical tasks in a typical usage environment.
2. When specific users and user tasks are not known, evaluators evaluate the document in terms of meeting all of the guidelines that are expected to be relevant.

PROCESS

As noted above, the evaluation process is a two step process:

1. The first step in the evaluation process is to determine which guidelines are applicable. The applicability of a guideline is based on:

   a) Whether the conditional statement, if included as part of the guideline, is true. A particular recommendation is (or is not) applicable when the conditional if-statement is (or is not) true. For example, if overlaid text is not used (guideline 3.15), guideline 3.15 would not be applicable.
   b) How the design environment pertains to the guideline. A particular guideline may (or may not) be applicable because of user, task, environment and technology features. For example, if the instruction was not computer or web delivered, guidelines in "4 Navigation" would not be applicable.

   The methods that are appropriate to determine applicability of a particular guideline include: system documentation analysis, documented evidence (e.g., prior studies), observation (the feature is included in the performance aid), analytical evaluation and empirical evaluation (see Chapter 8 for description of methods).

2. If a guideline is applicable on the basis of the criteria described above, the next step is to determine whether or not the guideline has been met. This can be determined by using one or more of the following methods: measurements (e.g., line width), observation, documented evidence, analytical evaluation or empirical evaluation.

Guidelines	Applicable	Met	Comments
1 Language and Grammar			
1.1 Reading level appropriate for learner and content and consistent throughout.			
1.2 Culture biased language and references avoided.			
1.3 Patronizing language or style avoided.			
1.4 Grammar, punctuation and spelling consistent with local standards.			
1.5 Short words and sentences used whenever possible.			
1.6 Transitions between sentences and paragraphs clear and adequate.			
1.7 Technical terms, acronyms and jargon used only when necessary to the content.			
1.8 If acronyms or technical terms used, they are defined.			
2 Layout			
2.1 Content organization (e.g., course title, objectives, prerequisites, lessons, exercises, summaries, etc.) clear and consistent.			
2.2 Graphics and text flow left to right and top to bottom (Western languages). (Information displayed so that the scan pattern follows the general scan pattern of the learner's native language.)			
2.3 Line lengths limited to provide sufficient "white space" in the margins of the page or window.			
2.4 Left margins should be justified and right margins not justified.			
2.5 Paragraphs single-spaced and separated with a blank line.			
2.6 Where possible, test messages broken at a phrase or idea boundary.			
2.7 Sentence and paragraph styles consistent throughout the course.			
2.8 Page breaks at appropriate points in the presentation.			
2.9 Text density should be less than 30% to create a clutter-free appearance.			

Guidelines	Applicable	Met	Comments
2.10 Navigation controls (e.g., back, forward, menu) clear and consistently located in all windows and screens.			
2.11 Directions (e.g., Press Forward to continue) placed in a consistent location on the window or screen (preferably at the end of the test).			
2.12 Input fields clearly titled and consistently placed within the content.			
2.13 Consistent headings used for content summaries and as navigational aids.			
2.14 Instructional presentation windows used in conjunction with application screens do not cover up screen fields or information needed by learner.			
3 Presentation			
3.1 Text and graphics used appropriately to describe the instructional content.			
3.2 Instructional content is accessibility.			
3.3 Goals and objectives, relevant to learners, stated clearly in the content prior to the lesson material.			
3.4 The content presented: a) relevant to the objectives, b) accurate and complete, c) at the appropriate level of detail and d) at the appropriate level of realism.			
3.5 More difficult topics emphasized in the content presentation.			
3.6 Unless inappropriate, the lesson organization conforms to subject-matter organization.			
3.7 If instruction is computer delivered, paragraphs should be short (6 – 8 lines).			
3.8 Where possible, content windows or screens should cover only one major concept or instructional step.			
3.9 Appropriate words displayed on the screen in idea units corresponding to the instructional strategy.			
3.10 Scrolling in windows and screens to view content minimized.			
3.11 Text attributes (e.g., font style, color, underlining, highlighting and reverse video) used only to aid comprehension of the material.			
3.12 Pace of presenting new information reasonable and as consistent as possible.			

Guidelines	Applicable	Met	Comments
3.13 Emphasis techniques (e.g., capitalization, italics, motion, blinking, color, etc.) used sparingly to draw attention to key parts of the presentation.			
3.14 If computer delivered, fonts are a minimum of 11 points.			
3.15 If overlaid text is used, it is easily located on the display (consistent overlay boarders should be used for differentiation).			
3.16 If incremental additions made to a growing graphic, clearly evident as to what part of graphic is new and what is old.			
3.17 Adequate detail provided to fully illustrate the thing being described.			
3.18 Animation and graphics are: **a) relevant,** **b) provide important information,** **c) at the appropriate level of detail,** **d) are aesthetic and** **e) have appropriate speed of display and motion.**			
3.19 Unnecessary or irrelevant graphics avoided (particularly the trivial use of animation and distracting scenes).			
3.20 Motion video used only when appropriate.			
3.21 If presenting audio: a) messages short and crisp, b) introduction of new ideas and the density of technical terms carefully paced, c) repeat control provided, d) Page turning approach avoided, e) echoing text with audio avoided.			
4 Navigation (Computer-based or Web Delivery)			
4.1 All windows (screens) have appropriate navigation buttons and keys to: **a) progress forward and backward through the content,** **b) return to the beginning of both the lesson and the course.**			
4.2 Navigation buttons (and keys) work correctly and consistently (e.g., same button and key used for same function).			
4.3 Input methods to navigate through the instructional content are accessible.			
4.4 If a particular lesson sequence is not required, a lesson menu provided to allow learners to access various lessons within the instructions.			

Guidelines	Applicable	Met	Comments
4.5 Learners able to exit a window, screen or the instruction whenever they wish without penalty.			
4.6 When exiting window or screen, upon re-entering returned to a logical point.			
5 Questions, Exercises and Tests			
5.1 Questions are: a) relevant, b) well spaced, c) promote response economy, d) emphasize comprehension, e) have variety and f) placed before or after the content.			
5.2 If question answering used, it is clear: a) how to respond, b) how to correct an answer, c) number of tries allowed and d) whether question can be left without answering.			
5.3 Results of the learner's choice displayed.			
5.4 Exercises relate clearly to the lesson objectives.			
5.5 Tests relate clearly to the end-of-course objectives.			
5.6 Capability provided to review the goals and data related to an exercise.			
5.7 Feedback provided for correctness of all question, exercise item and test item responses.			
5.8 Feedback is supportive, corrective, clear and identifies discrimination errors.			
5.9 Feedback is: a) of the appropriate type (text, graphic, markup, sound), b) attracts attention and c) is erasable when no longer needed.			
5.10 Prompt and feedback messages blend with, but do not complete with, the exercise.			
5.11 Replies provided that are varied and do not include disparaging feedback.			
5.12 Praise used sparingly.			
6 Learner Control and Interaction			
6.1 Unless inappropriate to the instructional strategy, the learner: a) controls the pace of instruction and b) is able to return to material previously visited.			

Guidelines	Applicable	Met	Comments
6.2 Temporary terminations and bookmarks available.			
6.3 If possible, learners able to enter comments in lesson material.			
6.4 Learner interaction: **a) frequent,** **b) comprehension enhanced,** **c) memory enhanced,** **d) transfer enhanced and** **e) provided by a variety of methods.**			
6.5 Learner interactions avoid creating false habits (i.e., not to teach misconceptions about the real world).			
6.6 Modes of learner control are easy to use, intuitive and have as much in common as possible with the work environment.			
6.7 Directions provided on how to take the course.			
6.8 Clear instructions and adequate warm-up practice on the interactions learners will engage in provided.			
6.9 A review of interactions, controls and their operations available during an interactive exercise.			

EPSS Evaluation Checklist

INTRODUCTION

The EPSS Evaluation Checklist provided in this appendix contains a shortened version of the guidelines for Electronic Performance Support products described in Chapter 7. It is highly recommended that users of the checklist read and become familiar with the guidelines as stated in Chapter 7 before applying the checklist in the evaluation of a product. This checklist format is based on the checklist designed by the author for ISO 9241-14 (Menu dialogues) and used in ISO 9241, Part 12 through 17. The procedure for using the checklist is essentially a two stage process (i.e., determining which guidelines are applicable; and then whether those applicable guidelines have been met). The evaluation procedure should be based on an analysis of typical users, their typical and critical tasks, and their typical usage environments. Evaluations generally fall into the two following categories:

1. When users and user tasks are known, evaluators evaluate the document in the context of users accomplishing typical and critical tasks in a typical usage environment.
2. When specific users and user tasks are not known, evaluators evaluate the document in terms of meeting all of the guidelines that are expected to be relevant.

PROCESS

As noted above, the evaluation process is a two step process:

1. The first step in the evaluation process is to determine which guidelines are applicable. The applicability of a guideline is based on:

    a) Whether the conditional statement, if included as part of the guideline, is true. A particular recommendation is (or is not) applicable when the conditional if-statement is (or is not) true. For example, if it was appropriate for the task for the interface to observe performance (guideline 6.6), guideline 6.6 would not be applicable.
    b) How the design environment pertains to the guideline. A particular guideline may (or may not) be applicable because of user, task, environment, and technology features. For example, if the EPSS product did not have a knowledge component, the guidelines in 3 would not be applicable.

    The methods that are appropriate to determine applicability of a particular guideline include: system documentation analysis, documented evidence (e.g., prior studies), observation (the feature is included in the performance aid), analytical evaluation and empirical evaluation (see Chapter 8 for description of methods).

2. If a guideline is applicable on the basis of the criteria described above, the next step is to determine whether or not the guideline has been met. This can be determined by using one or more of the following methods: measurements (e.g., line width), observation, documented evidence, analytical evaluation or empirical evaluation.

Guidelines	Applicable	Met	Comments
1 General			
1.1 Application provides the overall context for the process or work by creating a "big picture."			
1.2 Business/organizational strategy and goals reinforced through advice, options or underlying logic incorporating business rules.			
1.3 Application aids in goal establishment by presenting explicit goal options (e.g., presents "what do you want to do" dialogs).			
1.4 When appropriate, a means provided to compare goal options and consequences.			
1.5 Task centered work context established and maintained (employs task language and metaphors).			
1.6 Support for task progression or cognitive processing reflects most current and best known approach or content.			
1.7 Behavior, options, process, sequences and deliverables reflect the natural work situations and work flow (language, metaphors and actions).			
1.8 Application provides an interpretation of results, "Why did that happen?" "How did that happen?"			
1.9 Application utilizes a recognition approach, rather than recall of knowledge.			
2 Guidance Component			
2.1 Ongoing, dynamic, rich and explicit system or performer initiated advice provided based on data, time, options or performer behavior.			
2.2 Advice may be conditional, rule-based or "learned" and may be informational or directive.			
2.3 Content-sensitive access to support resources provided that do not break the task context.			
2.4 Whenever possible, support resources embedded within or immediately accessible from the primary displays.			
2.5 Information on the system, procedures, etc. tightly coupled to task context and			

Guidelines	Applicable	Met	Comments
available by context-sensitive access.			
2.6 Business logic and rationale access provided in a rich, dynamic and context sensitive form.			
2.7 Resources available concerning obvious options and next steps (e.g., "Show me" or "Tell me about" or "Do it" buttons).			
2.8 Provides answers to descriptive questions, such as "What is this?" "What are the differences," functional questions such as "What does this do?" and procedural questions, such as "How do I?"			
2.9 If appropriate, support (coaching or guidance) provided when needed based on proactive monitoring of user actions by system.			
2.10 Guidance helps users make decisions and solve problems.			
2.11 Users able to get help that is geared to their actions and knowledge.			
3 Knowledge Component			
3.1 Alternative search and navigation mechanisms provided to optimize the user's ability to find appropriate information.			
3.2 User able to search for answers to questions.			
3.3 Information layered to support performer diversity in prior knowledge, goals, motivation, available time and style.			
3.4 Access provided to underlying logic.			
3.5 Only relevant information provided.			
3.6 Users able to access a knowledge base relevant to their job tasks.			
3.7 Users able to obtain definitions for terms, objects and system components.			
3.8 Information provided to allow users to understand concepts.			
4 Instructional Component			
4.1 Instruction provided as necessary for users to learn to perform job tasks supported by applications that are difficult or rarely done.			
4.2 Instruction interactive and specifically aimed at supporting job tasks and improving performance.			
4.3 Unnecessary content avoided (in order to minimize time away from the job).			

Guidelines	Applicable	Met	Comments
4.4 Instruction provides practice on the task (using real or simulated system components) and provides appropriate feedback on performance.			
4.5 Available instruction accessible on demand by the user.			
4.6 If appropriate, the system provides instruction on the basis of apparent user difficulties.			
4.7 Instruction includes the use of the guidance and knowledge components when appropriate.			
5 Automation Component			
5.1 Where possible, data, cognitive and judgment tasks automated.			
5.2 Tasks automated when users: **a) do not like to perform them (e.g., are tedious and repetitive), or** **b) perform poorly.**			
5.3 Tasks automated that require: **a) forms-processing or document generation,** **b) repetitive distribution of standard information or** **c) calculations.**			
6 User Interface Component			
6.1 User interface provides access to all of the EPSS components in a straightforward and consistent manner.			
6.2 Elements of the EPSS integrated in the interface to provide a meaningful and whole context for the user to work within.			
6.3 Structure provided for the work process and progression through tasks and logic based on the proper or best known task or process sequence.			
6.4 Metaphors and direct manipulation of variables used (to capitalize on previous learning and physical reality).			
6.5 If appropriate to the task, the user interface observes performer context, prior decisions and physical interactions with the system.			
6.6 Alternative views of the interface and support resources provided to present a broad range of structure and freedom to the user.			

Guidelines	Applicable	Met	Comments
6.7 Interface provides evidence of task progression or conditions, or evidence of accumulated choices and system-generated outcomes.			
6.8 User able to tell where they are in the process.			
6.9 Rich, varied, explicit and continuous feedback provided related to performer actions, data, task requirements, performer attributes, etc.			
6.10 Feedback provided on what user did and where user has been.			
6.11 Primary displays contain embedded knowledge (e.g., obvious options, next steps, content displayed in multiple forms).			
6.12 Business knowledge and rules incorporated into displays, underlying system or programming logic.			
6.13 Where possible, customization of displays, task sequences, language and system behavior allowed according to individual differences and needs.			
6.14 Interface employs consistent interface conventions, language, visual positioning, navigation and other system behavior.			
6.15 Interface is forgiving (i.e., lets user make mistake, go back to previous state).			
6.16 Visual appearance of interface suggests its use.			
6.17 Relevant interface guidelines and standards are met (e.g., HFES 200.3 Interaction Techniques).			

Index

1st level deficiencies, 59
2nd level deficiencies, 59
3rd level deficiencies, 60
abbreviations, letters, words and
  numbers
  documentation, 206
access to users, 20, 22
accessibility, 184, 213, 260
accessibility features, 187
accuracy
  performance aids, 216
achromatic color, 171
action verbs, 88
adding new components
  PSS, 279
administrative/support
  documentation, 9
advantages
  performance aids, 210
advising, 122
advisor, **241**
advisors, 11, 239
aesthetic factors, 160
AICC, 260
alpha test phase
  EPSS products, 49
alpha testing, 291
  EPSS, 273
alphabetical or chronological
  order, 156
analogy models, 35
analytical evaluation, 284
analyzing and describing current
  performance, 77
applicability
  guidelines, 290
application components

online help, 230
application links
  online help, 238
area, 135
arranging information, 155
assumptions
  skill and knowledge
    derivation, 115
attention, 132
attention getting devices, 168
audio recording
  usability testing, 307
audit
  evaluation, 290
audition, 130
authoring tools
  instructional development, 259
Authorware, 259
automating, 122
automation
  EPSS, 271
automation component, 14
  EPSS, 265, 276
background color, 177
bar charts, 147
basic skills, 106
Basic Skills Derivation
  Checklist, 117
behavior
  instructional objectives, 249
Benefit-Cost Ratio (BCR), 68
beta test phase
  EPSS products, 50
beta testing, 308
  EPSS, 274
big picture
  EPSS, 268

breaking down activities, 96
brightness, 171
browsable help, 236
capturing tools
  usability testing, 307
categories of users
  usability testing, 297
cause of deficiencies, 61
causes of deficiencies, 67
centralized performance support
  development environment, 28
chromatic color, 171
clarity
  performance aids, 216
closure, 136
coach, **240**
coaches, 9, 11, 238
coaches, advisors and wizards
  guidelines, 246
coaches, advisors, and wizards
  need for, 240
cognitive walkthrough
  evaluation, 291
collecting source data
  task analysis, 78
color, 171
  accessibility, 187
  definition, 171
color combinations, 179
color definitions, 171
color discrimination, 173
color for information purposes,
  172
color meaning, 176
color ordering, 177
colors to display, 172
combining visual and verbal
  information, 164
Common Industry Format (CIF)
  usability test report, 313
comparative information, 140

comparing objects
  color, 176
complementary colors, 171
completeness and conciseness
  performance aids, 217
complexity, 154
comprehensibility
  online help, 237
Computer Based Training (CBT),
  13
consequences
  EPSS, 268
constancy, 134, 135
content outlines, 196
content requirements
  performance aids, 210
content variables, 33
contents tab
  online help, 223
context sensitive help, 230
  guidelines, 237
context-sensitive help, 10
contingency, 99
contingency analysis, 99
contingency tables, 100
continuity, 136
continuous reading of text
  color, 175
conventional use, 156
coordination, 20, 22, 24
corrective procedures, 99
cost estimation, 29
cost-benefit estimates, 68
criterion test
  instruction, 254
critical incident technique, 63,
  64, 311
Critical Information Survey, 70
data collected
  testing, 287
data collection forms

beta testing, 309
data form, 142
Data Form Selection Aid, 152
data graphics, 146
data objects, 83
database administrator's guide, 203
decision analysis, 91, 92
decision table, 93
decision tables, 145
deficiencies of execution, 61, 67
deficiencies of knowledge, 61, 67
deficiencies of skill, 61
deficiency, 58
deficiency analysis, 57
Deficiency Analysis Summary Form, 58
demonstration, 123
deriving activities, **88**
deriving tasks, 100
descriptive information, 140
design
    EPSS, 268
design document
    documentation, 197
    online help, 222
design phase
    EPSS products, 49
designing new performance, 84
determining information requirements
    steps, 141
developer skills, 20, 22, 24
developer variables, 33
development environment constraints, 54
development phase
    EPSS products, 49
development time, 24, 31
development time estimates, 40
development variables, 33

device objects, 83
dialog design principles, 288
directive information
    performance aids, 209
Director, 259
discussion, 124
display density, 154
display unit design
    performance aids, 213
documentation, 9
Documentation, 9, **195**
documentation analysis
    evaluation, 283
documented evidence
    evaluation, 283
Dreamweaver, 259
drill and practice, 123
education, 12
effective incidents
    critical incident technique, 64
effectiveness, 72, 301
    definition, 296
efficiency, 61, 72, 301
    definition, 296
e-learning, 4
Electronic Performance Support System, **265**
electronic performance support systems
    EPSS, vii, 1, 4, 13
emphasis
    color, 174
empirical evaluation, 285
enabling objectives, 249, 250, 251
environment related knowledge, 111
environmental requirements
    performance aids, 212
EPSS, **265**
EPSS product

need for, 266
estimating costs, 34
estimating effort, 30
estimating size, 30
Estimating the value of solving, 67
estimation approaches, 35
estimation tools, 39
Estimator, 266, 267, 268, 269, 271
  EPSS, 271
  EPSS, 272
  EPSS, 273
  EPSS, 274
evaluation, 124
evaluation methods, 283
exercises
  hands-on, 258
  instruction, 257
experience effect, 137
expert judgment models, 35
expert walkthrough
  evaluation, 291
exploration, 124
feedback
  EPSS, 271
fidelity, 168
field dependency, 139
file structure and naming
  conventions
  online help, 228
Finder's Guide
  Documentation, 200
finding information
  performance aids, 215
fisheye view, 198
flowcharts, 150
focal colors, 171
follow-up evaluation
  testing, 310
font styles, 159

foreground color, 177
foreground/background
  combinations
  color, 177
frequency of use, 155
functional models, 35
functionality, 156
funding, 22
games, 123
general design considerations
  color, 173
  media, 162
general layout guidelines, 160
general skills, 106
General Skills Derivation
  Checklist, 117
getting started guides, 201
Getting Started Guides, 9
goals of usability testing, 295
graphic information
  documentation, 207
gray scales, 179
group size, 155
grouping, 154
grouping distinctiveness, 155
guidance component, 13
  EPSS, 265, 275
guidelines
  CIF, 314
  documentation, 203
  EPSS, 275
  instruction, 262
  online help, 232
  performance aids, 215
hands-on practice, 124
harmonious colors, 174
headings and levels
  documentation, 205
help content, 229
help development tools, 220
help formats, 219

help menu
  to access performance support
    products, 279
help navigation and controls, 236
help product objectives, 222
help prototype
  online help, 229
help software, 229
help structure and content, 220
help system testing, 231
heuristic evaluation, 288
heuristics
  evaluation, 288
  evaluation, 288
hue, 171
human capabilities and
  limitations, 129
human factors engineer, 39
human factors/usability engineer,
  37
human information processing,
  131
Human Performance
  Engineering, 7
Human-centered design, 6
hyperlinking, 197
icons, 180
icons for media control, 181
icons for navigation, 181
ideal environment, 19
identifying target population, 56
identifying the target population,
  57
images, 150
importance, 156
index
  online help, 231
indexes
  online help, 227
indexing, 198
individual differences, 137

ineffective incidents
  critical incident technique, 64
information, 22, 24
information (about) help, 10
information categories, 140
Information Mapping, 157
information presentation, 140
information variables, 33
informational icons, 181
input and outputs
  accessibility, 185
input/output analysis, 84
inquiry or generative, 123
instruction, 9, 12, **247**
  delivery, 253
  need for, 248
instructional component, 14
  EPSS, 265, 269, 276
instructional content, 255
instructional delivery prototype,
  254
instructional design, 251
instructional designer, 37
instructional developer, 38
instructional modules, 254
instructional objectives, 249
instructional requirements, 249,
  250
instructional steps, 251
instructional strategies, 251, 252
instructional techniques, 123
instructor-led training, 12
Interactive Assistance, 5
interline spacing, 159
internationalization, 190
interpretive perception, 137
interview version
  critical incident technique, 64
interviewing managers, 71
interviewing users, 70
interviews

follow-up evaluation, 311
introductory topics
online help, 231
job aids. *See* performance aids
justified text, 159
key questions during needs
assessment, 56
knowledge
definition, 108
knowledge component, 13
EPSS, 265, 276
Knowledge Derivation Checklist,
120
knowledge management systems,
199
knowledge of basic theory
environment-related
knowledge, 112
knowledge of consequences
environment-related
knowledge, 112
knowledge of contingent
alternatives
process-related knowledge,
109
knowledge of discriminations or
decisions
process-related knowledge,
110
knowledge of effect
environment-related
knowledge, 112
knowledge of equipment layout
environment-related
knowledge, 114
knowledge of generalizations
process-related knowledge,
110
knowledge of overall function
environment-related
knowledge, 112

knowledge of performance aids,
tools and resources
environment-related
knowledge, 113
knowledge of policies and rules
process-related knowledge,
111
knowledge of principles
process-related knowledge,
109
knowledge of relationships
environment-related
knowledge, 113
knowledge of sequence
process-related knowledge,
108
Knowledge of special
precautions
process-related knowledge,
111
knowledge of terminology and
special symbols
environment-related
knowledge, 113
knowledge of what
process-related knowledge,
108
knowledge of when
process-related knowledge,
108
knowledge of why
environment-related
knowledge, 111
knowledge support, 4
Knowledge Support Systems, 5
labels, 158
language and grammar
instruction, 262
late involvement environment, 24
layout
instruction, 262

learnability, vii, 1, 2, 3, 15, 16, 295
learner control and interaction
    instruction, 264
learning maps, 251
learning support, 4
Learning Support, 8
lecture, 123
legibility
    performance aids, 217
lesson plan
    instruction, 256
lightness, 171
line width, 159
linear flow analysis, 90
lists, 143
lists and tables
    documentation, 207
localization, 190
logging software
    usability testing, 307
logical content
    documentation, 204
lower level flowchart, 96
major tasks
    developing performance
        support, 41
management needs, 69
matrices, 145
measurement
    evaluation, 285
media selection, 161
menu option groupings
    online help, 221
messages, 142
migrating to EPSS, 278
minimizing reliance on memory, 122
modularity, 199
more information button
    online help, 230

motion and animation, 166
moving products online, 278
multimedia, 161
multimedia use
    summary, 169
narrative data form, 142
navigation
    instruction, 263
needs analysis, 69
needs assessment, 53
needs assessment methods, 55
needs assessment reports, 75
nomographs, 149
non-disclosure agreement
    beta testing, 309
non-observed participants
    usability testing, 299, 300
non-observed user testing, 299
notes and warnings
    documentation, 205
number of performers
    task analysis, 78
number of users
    usability testing, 297
object descriptions
    accessibility, 185
object oriented task analysis, 82, 83
observation
    evaluatioin, 284
observations
    follow-up evaluation, 312
observed usability testing, 300
observed user testing, 299
online documentation and help
    accessibility, 189
online help, 9, 10, **217**
    need for, 218
Online help designers, 37
online help developer, 38
online help requirements, 219

online help system
  as an integrator, 278
online tutorial, 12
on-the-job performance, 124
on-the-job practice, 124
order of specificity, 156
organizational structure, 19
overall design configuration
  performance aids, 214
page (window) design
  performance aids, 213
pagination
  documentation, 206
parametric models, 35
participants
  beta test, 308
perceptual (cognitive) style, 138
perceptual organization, 135
performance aid design
  document, 213
performance aids, 9, 11, **208**
  need for, 209
performance aids vs. online help,
  208
performance support
  development tasks, 41
Performance Support Selection
  Aid, 125
performance support system
  PSS, 1, 4, 5, 13, 14, 15, 16, 20,
    21, 37, 39, 156, 180, 185,
    197, 248, 251, 278, 280,
    283, 286
performance support system
  attributes, 14
performance support usability
  objectives, 74
performance technologist, 39
performance technologists, 37
performance-centered design, 6

performer involvement and
  control, 169
personnel requirements, 37
Personnel Subsystem
  Development, 7
physical aspects of perception,
  129
physical sensory capabilities, 137
pie charts, 148
plan for the development of
  performance support
  deliverables, 41
planning activities for electronic
  performance support products,
  47
planning environments, 27
planning methodology, 36
planning phase
  EPSS products, 48
popups
  online help, 221, 230
positional constancy, 156
potential efficiencies, 61
potential for improving
  performance, 67
potential performance support
  solutions, 101
PowerPoint, 258
practice, 107
presentation
  accessibility, 186
  instruction, 263
presentation of help information,
  234
presentation of text, 158
preventive design actions, 99
printing considerations
  documentation, 207
procedural help, 10
procedural information, 140
procedures

online help, 227, 229
Procedures and Instructions
  documentation, 205
process and flowcharts, 150
process related knowledge, 108
product check lists, 290
product checklists, 290
product test phase
  EPSS products, 50
product testing, 24, 310
  EPSS, 274
progress indication
  EPSS, 269
progressive disclosure
  online help, 220
project scheduling tools, 40
prompting, 122
providing help
  EPSS, 271
proximity, 136
qualitative information, 140
quantitative information, 140
Quest, 260
Questionnaire for User
  Interaction Satisfaction
  usability testing, 303
questions, exercises and tests
  instruction, 264
realism, 168
recording test sessions
  usability testing, 300
recording tools
  usability testing, 306
reformatting and restructuring
  PSS, 278
remedial instruction, 258
reporting task analysis results,
  101
reporting test results, 293
requirements
  EPSS, 266

requirements phase
  EPSS products, 48
responsibilities
  task analysis, 80
Return on Investment (ROI), 68
role playing, 123
satisfaction, 72, 301
  definition, 296
satisfaction with the screens
  usability testing, 305
saturation, 171
schema differences, 138
SCORM, 260
screen shots
  EPSS, 268
secondary windows
  online help, 221
selective perception, 133
self-instructional text, 12
senior technical writer, 38
separate performance support
  development organizations, 29
sequence of use, 155
SGML, 199
show me help, 10
show me topic
  online help, 230
similarity, 136
simulation, 124
single-sourcing, 199
skill, 106
  definition, 106
skill and knowledge (S&K)
  requirements, 105
skill and knowledge derivation
  process, 116
skill deficiencies, 67
skill in discriminating, 107
skill making generalizations, 107
skills and knowledge, 250
software developer, 38, 39

software development
  environment, 27
Software Usability Measurement
  Inventory
  usability testing, 303
source/specificity
  instructional objectives, 249
specific skill, 106
Specific Skill Components
  Checklist, 118
Specific Skills Derivation
  Checklist, 118
spectrally extreme colors, 171
standard of performance, 58
standardization, 20, 22, 24
step
  task analysis, 81
storyboarding, 255
style guide, 278
style guides, 22, 24, 26, 190, 196
SuperBook, 8
supervised practice, 124
supportive information
  performance aids, 209
surveys
  follow-up evaluation, 310
symmetry, 136, 160
synthesis charts, 149
system administrator's guide, 202
system overview, 9
system overviews, 201
System Usability Scale
  usability testing, 303
system-initiated help, 233
Table of Contents (TOC)
  online help, 220, 223, 224
tables, 144
  online help, 224
tabular data form, 143
task, 80, 100
task analysis, 53, 77

task analysis for existing
  performance, 77
task characteristics, 101
task dependencies, 131
task scenarios
  evaluation, 291
  usability testing, 298, 299
task tutor, 13
task/information use
  dependencies, 141
technical writer, 39
techniques to enable immediate
  performance, 122
Telcordia Performance Support
  Project Estimator, 266
  Estimator, 39
terminal objective, 250
terminal objectives, 249, 251
test case specification, 292
test cases, 286, 291
test data
  usability testing, 301
test materials, 287
  usability test, 301
test participant questionnaire
  usability testing, 304
test participants
  usability testing, 297
test planning, 286
test procedures, 287
  usability testing, 305
test reporting, 312
test sessions
  usability testing, 299
test support software, 308
testing and revising instruction,
  261
testing performance support
  products, **283**
testing resources, 287
text, 142

text and narration, 165
text searching, 198
thin requirements
  EPSS, 266
time
  instructional objectives, 250
time dependencies, 131
ToolBook, 259
ToolBook Assistant, 260
ToolBook Instructor, 259
tools
  instructional development, 258
topic and text styles
  online help, 223
topic areas
  online help, 226
topic organization
  online help, 230
traceability
  testing, 286
training. *See* instruction
tutorial/dialogue, 123
type size, 159
typical performance support
  development environment, 22
typical use of media, 162
typographic layout
  documentation, 206
upper vs. mixed-case
  presentation, 158
usability, vii, 1, 2, 3, 8, 9, 15, 16,
  18, 19, 21, 22, 23, 24, 25, 28,
  37, 47, 49, 50, 51, **72**, 73, 75,
  86, 104, 197, 198, 213, 222,
  232, 266, 274, 281, 284, 285,
  286, 295, 297, 299, 303, 304,
  306, 308, 309, 313, 314, 315,
  316
  definition, 296
usability attributes, 72
usability criteria, 72

usability inspection, 288
usability inspections, 288
usability objectives, 53, 72, 74,
  195, 286
  online help, 222
usability test, 287, 295, 312
usability test phase
  EPSS products, 50
usability test results, 312
usability testing, 285, 295, 297,
  299
  EPSS, 273
  online help, 232
use
  instructional objectives, 249
use of individual media, 163
use requirements
  performance aids, 211
use scenarios
  evaluation, 290
usefulness, 1, 20, 40, 212, 295
user and management needs
  process, 69
User Assistance, 5
user control
  accessibililty, 188
user documentation, 9, 201
user interface component
  EPSS, 265, 277
user manuals, 2, 9, 201
user needs, 69
user preferences
  accessibility, 185
user requirements
  performance aids, 210
user sampling, 70
user satisfaction
  usability test, 303
user support, 4
user trials
  usability testing, 295

user-centered design, 6
user-initiated help, 234
variables impacting on effort, 30
video, 167
video recording
  usability testing, 306
vision, 129
visual search
  color, 175
visual spatial illusions, 135
web observing software
  usability testing, 308
window manipulations

  online help, 238
window naming conventions
  online help, 224
window/dialog help, 10
windows, 158
wizard, **243**
wizards, 9, 12, 239
work actions, 82
workflows, 77
worth analysis, 68
XML (Extensible Markup
  Language), 199